Jim and Jap Crow

Jim and Jap Crow

A Cultural History of 1940s Interracial America

Matthew M. Briones

PRINCETON UNIVERSITY PRESS

Princeton and Oxford

Published by Princeton University Press, 41 William Street, Princeton, New Jersey 08540

In the United Kingdom: Princeton University Press, 6 Oxford Street, Woodstock, Oxfordshire OX20 1TW

press.princeton.edu

Jacket photograph: Evacuee stands by her baggage. Centerville, CA, May 1942; by Dorothea Lange. Courtesy of The Bancroft Library, University of California, Berkeley

Library of Congress Cataloging-in-Publication Data

Briones, Matthew M., 1972–

Jim and Jap Crow : a cultural history of 1940s interracial America / Matthew M. Briones.

p.   cm.

Includes index.

ISBN 978-0-691-12948-8 (cloth : acid-free paper)   1. Kikuchi, Charles. Kikuchi diary. 2. Japanese Americans—Evacuation and relocation, 1942–1945. 3. Tanforan Assembly Center (San Bruno, Calif.)   4. Japanese Americans—California—Biography.   5. United States—Race relations—History—20th century.   6. Race discrimination—United States—History—20th century.   7. Japanese Americans—Social conditions—20th century.   8. African Americans—Social conditions—To 1964.   I. Kikuchi, Charles.   II. Title.

D769.8.A6K543 2012

305.8'956073092--dc23

[B]   2011026320

British Library Cataloging-in-Publication Data is available

This book has been composed in Minion

Printed in the United States of America

10 9 8 7 6 5 4 3 2 1

Contents

Acknowledgments

The story I have chosen to share is ultimately about one man's quest to find a family, whether it be biological, surrogate, or, more broadly, American. In the course of researching and writing this history, I myself have been fortunate enough to benefit from the advice and support of many "family members," both surrogate and immediate. I would like to thank my remarkably patient, reassuring, and talented editor, Hanne Winarsky, who has lent so much time and effort to this project, instilling the requisite confidence in me to bring my book to fruition; production editor Ellen Foos, for her steady oversight of the mechanics of its publication; two anonymous readers, for insightful advice that vastly improved this final version; copy editor extraordinaire Kip Keller, for his yeomanlike revision; and Thomas Broughton-Willet, for his precise indexing. My deepest gratitude, however, extends to Princeton University Press and its editorial board for supporting the manuscript and adding it to the Press's prestigious collection.

I am infinitely grateful to my primary dissertation advisor, Werner Sollors. Ever since I was a doe-eyed undergraduate in his Afro-Am seminar about twenty years ago, he has continually inspired, challenged, and cheered me. Without his encouragement, I surely would not have attended graduate school; without his belief in me, I would not have ever entered the profession. He has been my true mentor and friend. I am additionally indebted to Akira Iriye for his eminently wise and generous counsel. I came to him seeking help at the eleventh hour, but he has never wavered in treating me as if I had been one of his advisees all along: his grace and class will not soon be lost on me. I would also like to express my warmest thanks to John Stauffer, whose enthusiasm about my subject and limitless generosity have provided further proof of the master scholar-teacher we know him to be.

Cornel West has quite simply kept my spirit alive this past decade. From Cambridge to Princeton to Chicago, he has continually been a true brother to me, having more faith in me than I ever could myself. He is, first and foremost, the consummate teacher, and someone who not only preaches the love ethic but also practices it with every fiber of his body. He has taught me to see the person behind the scholarly mask, and in my darkest of days, he singularly revives my sagging spirit. When my mom was dying, Cornel propped me up: truth-telling bluesman in good or bad times. As is the case with all of my advisors, I can only hope to be a fraction of the man he is.

Reed Ueda of Tufts consistently went out of his way on my behalf, and I will always be especially grateful for his encouragement to pursue this particular project in late 2001. From 2002 to 2005, Gary Y. Okihiro kindly gave me the memorable opportunity to research and teach at the Center for the Study of Ethnicity and Race at Columbia University. Gary has not only taught me what it means to be a historian of Asian America, but also shown me what it takes to be a genuine friend in the academy.

Likewise, so many thoughtful men and women have aided both the project and its author the past decade: Arthur Hansen, who spent hours sharing his knowledge and resources with me, and with whom I could spend endless more hours conversing; John Modell, who entrusted me with years' worth of his collected archive on Charlie and who graciously passed the baton to keep telling his story; Brett Flehinger, who first introduced me to the Kikuchi diary; Jack Salzman, who provided two wonderful chances to publish in his critical annual, *Prospects*, but who, more importantly, always had the time to talk shop in a Lexington Avenue diner; Greg Robinson, who invested precious time in my project; my brothers and sisters at Harvard, such as Martha Nadell, Suleiman Osman, Hua Hsu, Salamishah Tillet, Dagmawi Woubshet, and Judy Kertesz; and the brilliant quartet of women in my dissertation writing group at Columbia—Amy Rasmussen, Susie Pak, Kathy Lopez, and Alia Yap. The magnanimous Tavis Smiley has been of immeasurable support through his publishing arm, but even more so through his warm friendship.

I owe many thanks to a number of scholars who generously took the time to read through drafts of this manuscript or offered indispensable advice along the way: Lane Ryo Hirabayashi, Paul Spickard, Dana Takagi, Evelyn Brooks Higginbotham, David Levering Lewis, Ann Holder, Moon-Ho Jung, Cheryl Greenberg, Todd Vogel, Arif Dirlik, Mary Yu Danico, Linda Vo, Steve Biel, the late William Gienapp, Thomas Underwood, Craig Wilder, John Ibson, Henry Yu, Jim Lee, Kariann Yokota, King-Kok Cheung, Robert Stepto, Bryan Wolf, Harriet Chessman, Shigeo Hirano, Richard So, Julie Reuben, Yunte Huang, David D. Hall, Henry Louis Gates, Jr., Laurel Thatcher Ulrich, Ada Savin, James A. Miller, Melani McAlister, and Joe Weixlmann. I was equally fortunate during this time to interview a historic triumvirate of writers who inspired the journey: I am thus endlessly thankful to Jessica Hagedorn, Yuri Kochiyama, and the late Hisaye Yamamoto.

At Harvard, I received generous financial support from the Committee on Degrees in the History of American Civilization, the Sarah Brady Gamble Fellowship, the Center for American Political Studies, and dissertation and summer fellowships from the Charles Warren Center for Studies in American History. The University of Michigan's Program in American Culture sponsored me for an Andrew W. Mellon Postdoctoral Teaching Fellowship in the Humanities from 2005 to 2007 and hosted a workshop of my manuscript with Nikhil Singh. The

Center for the Study of Race, Politics and Culture at the University of Chicago, through the auspices of Ramón Gutiérrez, has provided significant financial support for my project over the past two years (2009–2011). To all of these benefactors, I offer my sincerest thanks.

Through the unheralded efforts of wonderful colleagues at Michigan, I was privileged to stay on for two more years in Ann Arbor as a tenure-track faculty member. The following people nurtured me, as well as this manuscript, and unquestionably made me a much stronger scholar, colleague, and friend: Gregory Dowd, Damon Salesa, Jesse Hoffnung-Garskof, Paulina Alberto, Paul A. Anderson, June Howard, Vicente Diaz, Christina Delisle, Penny Von Eschen, Kevin Gaines, Mary Kelley, Geoff Eley, Regina Morantz-Sanchez, Richard Meisler, Larry La Fountain-Stokes, Lori Brooks, Evelyn Alsultany, Nadine Naber, Atef Said, Matthew Countryman, Michael Witgen, Kristin Hass, Stephen C. Ward, Angela Dillard, Alan Wald, John Carson, Joseph Gone, Tiya Miles, Magda Zaborowska, Amy Carroll, Jay Cook, and Judy Gray, along with her remarkable staff. I saved Phil Deloria and his inimitable mate, Peggy Burns, for last, because it was the most difficult to say goodbye to Phil. Like Greg, he had my back as chair, and stuck his own neck out to procure a line for me in AC. More than that, though, he is a kindred spirit, someone I can always speak to, and the consummate colleague and brother.

At the University of Chicago, I have been blessed with fantastic colleagues in the Department of History: Kathleen Neils Conzen, Bruce Cumings, Ramón Gutiérrez, Jane Dailey, Jim Hevia, Mark Bradley, Adam Green, Christine Stansell, Jim Sparrow, Ted Cook, Julie Saville, Thomas Holt, Leora Auslander, Dain Borges, Fredrik Albritton Johnson, Susan Burns, Jonathan Hall, Rachel Jean-Baptiste, Walter Kaegi, Emily Osborn, Tara Zahra, Kenneth Warren, Dean Mark Hansen, Dean John Boyer, and Cyndee Breshock, along with her amazing staff.

I would also like to shine the spotlight on my crack team of undergraduate and graduate researchers, whose hard work and persistent digging the last six years tremendously benefited this book: Danielle Beaulieu, Kati Lebioda, Alex Niemi Blaschczyk, and Hayley Taga. Michigan graduate students Annah Mackenzie, Kiara Vigil, Colleen Woods, Matt Blanton, Paul Farber, Robert Bell, Dean Saranillio, and Sharon Lee reminded me to laugh. Chicago graduate students Sarah Levine-Gronningsater, Tessa Murphy, Katy Schumaker, and Ramaesh Bhagirat similarly buoyed my spirits during the grayest of Chicagoland winters. I am tremendously appreciative of all my students at Harvard, Princeton, Columbia, Michigan, and Chicago: they have taught me so much more than I could ever have imparted to them.

Octavio Olvera and Jeffrey Rankin at UCLA's Special Collections deserve special recognition for their unparalleled kindness and professionalism in facilitating my project. I would also like to thank the Asian American Studies Center there for its helpful direction; Amey A. Hutchins and the staff at the University Archives and Records Center at the University of Pennsylvania; Don Skemer, Meg Rich, AnnaLee Pauls, Charles Greene, and the staff at Princeton's Rare

Books and Special Collections (excerpts from the Louis Adamic Papers were published with permission of the Princeton University Library); and Susan Snyder and the staff at the Bancroft Library, Berkeley (which granted permission to publish from the JERS Papers).

I surely could not have wholly understood Charlie without the thoughtful and exceedingly generous support of his wife, Yuriko Amemiya Kikuchi; his daughter, Susan; his son, Lawrence; and their entire family. They have been extraordinarily kind toward me, proving that Charlie had indeed found the family of his dreams by the end of his life. Charlie's best friend, the late Warren Tsuneishi, was equally encouraging of my project, carefully writing long letters and helping me appreciate the full measure of Charlie's life. His brother Paul was just as gracious with his aid. I feel honored to have gotten to know the Kikuchi and Tsuneishi families.

Finally, my own immediate family has been a capacious source from which to draw strength, sustenance, and motivation. I thank them all, especially my brothers, J. J. and Steve; they have always looked after their youngest brother, providing paths to follow (or occasionally avoid).

My daughters Cadence Skye and Ella West (named in honor of Cornel) are quite simply the reasons I wake up in the morning. My life rests with my partner, best friend, and wife, Eliza Parker. She has always believed in me, and her own brave example has consistently made me want to be a better man. Therefore, I can greatly appreciate the love Charlie felt for Yuriko over forty years.

In this spirit, my book is dedicated to Cade and Ella, and to the infinite possibility embodied by Yuriko and Charlie Kikuchi.

Preface: "Contraction and Release"

Meeting the spouse of the main historical figure in your book is an exhilarating, disorienting, and angst-inducing experience. Yuriko Amemiya Kikuchi was much more famous than her late husband, Charlie, for the length of their forty-two-year marriage. An acclaimed dancer in Martha Graham's avant-garde company and originator of the memorable role of Eliza in choreographer Jerome Robbins's *The King and I*, Yuriko—who went only by her first name for the stage, instantly recognizable like "Billie" or "Ella"—was the vibrant sun around which her husband, fellow dancers, critics, and guests in the couple's Lexington Avenue apartment constantly circled.[1] Now ninety years young, Yuriko still exudes an unmistakable grace and presence, and when she speaks, you listen. "Don't ever let your children see you and your wife fight," she advised. And: "Charlie and I always made sure that we wouldn't go to bed angry with one another." After such relatively benign and helpful bits of marital advice and a few more hours of bending each other's ears, she suddenly stopped, sat on her couch, and asked me to do the same. "You know, when Charlie and I were still young," she nearly whispered. "I became unexpectedly pregnant. I was so nervous, as I hadn't—*we* hadn't—planned for it." I was unsure whether she was referring to her daughter, Susan, her son, Lawrence, or possibly a child not brought to term; truthfully, that detail didn't matter, and all things being equal, it wasn't my business. A painfully long and silent pause sat heavily between us. Yuriko looked away for a few seconds. Then she smiled, the radiant sun once again: "But Charlie, you know, he comes to me and gives me a huge bear hug. He turns his head towards me and makes sure I'm looking at those big, kind eyes, while he says, 'Anything's possible, honey. Don't you worry.' This is what he told me whenever we had serious worries, problems, plans, or dreams: 'Anything's possible.' He always tried to be hopeful. And he meant we would always figure it out, no matter how complicated. We would always find a way."

Jim and Jap Crow

Introduction

An Age of Possibility

A young American with a Japanese face stares at a notebook. He is Nisei, a second-generation Japanese American, and a twenty-five-year-old master's student in social welfare at the University of California, Berkeley ("Cal"). The cacophony of the streets outside his apartment window serves as mere descant to the ringing in his ears, the palpitation in his heart, and the shaking of his hand as Charles Kikuchi writes:

> Sunday, December 7, 1941 . . . On this day the escapist pipedreams of paradise indulged in by the Nisei in their secluded university Ivory Tower was explosively shattered by the impact of the cold icy touch of Reality—by the ruthless treacherous "stab in the back" of America by Hirohito's brown slant-eyed warriors.[1]

> I think not of California or America, but I wonder what will happen to the Nisei and to our parents? They may lock up the aliens. How can one think of the future? We are behind the eightball, and that question for the California Nisei—"Whither Nisei?—[is] so true. The next five years will determine the future of the Nisei. They are now at the crossroads. Will they be able to take it or go under? If we are ever going to prove our Americanism, this is the time.[2]

Kikuchi offers an honest, immediate, and ambivalence-filled reflection in these two separate diary entries on "the day of infamy," otherwise known as the attack on the Pearl Harbor Naval Base in Hawai'i by the Japanese military (Operation Z). His reaction demonstrates the cynicism he felt about the Japanese American intelligentsia, of which he was certainly a part, but also a genuine concern for the diversity of Japanese living in the United States, from the first generation of immigrants (the Issei) to his American-born contemporaries (the Nisei) to another, "alien" class of Japanese immigrants, many of whom had just returned to America after education in Japan (Kibei). As he appropriately observes, this was not a defining moment just for those of Japanese ancestry in the United States, but for the nation at large: both stood "at the crossroads." Kikuchi makes his allegiance quite clear by emphasizing the need "to prove our Americanism," but

Figure 1. Kikuchi writing in his diary at the Gila River Relocation Center, ca. 1942. Photo courtesy of Yuriko Amemiya Kikuchi and the Department of Special Collections, Charles E. Young Research Library, UCLA.

the ensuing decade would sorely test Kikuchi's ideals and assumptions about his loyalty to the nation and that elusive term "Americanism."

Starting with Pearl Harbor, Kikuchi began a lifelong habit of writing a daily diary entry, not laying down his pen until his death from cancer in 1988 at the age of seventy-two while completing a peace march in the Soviet Union. More than 100,000 pages of diaries would be Kikuchi's legacy to his family, community, and nation. In particular, the immediate years after Pearl Harbor would afford him the opportunity to comment on nearly every significant moment of the war-time period: the fear-filled roundup of Japanese Americans on the West Coast into "assembly centers" or makeshift horse stalls refitted for human chattel; the eventual move of 120,000 men, women, and children to internment camps, or "relocation centers," eight of which were spread throughout the western interior and two of which were located in Arkansas; the denial of constitutional rights to citizens of Japanese ancestry in three pivotal Supreme Court cases; the ultimate resettlement of many Nisei in midwestern and East Coast cities and universities during the war; and the ultimate release of all internees by 1946, some of whom were rightfully frightened to return to their former ethnic enclaves on the West Coast for fear of nativist violence. Hence, Kikuchi's ambivalence—about his own people and his nation—was eminently understandable. The roller-coaster decade of the 1940s elicited Kikuchi's emotional vertigo: fear, anger, betrayal, sympathy, distrust, ignorance, hopelessness, and hope. In this sense, his initially "separate" diary entries on December 7—the first appears as a hidden insert in an essay for a psychology class (handed in on December 8), while the second appears in his original entry on December 7—adequately capture the seesawing, ambivalent feelings Kikuchi would experience throughout this disorienting, uncertain period. Later in the entry, he invokes Thomas Paine's "trying times," conceding that he could not adequately fathom the unknown challenges both he and the nation faced. The contradictory tones—again, fear filled, confused, and mildly assertive—found in his very first writing forecasts the diary as somewhat of a palimpsest. In the morning, he could write one thing, erase those thoughts in the afternoon (or at least begin a new paragraph), and in the evening record something wholly opposite of what he was initially thinking. The diary therefore comes across less like an exterior monologue (or one seamless narrative) than an internal dialogue, shifting between and among the various positions Kikuchi held, like various actors on a stage. In the midst of it all, he would mindfully write down and chart all the geographic and emotional shifts he and fellow Nisei felt throughout their collectively vertiginous experience in the wartime and postwar periods.

Kikuchi was not looking to be the face of Japanese America, its public intellectual. Certainly, other progressives would take on such visible roles. For example, Ina Sugihara graced the pages of the *Crisis*, the major news outlet for the National Association for the Advancement of Colored People (NAACP), pleading her people's case to a largely sympathetic audience. Larry Tajiri, the left-of-center editor of the *Pacific Citizen*, the mouthpiece for the more moderate Japanese American Citizens League (JACL), wielded greater influence by virtue of the editorial page he ran.[3] The league's chief executive, Mike Masaoka, had written the "Japanese American Creed," or oath of loyalty, in hopes of convincing fellow citizens of Japanese Americans' patriotism, but as the war and evacuation took place, his mien appeared too conciliatory, his actions too complicit with the government's desire to imprison his constituents. It is true that Kikuchi wrote the occasional article ("Joe Nisei Looks for a Job") for the progressive editor Jimmie Omura's *Current Life*, a Nisei weekly based in San Francisco. During internment, he even helped edit and write for the assembly center newspaper, the *Tanforan Totalizer*. But Kikuchi never explicitly sought the spotlight. He was not an activist intellectual, the Nisei equivalent of W.E.B. Du Bois. Nor would he become the definitive social scientist of Japanese America's "dilemma" as Gunnar Myrdal, or St. Clair Drake and Horace Cayton, became for African Americans' plight by war's end. Kikuchi nonetheless remains an indispensable historical link in the overlapping networks of intellectuals—immigrant, Black, Nisei, among others—that would dominate the landscape of democratic and ideological discourse throughout the 1940s. Kikuchi not only discussed the various possibilities of a multiracial American democracy with a number of intellectual players, but also invariably recorded these conversations in his trusted diary day after day, providing a road map through the winding and uncharted topography of the era. It did not hurt that, according to lifelong friends, Kikuchi also possessed an effortless, photographic memory, extremely useful for reports, case histories, and diary entries.

These well-preserved diaries and the man himself therefore represent a trail guide for a reconstructive investigation of why the various schools of American democracy—including Nisei intellectuals at Berkeley, pluralist advocates like the *Nation* editor Carey McWilliams and the immigrant activist Louis Adamic, Chicago School sociologists, and African American progressives, among other types—ultimately failed *in part* and, not insignificantly, of how some of their ideas managed to survive the larger society's capitulation to Orwellian, Cold War ideology in the late 1940s and early 1950s. Hence, a close examination of Kikuchi and his diaries provides a narrative through-line for the 1940s within the broader cultural history of home-front America and what I consider its unprecedented level of interracial interactions. His, then, is not the role of a downstage actor like Laurence Olivier or Paul Robeson, nor the bit part of a minor player who appears only sparingly; rather, Kikuchi and his diaries inhabit the traditional Greek chorus in an all-too-real staging of democratic America in flux during the 1940s: he touches upon almost every major historical event, records it in his diary, and ultimately fades ever so subtly into the background. His preservation of the time's key moments and meaning makers allows for a restaging of histori-cal actors and events, demonstrating that with the benefit of proper lighting and strategic viewpoints, we can clearly see the contours of their movements, their successes, the limits of their efforts, and their failures. Most importantly, through Kikuchi's narrative, historical actors reenact their earnest but fallible efforts at progressively redefining the idea of American democracy on a stage not quite prepared for the glare of klieg lights, a platform purposefully constructed for a "long winter."

The historian Michael Denning convincingly argues that the period preced-ing World War II came to be known as the "age of the CIO," one heavily shaped by the working-class culture of the 1930s, with its distinctive "cultural front." View-ing 1929 (the start of the Great Depression) and 1948 (most pointedly signified by Henry Wallace's failed Progressive presidential run) as bookends of the age, Denning acknowledges the victory of Henry Luce's triumphalist "American Cen-tury" (over Wallace's more critically minded "Century of the Common Man") as the world war turned to early stages of the Cold War in the late 1940s. However, as various scholars of the subsequent era have asserted, the "age of consensus" and Red baiting could not completely stop the radical, progressive elements that survived the war and shifted the fields of battle, specifically toward the anticolo-nial struggles waged abroad by Africans, Asians, and African Americans, and the continuing movement for civil rights at home.[4]

In considering these two bookend eras of heightened civil, political, and cultural activity, one might assume that the 1940s—particularly in the context of a worldwide war—represented an overwhelming consensus, a time when all Americans spoke with one voice to support "the good war." On the ground, however, and on the home front, an intermixture of existential insecurity and idealistic hope infused conversations about potential models of postwar American democracy: what would the country finally look like after the defeat of fascism and the mutual recognition of everyone's part in the war effort (even those behind barbed wire)? Networks of progressive intellectuals (like McWilliams, Adamic, and Margaret Anderson, along with "cultural front" novelists like Richard Wright, John Fante, and Carlos Bulosan), traditional institutional entities (such as the Black press), and university social scientists (at Cal and Chicago) all viewed the war—from decidedly different vantage points—as a useful vehicle and test for the advancement of American democracy, an opportunity for experiment and possibility, and evaluation of failures and limitations. Making their opinions and findings known through monographs, journals, editorials, fiction, and sociological studies, members of these "publics" and their arguments found purchase among a particular group of young Americans like Kikuchi. These young men and women, mostly second-generation ethnics, whom Adamic termed "the new Americans," strove to enter the discussion, affect the democratic discourse, and insert themselves into those very same "publics" that had influenced them. Taken as a whole, these networks were, by and large, in tension with the mainstream American public: against the internment; in favor of immigrants' and African Americans' civil rights; in favor of workers' rights; and skeptical of a growing American empire and extant colonialism. Hence, they can be considered what Michael Warner has termed a set of discrete "counterpublics," or "publics . . . defined by their tension with a larger [normative] public."[5] In a historical moment when conformity and lockstep support of the war effort was expected, these oppositional networks maintained and served the challenging but historically indispensable role of dissent in American political culture.

These counterpublics were not entirely autonomous, either, unaware of one another's discourses, members, and positions. In fact, if one could pinpoint each counterpublic or oppositional group on an imaginary cultural map of the 1940s, as well as draw lines between each point to mark the relationships among such groups, a remarkable web of interconnections—some fleeting, others more lasting—reveals itself. These relationships stretch expansively across the landscape of 1940s American culture, meriting more deliberate consideration and deeper exploration of the unexpected coincidences, unpublicized conversations, and unheralded interactions among these ostensibly segregated and unrelated groups of "democrats." Admittedly, I am arguing for the exceptionalist quality of the 1940s, documenting this home-front culture of interracialism and historicizing the era as a significant shift in democratic race relations. What other period in modern U.S. history has encompassed a world war, an unprecedented, wartime incarceration of hundreds of thousands of American citizens based on race, subsequent concerns about a "race war" at home and abroad, a second wave of Black migration for wartime jobs, and a confluence of institutional, activist, and cross-racial protest on behalf of one segment of the Asian American population? My admission does not deny the influence of "cultural front" ideology on this era's thinkers, or the fragmented intellectual legacy such actors bequeathed to anticolonial, anti-imperial movements of the Cold War. My examination acknowledges the foundation of the Popular Front as well as the torch carried forward by McWilliams, Du Bois, Nisei intellectuals, and others into the Cold War. But this narrative is largely concerned with telling the story of America during World War II, at a moment when the nation attempted to find "unity within diversity" but also, too often and too familiarly, turned a blind eye to the xenophobia, racism, and cruelty sanctioned by its constitutional democracy.

And 1948 marks the narrative's appropriate endpoint. Both domestically and internationally, a significant series of historical events took place that year, signposts of the next era in race relations, and markings of shifting geopolitical ideologies: desegregation of the U.S. armed forces; the reelection of Harry Truman and the advent of a civil rights plank in the Democratic Party platform, as well as an aggressive posture toward the USSR; *Shelley v. Kraemer*, the Supreme Court decision that prohibited courts from enforcing racially restrictive housing practices; the resumption of public witch hunts for un-American activity (e.g., the trial of Alger Hiss); the United Nations' Universal Declaration of Human Rights; the first of many Arab-Israeli wars over Israel's independence; Mohandas K. Gandhi's assassination, one year after the partition of Pakistan and India; the start of the Soviet Union's blockade of Berlin; and a failure to hold free elections throughout the Korean Peninsula, presaging the Korean War and the Cold War.

Before all these events, however, came the internment of Japanese Americans, a signal event of World War II and a repressed moment of shame in the nation's collective memory. Note well: not for the first or last time, America most publicly and unashamedly prioritized the paranoia of internal security over the principle of civil liberty in the 1940s, at the same time that it capitulated to a nearly unimaginable politics of fear, constructing a nationwide apparatus of domestic fascism based on racism while hypocritically claiming to abhor and dismantle the grotesque of international fascism.

Follow Charles Kikuchi, then, a diarist whose writings over this *longue dureé* provide the narrative touchstone or the historical trail map through this period of a reclamation of rights, this era of redefining democratic ideals, and this moment of infinite possibility.

Mapping the Networks

Kikuchi's story is at one time both exceptional and representative. On the one hand, it was highly unusual for Japanese American parents to orphan their physically abused child at eight years of age and leave him to fend for himself over a decade of adolescence and young adulthood while they lived with the rest of their children only an hour and a half away. Moreover, very few if any educated Nisei bucked their families' and peers' expectations by pursuing a social work degree (MSW) instead of a more prestigious social science PhD. Not many other twenty-something Nisei decided to rejoin their families of origin (after that decade in an orphanage) when the roundup and evacuation of Japanese Americans struck the West Coast. Through these examples, Kikuchi stands out as quite an original—ostensibly, a little like Robert Park's "marginal man" on the periphery of even his own marginalized, racialized group.[6] Notably, though, with the exception of his orphaning, Kikuchi actively made his own decisions for most of his young life; hardly a shrinking violet, he was not easily pigeonholed or blithely corralled by the herd's mentality. That type of toughness, a form of contrariness—most likely born out of his traumatic experience as an orphan—is what compelled me to delve deeper into Kikuchi's life story. He could have given up early in his life and wallowed in a dangerous (but understandable) depression, given the extremity of his family's neglect. He did not. Kikuchi could have then abandoned his own family in kind, especially since his work as a migratory laborer took him hundreds of miles away, traveling the length of the West Coast up through Alaska. But he did not. Instead, he returned often to San Francisco, a stone's throw from his family home in San Bruno. Knowing that he had unresolved business there, he made sure he occasionally saw his siblings in the city, keeping some kind of tether to his difficult parents. Last, choosing to share closeted space in makeshift barracks with those same parents during internment represents the most extreme example of how Kikuchi wished to see the whole issue through, emotionally charged and confounding as it might be.

On the other hand, Kikuchi always managed to find a place for himself among surrogate—and representative—families throughout his life. These units might be termed "networks" and "publics," but regardless of nomenclature, Kikuchi's participation in these groups reflected his profound desire to be a part of something bigger than himself, something larger than his own contrarian instincts and individualism. For example, even though Kikuchi conspicuously chose social work over sociology (the option for "serious" Nisei intellectuals) during graduate study at Cal, he nevertheless spent almost all his time with a cadre of radical, progressive Nisei at the university (most of whom would earn doctorates in the social sciences): his best friend, Warren Tsuneishi; Tamotsu "Tom" Shibutani; Lillian Ota; James Sakoda; and Kenji Murase (who, like Kikuchi, chose social work), among others. These intellectuals became his debate team as much as a bull-session social club. For many of them, lifelong friendships and long, unresolved intellectual and personal quarrels began at Berkeley.

As further proof of his seeking kinship networks, Kikuchi met Adamic in the early 1940s and attached himself to the Slovenian writer and his wife, Stella, in a fawning but shrewdly opportunistic manner. Kikuchi understood that he himself might not become one of the main interlocutors within the immigrant intellectual network, of which Adamic and his wife were a significant and recognizable part. But he realized that knowing Adamic represented a chance to gain precious social capital and valuable access to possible wartime and postwar opportunities. Adamic was, after all, the author of several well-received books and editor of the progressive, multiethnic magazine *Common Ground*: he hobnobbed and rubbed elbows with the likes of McWilliams, Fante, Bulosan, and William Saroyan. Surely, Kikuchi must have thought, Adamic could provide entrée into a worthy postwar prospect.

Furthermore, during the evacuation and resettlement itself, Kikuchi joined a few of the Cal Nisei mentioned above (and others) to work under the demographer Dorothy Swaine Thomas and her handsomely funded study of the internment. Here, Kikuchi became not only a member of the Nisei team on the ground in the camps, but also a protégé of Thomas and her well-known husband, the sociologist W. I. Thomas. Working in California and Arizona during the internment, Kikuchi also joined the Thomas team during the resettlement of 20,000 Japanese Americans in Chicago. In those heady days, he enjoyed unfettered access to the famous Chicago School of sociology, working at the University of Chicago campus in Hyde Park and living on the South Side, just on the edge of Bronzeville, the historic African American neighborhood studied and celebrated by a bevy of scholars.[7] In this limited context, Kikuchi became part of a generation of Asian American social scientists trained by Chicago sociologists; he once again strove to be part of a larger whole—consciously or unconsciously representative—however small his own contribution. My point here is that Kikuchi's life story is complicated and rich enough that he can be termed "both-and" rather than "either-or." As Kikuchi would self-diagnose in a letter to Adamic, he was a man with "a multitude of complexes."[8]

The Map's Legend

For most of the Popular Front era, Kikuchi himself was a teenager, but he was not entirely sheltered from the significant movements and issues affecting the sizeable migrant labor force or the number of Japanese relegated to domestic jobs. Especially toward the end of the 1930s, Kikuchi supported his own education at San Francisco State College through a panoply of odd jobs—chauffeur, domestic, cannery worker, fish scaler, and farmworker in the San Joaquin Valley, to name a few. While one would be hard pressed to include him among the historically recognized cadre of Communist Party USA members, like Karl G. Yoneda, or even term him a fellow traveler, Kikuchi nonetheless sympathized with—not to mention, experienced—the worker's plight. Even though considered part of the mass of workingmen and workingwomen, he kept a particular kind of distance from his own position as a worker and tried to maintain a putatively objective stance as a participant-observer (well before he would learn what this technical sociological term meant). Experience in the harvesting fields or in the kitchen of a well-heeled white employer certainly did not anesthetize Kikuchi to the feelings of being a laborer or prevent him from understanding the massive forces facing the proletarian class, especially immigrants in the United States. In fact, Kikuchi remained admirably committed to protesting the injustices faced by Mexican, Filipino, and Japanese migrant laborers, or longshoremen agitating for better work conditions and wages. He simply never labeled himself a party member, a fellow traveler, a Young Democrat, or any other moniker, for that matter. And for the most part, he eschewed formal organizations and mass movements in favor of direct, individual action and intervention. Up until the trauma of internment, it would be reasonable to say that class stands out as the main interpretive device in Kikuchi's analysis. It is, in large part, why he chose to attend a lesser-known college, San Francisco State, one associated with the working class of the Bay Area, rather than what he considered the bourgeois ivory tower for Nisei: Berkeley, an institution Issei parents easily recognized and respected. Conversations with other workers or students—highly personal, intimate, and dialogic—were his foundational fieldwork, while his memory, pen, and diary were tools for analyzing and ultimately working through the personal and the professional. The workingmen and workingwomen would be the catalyst and force for freedom, Kikuchi believed, as Marx had suggested. However, internment would radically alter the centrality of class in relation to race in his evolving belief system, forcing him to see many moving parts in the all-too-real process of an institutionalized exclusion based on race.

An immigrant himself, Adamic vigorously promoted the acceptance of "new Americans" (particularly second-generation immigrants) by "old Americans" through his numerous autobiographies and monographs, but primarily through *Common Ground*. In Adamic, Kikuchi found a surrogate father, an intellectual mentor whose levity and support counterbalanced the literal and figurative weight of Kikuchi's biological father. In Kikuchi, Adamic discovered an impressionable young man whose uniquely tortuous family story made his contribution to Adamic's immigrant-focused anthology *From Many Lands* (1940) that much more engaging and attractive to sympathetic readers. Close readings of Kikuchi's original twenty-six-page contribution to the book, and the ultimately slick revision published by Adamic, complicate characterizations of their friendship, revealing Adamic's liberal rewriting of his ward's work, and the puzzled but subsequently grateful feelings with which Kikuchi read the final draft. Once again, a thread of Kikuchi's web spins out in connection to another overlapping network here, but this time in more directly interactive, mutually dependent, and problematic terms.[9]

What I have loosely termed the "Common Ground School" (see chapter 3) in the 1940s was headlined by an informal, multiracial network of writers, including Adamic; Anderson; McWilliams; Langston Hughes; Zora Neale Hurston; the Nisei activist Mary "Molly" Oyama; the novelist D'Arcy McNickle; Roi Ottley, the *Chicago Tribune* columnist and award-winning author of *New World A-Coming* (1943); Bucklin Moon, the editor of the popular anthology by and about Black America *A Primer for White Folks* (1945); and Lillian E. Smith, a native Georgian and the left-leaning editor of *South Today*. These writers were all developing and improving upon cultural pluralist ideas first introduced in the early part of the century by thinkers as varied as Mary Antin, the author of *Promised Land* (1912), and the essayists Randolph Bourne, who penned "Trans-National America"

(1916), and Horace Kallen, who wrote "Democracy and the Melting Pot" (1924). Inclusive as they believed their conceptualization of pluralism to be, the older generation of intellectuals (and some in the younger one) possessed an uncannily similar blind spot. Their collective belief in universalism and in America as an exceptionalist, multiethnic model for the world often confused ethnicity for race in problematic and, frankly, unsatisfying ways.[10] While many of these thinkers focused on anti-immigrant prejudice and inclusion, their understanding of ethnicity did not fully encapsulate the native, racialized citizens already struggling for racial equality, namely, American Indians and African Americans. Even some of the Nisei (like Kikuchi)—clearly the sons and daughters of immigrants—considered themselves indigenous to the land, removed from unfamiliar "Oriental" traditions and customs. As Kikuchi's narrative demonstrates, some Nisei even viewed African Americans as the ideal "model minority" in America to emulate, given Blacks' long-standing, organized, and historical protest against oppression.

None of the writers in either generation, however, matched the ideal formulation conjured by the newspaper editor Hamilton Holt, whose farsighted, racially and ethnically inclusive *Life Stories of Undistinguished Americans: As Told By Themselves* (1906) earnestly wrestled with the arbitrary definition of what and who an American could be. As the scholar Werner Sollors has painstakingly documented, Holt believed "the elastic term 'American' to refer to a very broad spectrum of the populace." A veritable parade of Americans populates Holt's list, including " an Irish maid," "Agnes M., a German nurse girl," "a Syrian journalist," "an anonymous Negro peon," "a Chinese laundryman and businessman, Lee Chew," and "an Indian, Ah-nen-la-de-ni." Sollors highlights this diversity—"Holt includes everyone in his notion of the 'American': Black, white, Indian, Asian, native-born, immigrant, refugee, temporary migrant, sojourner, men, women"—and its implication: "The collection virtually transformed the inhabitants of the whole world into potential Americans."[11]

A tall order by any measure, the challenge laid out by Holt to see these disparate people as Americans was unusually formidable. Consciously or unconsciously following Holt's model, midcentury intellectuals nonetheless tried envisioning and actualizing the inclusive, rather than the exclusive, America. Some did it better than others, while leaders such as Adamic, Anderson, and McWilliams, Black newspaper editors like Robert Abbott and John Sengstacke of the *Chicago Defender*, Almena Davis of the *L.A. Tribune*, and Charlotta Bass of the *California Eagle*, as well as the *Pacific Citizen*'s Tajiri, provided superb outlets of publication for antiracist and pro-immigrant voices, like Kikuchi, Ottley, Smith, Cayton, Hughes, the novelist Toshio Mori, and the short-story writer Hisaye Yamamoto.

Well-funded institutional publics also grew very much invested and interested in the subject of race and ethnicity, particularly in studies of the internment of Japanese Americans. Recruited by Cal's Dorothy Thomas, Kikuchi embarked on the Japanese American Evacuation and Resettlement Study (JERS), which was heavily funded by the Rockefeller, Columbia, and Giannini Foundations. This enterprise—not to be confused with the government's own War Relocation Authority (WRA) study of the camps—has come under close scrutiny since the war, but it indisputably remains a remarkable archive of primary-source materials directly relating to the day-to-day camp experience, camp politics and governance, post-camp resettlement, and the uncensored views of internees.[12] Kikuchi's own contribution would result in the publication of fifteen interviews with Japanese Americans resettled in Chicago, found in the edited volume by Thomas (the second of three planned volumes) entitled *The Salvage* (1952). Mentored by Thomas, who quickly grew into an ideal surrogate mother figure, Kikuchi also managed to buttonhole and garner critical advice from Thomas's husband, W. I., the coauthor (with Florian Znaniecki) of *The Polish Peasant in Europe and America* (1918–1920) as well as (in)famous member of the Chicago School of sociology.[13] Thomas and Znaniecki broke methodological ground with their work by relying on intensive life histories, an approach that Thomas would encourage Kikuchi to master over twenty years later for the Nisei's work on JERS.

Focusing on JERS invites consideration of the efficacy and heavy involvement of these social scientists in their evaluation and analysis of internment camp life, culture, and politics. Some institutions continued their studies outside relocation camps, charting the generally difficult transition of internees to resettlement in new cities with new lives and new freedoms, but also facing familiar nativist anti-Japanese feelings and prejudices. From the Gila River Relocation Center in Rivers, Arizona, to Chicago, Illinois, a hub of wartime production, culture, and Japanese resettlement, Kikuchi witnessed and recorded remarkable violations of Japanese Americans and the Constitution as well. His subjectivity as a prisoner undoubtedly complicated the objectivity of his participant-observer status in the study. Additionally, seldom a day went by without tension with the older-generation Issei infecting his writings, and his self-confidence sagging. It was Dorothy Thomas's role (and that of her shadowy husband) to push, cajole, and encourage Kikuchi in these early days, reassuring him of his indispensable contributions to the study: his ability to listen, to remember conversations nearly verbatim, and to ingratiate himself with differing elements of the camp and resettlement populations. Kikuchi's work left him vulnerable but open to the intersecting and overlapping counterpublics of institutional entities like the Cal team of demographers, the Chicago School of Sociology, and young Nisei social scientists, stuck between the reality of their own alienated status and the promise of inclusion in a privileged set of nationally recognized, respected institutions.[14]

The diaries that Kikuchi kept at Gila reveal a maturing, highly political man who was much more sympathetic to the various Japanese groups than ever before. The historian Arthur Hansen has convincingly argued that two distinct moments in Kikuchi's life—his tenure at the orphanage in Healdsburg, California, and his graduate days at Berkeley—marked critical moments in his self-identification. At the orphanage, surrounded by boys of so many different races, Kikuchi found himself most at ease in a multiracial and multiethnic context, all the way through his time at San Francisco State, which was more working class and racially diverse than Cal. Even in his teenage years, Kikuchi ran against the grain, joining a multiethnic gang in San Francisco called the Yamato Garage Gang. When he attended Cal, Kikuchi's friends were the radical Nisei, who purposely stayed on the fringe of the mainstream Japanese on campus but were Nisei nonetheless. Gila thus became the place where Kikuchi's self-awareness as a Nisei was transformed into a broader-minded but still strongly self-critical identification as part of the Nikkei, or entire Japanese diaspora. Before his detention in Tanforan and Gila, Kikuchi derogatorily dismissed those who were not in his circle as "Japs"—Issei, Nisei, or Kibei, rural or urban—as mere abstractions, while he reserved his most venomous ire for the older and backward Issei bachelors, with whom he associated his abusive and distant father. In camp, the disdain Kikuchi had cultivated for most of his young life was transformed into measured but significant empathy as he officially took on the job of social worker, ministering to the neediest of the incarcerated the best he could, seeing them, at last, as individuals under extreme duress. Seeing firsthand how the camp administration treated "his" people and listening to their stories as a caseworker, Kikuchi grew into a much more knowledgeable, vocal, and fierce advocate for the rights and needs of his fellow Nikkei. This larger community taught him much that his own nuclear family had never imparted to him.

In April 1943, Kikuchi left the camp, even though much of his family remained behind. As described in Kikuchi's resettlement diaries—or "Chicago diaries"—he became immersed in another politically active, socially mindful set of counterpublics in the 1940s: the working-class African American population of Chicago's South Side and their middle-class brethren in San Francisco and Berkeley. Even though the majority of Kikuchi's fieldwork and life histories were recorded in Gila River and Chicago, he earned the rare privilege of reporting back to Thomas in person in Northern California during the war, as well as an opportunity to visit his old neighborhood and university. This marked an intensely attentive time in his life; Kikuchi was joined by two of his younger sisters in Chicagoland (for whom he was granted legal guardianship) and reunited with one of his brothers in San Francisco. With family members at his side, Kikuchi experienced the most riveting and engaging encounters with African Americans: strangers on the streets of Chicago, old friends from San Francisco, and rising intelligentsia at Cal. While it would be naïve to characterize Kikuchi's situation during this time as one of "being" Black, he inhabits what Craig Wilder has termed a "situational Blackness," a consciousness that cultivates a sense of deep respect for the African American struggle on the rough-and-tumble streets of the Black metropolis, for the national civil rights movement led by African Americans, and for culture, religion, and politics in everyday Black life.[15] What's more, Kikuchi was not the only Nisei to look up to African Americans as a model minority to emulate and follow into the promised land that could be the new multiracial American democracy. Unlike many of his Nisei colleagues, Kikuchi had experiential closeness to African Americans—living next to and interacting with them daily for decades—although this made his difference from other Nisei one only of degree, not of kind.

Kikuchi's rich conversations with a couple of these very Nisei—in person and by letter—accompanied the end of the Pacific War and the beginnings of the Cold War. His correspondence with two university friends, Tsuneishi and Murase, thus dominate the tail end of the book. As a microcosm of the Nisei network of intelligentsia from Berkeley, the three principals discuss their various experiences in the military, attempting to forecast the fate of Nisei and all Americans in a postwar world order. Despite the epistolary form in which their intimate conversations took place and the challenging context in which they wrote (i.e., as U.S. military personnel with family members still interned), the trio constituted a fascinating counterpublic—outsiders looking in, insiders looking out, neither marginal men nor fully realized democratic citizens. The precarious nature of their situations fittingly encapsulated the unease that the nation would collectively experience in the hazy aftermath of a hot war that quickly turned cold, with little time for any reevaluation. For example, the violation of constitutional civil liberties for the sake of internal security: had the society matured enough during the war to question that bald-faced, undemocratic act?

By the end of the 1940s, the foreclosure of transformative democratic possibilities in the United States appeared as inevitable as the counteractive rising tide of anticolonialist fervor at home and abroad. Paradoxically, then, melancholy and hope fill the Kikuchi diaries at this point, just as the historical reality sounded a corresponding blue note of political redefinition and ideological retrenchment.

Where the Map Ultimately Leads Us

On the one hand, as the scholar Charlotte Brooks convincingly argues, Japanese Americans felt the strangeness of being the middleman minority between "the twilight zone" of black and white in their relatively new home of Chicago.[16] Similar kinds of liminality affected the lives of Issei and Nisei in their old homes on the West Coast. By 1955, as the historian Paul Spickard has shown, the number of mainland Japanese Americans living next door to one another dwindled to a negligible statistic.[17] "Yellow flight" into the suburbs of major cities followed on the heels of white flight. As a metaphoric thread among the progressive counterpublics of wartime and postwar America, the Nisei had—for the most part— abandoned the interracial alliances that had held such pregnant possibility only a decade earlier. Of course, a significant and plausible explanation for this kind of exodus was the internment itself. A major consequence of the war was the fragmentation and dispersal of many Nikkei families, not to mention their former possessions, property, and businesses: it would be difficult to rebuild wholesale communities from such physical and emotional devastation. Even some of the most radical Nisei, like Kikuchi, believed that drawing attention to the group—by living in ethnic enclaves, for example—would only resuscitate the nativist sentiment and economic jealousy that had led to their incarceration in the first place.

Furthermore, the late 1940s and the 1950s brought an air of postwar relief, but also an unnerving cocktail of suffocating Cold War rhetoric, McCarthyism, and an alarming type of conformist culture that superficially papered over a pervasive existential anxiety regarding nuclear annihilation. In short, it was an era of paradoxes. For example, Chief Justice Earl Warren—the same man who, as attorney general of California a decade earlier, had vociferously encouraged the internment of Japanese Americans—remarkably reshaped the direction of the high court and ostensibly improved African American lives with a watershed, unanimous decision to desegregate public schools in *Brown v. Board of Education* (1954). However, the following year, the court would recommend the implementation of desegregation to occur, confusingly, "with all deliberate speed." In another example, a decade later the conservative William Petersen would sear the contested symbol of the "model minority" onto the body of Japanese Americans, in a *New York Times Magazine* article entitled "Success Story, Japanese-American Style." Despite the platitudes expressed in Petersen's premature article, Japanese Americans in the mid-1960s remained on the rolls of welfare agencies, still struggled with less overt forms of exclusion in housing and jobs, and continued to experience the lingering scourge of anti-Asian, nativist prejudice, in city and suburb, from farmland to fishery.

On a more personal level for Kikuchi, W. I. Thomas died in 1947, and his work with Dorothy Thomas had formally come to an end a year earlier. In 1951, Louis Adamic allegedly committed suicide at his farmhouse in New Jersey. In other words, the luminous polestars of Kikuchi's life had faded away. Additionally, Kikuchi would separate from many of his Japanese American friends, move to Manhattan with Yuriko, and raise their children, Susan and Lawrence. Meanwhile, politically, culturally, and socially, America inexorably entered an age of consensus. That kind of sterile conformity and emphasis on U.S. authority (vis-à-vis the USSR) would not sit well with a man who had crossed the brook of fire that was the 1940s.

Traveling Beyond the Edges of the Map

Fifteen years before Kikuchi conducted research for Thomas at the University of Chicago's Department of Sociology, one of its graduates and future professors, Louis Wirth, a pioneer in the field of urban studies and race relations, wrote: "If we knew the full life-story of a single individual in his social setting, we would probably know most of what is worth knowing about social life and human nature."[18] He was championing the importance and power of the personal document, as opposed to mere statistical evidence, in conveying the history of a person, time, and place.[19] Exploring history through the looking glass of a single life offers what the Yale scholar David Brion Davis deems "a concreteness and sense of historical development that most studies of culture lack . . . by showing how cultural tensions and contradictions may be internalized, struggled with, and resolved within actual individuals." By Davis's reckoning, "it offers the most promising key to the synthesis of culture and history."[20] In this context, the Kikuchi diaries provide not only a window into the evolution of an intellectual, but also a broader canvas upon which the history of racial and ethnic formation in wartime and postwar America can be projected, played out, and analyzed.

To that end, a reexcavation of the Kikuchi diaries reveals avenues of information and unexamined layers in the history of "democratic interracialism" at a time when America's democracy was hardly a foregone conclusion. A historical set of dynamics and processes in the 1940s allowed for, even actively provoked, the instability of defining key terms like "race," "democracy," and "citizenship." The multiple factors of the war, the internment, the ongoing civil rights movement, labor shortages and agitation, among other causes, encouraged an unprecedented set of overlapping counterpublics to interact and seek common cause, politically and ideologically. In the formation of such alliances, ostensibly immutable and preconceived notions of "how the races get along" were proved entirely provisional and contingent or, more simply, fluid. A new historical route renders old maps incomplete and long-held interpretations wanting. Charles Kikuchi thus stands at the center of these intersecting counterpublics. Under the influence of Adamic and his band of ethnic writers, the Thomases, fellow Nisei, and African American thinkers (of the "talented tenth" or not), Kikuchi enjoyed broadening the frames of his analysis beyond the dyad of black and white, incorporating the ideas and experiences of Asians, Jews, Mexicans, white ethnics, and indigenous people, as well as that of fellow travelers, migrant laborers, urban workers, and marginalized intellectuals in a fully globalized context. As John Stauffer wisely advises: "Only by changing perspectives, listening to multiple voices from different social groups and vantage points, is it possible to understand how racial identities get defined, blurred, and remade."[21]

What is more, Kikuchi's vision of the democratic experiment did not simply pour all racial and ethnic minorities, like molten lead, into homogeneous molds of white Americans. On the contrary, his ideal required a significant and moral transformation of society, one in which seeing Black or hearing Japanese engendered neither fear nor stigma in the eyes and ears of others. He most demonstratively put this philosophy into practice when counseling traumatized African American veterans of the Vietnam War later in life: Kikuchi recognized each man's individual problems, delineated consciously structural and systemic barriers to Black progress, and tried his best to provide aid and proper employment for these young men. Tragically, given its level of unprofessionalism, the Veterans Administration hospital where Kikuchi worked assumed that the psychotic tendencies of all Black soldiers were a tried and true matter of policy, systematically committing more and more Black vets to psychiatric wards without taking any in-depth case histories or spending measurable face-to-face time with the patients. Kikuchi retired from this position in the early 1970s, but not before he purposely took many of those African American men under his supervision in order to give them proper and professional treatment as individuals, vastly different from one another yet conveniently grouped together by his intellectually lazy colleagues as one dark and psychologically damaged monolith. His coworkers eventually left him alone with his Black patients or immediately referred them to him, but by his midfifties, Kikuchi decided he had had enough, and retired in 1973. Yet he needed to make one last point: he stood outside the hospital where he had worked for decades, strategically positioned on the public sidewalk across from the building's private property, and protested the Vietnam War in plain sight, with a homemade placard and the verve of his voice.

Deeply invested in plumbing the depths of racism, xenophobia, and the basic fear of the unfamiliar, Kikuchi initiated countless discussions with a variety of people—of various colors, religions, classes, ideologies, intellects, and prejudices—both in person and by letter. As a consequence, his diary weaves an intricate web of interconnected conversations, a large number of which focus intently on the intersection of race, class, ethnicity, and the possibilities for this elusive new American democracy. One might even posit that the young diarist hatched a "Kikuchi thesis" while living his last days in the crucible of an Arizona internment camp. On March 22, 1943, he soliloquized at length, asserting that racial history cannot repeat itself:

> Although we talk about maintaining Democracy, the defeat of the Axis is not going to solve any of the minority problems. I think that the very quality of future civilization is dependent upon the solution of these problems . . . If we can get them [the white majority] to have the same ideals of democracy, much of the world's ills will be solved . . . The Nisei group is important in that the problem will never be solved if rehabilitation is merely going to be a restoration of the status quo before the War.[22]

In this light, then, my work at first glance appears to be that of an eavesdropper on important debates or that of a translator of precious correspondence. But cartographer appears to be a more apt category: one who draws lines and connections between historical pinpoints on Kikuchi's map of innumerable conversations with mentors, friends, colleagues, strangers, family members, and other loved ones. Such dialogues prove not only that a discourse of interracial alliance was taking shape and evolving at this time, but also that the boundaries between the discussants were far more porous and arbitrary than initially drawn. Through Kikuchi's diary and my larger narrative of the period, the reader gains a greater sense of the substance and makeup of the oppositional groups in wartime, both formal and informal; the degree to which these networks were taken seriously and had an impact; and their revealing areas of overlap on many levels (intellectual, relational, geographic, ideological, and publicational). Cultural history as a field has not sufficiently considered the possibility of "the greatest generation" on the lower frequencies—previous narratives have not mapped out this especially challenging and untraveled route. My particular interpretation of this history therefore attempts to demonstrate not only the meaning making and agency of ordinary people under extraordinary circumstances, but also the structures and institutions against which they strategized and operated, sometimes successfully.[23] In the process, the contour and arc of a complex cultural history of race relations in the 1940s move into sharper relief, and one man's life comes to represent the through-line to a world of possibility.

A Note on Terminology

I wish to take this opportunity to clarify my usage of *internment camp* instead of *concentration camp*, or other similar euphemisms (e.g., *assembly centers* or *relocation centers*) regarding the forced removal and incarceration of Japanese Americans. I often use these euphemistic terms in my text as referents to the historical period, such as "during the era of internment." However, these terms—as widely propagated by the U.S. government—were consciously chosen to diminish the experiences of incarcerated Japanese Americans and blunt the language used to describe the severity and truth of these experiences. I thus strongly support the Power of Words Resolution (2010) passed by the National Council of the Japanese American Citizens League (JACL) and the most recent debate (November 2011) over terminology reform facilitated by community leaders and intellectuals, like Roger Daniels, Don Hata, Aiko Herzig-Yoshinaga, Karen Ishizuka, Tetsuden Kashima, Mako Nakagawa (author of the resolution), Barbara Takei and the Tule Lake Committee, among many others. Their work builds on earlier foundations laid by Paul Bailey, Allan Bosworth, Daniels, Richard Drinnon, and Ray Okamura.

To be clear, *internment camp* legally refers to the incarceration of "enemy aliens" by the government in times of war, a term which does not appropriately encompass the dehumanizing nature of Japanese American incarceration (throughout North America) which explicitly included citizens and noncitizens. To be sure, the reform movement is much more than a semantic debate, but also a sincere effort to address and revisit history, to accurately convey the injustice and violation of an entire population's civil and human rights.

Therefore, I wholeheartedly endorse the eradication of euphemistic terminology in respect to the historical representation of the World War II Japanese American exclusion and detention experience. However, I must also concede to the reader that I did not become fully aware of the reform movement and its far-reaching accomplishments until my book's publication process had, regrettably, reached a point of no return. This is not the fault of the Press, nor that of colleagues, advisors, or anyone else. I alone am responsible for the usage of such terms and I will hopefully have the opportunity to revise them in any subsequent edition of my book.

It is my equal hope that the history of interracialism told here, with courageous Japanese American men and women at the center, will not be lost amid this worthy and genuine concern over terminology.

Chapter 1

Before Pearl Harbor: Taking the Measure of a "Marginal" Man

On September 25, 1988, the writing finally stopped. Charlie Kikuchi had put his pen down at last. For forty-seven years, he had opened up a blank journal or slipped out a fresh piece of paper and started recalling that day's odyssey, from mundane to the epic, writing down whatever thoughts came to mind. For the first thirty-four of those years, he kept a personal diary, both hand- and typewritten, while over his final thirteen years, he substituted diligent correspondence with family, friends, and scholars instead. In the course of his observations, Kikuchi, a social worker by trade, ultimately penned more than one hundred volumes' worth of diaries and letters, totaling well more than one hundred thousand pages. While a preliminary argument may be made for the importance of his writings based on sheer size alone—they fill thirty linear feet of shelf space—a more persuasive and substantive claim can be staked on the content and historical significance of the "Kikuchi Diary" and his collected papers. They cover the most memorable events in twentieth-century American history: the bombing of Pearl Harbor; the U.S. entry into World War II; the internment of 120,000 fellow Japanese Americans; the Cold War; the civil rights movement; Vietnam; Watergate; and the illusory "morning in America." What is more, the settings (quite literally, where he sat) for his writing were as equally distinctive as the moments he reflected upon: San Francisco, where he spent his youth and young adulthood; the San Bruno, California, racetrack, former home of the celebrity thoroughbred Seabiscuit, which would serve as his temporary prison barracks for four months; an Arizona internment camp that squatted on an American Indian reservation during the war; the South Side of Chicago, or "Black Metropolis," the site of his postwar resettlement; the American South, which served as the base for his U.S. Army training; and his home of forty-two years, New York City. Kikuchi also traveled extensively in western Europe, East Asia, and the Soviet Union, thanks to his wife's occupation as a world-class dancer. Few contemporary historical figures would canvas as much landscape—in writing and in geography—with the same degree of Tocquevillian insight into America and its contemporary experiments with democracy. World War II had, after all, dislodged a number of the certainties and, in some cases, bedrock pieties, of American democracy; therefore, new routes to understanding what it meant to be an American and a democrat in the postwar era were just being mapped out.

Kikuchi first gained limited exposure as the author of "A Young American with a Japanese Face" in *From Many Lands*, the aforementioned volume edited by Adamic—himself an immigrant from Slovenia and the celebrated progressive activist and coeditor of the journal *Common Ground*. Kikuchi's chapter, however, was attributed to "Anonymous," thereby limiting knowledge of his authorship to select Nisei and members of progressive circles. In February 1942, President Franklin D. Roosevelt issued Executive Order 9066, which resulted in the evacuation of more than 120,000 Japanese and Japanese Americans from the West Coast to ten relocation camps far from the official military exclusion zone. In the course of his internment (May 1942–April 1943)—first at the Tanforan Assembly Center in San Bruno, and then later, during his prolonged incarceration at the Gila River Relocation Center—and during his resettlement in Chicago (April 1943–August 1945), Kikuchi was tapped by the Berkeley scholar Dorothy Swaine Thomas to collect data and interviews (case histories) for the Japanese American Evacuation and Resettlement Study (JERS), sponsored by the University of California at Berkeley. Kikuchi's reporting of Japanese Americans' experiences in the camps and in Chicago, combined with his personal diary, ultimately led him to make substantial, credited contributions to the study's second published volume, *The Salvage*, in 1952. Again, though, few knew of Kikuchi's contributions outside the community of Nisei intellectuals and some social scientists at Cal and Chicago.[1]

In certain social circles, some might have recognized Kikuchi as the husband of Yuriko Amemiya, the highly respected dancer famous for her collaborations with Martha Graham and Jerome Robbins during a sixty-year career on stage and in film. By his own lights, however, Kikuchi eventually earned recognition, in 1973, when the noted historian and former Thomas student John Modell edited and published *The Kikuchi Diary: Chronicle from an American Concentration Camp*, excerpts from the first nine months (December 1941 through August 1942) of Kikuchi's account, focusing on his stay at Tanforan. More than fifteen years later, Kikuchi himself submitted a reflective piece to *Views from Within* (1989), a collection of essays that analyzed JERS. In an extremely thoughtful and unconventional approach, the sociologist Dana Y. Takagi focused her essay on the importance of Kikuchi's case histories, privileging them with having broken "the Nisei silence" and contributed to the underdeveloped history of race relations and ethnicity and to the history of Nisei women (this last accolade was due to Kikuchi's number of unadorned case histories, or interviews, with resettled Nisei young women in postwar Chicago). Finally, the prominent oral historian Arthur Hansen recorded Kikuchi's life history a mere month before Kikuchi's death, planning to include it in the comprehensive Japanese American World War II Evacuation Oral History Project based out of California State University, Fullerton.[2]

My own examination of Charles Kikuchi builds on the sturdy foundation laid by these incredibly generous scholars, providing a more detailed portrait of Kikuchi over a longer period of time, based largely on his diaries, papers, and letters between 1940 and 1950. While these previous scholars analyzed the diaries by focusing mainly on the experience of the Japanese American internment, I attempt to read them as a synecdoche for the highly vexed but evolving relationships between ethnic and racial groups during this exceptional moment of the 1940s. Where scholars have considered only the diaries documenting Kikuchi's incarceration (approximately eleven months), I have broadened the sample to include a decade's worth of unpublished work. I have also included previously unexamined correspondence between Kikuchi and his mentors, colleagues, and family members, while incorporating original nonarchival materials given to me by his wife, his friends, and scholars who studied him, all in an effort to render a more complete portrait of Kikuchi before, during, and after the 1940s. The diaries reflect a young man's developing sense of himself and the world around him. Honest, direct, self-critical, witty, and thoughtful, Kikuchi writes with a dynamic voice and perspective: an intellectual in the making, a historical subject wrestling with questions of race, democracy, and individualism at the same time that the nation at large was struggling with very similar questions.

Viewed through this particular lens of Kikuchi's experience, the period's collective social and cultural history becomes clearer. Kikuchi's diary and papers provide substantive evidence of interracial alliances and conflicts at a time when the theory and practice of democracy itself were rigorously being tested and redefined. During the first stage of this period, or the early years of the internment (1942–1943), Japanese Americans experienced an extreme form of prejudice, oppression, and segregation, while fellow minorities initially feared for their own welfare, understandably hewing to shibboleths of unqualified patriotism. Eventually, though, the absurd arbitrariness of the evacuation compelled other American minorities to consider their own possible futures. African Americans, for example—having already borne separate and unequal treatment for more than three hundred years—recognized the all-too-familiar signposts: the segregation and mass incarceration of 120,000 U.S. citizens, rounded up like human chattel and placed in horse stalls with little or no consideration of constitutional rights. In the second stage—the resettlement of Japanese Americans, circa 1943–1945—growing populations of job-seeking minorities struggled over and negotiated the restricted urban spaces they were now forced to share with recently freed Japanese: after the roundup and evacuation were complete, African Americans, Filipinos, and Mexicans moved into low-rent West Coast neighborhoods, formerly known as "Little Tokyos," in San Francisco, Los Angeles, and Seattle. Meanwhile, a decent number of internees moved to new, unfamiliar cities in the Midwest and Northeast, some settling in established but small Japanese communities in Chicago and New York. In these more complicated and more crowded urban crucibles, blacks, browns, and yellows met in inevitable conflict, but also in common cause over jobs, housing, politics, culture, white supremacy, and the war itself.

Shaking the Tree

Whereas Alexis de Tocqueville arrived at his conclusions about nineteenth-century America as an outsider, Kikuchi lived America as both insider and outsider. Born in Vallejo, California, on January 18, 1916, Kikuchi struggled as the son of Issei immigrants, the second sibling among eight. His father, Nakajiro, had first arrived in the United States around the turn of the century, with great hopes of returning to Japan a wealthy man. However, after several years of toiling as a migratory farmworker, and an additional five years of service as a cook in the U.S. Navy, the elder Kikuchi put down stakes in the waterfront district of Vallejo, near the Mare Island Naval Base, opening up a barbershop that would eventually double as the family's home.[3] Kikuchi's mother, Shizuko, the educated daughter of a well-respected middle-class family in Japan, was seventeen years younger than Nakajiro. A broker arranged their marriage in 1913, for the sum of $500, and Mrs. Kikuchi did not meet her husband until the day he returned to Japan for their wedding. Her family took Nakajiro at his word that he was a wealthy American businessman, so Shizuko was greatly surprised when she discovered her new husband's occupation and living arrangements: a small barber's shack in the midst of dilapidated buildings, saloons, and brothels—the Wild West indeed. In Japan, the status of a barber was extremely low, since women usually filled such roles. According to her son, however, "[Shizuko] resigned herself to the situation."[4]

The Kikuchis gave each of their eight children Japanese names, but as was customary among Nisei, the names were Anglicized as they grew older. The first child was a daughter, who kept her name, Mariko, born in 1914. The siblings following Charlie were Sutekatsu, born in 1917 and called Jack; Haruka, born in 1919, who became Alice; Emiko, born in 1924, was known as Emi or Amy; Yoriko, born in 1926, changed her name to Bette; Takeshi, born in 1929, called himself Tom; and Miyako, born in 1931, became Marji. Charlie's Japanese name was quite beautiful, even fitting, in its translation: "Tatsuro," meaning "standing man."[5] He never revealed his "screwy Japanese name," according to Dorothy Thomas. In fact, she reported, he simply took to the nickname "Charlie" given him by his father's friends in the barbershop.[6] Similarly, Kikuchi's best friend, Warren Tsuneishi, confirmed his pal's extreme secrecy regarding the name, remembering an occasion when Kikuchi showed Tsuneishi a copy of his birth certificate with the middle name blacked out. He commented, "I never quite understood Charlie's attitude toward his Japanese middle name, except in terms of his profound desire to be considered an 'American,' and his consistent rejection of anything to do with Japanese identity."[7]

Despite her claims to the contrary, Mrs. Kikuchi found it challenging to adjust to her husband's career, and times grew difficult for Charlie's parents. In addition, because of his father's excessive drinking and gambling problems (habits he had developed long before starting a family), Kikuchi often faced the threat of physical and emotional abuse. In part because he was the eldest son, and in part because Nakajiro blamed him exclusively for Shizuko's threats of divorce, Charles alone suffered his father's beatings. The elder Kikuchi also cast aspersions on his younger wife's fidelity, inexplicably focusing the brunt of his suspicion and anger on Charlie. As a result, at the age of eight, the younger Kikuchi was placed in the Boys and Girls Industrial Home and Farm at Lytton Springs, an orphanage run by the Salvation Army, in Healdsburg, California (about eighty miles north of San Francisco). For all intents and purposes a ward of the state, he would enjoy little or no contact with his family over the next decade. Almost apologetic and certainly self-effacing, he would offer further rationale for his father's actions in a 1955 letter:

> My father never really believed I was illegitimate. He was extremely jeal-ous of my mother and this was his way of getting back at her. As I was a weakly child, it helped his theory since he felt that no first son of his could be that weak. I had defective hearing as a child and many illnesses, and my mother overprotected me and this gave my father further reason to take it out on me.[8]

Given these circumstances, Kikuchi created a surrogate family of his own at the orphanage, a diverse unit that included children from many racial and ethnic backgrounds; a veritable "League of Nations" he claimed.[9] This unique situation prepared Kikuchi for his numerous interracial and interethnic relationships later in life, predisposing him to an extremely high level of comfort in future multicul-tural or interracial milieus (like Chicago and New York). I further posit that this period of abuse and abandonment affected Kikuchi in two other specific ways. First, in the wake of violence at the hand of his father, Kikuchi developed a deep-seated, but ultimately reversible, resentment of all things Issei, deeming both the generation and all it represented as too "Japanese-y."[10] Second, as the book will demonstrate, Kikuchi was earnestly hypersensitive to the predicament of those most severely abused and violated in the proverbial American family: minorities in general, but African Americans in particular. Back at the orphanage, this early surrogate family undoubtedly helped Kikuchi navigate his parentless adolescence. In regard to this particularly challenging time, Modell thoughtfully—and I would argue, accurately—offers a psychoanalytic reading of the young man at this point:

> For the next decade Kikuchi would lead the life of an orphan at the home, developing there the mental qualities which life after such extreme trauma demanded. As Kikuchi recalls, he grew up in rather rough but basically humane surroundings, a self-motivated but entirely "regular" guy. Behind these qualities Kikuchi has guarded the deeper recesses of his psyche; of these, the present diary at best reveals fleeting images, for by 1942 his defenses were well set.[11]

After graduating from Healdsburg High School in the spring of 1934, hon-orably finishing in the top four of his class (despite a foggy, fifty-four-year-old claim to Hansen that he was salutatorian!), Kikuchi departed the area for San Francisco, contemplating both college and a job.[12] While his family invited him to return to live with them in Vallejo, Kikuchi chose to tough it out in San Francisco as a houseboy, one of the few Depression-era occupations open to many Japanese Americans. The money he earned helped him enroll in San Francisco State College in 1935, where he concentrated in California history (not the "Oriental History" major concocted by Adamic for the "touched-up" narrative of "A Young American with a Japanese Face"), with the hope that he might one day teach at the high school level; he knew, however, that few if any schools would willingly hire a Japanese American. All the while, Kikuchi maintained his position as houseboy, forming a unique relationship with the family that employed him. Although he cleaned and waited on the dinner table, Kikuchi eventually earned enough respect from his employers to sit in the front seat of the family car or join the family and houseguests in occasional conversation and debate (still in his servant's coat, however, despite his exaggerated self-inflation). Modell reports that Kikuchi even managed to convert "his employers from typical California contempt for Japanese Americans to a far more enlightened position." For Kikuchi's part, he told Modell that "living in that household was significant to me because . . . I began to develop [there] more and more identification with Americanism, so that it was not just an intellectual attitude, but an exposure to a way of life that I sort of accepted even though I was resentful of the so-called servant role (which was not really a servant role)." Modell further asserts that Kikuchi imbibed "the middle-class values of hard work and material success" from this surrogate family, and Kikuchi himself affirmed, "I didn't get that in my own home; I didn't get that in the orphanage."[13]

At other moments, particularly on weekends, Kikuchi found hours of recreation with another surrogate family, the Yamato Garage Gang, a group of young men who were unemployed, unmarried, and unfazed by outside attempts to corral them into organized activity. As Modell describes it, "Devoted mainly to gambling, mischief, whoring, and especially to talking about these exploits, the Yamatos provided Kikuchi with casual, undemanding amusement." Furthermore, Kikuchi may have been even more attracted to the gang for its multiethnic makeup: Italians mixed easily with Chinese, Japanese, and according to Kikuchi, at least one African American. Here, as Modell rightly points out, "the barriers of 'segregation' could at least temporarily crumble."[14] Kikuchi could well understand the lure of such a group for Nisei like himself: "I guess they were maladjusted individuals who were fighting very openly against the confining social structure, which was very inhibiting: being in a 'JA' community, working for a Japanese company, having these controls of the Japanese community on them."[15]

By his junior year at San Francisco State, Kikuchi had established himself as a leader on campus, first by helping "campus queens" pass a philosophy course in which he excelled; he devised a clever system of cheating on tests: "Raise this foot, it's true, raise the other foot, it's false."[16] In return, those same campus queens and their friends on the football team joined Kikuchi's International Relations Club, making it the most popular extracurricular group on campus. After graduating in May 1939, Kikuchi found himself in the midst of an identity crisis. He had deplored the self-segregating tendencies of the Nisei on campus and had similarly grown frustrated with the generational conflict (of Americanization versus tradition) he witnessed taking place between the Issei and Nisei of San Francisco. In a June 1945 letter to Dorothy Swaine Thomas, commenting on his postcollege blues, he conceded, "There were many times when I actually wished that I weren't a Jap. It wasn't because of any shame of my background, but I felt that economically I would be better off if I did not have a Japanese face." Kikuchi confided his misgivings to a professor at SF State, who unflinchingly joked that he should undergo surgery "to eliminate the slant-eyed effect." Kikuchi considered the procedure, but ultimately decided against it: "It was a silly idea, but it indicates the mood of my thinking at that time. The two years after graduation from college were extremely frustrating in many ways."[17]

To be fair, Kikuchi certainly was not the only Nisei to entertain such a drastic measure. Fred Korematsu, a Nisei from Oakland who would eventually gain prominence for his role in the Supreme Court case bearing his name (*Korematsu v. United States*, 323 U.S. 214 [1944]), actually underwent such surgery in the immediate aftermath of Pearl Harbor. In an effort to avoid the roundup of West Coast Japanese, and aided by his Italian American girlfriend, Korematsu changed his name to "Clyde Sarah," barely passing as a Spanish Hawai'ian, while he pursued an advertisement he found for an eyelid lift. Many years later, he recalled, "The doctor just slit my eyes and put some of the skin up. It didn't work out right because my mother recognized me."[18] The authorities eventually caught Korematsu in May 1942 as he waited on a street corner for the girlfriend, who never showed up. Arrested for remaining in a military zone barred to anyone of Japanese ancestry, Korematsu was sentenced to five years of probation and placed in military custody at a relocation center in Topaz, Utah. Spurred on by some of his campmates, including Kikuchi, he subsequently challenged the government's right to imprison him, lost the case, and appealed unsuccessfully to the Supreme Court in 1944. By a margin of six to three, the majority based its ruling solely on Korematsu's failure to leave an enforced military zone, not on the lack of due process or the constitutionality of the internment camps. The three dissenting judges (Robert H. Jackson, Owen J. Roberts, and Frank Murphy) vigorously cast doubt on the decision, decrying "this legalization of racism."[19] It would later be revealed that the government had withheld crucial facts in the case, and forty years later, Korematsu would finally gain justice and a reversal on the grounds that he was not initially provided a fair trial. This particular case demonstrates that to an American of Japanese ancestry at this specific historical moment, a procedure as terrifying as invasive plastic surgery was a *reasonable* way to cope with an atmosphere of systematic repression and terror.

Sander Gilman provides context for this type of elective surgery: "Ethnic difference among groups that are perceived as 'ugly' and of 'poor character' remains unacceptable even in a multiethnic society. One can look different, but not *too* different. Thus Asian American men have been 'stereotyped as being short people with flat faces and slanted eyes.'" In an effort to appear less Asian, or more Caucasian, Gilman argues, some of them seek common aesthetic procedures, like rhinoplasty (nose surgery) and blepharoplasty (eyelid surgery). He concludes, "The shrunken nose coupled with the revealing eye take on yet other meanings as a sign of difference and visibility."[20] In Korematsu's case, however, the desired goal was *in*visibility. If the surgery had been done before Pearl Harbor, he might have wanted to look more Caucasian strictly for aesthetic purposes. After December 7, however, the surgery was undoubtedly an act of desperate self-preservation. He even admitted to the Federal Bureau of Investigation (FBI) that it was an effort to conceal his racial identity in the face of being rounded up for internment.[21]

Unsurprisingly, Kikuchi met Korematsu at Tanforan, where many Bay Area Japanese Americans were sent. He remarks on the superficial issues first: "According to paper reports he had his face lifted, but he looked quite Japanese to me. The only thing was that he had an operation on the slits of his eyes."[22] It is an odd observation: one wonders what exactly Kikuchi means by "looked quite Japanese," because he clearly notices Korematsu's surgery; in other words, it is not simply the slant of one's eyes that essentially defines Japanese-ness. Something else assured Kikuchi of Korematsu's "authenticity." As Kikuchi's account continues, one gains the sense that he considers Korematsu's determination to challenge to the constitutionality of the evacuation to indicate much more of his true character. After Korematsu and his brother Hi solicit the advice of Kikuchi and other Tanforan evacuees, Kikuchi asserts:

> Fred has the "guts" to fight the thing. I don't believe that the group would suffer by it. In fact, we have everything to gain. We are not prisoners of war and our civil rights have been taken away without due process of law. Fred has not made up his mind yet, but he is thankful that many Nisei believes as he does in regard to this situation.[23]

As both a confirmation of his past work with other minorities (e.g., his migratory farmwork experience with Filipinos and Mexicans), and as a foreshadowing of Kikuchi's growing belief in the need to broker differences across various ideological or racialized lines, he concludes that those meeting with Korematsu were "a well-rounded group representing the 'radicals,' the progressives, JACL reactionary and church elements." And this diversity was important: "We believed that unity would be helped in the war effort."[24] Even when that unity (for Korematsu's court appeal) seemingly ran against the grain of the "war effort," serving to challenge the very structure and set of institutions that had imprisoned Kikuchi and his fellow Nikkei on the grounds of "military necessity."

For Kikuchi, however, this dilemma of being, and looking like, a Japanese American predated America's entry into the war and the trials of Korematsu. As he later conceded about the year after college graduation:

> I was one of the most confused young men in the Bay Area. There just did not seem to be any answer to things, and often the situation looked quite hopeless in spite of my determination to be optimistic. Instead of becom-

ing extremely bitter about it, my attitude developed more and more into "I'll show them that I'm an American."[25]

Even when trying to follow up on these surges of patriotism, though, Kikuchi encountered great frustration. One of his college friends—presumably white and identified only as "Frank"—who had been heavily involved in the labor movement offered to help Kikuchi find work through union connections. "But it was the same old story," Kikuchi remembered. "I couldn't join the union because I had a Japanese face." This was even after Kikuchi had joined his friend at the waterfront to picket ships hauling cargo to Spain and Asia. On one occasion, they had set up outside the Japanese consul's office.

> Frank and I strolled up and down the street with an American flag and placards. When the Japanese officials came out for lunch, they looked at me in amazement and made some comment; but I didn't understand what they were saying. I felt that the embargo of American goods to the Orient had to be strictly enforced because of the aggressive ambition of Japan. It never occurred to me that some day I would be looked upon with suspicion and regarded as a Japanese.[26]

In essence, the "American" (read: "white") union rejected Kikuchi for being too Japanese, while Japanese nationals scoffed at him for being too American. His sense of being on the margin seemed only to deepen. Even as Kikuchi's enthusiasm for labor unions subsided, his friend attempted to recruit him for the Young Communist League (YCL), but Kikuchi demurred: "I personally liked many of the young fellows in this organization, but my political sentiments were not quite this far to the left." In fact, his faith in America still remained strong, perhaps buoyed by a wishful hope in its progressive possibilities:

> I still had a firm belief in democracy, and I felt it would be a betrayal to overthrow it simply because I was having a difficult time finding a job. I tried to remain consistent in my attitude that a large part of it would be up to the individual's efforts and that I could not blame the system entirely for failures on my part.[27]

At the same time, despite misgivings about appearing too "Japanese-y," Kikuchi could not entirely extricate himself from the Nisei group. For example, in the wake of leaving SF State, Kikuchi had no choice but to live in the Japanese community. Rent and food were markedly cheaper there, and other neighborhoods simply excluded Japanese Americans with restrictive covenants and other discriminatory practices. He felt a certain amount of unease, however, going so far as to exclaim, "It grated upon my ears to hear the strange Japanese tongue everywhere. It seemed that even the young Nisei used the language exclusively." But he immediately acknowledges having made an error: "This was a mistaken impression, since I later found that they [the Japanese-speaking Nisei] were quite Americanized and that many of them were going through similar conflicts as I was."[28] Again, Kikuchi consciously distinguished between the backwardness and "old country" habits of the first generation—most intensely associated with his father—and the seeming capacity for change in the second generation.

Like so many young Nisei, Kikuchi was intent on figuring out who he was, emotionally, intellectually, and possibly even ideologically. His resistance to authority figures, for example, still manifested itself in his living in San Francisco during the school year and working in the fields, factories, or canneries during the summer, all efforts to stay away from the family home in Vallejo. Furthermore, he continued to fraternize with the Yamato Garage Gang on the weekends, a relief from the mainstream Nisei "squares" on campus. The irony was that by choosing such a multiracial gang of ne'er-do-wells, drinkers, and fighters, Kikuchi conceded that the gang was an entrée of its own into the Nikkei community, at the time his "strongest tie to the Japanese community."[29] Simple things like being invited over to eat home-cooked Japanese food or knowing other gang members who sympathized with the issue of Nisei unemployment were powerful incentives to keep up his "membership" as well as reassuring and educative experiences for a young man who knew very little from whence he came. Eventually, though, he admitted to tiring of such company, citing the gang's lack of purpose, and he regularly returned to school each semester, energized in his pursuit of a degree. But he would still see these gang members on weekends when he wanted to get away from the eggheads, or when he would bring an intellectual but sexually active buddy to one of the gang's regular whorehouses. Again, these loose, informal habits for Kikuchi inevitably informed how he began to think of his own Japanese-ness, consciously or not. In other words, lines were much more flexible and porous in reality, challenging his theoretically discrete lines of Nisei versus Issei, or working class versus mainstream.

Ironically, the gang enjoyed modest success over the years. A couple of the Nisei members became decorated war heroes, and other members were successful horticulturalists and small business owners. And in the most celebrated case, Goro Suzuki changed his name to the Chinese-sounding "Jack Soo," subsequently starring in Rodgers and Hammerstein's *Flower Drum Song* (1958), but Soo was best known for his memorable wisecracking role of Detective Nick Yemana on the sitcom *Barney Miller* (1975–1979). Of course, there were less romantic outcomes for other members, as Kikuchi wistfully recalled a few suffering from alcoholism or succumbing to suicide. The gang also imparted a skill that Kikuchi would take with him to Cal, to the benefit of all his Nisei pinhead pals: Robin Hood–like thievery. Kikuchi remembered one major football game with rival Stanford held in Palo Alto that year. As he tells it, his friends were penniless and hungry, but none of them wanted to accompany Kikuchi to burgle empty Stanford fraternity houses, for fear of being caught or beaten up. So he drove his Model A to Palo Alto, absconded with money from the wallets of absent frat boys (and allegedly nothing else), and came home to fill the food pot. That night, he and the boys ate like kings. Without shame, he admitted to Modell, "To the people there, and to me, this was economic justification; they owe it to us!"[30]

This was not the kind of behavior expected from aspiring Nisei, but Kikuchi was a big enough personality within the group that no one really questioned him, at least not to his face. While he demonstrated his yen to redistribute money like a good communist, he tried on different ideological clubs at Cal, including the Young Democrats (YD), not to be confused with his earlier brush with the YCL. Having considered the conservative Japanese American Citizens League (JACL) on one extreme, Yamato friends on the other, as well as his siblings on the occasional weekend, Kikuchi was pulled in many different directions. He tended to remember the Young Democrats' participation on campus and then in camp as being very much "half-assed" and found them, like the JACL, surprisingly accommodationist. As he puts it, everyone at Tanforan thought the YDs were communists, but at the end of the day, they were incrementalists who did not want to rock the boat. For example, when Korematsu finally decided to press his case in court, the Young Democrats demurred, not "wanting to disturb the war effort." Even worse, in Kikuchi's estimation, the YDs would not protest the evacuation because, with the Soviet Union in mind, they wanted a second front in the war opened up. He derisively recollects: "Because they didn't want anything to be disturbing the Russian part of the war, they were willing to have [our] constitutional rights violated."[31] Providing broader historical context, Harry Kitano and others remind us that Ernest "Ernie" Iiyama, one of Kikuchi's buddies who strategized with Korematsu at Tanforan, "recalled a group of approximately forty Nisei who formed the Young Democrats of the East Bay (Berkeley and Oakland, California) in the mid-1930's." They "discussed discrimination, political participation, and civic issues," although "they were ignored by the vast majority of their Nisei peers." Moreover, they point out that "the [YDs] were considered too radical by the majority of Japanese Americans," while folks like Kikuchi and his Cal circle thought they were not radical enough. Kitano makes the pertinent and glaring point, however, that among left-leaning Japanese Americans, "even more 'radical' were the Japanese American Communists, such as Karl Yoneda."[32]

Japanese America's Popular Front: "An Ordinary Working Stiff"

The legendary Yoneda and Kikuchi never met during this time, but Yoneda's example provides tremendous insight into the relatively unknown sphere of Communist Party (CP) Nisei who cut their teeth during the Popular Front in the 1930s and into the early 1940s. One might even informally position Yoneda as a prototype of the radical-progressive Nisei of Kikuchi's sort a decade later (the two men were, after all, ten years apart in age). A comparison of their lives also helps underscore what differentiated Kikuchi from Yoneda and other CP members—to distinguish what limited Kikuchi from seeing himself as an explicitly political animal and a potential far leftist, and, possibly, from finding the road he could have traveled had he sharpened his focus exclusively on socioeconomic issues in the prewar era.

By any measure, the leftist labor activist Goso "Karl" Yoneda (1906–1999) wore many hats: a loyal member of the International Longshoremen's and Warehousemen's Union (ILWU) and the Congress of Industrial Organizations (CIO), and the editor (from 1933 to 1936) of *Rodo Shimbun* (*Japanese Labor News*), the official newspaper of the Japanese section of the Communist Party USA (CPUSA). A Kibei-Nisei originally from Glendale, California, Yoneda was one of the first American-born Japanese in the continental United States, but in 1913, at the age of seven, he returned to Japan with his parents to study until 1926, the year he expected the Japanese Army to conscript him. Yoneda grew up in Hiroshima Prefecture, where a third of the laborers from Japan lived before thirty thousand of them left to work on the Hawai'ian sugar plantations between 1885 and 1894 after the Japanese government and the Hawai'ian monarchy reached an immigration agreement. As a youth, Yoneda had taken a profound interest in the writings of anarchists and socialists, and when not in school, he was attending labor rallies. He especially followed the writings of the Russian anarchist Vasily Eroshenko, who was kicked out of Japan in 1921 and had taken refuge in China. Yoneda admired Eroshenko to such a degree that he traveled to China and met with the blind Russian in 1922 to study under him for two months.[33]

When he returned to the States via a brief stop in Japan, Yoneda was stranded in immigration processing on Angel Island until a cousin finally picked him up two months later. Immediately thereafter, though, he began his life of hard work and active labor organizing.[34] To wit, he was one of the earliest members of the Communist Party, whose American branch was cofounded by Sen Katayama (1859–1933), the man best known for initiating the modern labor and socialist movements in Japan. With Katayama as a prominent Party leader, many Issei communists established branches of the Japanese Workers Association (JWA) in New York, Los Angeles, Seattle, and San Francisco. In 1927, Yoneda joined the JWA and officially became a member of the CPUSA. He deeply respected Katayama, whose internationalist multiracialism would be familiar and appealing to Kikuchi:

> "Labor in the white skin can never be free so long as labor in the black skin is branded." These profound words of Karl Marx, which first saw the light of day over a century ago and to which Katayama adhered with intense proletarian internationalism, are still true. However, written or spoken in the context of present day struggles, they include red, brown and yellow skins as well.[35]

Despite such fervor, multiple attempts by Japanese American workers to join an American union were initially rebuffed. The American Federation of Labor (AFL), for example, imposed racial restrictions on its membership. By contrast, the CIO viewed industrial unionism as favorably as craft unionism and openly opposed the racist policy of the AFL. Led by Harry Bridges, a longshoreman, the CIO arrived on the West Coast in 1937, and subsequently, many Asian American laborers, including Yoneda, appreciatively signed up. That is not to say, however, that Yoneda's entry into the ILWU the previous year had gone without a racial hitch.

In his autobiography *Ganbatte: Sixty-Year Struggle of a Kibei Worker* (1983), Yoneda recalls how he requested the help of an African American friend, Len Greer, a well-respected member in the union community and one of five officials on the crucial Investigating Committee for the ILWU, an admissions committee for all intents and purposes. Without any official restriction against Asians' joining the ILWU (but with no actual Asian constituents to show for it), Greer and Yoneda thought the four other members of the committee, coincidentally all white, would not waver in accepting Yoneda. But their hesitation was palpable as they rudely failed to acknowledge any of his answers to their questions. Yoneda remembers:

> Len, surmising the situation, broke in with, "Well, you fellows seem to be disinclined to accept this brother. This is what I'll do. As our union has a tradition of issuing a work permit or book to the son of a member, I adopt Karl right here and now as my son!" With this unexpected proposition, [the chairman] interrupted Len and turned to me saying, "Okay, you can go to the union office tomorrow morning, pick up a permit and go to work." That's how I became the first Japanese-American union longshoreman on the mainland.
>
> On the way home Len told me, "Sometimes you have to use strong language to call their bluff, especially where racial prejudice is concerned."[36]

Given his anti-imperialist and antinationalist (i.e., anti-Japanese) ideology and writings in *Rodo Shimbun*, Yoneda was closely watched by the Japanese government for his frequent editorials decrying Japan's militarism, particularly the nation's aggression in China. Unlike Kikuchi, who occasionally protested exports to Japan at the wharf or confronted officials at the Japanese consulate in the mid to late 1930s, Yoneda made a regular habit of attending political rallies, boycotting the import of Japanese-made goods, and persuading other Asian longshoremen not to work as nonunion scabs on the San Francisco docks. For his American-based activism, Yoneda not only earned his own FBI file but also sustained numerous and violent beatings at the hands of the police's anticommunist, antiunion, and antianarchist special unit, aptly named the Red Guard. After one particularly gruesome beating in 1931, a sympathetic cop called the International League Defense's Elaine Black, nicknamed the "Red Angel" for her fearless defense of jailed unionists and communists, and asked her to pick up Yoneda, who had been beaten within an inch of his life. Four years later, the two fast friends and ideological comrades married in Seattle (because of antimiscegenation laws in California—Black was white), fighting their common enemies as a remarkably committed duo until Elaine's death in 1988. Yoneda liked identifying himself simply as another "ordinary working stiff"; given his tortuous story, he was anything but.[37]

Relatively soon after Pearl Harbor, Bay Area Nisei leaders from diverse political backgrounds and various organizations began acting out an internecine battle—not exactly of Shakespearean proportions, but of sufficient vitriol that the riots at internment camps in the next few years would not seem at all surprising. In early 1942, California congressman Leland Ford, buoyed by pressure groups of nativists, American Legionnaires, and farmers' organizations, lit the match of hysteria by vociferously encouraging the West Coast Japanese Americans to voluntarily evacuate their homes. Bald-faced racists and venal economic competitors now had an advocate in the national government. The JACL naturally tried to take the initiative in mounting a response. But James Sakamoto (the editor of the *Japanese-American Courier* in Seattle) had beaten them to the punch, informing Ford that, last he checked, Japanese Americans were still loyal citizens, born and raised in the United States and possessing certain inalienable rights. Nonetheless, Sakamoto's appropriate and direct message made the rounds only in Seattle and the Pacific Northwest. The rest of the West Coast, the JACL insisted, needed a more organized response.

At the same time, the famous sculptor and artist Isamu Noguchi was trying to establish a progressive organization called the Nisei Writers and Artists Mobilization for Democracy in LA and San Francisco. This group was to be more politically engaged and more formal than, say, precursors like the John Reed Clubs or the LA-based Japanese Proletarian Artists' League (JPAL), which were part of the cultural politics of the Popular Front. (In *Ganbatte*, Yoneda mentions that he contributed a few poems to JPAL's literary arm.) Noguchi approached Jimmie Omura, the progressive editor of *Current Life: The Magazine for the American Born Japanese*, who had published articles by Kikuchi, Tsuneishi, and Murase, and asked him whether he was interested in joining the group. After an informational session in Hollywood, Omura demurred: "I was still bothered about the purpose of this. It seemed like Washington was going to feed the news and we were going to break it to the Nisei media, Japanese media, whatever. I didn't like it because . . . I didn't like to take orders from the government anyway."[38] As an alternative, Omura suggested a power-sharing council comprising all the area's Nisei groups, even the JACL, just so everyone would be singing from the same hymnal. Apparently, however, Omura discovered that the JACL had already tarred him and his ilk with the brush of communist red, attempting to cast doubt on his patriotism in case he wanted to take a leading role. To the JACL, Omura was too much a radical with a big, critical voice.[39]

Likewise, Larry Tajiri had been organizing groups like Oakland's Young Democrats, whose members, Omura joked, treated Tajiri like "the Godfather."[40] He additionally recruited other JACL-minded outfits, pushing for a more accommodationist agenda under the tentative name of the Bay Region Council for Unity. Politically, this option was not necessarily any shock, given the JACL's sponsorship, but the fact that Tajiri was spearheading the movement came as a true surprise to many. In later years, his progressive streak would shine more prominently, but at this early moment, he was more invested in jockeying for power among a majority of accommodationists. The lefty reputation of the YDs (for example, Tsuneishi had gone to one of their meetings with Kikuchi, frightfully calling them "Communists") withered under duress as well.[41] Tajiri had apparently co-opted the normally leftist YDs, persuading them of the advantages of voluntary evacuation as a way to display Japanese American patriotism right away and to neutralize any fifth column accusations, in hopes of avoiding a government-run evacuation. When the Bay Region Council finally convened, Omura suggested Noguchi as a politically neutral chair, but Tajiri had already decided that he himself was going to lead the group. Additionally, knowing how Omura's overtly progressive reputation might gum up the works, Tajiri unexpectedly and brashly called for Omura's expulsion from the council on the shaky grounds that he represented a publication, not an organization. Such a transparent power grab stunned most of the audience. As Omura remembers it:

> There was a moment of silence after he said that. Noguchi was leaning against the jamb of the door right nearby. Then he spoke up. He said, "Under that interpretation, I would have to withdraw also." After he said that, Karl Yoneda got up and said, "I represent the *Doho* of Los Angeles, which is a newspaper. I would have to withdraw also" . . . Lincoln Kanai was down in the corner . . . He was the executive director of the Japanese YMCA. He said, "If *Current Life* is banished, I'm going to walk out of here." So three of the key people said they would go with me. So they called for a vote. They overwhelmingly overturned that motion, so naturally I could participate. But I was shocked at what Tajiri would propose.[42]

Tajiri's actions reflected deeper schisms within the national JACL; tectonic shifts would take place as the war progressed. Suffice it to say that in this instance, with the exception of Omura and Kanai (now both blackballed), the entirety of the Bay Area Nisei community (even Noguchi and Yoneda) accepted the JACL rationale and decided to willingly volunteer for evacuation as a gesture of goodwill and community self-preservation. This meeting (the same one with the motion to expel Omura) took place on February 16, 1942, only three days before Roosevelt issued Executive Order 9066. This may as well have been another Noh play for everyone to enjoy: the government had already made its decision to round up and evacuate the West Coast Nikkei by this date and meeting. According to Omura, Tajiri and Noguchi must have already known this fact, and if so, they were simply indulging the community in order to make it feel as if it had a say—a way to blow off steam, one might say, or release the historically reliant "safety valve" for the feverish masses.

While it is disappointing that Yoneda did not see the forest for the trees—the unconstitutional violation of more than 100,000 Americans' civil liberties—one must note that he was at least philosophically consistent: antifascist, anti-imperialist, unquestionably against Japanese nationalism, and, consequently, a zealous American patriot (as defined at that historical moment). Depending on one's viewpoint, Yoneda's principled or stubborn antifascism was what ultimately compelled him to voluntarily evacuate his entire family to the Manzanar Relocation Center and later to enlist and serve in the U.S. Army as a language specialist with the Military Intelligence Service in the China-Burma-India theater. Although disappointed by the CP's racist and hasty decision to suspend all Japanese Americans' membership because of fears of fifth column activity, he rejoined the party after the war and survived the witch hunts of McCarthyism. What is more, Yoneda not only telegrammed Roosevelt an unmitigated declaration of support for the American war effort on behalf of the *Doho*, the newspaper he edited, but also received an unanticipated letter of recommendation from none other than J. Edgar Hoover, the director of the FBI. All hands off Yoneda and his wife seemed to be the message (even if Hoover kept thick FBI files on both of them). The April 23, 1942, memorandum awkwardly stated: "Yoneda is one of those rare individuals who is of Japanese descent, but is open and avowed in his Communist sympathies and anything but in sympathy with the present militaristic regime in Japan."[43] For the moment, at least, the old adage held true: "The enemy of my enemy is my friend." Important to note, too, is that in a macrocosmic sense, all the democratic and capitalist Allied nations had temporarily joined forces with the communist Soviets to defeat the fascists Hitler and Mussolini. Strange bedfellows all around, but at least Yoneda was not alone in his opportunistic antifascism.

At first blush, then, Kikuchi and Yoneda seem similar only because of their race and common friendship with Omura. By contrast, they were ten years apart in age. Kikuchi was an unusually self-critical twenty-six-year-old Nisei bachelor at Gila, while Yoneda was an extroverted CP Kibei-Nisei married to a white woman and had fathered a son by the time he entered Manzanar. However, both also embraced America, joining the military to demonstrate their loyalty. Each man, in his respective moment, lobbied for and strongly believed in the necessity and promise of interracial alliances. Both men worked closely with Mexican and Filipino farmworkers to protest unfair, exploitative practices by Japanese growers while investing significantly in the plight and future of African Americans as well. As Yoneda would recount, regarding the early 1930s: "In discussions Japanese comrades all agreed that racial discrimination against Japanese in this country could not end without the support of the Negro, other minorities, and white workers. The Scottsboro case, a vicious example of anti-Negro racism, had been an eye-opener for Japanese CPers, including me."[44] A long-standing member of the multiracial League of Struggle for Negro Rights, Yoneda partook in many antidiscrimination or Jim/Jap Crow protests, including those to desegregate the landmark Sutro Baths, the Golden Gate YMCA pool, and a Turk Street barbershop that would cut only white men's hair (these institutions had indignantly refused service on the basis of inferior "hygiene").

In this light, then, their similarities outweigh the differences: the CP aside, these two were indubitably lefties who believed in the class struggle, experienced it themselves, and were strongly committed to racial equality. Additionally, they both hated their fathers, renaming themselves in symbolic rebirths: Kikuchi dropped his Japanese-given name and became "Charlie," the nickname he had enjoyed when U.S. Navy boys came to his father's barbershop; Yoneda replaced Goso with "Karl" in honor of his hero, Karl Marx. The parallels between the two men are not perfect; after all, the diversity of Nisei remains infinite. It might be more accurate—historically—to acknowledge the overlapping cultural and political networks in which both men circulated (over two different decades). Nonetheless, Yoneda figures as a proper historical precursor and prototype for the radical Nisei (men or women) in Kikuchi's group and for the diarist himself. In *The Cultural Front*, Michael Denning emphasizes the originating role played by authors of "proletarian literature" in building greater appreciation and historical recognition of the common, the ordinary, and the worker in literature and art: culture's sturdy front in the ideological struggles of the 1930s and early 1940s.[45] Kikuchi was meeting and reading the artists whose work Denning placed at the fore of the cultural front: John Fante, William Saroyan, Louis and Stella Adamic, Carey McWilliams, Toshio Mori, Carlos Bulosan, and Richard Wright. The point here is that Yoneda was living through and contributing to this era's cultural apparatus, while Kikuchi was enjoying the fruit (i.e., reading and meeting these authors) of seeds sown in the decade or two before. Kikuchi and others did not have to "wait for Lefty," in other words: a template already existed.

Although Kikuchi felt undue shame over his Japanese name, Tatsuro, its meaning, "standing man," still captured him very well, as the next few chapters will demonstrate. Likewise, Yoneda deemphasized his Japanese first name, Goso, opting instead for the Marxist "Karl," and entitling his autobiography *Ganbatte*, which means "steadfast." These were two long-distance freedom fighters running similar paths.

Demography and Intergenerational Fault Lines

As a whole, the Nisei were growing rapidly by wartime: in 1920, they made up little more than a quarter of the mainland Japanese American population (totaling 111,000), but a decade later, they constituted almost half (of nearly 139,000). By 1940, close to two-thirds of the community (79,000 out of 127,000) were of this younger generation. Of course, this upsurge in the percentage of Nisei in the Japanese American population between 1930 and 1940 paralleled a steep decline in first-generation numbers. All told, the entire Japanese American populace fell by nearly 10 percent over this decade, a direct result of the Immigration Act of 1924 and its mandate to repel Asia's and southeastern Europe's unassimilable hordes. Vigorously supported by nativist organizations and shaped by the language of eugenics, the law established a national-origins quota system that restricted total immigration to 155,000 per year and instituted temporary quotas based on 2 percent of the foreign-born population in 1890. It also excluded immigration for all persons ineligible for citizenship, "a euphemism for Japanese exclusion," as Mae Ngai puts it. She states that even though support for a Japanese quota (not outright exclusion) persisted through the late 1920s and early 1930s, "Japanese immigrants felt thoroughly dejected by the 1924 immigration act, which foredoomed them to permanent disfranchisement and social subordination. Their only hope lay in the Nisei."[46]

The late Ronald Takaki rightfully characterized this generation as a hyphenated one, caught between two cultural poles (Japanese and American), giving rise to his observation that "the Nisei had their own peculiar view of the world."[47] As Kikuchi recognized, other Nisei were experiencing American life and culture in similarly painful and confusing ways. Takaki likened this conundrum to a Du Boisian "twoness," insofar as Nisei found that

> their lives and their identities were bifurcated between the land of their parents and the land of their birth, folk stories about the peach boy Momotaro and children's tales about Jack and the Beanstalk, the Japanese love songs their mothers sang in the kitchen and the popular songs they heard on the radio, the summer *obon* dances and the weekend jitterbug dances, Japanese New Year's Day and Christmas, the annual *kenjinkai* picnics and high-school outings, banzai to the emperor's health and the pledge of allegiance to the flag of the United States.[48]

The divergence further manifested itself in language. Citing the fact that Nisei spoke English to one another but Japanese to their parents, Takaki shares a comical exchange between a Nisei and her father:

> One day, when I was young, I had been with a boy and didn't come home for lunch. My father asked me what Roy and I had been doing. "We were fucking," I replied in English, thinking he wouldn't understand what I said. Suddenly his face turned white. I felt betrayed. He knew more English than he had been letting on.[49]

For their part, the Issei felt equally betrayed as they attempted to maintain their authority and the cultivation of time-honored traditions, but their hold remained tenuous at best. Bill Hosokawa elaborates on this theme:

> The *Issei* viewed this Americanization of their children with mixed emotions. They were proud that their offspring took so naturally to a language that they themselves were incapable of mastering . . . But they were also disturbed that the *Nisei* were ignoring, and in some cases, rejecting, their Japanese heritage.[50]

Furthermore, the strengths of both cultures worked at cross-purposes.

> In [public] school, the *Nisei* were taught to question and challenge, encouraged to make their own decisions, to be aggressive, to assert their individuality. To make matters even more confusing, the parents whom one was taught at home to honor, respect and obey, in turn urged the *Nisei* to honor, respect, and obey the teachers who, unconsciously and unintentionally, were indoctrinating the youngsters in a conflicting philosophy.[51]

Issei tried to neutralize their children's slackening cultural retention by enrolling them in Japanese schools, which specialized in both language and cultural practices and were attended after the public school day. As the two following examples will demonstrate, identity crisis and cultural conflict struck many Nisei, not just Kikuchi, and with ostensibly equal effect on both genders. Monica Sone, for instance, lived in the relatively unseemly Skid Row area of Seattle before evacuation. Her father ran a hotel there, which in turn provided living quarters for his entire family. In an effort to counter the influence of her immediate surroundings, Sone's parents desperately turned to the principal and teacher of the local Japanese language school for help:

> Mr. Ohashi and Mrs. Matsui thought they could work on me and gradually mold me into an ideal Japanese *ojoh-san*, a refined young maiden who is quiet, pure in thought, polite, serene, and self-controlled. They made little headway, for I was too much the child of Skidrow. As far as I was concerned, Nihon Gakko [Japanese school] was a total loss.[52]

Compare this to a strikingly similar passage from Jeanne Wakatsuki Houston's *Farewell to Manzanar*, a 1973 memoir of her internment as a young girl at the Manzanar camp in the desert of southeastern California. Houston recalls being a baton-twirling fourth grader sent by her parents to try something new but foreign.

> [An old geisha] was offering lessons in the traditional dancing called *odori*. A lot of young girls studied this in order to take part in the big *obon* festival held every August, a festival honoring dead ancestors, asking them to bring good crops in the fall . . . I sat across the room from her for an hour trying to follow what was going on . . . When she bowed to me from her knees at the end of the hour, I rushed out of there, back to more familiar surroundings.[53]

Unlike other moments in his life (most notably his time at the orphanage), Kikuchi's experience during this prewar stage mirrored that of many other Nisei coming out of college and struggling to enter a national workforce heavily debilitated by the lingering effects of the Great Depression. On one flank, they faced the threat of clashing cultural influences within their own community. On the other, they had to brave the external pressure imposed from without: that is, confinement to an ethnic labor market. Most Nisei either could not find or were flatly denied work in white-owned businesses: for example, only 5 percent of the Nisei population answered to white employers in Los Angeles in 1940. Most of the remaining 95 percent were self-employed or worked for other Japanese in laundries, groceries, barbershops, hotels, flower shops, and Japanese art shops. Twenty percent of all people of Japanese descent in LA worked for family-run fruit stands. Civil-service jobs were simply off-limits: in 1940, with a Japanese population in excess of 30,000, Los Angeles could not boast of *one* Japanese fireman, policeman, mailman, or public school teacher.[54] Kikuchi would offer his evaluation of these kinds of conditions:

> Coming into a situation of this sort, it was more difficult for me because of the language handicaps. I also had a certain amount of false pride, and

I didn't want to do menial work because I felt that this would be admitting defeat to myself. But hunger is a powerful force, and I soon had to swallow my pride and take any kind of job.[55]

Kikuchi then milled around Japanese employment agencies but encountered intense competition from Issei, Nisei, Kibei, and Filipino workers. He managed to find a number of odd jobs, living a hand-to-mouth existence for several months. In 1945, he tried to put his circumstances in perspective:

It was a frustrating experience because I found that I wasn't qualified for many of the ordinary types of work because most of my previous activity had been directed towards educational ambition. I consoled myself with the thought that a lot of the less fortunate workers that I competed with had to do jobs of this sort all of their lives, while my break would come eventually if I remained patient.[56]

The uncertainty of the job market led Kikuchi, along with many other Nisei, to a peripatetic existence in migratory farmwork. Again, though, because of his lack of proficiency in Japanese, Kikuchi stood very little chance of breaking into Japanese work gangs, and was thus compelled to join Filipino, Mexican, and Great Plains laborers—the last of whom were poor, largely white migrants coming from the Dust Bowl (Oklahoma, Texas, Arkansas, and Missouri), where farms had dried up and dust storms (1932) compounded the ignominy of what would be a seven-year drought (1931–1938). These workers tended to inhabit the Central Valley landscapes described by John Steinbeck. Kikuchi later offered astute impressions of his colleagues in the detached but paradoxically involved tone of a "participant-observer":

Most of these workers were deadened in their ambition and were only existing from season to season. It was not difficult to understand why they looked forward to Saturday nights when they could get drunk, go see women, and gamble. It was a release from the humdrum life that they were living.[57]

For the moment, he lived a similar life, canvassing as far north as the Sacramento Valley and as far south as Fresno, all the while mentally preparing to return to graduate school. He had always been partial to studying history, but his experience with migratory laborers transformed those career aspirations. At this point, the activist impulses in Kikuchi that would come to define the rest of his life were already detectable as he made the significant move away from intellectualizing about a problem to tackling it head-on. "This experience was quite illuminating to me," he remembered,

because I saw first hand how these workers were exploited. I wanted to do something about it. One day I picked up a social work book and I became intrigued with it so much that I decided to become a social worker. I felt that in this way I could work upon minority problems and attempt to solve them in some way.

He pointed to the example of his fellow migrants, deploring their working and living conditions, their dilapidated shacks without electricity or running water. He testified to the number of dead Mexican babies he saw "casually [buried] in some lonely and deserted spot" in the migratory camps. He painfully concluded: "It was shocking to me because I had naively swallowed everything, or almost everything in college, and I had an impression that this country had the highest living standards in the world."[58] Growing up in the New Deal era, Kikuchi still maintained a deep faith in the abstract power and reach of the government in such dire situations, but faced with the stark reality of these workers' lives, he learned very quickly that what was possible—what constituted the ideal—was still beyond his, and these laborers', reach.

The impediments to a truly egalitarian and multiracial democracy became deeply apparent to Kikuchi, as events unfolding in his workplace would prove. In the summer of 1940, a friend of Kikuchi's told him about a job opportunity at a celery ranch near Stockton, California, eighty miles east of San Francisco in the heart of the San Joaquin Valley. For two months, Kikuchi pulled celery stalks out of the ground for a mere twenty-five cents an hour. As he put it, "There were many times that I wanted to quit because I rebelled against the thought of being exploited like this, especially by a Japanese foreman." Notably, the presence of Issei spurred on Kikuchi's class consciousness. "It seemed to me," he continued, "that these Japanese farmers were inhuman in their attitudes toward the workers and their only interest was to get as much out of them as possible."[59] Two crews worked on this particular ranch: Japanese and Filipino. Most of the Japanese were Issei who had worked in such gangs for twenty-five years, but nine were Nisei who mostly stuck together. While the Japanese labored in the fields, the Filipino crew was responsible for cutting the celery stalks inside sheds, so neither the work nor any common interest compelled the two gangs to interact. According to Kikuchi, bad blood existed between the two groups, and historical prejudices gave way to despicable practices. For example, a battle royal nearly erupted over the use of a common bathtub. Despite preconceived Japanese notions that Filipinos, like Blacks, were filthy and uncivilized, both groups regularly bathed every day. A problem arose, however, since the two competed to be the first to use the tub each night, since Filipinos did not want to follow Japanese into the water on principle, while the Japanese feared that all Filipinos had syphilis. Eventually, moved by the intensity of the conflict, the foreman built two separate bathhouses, and the crisis was temporarily averted.

The heated rivalry also stemmed from basic economic competition. Kikuchi recognized this: "The Japanese workers accused the Filipinos of strike-breaking tactics and being troublemakers, while the Filipinos felt that the Japanese workers did not have the guts enough to demand a living wage."[60] Much like the obstacles that have stymied the convergence of the white working class and Black working class, Filipinos and Japanese allowed racial differences to trump potential alliances based on class (to agitate against the farmers).[61] As a result, understandable conflicts that would normally arise when so many men worked and slept in such close quarters escalated into miniature race wars. Kikuchi found himself caught in the middle of one such skirmish that summer and attempted to bridge the racial divide, one of the first of his many lifelong efforts to effect some degree of interracial unity.

It all began inauspiciously; as noted above, both groups not only resented each other's race, but also their limitations as class-conscious workers. In this spirit of ill will, the Japanese crew decided to speed up its productivity in an effort to pile up celery stalks on the cutters' tables, thereby forcing the Filipinos to do extra work. This practice overwhelmed the Filipinos until a few of the Japanese were called into the shed to balance the load. Even closer in proximity at this point, the two groups were primed for a dustup. Kikuchi, meanwhile, found himself on a break in the shed, sitting between a fellow Nisei hand named Kenji and a large Filipino named Manuel. Being the genial and outgoing person that he was, Kikuchi struck up a friendly conversation with Manuel, discovering that he was a graduate of Ateneo de Manila University who had arrived in the States to attend Cal. Having run out of money, Manuel sought work on the farm gangs, but after ten years had yet to return to school. Like many immigrants, Kikuchi noted, Manuel refused to return to the Philippines "until he was a success." In the midst of this casual conversation, a crisis erupted when Kenji threw a crate out of the shed that inadvertently struck a Filipino on the head.

> For a moment there was a stunned silence. Then the Filipino man sprang up and started swinging his knife. The first thing I knew . . . this 12-inch knife came swishing through the air, cutting the tip of my nose. There wasn't anything I could do because my back was to a board and I could not make a retreat. A general riot was about to burst loose when Manuel jumped to my protection and he shouted to the other workers that this was a personal matter.[62]

Each group of course demanded that the foreman dismiss the other, but cooler heads eventually prevailed, and the two gangs simply kept their distance. For his part, Kikuchi rejected tribalism, instead choosing to enjoy more dialogue with his new friend. Because of his principled yet somewhat naïve attempts to model interracial friendship for his Japanese workmates, Kikuchi was told that he was a discredit to the race and was forced to leave their bunkhouse. Contentedly, he found a spot in Manuel's bunkhouse and worked with the Filipino crew for the rest of the summer.

While it might have been reasonable for Kikuchi to simply shun other Japanese after his treatment on the farm, he decided to take the opposite tack. He returned to San Francisco at the end of the summer with a clearer picture of his future:

The experience had not been unfruitful for me, because it had given me an objective picture of migratory workers and I had also learned that the Japanese workers were in a similar predicament. The experience had also helped me to determine what my field of study should be. From that time on, I worked for this goal.

This particularly challenging summer of exhausting fieldwork had, ironically, energized Kikuchi. "I was intensely interested in the Nisei predicament," he concluded, "as I could see no good coming out of the segregated community which could never be self-sufficient [by] itself."[63] Thus, he headed to the offices of the National Youth Administration (NYA) and proposed a survey and analysis of employment opportunities for Bay Area Nisei. The New Deal agency welcomed his project and promised him $24 a month. Nearly two hundred pages in length, the study is a striking document: Kikuchi had not yet received any kind of formal training in the social sciences, although he notes in the study's introduction that he gleaned sampling and interviewing techniques from the Federal Youth Survey of 1939, administered by the Works Progress Administration. It would be another year before Kikuchi was introduced to Dorothy Thomas and sociological methodology, but he already demonstrated a near instinctive understanding of the participant-observer process, noting "the interviewer throughout the period of the study was in intimate daily contact with the Japanese colony in San Francisco."[64] Notably, this intimacy would be the trademark of his future work for JERS, his diary entries, and his twenty-four-year career as a social worker in New York.

Interspersing interviews in the community with protoscientific analysis, Kikuchi attempts a social and cultural history of the Nisei before focusing on the economic opportunities (or lack thereof) for the group. Given his own initial prejudice against the older generation, Kikuchi arrives at some surprising conclusions. For example, with regard to the fundamental gulf between the traditional Issei and the Americanized second generation, his prescription was conciliatory: "A slow and sure growth with the retention of the best of the old and addition to this foundation with the best of the new is more healthy, and better for America, than an indiscriminate discarding of old things and the unthinking appropriation of new things."[65] This is Kikuchi the objective social scientist, his personal biases in check. The main thrust of his study, and ultimately its most valuable contribution, lay in examining what factors affected job searches in the Bay Area and, specifically, what the Nisei themselves felt posed the greatest stumbling blocks. Kikuchi sprinkled his collected data with observations and commentary from the representative sample he interviewed ("I guess I'm a misfit. No experience, no job; no job, no experience. So what?" "Because I was a 'Jap,' they wouldn't give me a job." "All I want is a job. I don't care what color of skin the boss has."). The analyst fixates on a portion of the data with large implications for the future:

A significant factor was that 15.7% of the Nisei considered racial discrimination as the chief difficulty in not securing jobs . . . Psychologically, it is important, since many of the Nisei may become totally disillusioned with the failure to find work and not realize that economic factors are equally as important as discrimination.[66]

These observations reveal Kikuchi's preoccupation with class, unsurprising given his experience as a migratory worker. However, one must also take note of the rhetorical distance he seems to place between the Nisei and himself. At this point, he no longer appears to separate himself only from Issei, but possibly from his own generation of Nisei as well. It will be extremely helpful to keep this early worldview in mind as the year 1941 inches closer to the "day of infamy" and especially as Kikuchi himself evolves, both intellectually and emotionally. Class will always remain an important factor in Kikuchi's calculus, but race (and, as a corollary, discrimination) takes on greater importance in his thinking as the years pass. Watershed racializing events, like Pearl Harbor and the internment of Japanese Americans, would give him ample reasons to change his mind.

In the end, previously ill equipped to deal with the increasing number of Nisei job seekers, the Junior Counseling Service of the NYA and the California State Department of Employment enthusiastically accepted the report and were finally able to provide adequate guidance to the "New Americans" about whom Kikuchi wrote. Of course, even with the newly adopted recommendations, Japanese still struggled to find steady work. Earlier in the year, Kikuchi had written an article, "Joe Nisei Looks for a Job," for *Current Life*. This periodical—despite having a short life of only fourteen months (October 1940–January 1942)—prided itself on being the progressive voice for the Nisei community, focusing on the arts and politics and counting noteworthy intellectuals as contributors: the short-story writer Hisaye Yamamoto (writing under the pseudonym "Napoleon"); the aforementioned immigrant scholar and Kikuchi acquaintance Louis Adamic; two future "batch" mates of Kikuchi's at Cal, Murase and Shibutani; and Kikuchi's sister Alice.

The magazine's editor, Omura, mentioned above (in political tugs-of-war with Tajiri) was a remarkable figure in his own right. Born on Bainbridge Island, Washington, he was an outspoken critic of the evacuation and, of course, of the JACL, its moderation, and its unrelenting support of the government during the evacuation and internment years. When *Current Life* folded in 1942, though, Omura moved to Denver, keeping tabs on the goings-on at the nearby internment camp at Heart Mountain, Wyoming. Shortly after the government's reinstatement of the draft for Nisei in camp in January 1944, Omura was the only journalist to encourage resistance, offering thinly veiled advice to camp readers in his columns for *Rocky Shimpo*, one of many Japanese vernacular newspapers in Denver. Citing his support of the Heart Mountain Fair Play Committee (formally established by internees in January to explicitly resist the draft), the government charged Omura with conspiracy to counsel draft evasion. Ultimately, he was the only defendant acquitted on First Amendment grounds of freedom of speech and the press.[67] As the redoubt of many Nisei intellectuals, Japanese American newspapers and magazines—such as *Current Life, Sangyo Nippo, Rafu*

Shimpo (*L.A. Japanese Daily News*), *Nichi Bei Shimbun* (SF), and the *Pacific Citizen* (JACL's paper), among others—offered the space, both literally and figuratively, for these second-generation thinkers to take controversial, and subversively oppositional, viewpoints.

Published in 1941, Kikuchi's contribution to Omura's magazine was a semiautobiographical tale chronicling the brief success and ultimate failure of a prewar Nisei jobseeker. Kikuchi conceded that much of the story was cribbed from the experiences of one of his roommates, a former student and boxing champion at San Jose State College. The narrator begins with an air of naïveté, quitting school to make what he believes will be "easy money": "I kept thinking about how adventurous it was going to be for me to actually be a working stiff instead of a quiet, bespeckled [*sic*] college student confined in the cloisters of an Ivory Tower."[68] Told by the Japanese employment agencies that they had leads only on domestic work, the narrator asserts that such work is beneath him and tries a white employer instead, only to find that the manager (of a shirt shop) fears the narrator's being Japanese will scare away his white customers. "It's such a vicious circle," Joe Nisei remarks. "Can't get work without experience. Can't get experience because you're a Jap. And who would hire a Jap?"[69] The individual's lived experience (albeit fictional) echoed that of the collective group as reported in Kikuchi's NYA study.

In Kikuchi's life, positions came and went: janitor at a Japanese beer parlor, art-store clerk, fish scaler, window cleaner, peach picker, and factory worker. At one point, fed up with the poor treatment doled out by his Japanese employers, he attempted to organize a union amongst his Nisei coworkers, but they demurred, citing respect for their elders. At another point, thoroughly demoralized by dim job prospects, he visited the army recruitment office and volunteered for service. This was the second time since December 1940 that he had tried to register, but the army refused, as before, citing his race. "This sort of answer made me boil inside," he remembered, "but there was nothing I could do about it."[70] In the spring of 1941, a meeting arranged by Adamic with the author and playwright William Saroyan, himself the son of Armenian immigrants, helped give Kikuchi a temporary rush of inspiration. As he explained,

> He was interested in the Nisei problems [and] it was through his influ-
> ence that my philosophy on life changed drastically for a while. I had
> been rather discouraged by my failure to achieve economic stability, but
> Saroyan emphasized . . . that everything was good and beautiful and that
> one should expand one's experiences as broadly as possible.[71]

Despite the slightly ethereal (and likely drunken) quality of this advice, Kikuchi nonetheless found a thread of motivation in it and made his way down to the Merchant Marine office, only to discover, once again, that they would not accept him because of race. However, Saroyan's positive attitude must have rubbed off on him a little bit, since the School of Social Welfare at Berkeley shortly thereafter notified

Kikuchi of his admission for the fall of 1941. Now eligible for loans and professional training, Kikuchi could at least temporarily leave the grind of the working world.

Arriving at Cal, Kikuchi intended to earn his certificate in social work by the end of the academic year (spring 1942) and then proceed directly onto fulfilling requirements for his master's degree. Schoolwork did not pose too formidable a challenge to Kikuchi, but the culture of the university certainly did. It is important to recall that Kikuchi had attended San Francisco State during his undergraduate years, an institution that enjoyed less prestige than Cal, especially within the Japanese American community, and one that, consequently, fewer Nisei attended. It was definitely less expensive than Cal, thereby attracting a wide sample of students from different racial and socioeconomic backgrounds, which Kikuchi appreciated. In his mind, "it was possible to get a real college feeling there," while Cal seemed snobbish at best. Upon setting foot on the Berkeley campus as a graduate student, he was floored by the sheer number of Nisei students, and somewhat dismayed that three hundred to four hundred made up a Japanese Students Club: "I couldn't understand why they had to be so isolated."[72] He would later tell Dorothy Thomas, "I soon discovered that most of the Nisei students were quite limited in their outlook, and they did not care to mix with the general student body. I did not wish to be segregated on campus, so I began to avoid the Nisei group entirely."[73] He made most of his friends in the Social Welfare School, many of whom were Jewish and who willingly educated Kikuchi about the various problems affecting their community. On occasion, he went out socially with a Swedish woman from the department, a choice that drew sharp looks from the Nisei students. Characteristically, Kikuchi simply ignored the raised eyebrows.

At last, however, Kikuchi encountered a group of Japanese he liked. Labeled "radicals" or "queers" by the conservative Nisei on campus, they joined multiracial clubs, were politically active, and assumed leadership of the entire Nisei student body after the bombing of Pearl Harbor. Young men and women of "varying levels of liberal thinking," they distanced themselves from the Issei generation as well as from the "moderate" and "conservative" leadership of the JACL.[74] This aforementioned group included Warren Tsuneishi (Kikuchi's lifelong best friend who went by the nickname "Wang," based on his sympathies for the Chinese in Japanese-occupied Manchuria); Kenji Murase (formerly of *Current Life*); James Sakoda (who would be the first to encourage Kikuchi to keep a diary); Tom Shibutani (who introduced Kikuchi to Dorothy Thomas); and Lillian Ota (who became a well-regarded professor at the University of Connecticut).[75] Undergraduate roommates at Cal, Murase and Tsuneishi would go on to complete PhDs in social work (Columbia) and political science (Yale), respectively. Murase would retire from San Francisco State in 1990, while Tsuneishi served as curator of the East Asian Collection at Yale, and then retired as chief of the Asian Division of the Library of Congress in 1993. Sakoda (social psychology) and Shibutani (sociology) would also earn PhDs (Berkeley and Chicago, respectively) and enjoy successful academic careers (retiring from Brown and UC–Santa Barbara). Well before that, though, "Jimmie" and "Shibs" would convince Kikuchi to work with them under Thomas for the wartime JERS.

Unlike his peers (the exception being Murase), Kikuchi chose social work over sociology, despite warnings from Shibutani and others: "Well, you don't want to go into social work. Social work is sissy work. Men go into sociology and then women go into social work."[76] This choice seemed to fit Kikuchi's predilections and consistently reflected his feelings after working as a migrant, as he would tell a friend: "Got a letter from Louis Adamic today and he wants me to write some stuff for him but I am not too interested. *I want to be active, not academic*—let those people that can write do the reflecting after things have already happened. I'd rather be in on the actual process."[77] Ironically, though, Kikuchi would shortly be immersed in sociology, eventually meeting Thomas, an expert in social demography and wife of W. I. Thomas, the "Chicago School" sociologist who emphasized the use of life histories in his research.[78] The "Thomas school" would heavily influence Kikuchi in the ensuing years, providing him with hands-on training and a foundation in social science methodology that he might not have otherwise received in graduate school. The most fruitful period of their friendship and work was still to come, though, after Kikuchi had already suspended his studies to join his family at the internment camp in April 1942. Before that particular stormy period, however, Kikuchi would learn to appreciate the contrasting, relative calm that Berkeley and his friends had to offer.

The Quest for a Family

"Kenny" Murase shared a passion of social work with Kikuchi, but not much else. The two would correspond during the war, but their friendship always remained fairly strained. Nonetheless, nearly sixty years after first meeting "Charlie," Murase still expressed a genuine respect for his fellow Nisei, speaking of him in the prewar context of the Berkeley "talented tenth."

> Charlie, I guess I didn't take him that seriously because he was always making wisecracks and he was always really running down other people's accomplishments. At the same time, I knew he had a certain flair for relating to people of a certain class, the working class. He was very gifted in being able to relate to people who were certainly much less educated than he was . . . He was always for the underdog. So I think I will always be indebted to him for that kind of influence.[79]

Kikuchi's ability to relate to marginalized members of society—migratory workers, gang members, laborers, African Americans and other ethnics—stemmed in large part from his own status as a marginal man. In a broad sense, he lived the life of "double consciousness," a concept wrestled with by thinkers from Hegel to Emerson, but arguably made most memorable by W.E.B. Du Bois in *The Souls of Black Folk* (1903). At the time, of course, Du Bois spoke mainly of the plight of African Americans, but replacing "Negro" with "Japanese" in his expression of double consciousness would not be unreasonable in the context of Kikuchi's situation: "One ever feels his two-ness,—an American, a Negro; two souls, two thoughts, two unreconciled strivings; two warring ideals in one dark body, whose dogged strength alone keeps it from being torn asunder."[80] Indeed, Kikuchi recognized this conundrum when generalizing about the entire Nisei group. "On one extreme," he wrote,

> a large number of the Nisei are trying to be intensely "American." They have completely adopted "American" conventions, but this does not seem to be a solution to their difficulties. They are not "accepted" by the dominant group as "Americans."

He continued,

> On the other extreme, in much smaller numbers, are the Nisei who pretend to accept their parents' Japanese traditions . . . The majority of the Nisei belong to neither of these extremes, but move more or less confusedly between them. They are the true "marginal man" or "cultural hybrid."[81]

Evidently, Kikuchi read the work of Robert E. Park, the eminent sociologist from the University of Chicago who popularized the theory of the marginal man.

In his 1928 essay entitled "Human Migration and the Marginal Man," Park argued that increased migration of populations and amplified cultural contact between them tore down walls that traditionally separated cultures and societies. As a result, "there appeared a new type of personality, namely, a cultural hybrid, a man living and sharing the cultural life and tradition of two distinct peoples . . . a man on the margin of two cultures and two societies, which never completely interpenetrated and fused."[82] Despite the permanence of this "in between" status, Park nonetheless celebrated the birth of such a type, seeing him as a "cosmopolite" and a "true citizen of the world," privileged to understand and freely explore other cultures. In the same article, however, he conceded that acculturation and assimilation would not come as quickly, if at all, for Japanese immigrants. Harking back to an argument he had made in 1914, Park wrote:

> The Japanese bears in his features a distinctive racial hallmark, that he wears, so to speak, a racial uniform which classifies him . . . The Japanese, like the Negro, is condemned to remain among us an abstraction, a symbol—and a symbol not merely of his own race, but of the Orient and of that vague, ill-defined menace we sometimes refer to as the "yellow peril."[83]

Ultimately, Park believed the assimilation of "secondary" groups like the Japanese was inevitable. They too would enjoy the liberation afforded to other marginal men. Such status nevertheless remained extremely vexing. Henry Yu offers explanation:

Strangely . . . the region of marginality lay not in the middle of the spectrum, as the representation of the "marginal man caught between two worlds" suggested. Rather, feelings of marginality increased when the Nisei identified too closely with Caucasians. Moving toward being American did not remove the Nisei from the margins but only furthered their marginality by increasing their distance from the Japanese in-group.[84]

Such was the case with the loosely organized group of Nisei radicals at Berkeley. Each of them, for one reason or another, was seen as deviating from the mainstream Nisei on campus, whose attitude was, generally speaking, virtual isolation from or minimal intermixing with other racial groups. Murase had informally been the point man who brought all of these so-called marginal Nisei in contact with one another. What made him an outsider was his progressive credentials: he had been quite active in the Young Democrats, often attended meetings on race relations, wrote for Omura's *Current Life*, and "seemed to collect those *outside of* organized Nisei groups."[85] Ota, meanwhile, was the only Nisei writer on the campus newspaper, the *Daily Californian*, and despite living in the Japanese women's house, she allegedly harbored "contempt for other Nisei."[86] In addition to his iconoclastic personal history, Kikuchi had, by this time, often expressed disdain for the self-segregating tendencies of the mainstream Nisei, while Tsuneishi—unique for his political stance on China—complained to Sakoda of the "bovine complacency" of the Nisei.[87] As for Shibutani, Yu succinctly captured the scholarly mien that made the young Nisei an appropriate fit for the "radicals": "Shibutani had a penchant for thoughtful reflection and detachment from the world, and the role of participant observer/sociologist suited him perfectly. Perhaps he was the kind of person who had always felt a little apart from the world around him, but within social science he was amply rewarded for his ability to remove himself from the subjects he studied."[88] Lastly, Sakoda, who had grown friendly with Murase through rooming with him, was even marginal to the "marginal group," since he was a Kibei (like Yoneda), having lived for six years in Japan before returning to Cal for college.

Modell reports: "It was these 'radicals,' most of them now occupying (as [did] Kikuchi) positions of responsibility in the general community, who introduced Kikuchi to the intellectual value of 'marginality.'" Being on the margin provided these particular thinkers a distinctive vantage point: "The Nisei, or so it was argued, could gain from his discomfort a perspective on the broader workings of the society which contained but did not integrate 'whites' and 'Japanese.'"[89] In this sense, Kikuchi was one of a rare handful of ethnic intellectuals who perceived their own social location in terms of Chicago School terminology. Based on his experiences up to this point, he did at least seem like the archetype of the marginal man. His childhood at the orphanage made him a temporary outsider in his own family, but a cultural hybrid among so many different racialized and ethnic children there. Attending SF State instead of Cal extended his detachment from the mainstream Nisei crowd, but once again exposed him to a multitude of racialized, ethnic, and working-class students. Working on labor gangs certainly drew him closer to Nisei workers, while it also afforded him frequent interaction with Mexicans, white migrants, and Filipinos. Even the street-corner gang he joined boasted both Japanese (with them, he was on the margin of mainstream Nisei) and other ethnics (with them, a cultural hybrid). His graduate-school year at Cal would be no different: he would still interact with various racial and ethnic groups, but his marginalized affiliation would be with other Nisei of similar persuasions. In fact, some of them were his roommates. I emphasize the point of his identification with this unique cadre of Nisei intellectuals because as time passed, at least one scholar (among others)—the late Yuji Ichioka—strongly criticized Kikuchi for not being, in Ichioka's words, "a typical Nisei."[90]

As Modell corroborates, Kikuchi *was* an "atypical Nisei," but not at all with the negative connotation Ichioka implied.[91] For Modell, because of, not despite, what he observed about Kikuchi as an "extremely individualistic, almost detached, young man," he was sure that "something of the *central* theme of the Japanese American experience was contained in the biography of this man."[92] That is to say, as one reads Kikuchi's unpublished diaries, his atypical nature does prove extraordinary and exceptional, but more for his prescience and broad vision than for any societal incompatibility. In effect, he earnestly attempts to expose others to his atypical and unpopular views—regarding race, ethnicity, class, integration, "Americanism," and democracy—in the hope that such ideas would be heard, possibly shared, and potentially accepted as typical by other Americans—Asian, Black, white or otherwise.

In service of that goal, Kikuchi would strategically try to marry his individualism to the aims of the group. In fact, the main arc in my narrative of Kikuchi's life is that because of the signal experience of being orphaned and effectively abandoned at such a young age, he constantly seemed to be in search of the security and interconnectedness of groups that resembled, or at times re-created, the family unit. Psychologically, such an adaptive practice would have been his lifelong (and life-saving) coping mechanism. Beginning with the surrogate brotherhood at the multiracial orphanage during his youth, Kikuchi eagerly sought fraternal ties: in the 1930s, they came in the form of Filipino migratory farm workers and the cadre of Nisei intelligentsia at Cal; in the 1940s, they were African Americans in the "jazz city," other high-octane JERS researchers in camp, and barrack mates in the U.S. Army, as the remaining chapters will show. Equally, perhaps even more, important was his need to find guidance, mentoring, and support from parental figures throughout this time. Louis Adamic and his wife, Stella, and then Dorothy Thomas and her husband, W. I., filled these surrogate roles for Kikuchi at various stages of both his academic and emotional development. While he did reunite with his biological family at Tanforan and Gila, even going so far as to assume guardianship for two of his younger siblings during resettlement, the experience, in truth, never fully lived up to his imagined expectations. In the end, his greatest comfort and connection would derive from membership in another Kikuchi family: his own union with Yuriko and their two children in New York City.[93]

Admittedly, Kikuchi bore some markings of the marginal man, for as Park reminds us, "It is in the mind of the marginal man—where the changes and fusions of culture are going on—that we can best study the processes of civilization and progress."[94] Kikuchi's diary and the abundant experiences recorded therein support that characterization. But at the same time, as his best friend put it:

> Charlie is one guy who cannot be labeled. He was, as I have said before, unique. Charlie himself did not like labels, either for himself or for others. I would say that he was very broad-minded and also very accepting of people, understanding them and not passing judgment on their only too human foibles and weaknesses. At least that is how he treated me, and I don't think I have ever met anyone quite like him.[95]

Chapter 2

"A Multitude of Complexes": Finding Common Ground with Louis Adamic

On Sunday afternoon, December 7, 1941, a bull session among a few Nisei friends at Cal grew increasingly contentious. Topic A was the simmering relationship between Japan and the United States: only four months earlier, President Roosevelt had ordered the freezing of Japan's assets and a de facto embargoing of oil exports to Japan in response to the Japanese occupation of southern Indochina. Kikuchi and his buddies had been closely monitoring the failing negotiations between the United States and Japan, and they suspected that America had little choice but to enter the war soon. In a matter of seconds, they came to realize that choice would have nothing to do with it.

"Right in the midst of this conversation, another Nisei boy rushed in to announce that Pearl Harbor had been bombed by the Japanese Air Force," Kikuchi recalled. "We all took it as a joke and continued our discussion. Finally, one of us turned on the radio, and the news flash came over. Our group quietly broke up, and I suppose that we were all pretty shocked."[1] In the immediate aftermath of the announcement, Kikuchi expressed a "vague fear," anticipating that he might be identified with the enemy. He rushed to the campus library in an attempt to blend in with the host of other students studying for final exams, but all conversations swirled nervously around the attack, and Kikuchi could find little solace in anonymity. On December 8, he found time to record some of his anxiety-ridden thoughts:

> I was very upset yesterday as we are in a war now. I am afraid that there will be violence and it is a hell of a mess. I should have confidence in the democratic procedures, but I'm worried that we might take a page from Hitler's methods and do something drastic towards the Issei. I hope not. I don't give a damn what happens to me, but I would be very disillusioned if the democratic process broke down.[2]

At this point, Kikuchi already suspected that his belief in his inalienable rights as a citizen would be severely challenged. His immediate concern for the first-generation immigrants was somewhat surprising, given his long-standing personal tension with his father's generation, but the worry he expressed at that moment seemed as genuine as it was justified. A year earlier, for example, Congress had passed the Alien Registration Act, requiring the registration and fingerprinting of all aliens over the age of fourteen. The law had passed in large part due to un-substantiated rumors of fifth column activity and espionage on the part of enemy aliens, especially German Americans. At the same time, Roger Daniels reports, the Department of Justice and the FBI were compiling a short list of dangerous or sub-versive aliens—German, Italian, and Japanese—who were to be arrested as soon as war broke out with their particular countries.[3] Understandably, given these legal precedents and his current circumstances, Kikuchi viewed the situation through a racial lens—citing Hitler's anti-Jewish pogroms—whereas he had been preoccu-pied with class after his migratory work in the San Joaquin Valley. Kikuchi optimis-tically but incorrectly forecast that "nobody can predict the future and things do look bad, but I just feel that we will win the war and I will survive nicely as things do turn out for the best," adding hopefully, "I'm not pressing my luck any, since it won't get any worse."[4] His wishful thinking would soon come up against the harsh reality of a democracy under siege and significantly compromised.

Demonstrating the confusion that permeated the Nisei community, and the country at large, he concluded this diary entry by declaring:

> Having bull sessions is meaningless now. It's action which counts, no more words. FDR says Pearl Harbor will be a day of infamy. Last fall I tried to get into the Army, but now I want to be a student, as it is going to be hell in the Army.[5]

That same day, however, as war on Japan was declared, Kikuchi quietly made his way to the Civic Center in San Francisco and, despite his misgivings, requested induction into military service; once more, he was rebuffed, this time based on the fact that no government policy had yet been established for Nisei.[6] At the same time, the Justice Department and military were issuing thousands of search warrants for homes in which an Issei enemy alien lived, claiming there was rea-sonable cause to believe that contraband—defined as any potential weapon, ex-plosive, radio transmitter, short-wave radio, or camera—was on the premises. Although the FBI ultimately determined that "none of [the contraband found] was sinister . . . [or] intended for subversive use," the damage was done in the court of public opinion: reports of the searches, regardless of outcome, simply affirmed suspicions held by many Americans about their Japanese neighbors, citizen and alien alike.[7]

By early January, General John DeWitt, the Western Defense commander, wanted another policy implemented: registration of all aliens through fingerprints and photographs, and records kept in duplicate (one in the community in which the alien lived, and one at a central office). A "Pass and Permit" system would effec-tively be put in place, random raids of alien homes would continue, and two zones would be established: the first, around military installations, would be strictly for-bidden to all civilians, and the second, in the rest of the West Coast, where Japanese American citizens and Japanese aliens would be able to live and work, but only under strict supervision. Ultimately, however, more severe measures would be taken, propelled by a confluence of DeWitt's paranoia about subversive activity, vocal fearmongering among western congressmen and nativist groups, and Roosevelt's own personal distrust of all Japanese Americans, alien or not.[8] On February 19, FDR would issue Executive Order 9066, authorizing the army, through Secretary of War Henry Stimson, to designate specific military zones on the West Coast from which "any and all persons may be excluded," thereby allowing for the removal of nearly all Japanese Americans from their homes in California, Washington, Oregon, and parts of Arizona. The distinction between Japanese American citizens and Japanese aliens was rendered moot.[9] However, in a bald-faced, hypocritical policy exception, the government detained and evacuated only a handful of Hawai'ian Japanese it deemed potentially troublesome. Had 9066 been implemented in Hawai'i, the absence of a majority-Japanese workforce would have ground the island economy to a halt. Sugar, pineapple, coffee, and other lucrative industries, owned by white businessmen, heavily relied on the labor of Japanese Americans (along with indigenous Hawai'ians, Chinese, Filipinos, and many others): more than $100 million worth of exports would have been at risk. Hence, the government bowed to its elites in the tropics and exempted Hawai'ians of Japanese descent from evacuation, allowing the uninterrupted production of profitable crops on island plantations. Despite the Japanese having attacked naval assets in Hawai'i, authorities saw no need to rearrange the economic priorities of the American empire in that part of the Pacific.

Kikuchi later recalled his feelings at the time: "When the general evacuation was declared, I became quite angry, because I felt it was a violation of our constitutional rights, and I thought that the Nisei should take a strong stand against it and refuse to move, but they were all too worried about their families to fully realize the implication of the military order."[10] Kikuchi himself was no exception, admitting that 9066 had convinced him "to take an active concern in my family in Vallejo for the first time in my life."[11] In the immediate aftermath of Pearl Harbor, and compelled by rumors on the Berkeley campus that FBI spies had "picked up some suspicious Japanese already," Kikuchi initially grew anxious about his parents' remaining at home:

> It may be dangerous for [Pop] in the barber shop with all those Mare Island [navy] guys coming in. I told Alice to tell Mom to have Pop's Navy discharge framed and put on the wall next to the barber license and take that Buddha statue the hell out of there. Alice says the Army should put me in charge of patriotism because I am suspicious of my own father.[12]

The family situation he reentered, of course, was not uncomplicated. Like most Issei, his parents had been classified as enemy aliens and could not remain in Vallejo, too close to the Mare Island Naval Base so soon after the Japanese attack. White friends petitioned on behalf of the elder Kikuchis, but to no avail. After a conference among the brothers and sisters, it was decided that Kikuchi's parents would move to San Francisco for the time being, while Mariko, the eldest child, would assume a position of authority and remain in Vallejo to look after the youngest Kikuchi siblings (Tom and Miyako) while they finished their school terms. Mariko had been working in Los Angeles as a domestic, but like her brother Jack, a student at San Francisco State, she returned to Vallejo to assist in the transition. Up to this point, the bulk of familial responsibility had fallen on Alice, who had filled the role of leader in the wake of each of her older siblings' departures. Although she had graduated at the top of her class at Vallejo High and completed a course in secretarial work, Alice—like Mariko—had been forced into domestic service to help support the family. To complicate matters, Kikuchi père completely reversed his attitude toward Charlie, considering the eldest son, by default, the leader of the family in a time of crisis. Coincidentally, the school of social welfare had required Kikuchi to conduct fieldwork at the Public Welfare Department: through this connection, Charlie was able to arrange for emergency assistance for his family through the Federal Security Funds program, but as Dorothy Thomas observed, "Alice and Mariko welcomed [Charles'] aid but resented his exercise of authority, and the struggle between them was to mount in intensity over the next three years."[13] In his sisters' opinion, he had not quite earned the title of head of house after spending all those years at the orphanage and away from home.

Charlie nonetheless contemplated quitting school altogether to help his family full-time, but thanks to the encouragement of his fellow students and instructors at Cal, he stayed the course until his family's evacuation at the end of March. All the while, Kikuchi struggled with accepting the rationale that the evacuation was an issue of national security. His Nisei peers, on the other hand, barely gave it a second thought—"They all took it for granted that it actually was a military necessity, because of the scare headlines about an imminent invasion by the Japanese forces"—but Kikuchi always had doubts: "I began to rationalize that it was a military necessity, but I never could convince myself of it." While trying to remain clear headed during this challenging time, Kikuchi harbored deep suspicions about the true motivation behind the evacuation orders: "I couldn't understand how minority pressure groups could sway the military to the [point] of ignoring constitutional provisions."[14]

My Native Land

The "pressure groups" Kikuchi referred to were the rabid anti-Asian, nativist organizations like the American Legion, the California Joint Immigration Committee (CJIC), and the Native Sons and Daughters of the Golden West. The résumé of these putatively patriotic organizations had been long established before America's entry into war, but in the immediate context of the Japanese attack and the evacuation of Japanese Americans, the same groups substantially padded their credentials.[15] For example, two years before the war, the national defense committee of American Legion Navy Post 278 in Los Angeles and the CJIC had jointly proposed a bill that would have forbidden anyone but U.S. citizens from operating fishing boats off the California coast. Supported by the navy, the bill was specifically targeted at preventing Issei from fishing in any areas where the U.S. Navy was engaged in maneuvers. Clearly, as an intentional consequence of the bill, any financial losses by Japanese fishermen would become gains by white fishermen.[16] In early 1941, the CJIC also lobbied California lawmakers to ban the teaching of Japanese language and history in the 248 Japanese-language schools in the state.[17] At the time, both measures failed. After December 7, however, the stakes were raised, and the three groups subsequently led the vociferous anti-Japanese charge by flooding newspapers with opinion pieces and spearheading letter-writing campaigns, all calling for the confiscation of Japanese property and the rounding up, detention, and incarceration of the Japanese. By mid-January 1942, the entire congressional delegation from Washington, Oregon, and California joined the Native Sons and Daughters and CJIC in demanding that Roosevelt remove "all persons of Japanese lineage" from the West Coast.[18] "This is our time to get things done that we have been trying to get done for a quarter of a century," remarked one member of the CJIC.[19] These groups' actions dovetailed with those of agricultural competitors of the Japanese, like the Grower-Shipper Vegetable Association of Central California, whose managing secretary declared: "We're charged with getting rid of the Japs for selfish reasons. We might as well be honest. We do. It's a question of whether the white man lives on the Pacific Coast or the brown man."[20]

Kikuchi, like many other Japanese Americans, was painfully aware of such economic motivations behind the evacuation: "Many citizens, in the name of loyalty, are using the present war as a weapon to shove all Japs out while they have a theoretical legal chance. If we examine the motives behind many of the individual acts, I am sure that we will find personal and selfish reasons why they want the Nisei property to be confiscated and business competition eliminated."[21] A consistent ally since the beginning of evacuation, Du Bois courageously and frequently spoke out against the internment. For example, in February 1942, he was the sole African American leader to sign Norman Thomas's open letter to FDR protesting the order, while intellectuals, editorial boards, and national organizations initially remained silent, fearful of the potential charges of un-American activity for supporting enemy aliens.[22] Two years later, in 1944, Du Bois would remind readers in his "As the Crow Flies" column that economic competition and deeply ingrained racism colluded to scapegoat their Japanese American brethren:

> The driving out of people of Japanese descent on the West Coast was not only the attempt to confiscate their savings without return, but to foment and prolong racial antagonism. The persons back of this wanted to keep serf Japanese labor in the Hawaiian Islands and prevent the Japanese from working anywhere in the United States outside the West Coast.

The federal government hardly needed to exert itself, since nativist, militia-like citizen groups hungered for a racialized witch hunt. Du Bois continues, "Among the organizations back of this movement is the Americanism Educational League, and the Homefront Commandos, Inc., whose slogan is 'Slap the Rat Jap' and 'No Jap Is Fit to Associate With Human Beings.'"[23]

Even after Japanese Americans had been interned and safely removed from the coast, American Legion posts decried the (mythically) excessive birth rates of the Japanese; picking up on this charge, the Native Sons and Daughters went one step further, passing resolutions calling for separation of the sexes within the camps in order to prevent the Japanese from reproducing at the taxpayers' expense.[24] Both types of anti-Japanese activists (i.e., economic and nativist) filed suit to force the registrars in San Francisco and Alameda Counties to strike the names of Japanese Americans in camps from the voting rolls, and in the summer of 1942, a former attorney general of California, U. S. Webb, filed suit on behalf of the Native Sons to rescind the citizenship of all Japanese born in the United States.[25] Du Bois unequivocally threw his lot in with the Nikkei: "The Native Sons . . . the real force behind the movement in California . . . have a membership of 25,000 and are not merely anti-Japanese, but anti-Oriental, anti-Mexican, and anti-Negro."[26] Clearly, Du Bois interpreted these unconstitutional, unjust, and chillingly self-interested acts as a collective and quickly developing assault on the civil rights of vulnerable, relatively voiceless citizens. Furthermore, in 1943, a congressman from Michigan spoke for the American Legion in the House of Representatives, criticizing the policy that permitted Nisei students to leave camps and continue their studies at colleges far removed from the military zone. Shockingly ignorant of the nearly 12,000 Nisei volunteers who had reported for service to the War Department in January 1943, but nonetheless quoting from an editorial in the legion's mouthpiece, the *National Legionnaire*, Rep. Paul Shafer propagandized:

> There is a rankling hurt in the bosom of good, honest, patriotic, loyal, and devoted Americans when they see their sons come to the crossroads— their sons take the road that leads to war and the battlefield. The Japanese boy takes the road that leads to college, and, to use a trite phrase worn rather thin and threadbare, the abundant life.[27]

Shafer's use of American "sons" versus Japanese "boys" is sadly telling of the hyperbole and racialized hysteria common to domestic discourse. In December 1944, the Legion sank even lower, when a post in Hood River, Oregon, agitated for the removal of the names of sixteen active-duty Japanese American soldiers from its honor roll.[28] The native sons had indeed risen.

Off to the "Races"

Back in San Francisco, Kikuchi was trying to fulfill his newfound filial duty of caring for the family while preparing for the impending evacuation. At the eleventh hour, his older sister, Mariko, had bowed out of overseeing the two youngest siblings and fled to Chicago, avoiding evacuation but leaving her brother with even greater responsibility: he was now looking after both of his parents and six of his younger siblings. Kikuchi readily admitted that he wanted to escape to the East Coast or Midwest, but after taking stock of his financial situation and the uncertainty of his job prospects, he decided that joining his family would be the most reasonable thing to do.[29] In late April, the Kikuchi family was finally evacuated to an assembly center at the Tanforan Race Track in San Bruno, California, a site most famous for one of its previous VIPs, the underdog-turned-champion thoroughbred Seabiscuit.

The first inmates arrived at Tanforan on April 28, 1942, and the last ones departed on September 4, 1942, destined for longer stays at relocation centers throughout the western interior and Arkansas. The center's population, which at its peak reached 7,816 people, tried very hard to make a livable existence out of what Sandra Taylor has appropriately called "a prison city."[30] The most recently constructed barrack sat in the center field of the racetrack, with a set of grandstands lined up along one side. All told, there were 180 buildings, 26 of which were converted horse stalls. The residents lived in either shoddily made barracks or these poorly fumigated horse stalls. Miné Okubo, the talented artist who narrated and illustrated her internment experience in *Citizen 13660*, was a young art student from Cal at the time. She remembers seeing Stall 50 for the first time, the space in which she and her younger brother would spend the next four months together. "Spider webs, horse hair, and hay had been whitewashed with the walls," she wrote. "Huge spikes and nails stuck out all over the walls. A two-inch layer of dust covered the floor, but on removing it we discovered that linoleum the color of redwood had been placed over the rough manure-covered boards."[31]

Deprived but unbroken, residents made as much a home as they could behind the barbed-wire fences: playing sports or Japanese versions of checkers and chess (*shogi* and go); hosting dances and talent shows; watching movies; planting victory gardens; attending school (children) and Americanization classes (adults); reading in the makeshift library; and putting up family nameplates over barrack entrances. Okubo notes, "All signs in Japanese were ordered removed but many fancy names, such as Inner Sanctum, Stall Inn, and Sea Biscuit, lent a touch of humor to the situation."[32] Most impressively, despite the temporary nature of the camp, a group of landscapers decided to build a lake in the center field, completely lined with trees and shrubs around its perimeter. "The lake was a great joy to the residents, and presented new material for the artists," she remarks appreciatively. "In the morning sunlight and at sunset it added great beauty to the bleak barracks."[33]

Hence, even in the face of an oppressive and depressing prison-like atmosphere, surrounded by armed guards and suspicious administrators, the internees—in many ways exemplified by Okubo herself—refused to give up their own agency and creativity, or their right to make something their own. It would be absurd to idealize the situation and misrepresent the internees as well adjusted to or content with the situation. Nor were they, as the War Relocation Authority would have liked, comforted by the fallacy that they were in camp "for their own protection," safely removed from hysterical mobs outside the camp. By showing their resistance, however, the internees certainly proved beyond any doubt that they could be imprisoned in body, but never in spirit.

What's Your Name? The Influence of Louis Adamic

On December 11, 1941, four days after the bombing of Pearl Harbor, a letter written by Kikuchi indicated that he had renewed correspondence with an old acquaintance. He began:

> Dear Mr. Adamic:
>
> You have asked me to send you some comments on reactions and developments out here. I am afraid that I cannot do this too calmly. I will try to give you some of my personal observations on the immediate reactions of the San Francisco and Bay Area Nisei. I don't think I can be too objective about it. I know where I stand.[34]

Approximately six months had passed since their last exchange of letters, but the unusual circumstances prompted Kikuchi to type a four-page single-spaced letter full of anxiety, the first of several such letters to Adamic in the ensuing two weeks. For his part, Adamic was extremely obliging and especially concerned for his young friend.[35] Only four days later, on December 15, he replied:

> Dear Charles:
>
> Thank you for your letter. Please write me once a week, giving such details and observations as you can. This is very important. I shall help all the loyal nisei, which doubtless means the overwhelming majority, but I need information, etc.[36]

He concludes the brief, three-paragraph note by averring, "Japan has to be licked, but equally important is that in doing this nasty job we don't distort America all out of shape." This particular exchange captures the history of their correspondence quite accurately: Kikuchi wrote long, involved letters in multiple pages, while Adamic, in general, sent only short, one-page notes, mechanically acknowledging receipt of Charlie's letters. In fact, judged by the correspondence alone, it was clearly a one-sided relationship.[37] Merely tallying up the letter count, however, misrepresents the weight and significance of their relationship. Kikuchi himself never denied the importance of his friendship with Adamic. The day after Adamic's mysterious suicide in September 1951, Kikuchi reflected: "I feel that I have lost a close friend and it is undoubtedly true that he was one of the great influences in my life ever since I first met him in 1940 in San Francisco."[38]

How the two men came to meet was by happy coincidence. Kikuchi had just recently graduated from San Francisco State, and two of his former instructors, a professor of social welfare, Bertha H. Monroe, and a philosophy and religion professor, Alfred G. Fisk, kept the young man in mind when they wrote separate letters of inquiry to Adamic in the fall of 1939. Kikuchi recalled Monroe's "instrumental" influence nearly fifty years later:

> She wanted us to write a life history of our own as part of a course requirement. So I had written a section of my experiences before I came to the university, and she thought it was so interesting that she discussed it with someone else in the college, who happened to be another professor of mine.[39]

The other teacher, of course, was Fisk, who would subsequently publish two solo projects: a book on apologetics, and a pamphlet on world disarmament. He was also a Presbyterian minister, and much like Adamic and Kikuchi, Fisk was deeply interested in interracial relationships: he would later cofound the Church for the Fellowship of All Peoples in 1943 with the African American minister Howard Thurman. It was considered the era's first interracial and intercultural church. He would also gain modest benefit from introducing Kikuchi to Adamic, publishing an article on "intercultural education" in the winter 1947 issue of Adamic's quarterly.[40] Encouraged by Monroe's endorsement of Kikuchi, Fisk saw an opportunity of mutual benefit for Adamic and Kikuchi when he contacted the Slovenian American scholar and writer, already well known for his two autobiographies, *Laughing in the Jungle* (1932) and *The Native's Return* (1934).[41]

Born in Blato, Slovenia, in 1898, Adamic decided at an early age that he was going to America. He remembered hearing stories as a child of places called Texas and Oklahoma, where ranches were as big as the entire province of Carniola, and it took a man on horseback a whole day to traverse the property; he truly believed that "in America everything was possible."[42] At the same time, an American immigrant who had returned to Blato a broken man told the young Adamic, "The jungle swallows many who go there to work. She squeezes the strength out of them, unless they are wise or lucky to enough to escape before it is too late."[43] Indeed, after arriving in New York in 1913, Adamic traveled a tortuous path, working for a Slovenian immigrant newspaper and translating articles from English into Slovene while taking English classes at night. He then swept floors at a silk mill in Paterson, New Jersey, before enlisting in the U.S. Army in 1916 (and becoming a citizen in 1917). In 1921, following a year of work aboard merchant ships came a succession of odd jobs as a printer, a field hand, and an auto factory worker, prompting Adamic to call himself a "workin' stiff with no particular trade."[44] By 1925, he had gained more stability, taking a clerk's position in a ship pilot's office in San Pedro, California, where he found time to read and write, thus producing a few articles for *Pearson's Magazine* and the *American Mercury*. The pieces shed light on Adamic's experience as an immigrant in America and emphasize the contributions of other immigrant and minority laborers in performing "most of the dirty work in the United States," themes that would dominate his string of books published in the two following decades.[45]

Adamic made it the passion of his life to promote the diversity of American immigrants and privilege their experiences as the central narrative of American history. Along with Read Lewis, a genteel lawyer from New England involved in the settlement-house movement, and M. Margaret Anderson, an unheralded author and former high school teacher, Adamic edited and published *Common Ground* (1940), a progressive quarterly that fulfilled his aim of honoring immigrant history in the United States and preaching "unity within diversity." In the inaugural issue, Adamic explicitly shared his vision for America:

> Democracy, if it is to be a positive way of life, requires something more than tolerance. The diverse elements of the U.S. population will have to try to accept one another. We need to look at each other, closely, objectively, critically, but without fear and with active effort toward understanding.[46]

For Adamic, Ellis Island and Angel Island symbolized the greatest origin stories in the collective American imagination, as did Plymouth Rock. He called for an intellectual-emotional fusion: "We need to work toward a synthesis of the old-stock and the new-immigrant America, of the Mayflower and the steerage . . . of the Liberty Bell and the Statue of Liberty, of the New England wilderness and the slums of modern industrial cities, of the American Revolution and the Industrial Revolution."[47] A recent biographer of Adamic proclaims, "Of course, Adamic was not the first person to champion America's diversity." Writers as varied as Walt Whitman, Israel Zangwill, Emma Lazarus, Randolph Bourne, Mary Antin, and Horace Kallen had already established theories of America's "multifaceted character," its ethnic and racial underpinnings, as well as its endlessly replenishing fount of transnational immigrants. Building on these foundational thinkers, and like Antin and Kallen before him, Adamic "wrote both as an immigrant and as one deeply aware of the broader and varied currents within American society."[48]

One of those currents carried Adamic toward studying the importance of second-generation Americans, both in comparison to their parents and with regard to their own attitudes and acculturation. Cognizant of Adamic's recent investigation of such individuals, Fisk made his innocent plea in a letter dated October 27, 1939. "A very interesting case of a second-generation Japanese American has come to my observation," Fisk began, "and I thought that you might be interested."

> He graduated last May from this college with highest honors, one of our most brilliant students. His personality, however, is not particularly attractive. He hates the Japanese, criticizes them unmercifully, and yet occasionally champions their part when others criticize them. He has had to work his way through school and yet resents working at tasks which (like dishwashing) seem to put him (and his race) in an inferior position. Altogether, I think that he is a very interesting—if perplexing—psychological study.
>
> His name is Charles Kikuchi.[49]

This introduction led to a meeting between the two in San Francisco at the Clift Hotel, after which Adamic asked Kikuchi whether or not he would be willing to contribute his life's story to a collection Adamic was editing entitled *From Many Lands*. This particular volume brought together testimonials and narratives from a diverse sample of second-generation immigrants: Dutch, Finnish, Croatian, Greek, and Mexican, among others. To Adamic, the aim of his project was ambitious but necessary:

> Many people of the second and third and later generations, to whom America is a platitude, have never glimpsed its power. They are the majority of the youth today. What if we could revive it, lift to bewildered and cynical eyes the vision of new frontiers, rich in culture and spirit, wide and deep as the best in man—an America with a sweep to which a continent's breadth is narrow—a democracy not only of political inheritance but of the heart and the handclasp?[50]

Kikuchi happily obliged: "The way I feel towards the matter is that you are doing a great service for the second generation group in this country and capable of reaching a wide audience. It is sufficient reward for me to feel that I was able to contribute something—little as it is."[51] The "little" contribution to which Kikuchi referred was a twenty-six-page, single-spaced, typed letter sent to Adamic two months earlier. Attached to the end of Kikuchi's letter were answers to three questions Adamic had asked regarding San Francisco's Japantown, the literal timbre of Nisei voices ("I noticed that your voice was quite deep"), and intermarriage. Kikuchi had culled much of the Japantown information from his current research on Nisei youth for the NYA. Adamic inquired of him:

> To what extent may I use it, should it fit into any of my current writings? I mean: do you expect to have some use for it later? Or might not the NYA object if your stuff, or the results of your research, should appear in my writing? Could I credit the research to you? . . . Might not then your name become connected with the personal story, which I plan to call "A Young American with a Japanese Face"?[52]

Adamic subsequently took both Kikuchi's letter and NYA material. After generous editing and paraphrasing, he turned the twenty-six pages into a fifty-page narrative entitled (true to his word) "A Young American with a Japanese Face," published anonymously in *From Many Lands* later that year (1940). Kikuchi put it bluntly, if not sarcastically, fifteen years later: "Mr. Adamic re-wrote all those parts which had interpretation in it, although my observations about the Nisei [were] generally included."[53] To be fair to Adamic, however, he was not the one who decided that the piece should run without an acknowledged author. "Personally," he wrote to Kikuchi,

> I feel you ought not to worry about being identified as the Young Man in the story. It may be a little awkward, but I'm sure the story will make your

life very dynamic and open all sorts of things for you and do a great deal for Japanese Americans, and for the second generation generally.[54]

Kikuchi's early life, as this chapter will later demonstrate, was not a particularly happy one; in other words, he had plenty of reasons to distance himself from his parents and the embarrassment of airing his family's dirty laundry (which the narrative certainly did).

Two-Way Passage

Before delving into the themes and objectives both authors commonly sought to highlight in this ostensibly autobiographical narrative, it is worth noting a few examples of the aesthetic and stylistic differences between the original letter written by Kikuchi and the reinterpreted final version published by Adamic. First, Kikuchi's letter is fairly conventional and straightforward, more along the lines of reportage with little embellishment. He shares his story in a linear, chronological fashion with a few short asides. Adamic's interpretation, on the other hand, divides Kikuchi's narrative into four thematic sections: "He Begins His Story," "Father and Son," "A Job and College," and "'What a Country! What a Country!'" At first glance, such an editorial choice to organize and categorize Kikuchi's life story is not unusual or particularly noteworthy. Like a good editor, Adamic simply decided that the narrative needed some shape and focus. However, when one compares some of the content in the original letter with its analogue in the published version, it becomes obvious that Adamic took substantial license in revising Kikuchi's story to make it fit smoothly within the overarching analytical framework for the collection. Adamic's ultimate hope was that readers would recognize that America had yet to realize its full potential as a democracy, one that would include all its citizens as participants and be defined nearly equally by the various ethnic groups of which it was composed.

For example, early in his letter, Kikuchi explains how he came to be placed in an orphanage by his parents and how he subsequently became acclimated to the new surroundings:

> I quickly adjusted myself to this new life, and took part in the activities of this complete community. All in all, my childhood from then on was fairly happy. I had to work and help pay for my upkeep starting at the age of nine, but this experience did not hurt me much. Thus, I feel that any personality difficulties that I may have are a result of my being reared as an orphan rather than a result of being a second generation person. It's an awful feeling for a child to have burnt into his memory that he is not wanted.[55]

Adamic essentially rendered this passage in good faith, especially the last section, in which he states, "Of course, the place could not give that unquestioning love which children need, and in my case it could not overcome the salient fact, which overhung my thoughts and feelings like a vague threat, that I was an orphan although my parents were alive."[56] What is striking about this set of passages, however, is that the former excerpt is the only time Kikuchi explicitly comments on his being an orphan. As mentioned in the previous chapter, Kikuchi fiercely guarded that orphanage experience (leaving the actual institution nameless, for example), and as Modell correctly pointed out, "his defenses [about the experience] were well set."[57] Therefore, in the letter, it comes only as a passing observation, and its theme does not persist throughout the rest of his draft. Adamic, on the other hand, runs with this fleeting moment of self-revelation and takes significant license in telling Kikuchi's story thematically. Toward the end of the published narrative, Adamic seizes on this seed of Kikuchi's thought and crafts a stirring monologue—not a trace of which can be found anywhere in Kikuchi's original letter. Adamic's version waxes rhapsodically:

> Isn't Americanism, perhaps, an attitude of one's mind and feelings that issues out of an inner harmony which is respected by one's environment and should endure anywhere? I haven't that harmony. Nor has most of the second generation of Oriental descent. *We are all orphans* psychologically, confused; cluttered up with our past, with the past of our immigrant parents; afflicted with our faces—all of which, of course, involves also America, which cluttered up with her own past, thinks she is still the America of a hundred or fifty years ago, when the majority of people here were Anglo-Saxon Americans.[58]

Rightly or wrongly, at this point Adamic co-opts the narrative, imposing his own ideological template upon it (no matter how similar Kikuchi's philosophy might have been). Granted, Kikuchi had few if any other public venues in which to give voice to his experience, like many other contemporary immigrant writers and thinkers. Nonetheless, Adamic changed the timbre of Kikuchi's voice, and instead of allowing the writer's youthful and contradictory experience to unfold on its own, Adamic made certain that the narrative hewed to his own vision of America. Ironically, like those in Old America whom he chastised, Adamic was shoehorning Kikuchi's original story to fit conveniently into his own master narrative.

While one should not overstate the conspiratorial nature of the revision or devalue Adamic's unquestionably admirable intentions overall, one must still draw attention to the differences between the original and published documents, if for no other reason than to highlight the imbalance of power between Adamic and Kikuchi. The latter was certainly indebted to the former, but Kikuchi's thought process and ideology were all his own. As further proof, one might consider the concluding remarks in both Kikuchi's letter and Adamic's adaptation. Note that in Kikuchi's version, he contradicts his earlier claim that his problems stemmed more from being an orphan than from being a part of the second generation, which would not be the only time Kikuchi revealed himself to be an age-appropriate, paradoxical, or confused young man in his twenties. While he does not conflate the terms "orphan" and "second generation" here (as Adamic does in the earlier passage), he still blames social and economic reasons for his maladjustment:

> In myself I see a multitude of complexes. I have at different times noticed glaring contradictions in my thoughts. In essence, I am a "Jittery New American" as you would state it. The basis for all my maladjustments lie in the economic and then social realm. (I think economic problems are the root of all racial problems. Solve it, and you solve the second generation problem, as well as all world problems. This is Utopia, but a worthy goal. Meanwhile as long as we have room for progress and change in a Democratic society, life is worth living.)[59]

By contrast, Adamic is not quite sure how to deal with the complexity of Kikuchi's self-evaluation: the contradiction, the concern with the intersection of class and race, and the naïveté of his utopian vision. Instead, in his published conclusion, Adamic focuses on the hopefulness expressed by the young Nisei. Having shared a Kikuchi anecdote about being rejected by the naval recruiting office based on the diarist's being a "Jap," Adamic once again ventriloquizes Kikuchi's voice, customizing the young man's story to advance his own thesis and impression of America: "After the interviews at the recruiting offices I rode uphill in a cable car . . . I thought of my brother, of the artistic arrangement of fruits and vegetables in the store where he worked, of the fruits of the earth brought together and arranged in a pattern of beauty, harmony, and color . . . The car groaned and jangled."[60] Adamic employs a Whitmanesque flair and Pearl Buckian imagery, presciently anticipating the "salad bowl" (here, fruit bowl) analogy of America's diversity while simultaneously reaffirming the difficulty of the road ahead (the modernist cable car's literal pitching and heaving uphill) for the country as a whole. Noble in its sentiment, the passage nonetheless demonstrates that Adamic too broadly interpreted key passages of the letter, essentially substituting his own beliefs and words for Kikuchi's. Such flights of fancy are especially glaring, given that in other sections of the story, particularly with regard to straight plot lines, he merely transcribed the young man's narrative.

My argument here is not an indictment of Adamic; I believe that he was one of the few, and one of the most reliable, allies whom people of color and immigrants could trust. And, once one absorbs the entirety of Adamic's complicated relationship with Kikuchi, one gains even greater appreciation for Adamic's acting as a true friend and mentor at a time when barely anyone wanted to stick their necks out for any "enemy aliens." Rather, I want to delineate the structural inequality behind these two texts. Too often, lines blur between mentor and charge, or between teacher and student. In the case of Kikuchi, his being an American of Japanese ancestry (or in the parlance of the time, an Oriental) magnifies this ambiguity. As Henry Yu points out in his critical study of Chicago School sociologists and Asian Americans under their tutelage during the mid-twentieth century, the dynamic between these scholars and their students could be characterized by an imbalance in power and representation:

> Professional academics, in defining an interest in the exotic, and at the same time producing knowledge about the unknown, also produced themselves as the expert knowers. Seeing themselves as enlightened and cosmopolitan at the same time they defined working-class racists as ignorant and provincial, progressive and liberal elites crafted themselves as the knowing subject through which others became important.

Further he observes:

> Their intellectual project was a progressive program, but . . . it built an institutional structure that was Orientalist. . . . Individual sociologists and their intentions cannot be divorced from the structural effects of their practices.[61]

To be clear, Adamic was neither a sociologist nor related in any official capacity to the Chicago School. While Kikuchi would later study with some of the Chicago sociologists, at the time of the publication of Adamic's collection (1940), he was still a recent college graduate looking for work or a graduate degree program. Nevertheless, Yu's analysis does provide a useful analogue and theoretical framework for understanding the relationship between Adamic and Kikuchi.

Adamic, akin to the luminaries in the Chicago School—Robert Park, Louis Wirth, Ernest W. Burgess, Herbert Blumer, and W. I. Thomas—was responsible for helping shape the image of Asians (and immigrants generally) in the eyes of the general American public. Unlike most members of the Chicago School (with the exception of Wirth, who migrated from Germany in 1911), Adamic was a recent foreign immigrant himself, having arrived at Ellis Island in 1913.[62] He therefore had an arguably deeper personal investment than his native-born peers in studying the perceptions of these New Americans and promoting the roles of foreign immigrants in American culture. Additionally, with the publication of several books and his editing of *Common Ground*, Adamic wielded relatively significant power in directly influencing the public's understanding of the immigrant experience. His articles appeared in large-circulation periodicals like *Harper's*, the *Nation*, the *American Mercury*, and the *Saturday Review of Literature*, while *The Native's Return* sold 70,000 copies in its first two weeks, becoming a Book-of-the-Month Club selection in 1934. To paraphrase Yu, Adamic had indeed become the knower of all things immigrant, and through his interpretation of what was previously unknown, "others became important." One of those "others," of course, had a Japanese face. Continuing along the line of argument drawn by Yu, Adamic's intellectual project—while admirably progressive in its goals—still cannot be decoupled from the institutional or, better yet, ideological structure it reinforced: Orientalism.

Put another way, Adamic circumscribed Kikuchi's desire to speak for himself on his own terms, to define himself as the "multitude of complexes" he believed himself to be. Instead, in keeping with the dichotomy between Oriental (quiet, calm, detached, exotic, and submissive) and Occidental (robust, individualistic, enterprising, and knowable), Adamic seizes upon Kikuchi's single line of being an orphan and transforms all second-generation Asians into "psychological orphans," contrasted with first-generation immigrant "families," who knew their own far-away history, and the family of established Old Americans, secure in their "common" Anglo-Saxon heritage. Adamic thus conflates the terms "second-generation Oriental" and "psychological orphan," simultaneously defining an Oriental and placing it outside the bounds of a conventional American experience (i.e., exoticizing it, branding it a problem). In fairness, Adamic generally diagnosed all second-generation immigrants as suffering from perpetual outsider status, cultural rootlessness, and civic disengagement. In *My America*, he writes: "The majority of the grown-up New Americans just hang back from the main stream of life in this country, forcing a tremendous mass of neutral, politically lifeless citizenry; while their younger fellow New Americans . . . show dangerous signs of becoming the same kind of neutral, unstirring citizens, unless something is done about it."[63] However, in the case of "A Young American with a Japanese Face," Adamic delivers his critique of Nisei and other second-generation Asian Americans in a manner that Kikuchi never explicitly conveyed in his letter. Adamic therefore reinforces Orientalist thought not only by silencing an Asian American voice but also by attributing an unfounded criticism of all second-generation Asians to that same stolen voice. Adamic's readers did not realize, however, that he had donned the cloak of authenticity in appropriating Kikuchi's text.

Kikuchi himself did not initially seem overly concerned about Adamic's revisions. Recalling the collaboration nearly fifty years later, he said only that he did not have time to correct the proofs of the essay before Adamic submitted the final version to the publisher: Kikuchi had been too busy working on farms up and down the Pacific Coast.[64] In subsequent conversations, however, he eventually conceded that parts of "A Young American" were factually incorrect (e.g., his mother was not "lady-in-waiting to the Empress Dowager," a fiction drawn to overemphasize the class anxiety felt by Nakajiro toward Shizuko).[65] Or other details in the narrative were exaggerated to overdramatize the family's fall from "respectability." Kikuchi laughs when he recalls:

> We were always poor [and on relief for awhile]; we were never wealthy. But Adamic seems to have gotten the impression from me that we were well-off and my father drank and gambled all the money away, which was not true. My father drank heavily but he did not gamble, as far as I remember.

Adding for good measure: "And we did not come from this noble family."[66] Finally, some of the "license" Adamic took—especially in characterizing (or perhaps simply revealing) Kikuchi's caustic disdain toward most things Japanese—adversely affected how campmates in Gila perceived him; through reading "his" story, they believed they already knew this pompous, self-righteous expatriate. For example, some questioned the publicizing of actions that should have remained private within the Japanese American community: the airing of dirty laundry was not meant for everyone's viewing pleasure and was not culturally Japanese. "The more negative feeling," Kikuchi remembers, "was in relation to 'How come you went to the waterfront to boycott sending scrap iron to Japan? How come you resist learning Japanese?' As if this was a deliberate thing."[67] Admission of these explicitly political acts did not sit well with some campmates, which made his work as a counselor in social welfare with those same internees—an extremely intimate dynamic—doubly hard, since he had to overcome hostile first impressions. In the end, though, Kikuchi still wrestled with the complexity of his curious collaboration with the famous Louis Adamic: "It [the revision] didn't distort it [the actual story] that much, but when I read it . . . my feeling was that this isn't true."[68]

On the heels of Adamic's reported suicide in September 1951, however, Kikuchi naturally shared his most grateful memories of Adamic in his diary. After all, nearly a decade had passed, much had happened to both of them, and enough water had passed under the bridge. "At that time [1940]," he wrote, "I was a very bewildered recent college graduate getting disillusioned about America because I could not get any sort of a job except domestic work, and he encouraged me to keep on striving because the time would come when I would gain full acceptance in our society." He continued:

> I was confused about my status in California society which discriminated against Japanese and their offspring and feeling most frustrated in my inability to resolve my conflict about it. My talks with Adamic and in subsequent letters and articles I read written by him helped me to gain a much better perspective about the status of minorities in this country and it helped me to see beyond my immediate problem.[69]

As will be shown, Adamic eventually persuaded Kikuchi that all minorities, not simply the Japanese, would finally integrate fully into America's social and cultural fabric. Adamic made it clear to him that it would not be easy, and Kikuchi understood that integration would not simply mean the "whitening" of these immigrants and minorities after the melting away of their Old World habits, but rather the acceptance and inclusion of these diverse cultures in a new America redefined by its various colorful strands. Finally, he assisted Kikuchi in seeing his "maladjustments" within the larger context of challenges facing all second-generation Americans, and inspired the young Nisei at a historical moment when Kikuchi's internal compass was pointing in so many different directions.

"This Crisis Is an Opportunity"

Within this historical arc, then, *Common Ground* ultimately proved to be one of the impresario's most effective vehicles for conveying the message of "unity within diversity"—through the work of writers, artists, and thinkers much like

Kikuchi. The Common Council for American Unity (CCAU), an organization through which Adamic aimed to help both New and Old Americans learn about one another, published the progressively minded journal. As early as April 1940, Adamic had informally offered Kikuchi a job with the CCAU, without putting too much pressure on him. "You seem to be very capable," he wrote to Kikuchi. "Would you be interested in coming East eventually and see if you might not fit into something? . . . Of course, don't take this too seriously; it is only a suggestion, hint of a possibility!"[70] Kikuchi declined, but kept abreast of Adamic's work with the council. The CCAU had been reorganized in 1939, the institutional heir to the Foreign Language Information Service (FLIS) established by President Woodrow Wilson in 1917. During World War I, FLIS educated Americans about the nation's entry into the global conflict, but in the postwar years, it became an independent agency and a leading advocate for foreign-born citizens in the United States. In its reincarnation as the CCAU, the organization retained its mandate to lobby for recent immigrants, celebrating their diversity and cultures and actively aiding them in adjusting to American life.

As one of its most influential members, Adamic set out to privilege the Japanese American experience. For example, between the fall of 1940 and the summer of 1942, he invited at least six Nisei to share their stories in the quarterly, including Mary ("Molly") Oyama, Mike Masaoka, and the short-story writer Toshio Mori. In the spring 1942 issue, Oyama contributed "After Pearl Harbor: Los Angeles," wherein she passionately wrote:

> After this stressful period of inevitable intensified prejudice, intolerance, and discrimination, we hope for—and we fight for—a new era wherein we Nisei will be accepted as full-fledged Americans. By that time we will have proved our loyalty; our Nisei soldiers will have died to preserve the ideals of the only country we know. Somehow we will see this hard interlude through.[71]

Coincidentally, Oyama lived in a home subsequently taken up by author Chester Himes during the evacuation. In his most popular novel, *If He Hollers Let Him Go* (1945), Himes's protagonist curses the white supremacy faced by many Angelenos of color, remembering the internment of his former, pseudonymous neighbor, "Little Riki Oyana."[72] (One of Oyama's sons was named "Rickey.") In the same spring issue, Adamic highlighted Masaoka and the JACL's controversial "Japanese American Creed," which immediately followed an article by the honorary chairman of the National Committee of the CCAU, First Lady Eleanor Roosevelt. Read before the U.S. Senate and officially entered into the *Congressional Record* in May 1941, the "Creed" was intended to formally express the patriotism of Japanese Americans and their support of the war effort. The wording of the creed, however, soured many Japanese Americans; the statement proclaimed that if discriminated against, Japanese Americans would "*never* become bitter or lose faith," and would discourage such external prejudice by "doing it the American way: *above-board*, in the open."[73] Such overwrought phraseology made it seem as if prewar rumors of Japanese fifth column activity were true, or as though shifty Orientals were indeed conducting themselves "below-board," suspiciously and with ill intent. Without any controversy, on the other hand, Adamic published Mori's story "Lil' Yokohama," which depicted a rural community of Japanese Americans—most notably, like any group of Americans—playing a game of baseball.[74] Mori would go on to write a well-received collection of short stories, *Yokohama, California* (1949), introduced, not coincidentally, by Adamic's friend William Saroyan. Consistently over the next few years, other prominent Nisei joined *Common Ground*'s efforts, most notably the cartoonist Miné Okubo, whose work was published in the spring of 1944, and the editors even included snippet reports from camp newspapers (most frequently from the *Manzanar Free Press*, Oyama's paper).

The late dean of Japanese American history, Yuji Ichioka, generally praised Adamic for taking such a genuine interest in Japanese Americans and for drawing attention to their plight, particularly during the internment years. He did, however, issue one major criticism about Adamic's pet project: "Common Ground articles by and on Japanese Americans all stressed the Americanism and assimilation of the Nisei, saying nothing about any aspect of Japanese culture with which the Nisei might affirm their ethnicity."[75] A tall order to fill in a time of war, Nisei writers knew all too well that the harsh spotlight was on them, and it would have been quite difficult to publicly celebrate the cultural traditions of sumo, go, *obon* festivals, or Momotaro (a young Japanese folk hero), as Ichioka might have desired. Such affirmations would have potentially been an invitation to violence. Ichioka's overemphasis on Japanese culture would likely have rankled not only Kikuchi, but also many of his radical friends looking to shed Old World ways. However, Ichioka raised a more reasonable criticism: Adamic had "tended mistakenly to equate the racial problems of the Nisei with the ethnic problems of European ethnic groups."[76] As Yu's analysis of the Chicago sociologists and Ichioka's commentary on Adamic suggest, many intellectual allies of Japanese Americans did not fully understand the complexity of the simultaneous intersection, overlapping, and rupture between ethnicity and race.

Werner Sollors has most lucidly argued that the era's " 'old-stock'/'new immigrant' distinction on which much of the thinking about 'America' and 'ethnicity' rested did not, of course, apply to all ethnic groups." After pointing to the vexing and nonconforming cases of American Indians, Mexican Americans, African Americans, and Asian/Pacific immigrants, he reminds us: "Among immigrant groups proper, American citizens of Japanese descent were, *at the very time* that Adamic popularized the reinterpretation of the immigrants as new Puritans, stripped of their rights as citizens and property owners and interned in detention camps—as a *race* (unlike German or Italian enemy aliens, who were generally detained only on the grounds of individual affiliations or political acts)."[77] In other words, the Japanese immigrant certainly looked different enough (phenotypically and, probably, physiologically) from the white ethnic immigrant (as long as the latter did not display overtly anarchist or fascist tendencies). The federal government, for one, could easily identify the former as a racialized immigrant and segregate him, as it would red, black, brown, and other yellow "races," while compensating the latter with "honorary wages of whiteness" (even if they were German POWs, for example).[78] Sollors has also cautioned against accepting a duality of ethnicity and race separated by a yawning gap, a false construction that belies the mutually constitutive nature of the concepts. One must then contextualize the phenomenon of *Common Ground* within this admittedly complicated framework of defining the terms "immigrant," "minority," "ethnicity," "race," and "racialization."

Publishing Issues

As the United States entered the war, Adamic's attention grew more distracted by goings-on in eastern Europe (specifically Yugoslavia) and the Soviet Union. Consequently, Anderson and Lewis largely planned and shaped the trajectory of the quarterly over its remaining life (until 1949), publishing it through Princeton University Press. The Carnegie Corporation eagerly funded the quarterly: the foundation hoped to unify morale on the home front and promote the relatively unsuccessful philosophy of intercultural education during the early to mid 1940s. Thus, the magazine enjoyed reasonably high circulation and subscription rates for its first six years, when the Adamic-inflected theme of immigrant diversity reigned over the majority of volumes, while attracting the finest writers and thinkers of the day: the folklorist Zora Neale Hurston, equally iconoclastic George Schuyler, the immigrant activist and author Mary Antin, University of Chicago president Robert M. Hutchins, literary giant Van Wyck Brooks, the novelist Mary Ellen Chase, the Chinese author Lin Yutang, and Hurston's erstwhile writing companion, the polymath Langston Hughes, the last four of whom were editorial board members for the magazine. What is more, the column space the editors reserved for Nisei writers proved to be one of the only outlets available for comparatively unfiltered news from the camps. While these Nisei knew full well that they had to keep up an air of unquestioned loyalty, some pieces managed to convey the exasperation and betrayal felt by internees. As a historian of *Common Ground* tellingly noted, Anderson did nothing to mask such overtones (in stark contrast to the WRA administrators' *ad absurdum* censoring of camp newspapers). William C. Beyer astutely observes:

> Mary Oyama could joke about life at the hastily arranged assembly center in the stables at the Santa Anita racetrack, but her hints at generational strains, the bitterness, and the fear told of life in the camps more honestly than did Robert L. Brown, public relations director at the Manzanar center. His facile account made Manzanar sound like a summer camp where internees, "stomachs full of good substantial food," sacked out on cots and became irritated only on the odd occasion when a "playful" sol-

dier awakened someone by shining a searchlight from his sentry tower through the sleeper's window.[79]

In line with Beyer's critique, it is hard to discern the greater offense to a reader's intelligence: Brown's self-serving, fairy-tale version of Manzanar, where an intergenerational riot took place in December 1942, or the fact that an internment camp fielded its own public relations director, as if it were a cruise ship.

It is, however, little surprise that such governmental updates and reports appeared in *Common Ground* from the likes of Brown, WRA administrators Dillon Myer and Robert Frase, or even guilt-ridden U.S. attorney general Francis Biddle (who had authorized warrants for FBI searches and seizures of Nikkei households and whose January 1942 announcement of enemy alien evacuation from West Coast military zones set the precedent for 9066). Superficially, the quarterly was doing the government a favor by educating a broad audience on procedures and arrangements regarding the internees—transparent, forthright, and ostensibly honest communication between the wartime administration and its citizens. These leaders may have in fact believed in the purely educative aspect of such communiqués, but some elements of the administration also considered it effective and free propaganda (hence, the camps' PR directors). While Adamic and the editors did not explicitly address the rationale for cooperating with the WRA, the inclusion of official pronouncements unquestionably made the magazine look patriotic and unobstructive. On another level, however, one should consider why the editors strategically sandwiched sterile updates on camp conditions or hypocritical pleas for help with evacuee relocation in between obliquely stinging indictments of the government whose spokesmen wrote those puff pieces. Absurd agitprop amid thoughtful intellectual discourse stuck out like a sore thumb, making the WRA authors, and by extension, the government, look like melon-sized piñatas, ready to be whacked and severely disemboweled.

Brown's and Frase's articles, for example, were bookended by Anderson's excellent and subtly entitled article "Get the Evacuees Out!" and the lengthy "Blueprint for a Slum," a trenchant reflection on a camp's collective psychological damage, by Eddie Shimano, an internee at the Jerome Relocation Center in Arkansas and editor of its newspaper, aptly entitled *Communiqué*. Tellingly, Myer's oxymoronic "Democracy in Relocation" appeared in an issue with "Democracy Was Not a Candidate" by Lillian E. Smith, the publisher of the liberal *South Today*, and Mary Ellen Chase's "Ancient Democracy to a Modern," which purposefully reminded readers of the tortuous path of democratic history from Athens to wartime America. And finally, Biddle's regret-filled article "Democracy and Racial Minorities" was followed by "No Short Cut to Democracy" (Lester B. Granger), "Democracy Is for the Unafraid" (Himes), and "Farewell to Little Tokyo" (Larry Tajiri).

Anderson's article, though, merits further deliberation and analysis. Written for the summer 1943 issue, the piece searingly criticizes the nationwide readership and larger majority population for an unearned self-satisfaction and the sin of omission for remaining largely silent as fellow citizens were herded into incarceration camps. She immediately sets down her marker:

> There are readers who go with us in COMMON GROUND on everything except those of Japanese descent; there are others who go with us on everything except the Negro or the Jew. But democracy is no such halfway process. It is a tough belief, and it brooks no emotional withdrawals. We really mean democracy—at home and abroad—or we don't.[80]

On the fear-filled roundup and indefinite evacuation, Anderson does not equivocate: "It seems crystal clear that against our Japanese Americans democracy has done deep wrong." Imbuing her message with passion and measured anger, she personifies democracy itself as having unconscionably blundered, and implicates every American as personally obligated to the collective remedying of this horrific error. At the time she was writing (mid-1943), the government had finally permitted significant numbers of "loyal" internees to "relocate and resettle" in urban and rural areas of the unfamiliar Midwest and East Coast. "To undo the wrong *we* allowed to happen will not be easy," she proclaims. "Wrongs breed evils; and *no one* can read the account later in these pages of the spiritual crack-up of families and individuals in the centers and not realize the size of the social problems *we* have created for *ourselves*."[81] She uses first-person pronouns, the active voice, and a declarative tone, all of which hammer readers with the guilt of complicity and indict them for negligence in failing their Japanese American brethren. If America metaphorically represents the whole family, smaller parts of that whole—the units of families and individuals in the camps—have "spiritually crack[ed]-up," in Anderson's words, fallen from the whole, and now it is up to the smallest but most important element to help in the reconstitution, "resettlement," and healing of that wound in "the national body."

> The close reader will find many areas in which he can take hold individually and help . . . He can take some of them under his wing and see they meet people their own age, go to movies with them, help them pick up the old normal strands of taken-for-granted living, help them find their way back to what they thought was America. He—the individual at the base of American society—can create the true climate of democracy.[82]

Stirring, lucid, and bracingly direct, Anderson issues a further challenge: "It is time we stopped being intoxicated with ourselves and our mission and our ideas, and really had a look at what we are doing here at home. It is understandable why we like to look away." Instead of turning a blind eye to the violation of civil liberties in the name of internal or national security, or navel-gazing at America's exceptionalism, "we, the people" need to recommit to ushering in "the true climate of democracy," not, as the nativists would like, the wartime climate of fear. Raising the stakes, she dares her public to risk individual and national failure for collective, global success:

For this is the true test of democracy. If we cannot solve so small and tidy a problem as the dispersal resettlement and assimilation of 110,000 people of Japanese descent within our borders, what hope is there for our own 13,000,000 Negroes and for the great masses of the people of the world who look hungrily to us for moral leadership?[83]

Her friend Adamic could not have improved upon her message, while the magazine could not have placed its reputation in surer hands than hers.

As the nation's attention pivoted from immigrants toward Americans of color, so too did the magazine. African American literati such as Hughes (published sixteen times), Schuyler, Himes, Roi Ottley, Melvin B. Tolson, and the political cartoonist Ollie Harrington found an inviting editorial board and ideologically welcome outlet in *Common Ground*, which was complementary to black newspapers and, in some cases, much less conservative than those papers. But the magazine began to sag under the burden of discomfited readers put off by the greater emphasis on racism, pointed discussions of race riots (such as those in Detroit, LA, and Beaumont, Texas, all in the summer of 1943), and discussions of a possible race war occurring in the Pacific theater. Additionally, Carnegie pulled its indispensable financial support, citing the CCAU's need to avoid any further "efforts whose primary function is to facilitate harmonious relationships between racial groups—the Jew and the Negro—and the old-stock Christian or 'general' American public."[84]

In the same issue as Anderson's noteworthy evacuee piece, Tajiri deftly "couple[d] . . . the Japanese American situation with the Negro problem." Characterized by Anderson as the "vigorous editor" of the JACL's *Pacific Citizen*, Tajiri demonstrated precisely why others, like Kikuchi, would later take note of how dramatically Tajiri diverged from Mike Masaoka and the mainstream JACL.[85] "Farewell to Little Tokyo" was not just a quaint update from Tajiri, but also a deadly serious cautionary tale for other Nikkei. Japanese Americans, he recommended, would do well to pay attention to the "Negro question" and find common cause with African Americans. "This fact is slowly seeping into the consciousness of the group," he wrote. Nisei themselves had been perpetrators of terrible racism toward other groups.

> But the racial nature of evacuation developed a recognition among many Japanese Americans that they were inescapably relegated to a place on the color wheel of America, that their problem was basically one of color and is part of the unfinished racial business of democracy. With this realization came a corresponding awareness of the urgent and demanding color problem of the American Negro.[86]

Tajiri then reminds his audience that 16,000 evacuees had been sent to two camps in Arkansas (Jerome and Rohwer) while 5,000 Nisei soldiers were training relatively nearby at Camp Shelby, Mississippi. These folks witnessed firsthand how white southerners regularly and casually deployed acts of racism and dehumanized Black southerners, the elemental fabric of Jim and Jane Crow society. Whites could define themselves against what Blacks were not allowed to possess, where they were not allowed to go, and how they were not allowed to act. "When instances of race violence, though minor in nature, were reported against the evacuees, 'Jap Crow' became an inevitable corollary of 'Jim Crow,'" he reports. Almost in relief, Tajiri concludes, "Thus, fact by fact and incident by incident, Japanese Americans are coming to the realization that theirs is only a part of the nation's race problems."[87] Much like Anderson, Tajiri here takes on readers who cannot see the forest for the trees, urging them to see "the *Nisei* problem" or "the Negro problem" as synchronized parts of the whole "American problem." With regard to democracy: to paraphrase Anderson, Japanese Americans should either commit all the way or not at all. After all, the Double V campaign, initiated by the African American *Pittsburgh Courier*, had called for democracy's victory at home and abroad.

Hughes's essay "White Folks Do the Funniest Things" (1944) marked a turning point for the quarterly. Full of satire and purposely putting the shoe on the other foot (i.e., making white people the butt of jokes), the article revealed to white readers what many Black readers had known all along: American democracy was a downright hypocrisy, a dream almost completely deferred and essentially out of reach. Commenting on how white Americans heralded the victory of democratic forces abroad while simultaneously paying no heed to time-honored undemocratic customs of Jim and Jane Crow back home, Hughes sneers: "Negroes think democracy's left hand apparently must not know what its right hand is doing."[88] Hughes characteristically sent up the absurdities of Jim and Jane Crow, with great success, and despite a negative backlash, circulation and publicity for the quarterly temporarily spiked. Significantly, Anderson's "Letter to the Reader" in the next issue attempted to assuage some of the anxiety felt by the growing part of the audience that took offense at "White Folks." Not entirely sympathetic to the complainants' moaning, Anderson also pinpointed and exposed the "soft targets" of discomfort in these readers, noting that they enter into "very real emotional or intellectual withdrawal when we touch too frankly and too vigorously upon matters of color."[89]

As in her earlier, vigorous defense of encouraging a complete commitment to the resettlement effort of evacuees, when she plainly stated that the enterprise of democracy "brooks no emotional withdrawals" and is no "half-way process," Anderson calls out those who comfortably deny, sublimate, or completely shut down when confronted with issues of race that prove too complex, too unnerving, and too immediate. After all, many African Americans worked in these people's homes, clubs, and restaurants and provided sundry other services. By contrast, Japanese Americans were imprisoned, comfortably removed from the readers' experience (and therefore safe to discuss). They resembled diorama figures in a natural history museum: distant, abstracted, and exotic (until resettlement brought them into adjacent neighborhoods, and then housing covenants accordingly shot up). African Americans were an unidentifiable blur, too close to the lens even to be recognized. Why talk about the pressures that one's nanny must face as she spends all day in one's kitchen, tending to and feeding one's children, seeing her own kin only when they are asleep? How can a white club member envision a waiter or attendant as anything more than a nameless object that retrieves other inanimate objects, like drinks, cigars, raincoats, and newspapers? Acknowledging the individuality, let alone the humanity, of such persons would be overwhelming, a breach of the racial code, and an unnecessary challenge to everyday social norms. Anderson argues that all of these discomfiting "truths" compel the denier "to look away" and seek "emotional withdrawal." This is akin to a psychologist's way of saying that a neurotic patient possesses inadequate coping mechanisms and will remain stuck at a particular emotional impasse, intellectualized roadblock, or self-centered, irrational fear of difference, of an Other. The editors' objectives of persuading Old Americans to understand and mix with the New, and of constructively bringing the various races and ethnicities together in conversation "lie ultimately in our own hearts, in our own creative imaginations, in reaching out across the barriers of color to what . . . are only other human beings like ourselves, now torn by fears and despair and bitterness and aspiration and yearning."[90] "Everyday people" longing to find common ground.

Chapter 3

"Unity within Diversity": Intimacies and Public Discourses of Race and Ethnicity

He was a myth-maker. A spinner of tales.
—Carey McWilliams, "Louis Adamic, American," *Nation*, September 22, 1951

Familiar with Adamic's œuvre and well aware of *Common Ground*'s timely appeal to particular writers and readers, Kikuchi shrewdly (and opportunistically) understood that cultivating a relationship with a figure as influential as Adamic could only help his future career and long-term interest in matters of race and ethnicity. On a personal level, he knew that maintaining such prominent connections could yield more immediate help if necessary; after the Japanese bombed Pearl Harbor, Kikuchi indeed counted on the Adamics for practical and emotional support. As the war progressed and his family was interned, Kikuchi asked both Louis and Stella to aid his brother John in securing a full-time job that would allow him to leave the Tanforan camp. Encouraged by his older brother, John wrote to the Adamics in August 1942:

> My ambition is still to continue in the study of medicine, but the situation at present does not look very promising . . . I have been trying desperately to get out through the Student Relocation Committee but it does not seem very likely that all the students here will benefit through it . . . Otherwise the government requires that a student have a job offered to him and be accepted by the college before he can get a release. As I have no contact outside of the western defense area it is practically impossible for me to make any sort of arrangements.[1]

In response, Stella instructed her husband,

> Will you add a note to this; it will strengthen the request if you do. I think we should definitely help John. I asked John about full-time, part-time

job and schedule for studies. He wrote back he'd better take a full-time job—since it would be easier to obtain—and save money for a while and then go on with his studies. But he'll take anything he can get, he said.[2]

Adamic signed and okayed the request. Eventually, their lobbying helped John find work outside the camps and gain readmission to college—at Drew University in New Jersey—to take premedicine courses. Ultimately, the younger Kikuchi completed his medical degree at Stanford Medical School and joined the U.S. Air Force as a flight surgeon.[3]

Numerous later letters showed that Charlie considered Adamic's mentoring a welcome development, something he had lacked for so many years while away from his biological parents. Even in his initial letter to Adamic (the one on which "A Young American" is based), Kikuchi reached out to the scholar in a confessional, psychoanalytic tone: "After reading this, you will no doubt conclude that I am suffering from an inferiority complex and that I am a typical 'jittery' New American. Naturally, this will hurt my egotism; but if you could give me an analysis of my personality, I would appreciate it very much." Equally clear is the fact that Kikuchi knew whom he was dealing with: "From your books, I know you are an expert in character dissection, and it might do me a world of good if I received suggestions on how to develop my fullest possibilities (if I have any). Even if you don't, I will at least have the satisfaction of getting the thing off of my chest."[4]

A series of letters from Kikuchi followed in the next few months, but Adamic responded in significant length only twice during this period (first, in April 1940, as described above, and second, as follows). On March 26, 1940, he directly answered Kikuchi's request to have his character dissected: "My dear Kikuchi: Later I'll try to give you an 'analysis'—although my first impression is that you're all right; you don't need a hell of a lot of help from anybody." It was quite a generous gesture, indulging a young man still trying to find himself. In this early stage of their relationship, Adamic did his best to nurture Kikuchi and affirm his contribution:

> Yesterday I gave a careful reading to your notes [a reference to the 26-page letter from February]. I think they are fine, and I shall be able to make good use of them. I wish you'd let me send you a little check. The stuff is really valuable to me. If not a check, may I send you a few more books—my own and others? . . . Have you read this recent Negro novel called Native Son? If not, I want very much to send it to you.[5]

This last reference, to Richard Wright's *Native Son*, a highly successful Book-of-the-Month Club selection, is worth noting, given Kikuchi's eventual and frequent interaction with African Americans after his move to Chicago in 1943 (see chapter 6), which led to a vastly experiential and educative exposure to Wright's black metropolis (Kikuchi lived on Drexel Boulevard between the University of Chicago and Bronzeville).[6]

As Kikuchi recorded at a later point in his diary, he animatedly discussed Wright's autobiography *Black Boy* (1945) with his younger sister Miyako in Chicago when she was still in high school:

> While we were walking down Randolph Street, Miyako said: "That Black boy is pretty good."
> "What black boy?" I asked.
> "You know, the book you have."
> "You mean you are reading Black Boy," I asked in surprise.
> "Yah," says Miyako, "It's pretty good. I read it all day. I got so scared when he set the fire to his house and his father chased him under the house. I'm going to read it all day tomorrow too."[7]

Also living with Kikuchi and Miyako was their sister Bette (born Yoriko), who also was strongly invested in learning much more about the predominantly African American world around her. Proudly, Kikuchi writes:

> Bette is interested right now in the Negro problem because they are discussing it in her social problems class. She bought a recent New Republic magazine because there was a very interesting section in it on the whole Negro situation. I think that both Emiko and Bette are getting much more socially conscious now and the school experience is beginning to show on them.[8]

In a moment of great pride, Bette gleefully shared

> that she went to the meeting sponsored by the Negro students on the campus yesterday and she got to personally meet Paul Robeson. She even got his autograph to prove it! She said that he was interested in what she was doing as she was the only non-Negro student at the gathering. He told her that he was using the stage as a vehicle to foster better race relations and treat other social problems.[9]

(The popular African American figure would repeat this sentiment a year later in Chicago, invited by Japanese Americans to help honor Nisei veterans on Memorial Day.) As these few passages demonstrate, Charlie was not the only Kikuchi sibling interested in the cause of African American equality. In fact, Bette became deeply involved in the concerns of African Americans; coincidentally, she would also later fall in love with and marry an African American named Gene Orro.

Although Adamic did send Kikuchi many other similar texts, he rarely communicated with his acolyte at any great length or with any immediacy. Kikuchi nonetheless persisted, using his missives to Adamic as opportunities to comment upon various scholarly and mainstream articles about Asians in America, thereby previewing the informal but analytical style that would mark his future diaristic efforts in camp and beyond. One also gains the sense in reading Kikuchi's letters to Adamic during this period that he treated the senior scholar not only as an academic advisor, but also as a true confidant, a man with experience and knowledge to impart. Undoubtedly, he viewed Adamic—albeit distantly—as the paternal figure that he never truly had. For example, in May 1940, he disclosed:

> As far as my personal problems are concerned, I am still at a standstill. It seems that I will never get started. I only wish that economic conditions were better so that there could be more jobs for young people like me who want to work, but can't.[10]

Adamic's relative silence must not have been too jarring to the young Nisei, given that his real-life father rarely if ever communicated directly with him (e.g., while Charlie was in the orphanage, the Kikuchis sent a lawyer to speak with the young boy on their behalf). When Adamic answered, it was usually in the most general terms, often offering Kikuchi other opportunities to contribute to his or other publications. In this sense, Adamic treated the letters more like reportage from the field, a continuous update from a Japanese American correspondent. Kikuchi did not mind, though, humbly revealing to his newfound mentor:

> I hope that I haven't taken up too much of your time. Please excuse my rambling. It makes me feel better when I can tell my problems to a person that understands my situation.[11]

As Kikuchi understood, his and Adamic's commonality had at least two sides: their visions and hopes for America coincided, and the two men's lives were similar versions of the immigrant's tale.

While Adamic himself was a first-generation immigrant and Kikuchi the son of immigrants, both men left their families at relatively young ages: Kikuchi lived in the orphanage from eight until eighteen years old, and Adamic ran away from his Slovenian home at the age of fourteen (a year later he boarded the *Niagara* in Le Havre on its way to New York). Additionally, while labor was not necessarily their very first exposure to multiethnic or multiracial environments (Kikuchi's orphanage provided him with such contact), hard, menial work experiences deepened both men's understanding of the obstacles facing immigrants and minorities in this country. As previously noted, Adamic's second job in America was as a floor sweeper in a New Jersey factory; witnessing the struggle of fellow immigrants, according to Daniel Shiffman, "gave him a broader appreciation for the multiethnic drudgery of American labor."[12] After he joined the army, his tours of duty took him to Louisiana, Hawai'i, the Panama Canal Zone, South America, the Pacific Islands, and Europe. Like Kikuchi, Adamic led a peripatetic existence thereafter, enduring manual labor stints until his break into publishing in the late 1920s.

More than a decade later, Kikuchi would forge a separate path, albeit one with familiar signposts: migratory farm laborer, houseboy, art salesman; induction into the U.S. Army with training in Illinois and travel to Virginia and New Jersey; and eventual globe-trotting as far as the Soviet Union and East Asia. Sometime in February 1940, he sent an update to Adamic, highlighting a theme common to both of their experiences:

> I just returned from the country where I made $28.00 in nine days paint-
> ing the insides of a house. What a combination we were! There was an
> Italian plumber, an English carpenter, a Jewish linoleum layer, a German
> electrician, and a Japanese painter (me) all working for an Irish boss with
> a Chinese houseboy who came around and pestered us. At lunch times,
> we argued about whether America should aid the allies or not![13]

Even though this time Adamic could not have possibly overwritten Kikuchi's
letter, the imagery Kikuchi paints has all the hallmarks of an Adamic-inflected
metaphor for America: a house in order (the nation), built, colored, and polished
by a multiethnic workforce (the proletarian citizenry).[14]

Furthermore, as one reads the corpus of letters Kikuchi sent to Adamic over
time, one notices additional markings of Adamic's influence on Kikuchi or, at
the very least, the confluence of their respective philosophies. Granted, Kikuchi
was a young, highly impressionable twenty-something during this period, but
Adamic's analytical framework did seem to fit him like a glove. For example, as
noted above, he often referred to himself as a "jittery" New American with an
inferiority complex, echoing Adamic's refrain that all second-generation Americans were constantly struggling to find their identity and place in the society. In
this regard, Adamic placed a great deal of both responsibility and blame on this
generation, writing in 1938:

> Most of them merely hope to get along, to get by, somehow. Without a
> vital sense of background, perennially oppressed by the feeling that they
> are outsiders and thus inferior, they will live outside the main stream of
> America's national life.[15]

Two years later, Kikuchi corresponded with his mentor, commenting on San
Francisco's Girls' High School and the segregation of pictures of Japanese American girls and white girls in the school's yearbook. Read closely, the passage demonstrates both Kikuchi's deep familiarity with Adamic's analysis of the second
generation and the dovetailing of their critical thinking:

> I was all burned up the first time I read it; but after reflection, I think
> it serves the girls right. The Girls' High is the only high school in this
> city that would do such a thing. The reason for this is that the Japanese
> American girls there do not take any part in the school activities and are
> willing to be "pushed around." In all of the other high schools in this city,
> the Japanese youths have taken an active part in sports, student body, etc.
> Perhaps these girls will wake up now and do something about it.[16]

At the end of this excerpt, Kikuchi even characterizes the young women as
zombie-like, in need of reawakening, a direct nod to Adamic's diagnosis of New
Americans as lifeless, unstirring, and neutral. At the same time, it is important
to bear in mind that as much as he laid blame at the feet of New Americans,
Adamic ultimately held Old Americans—and the nation as a whole—responsible

for their failure to realize the potential of a multiethnic America invigorated by these recent, diverse generations. In fact, his privileging of new immigrants far outweighed his scolding of them.

"I believe that the majority of the New Americans and the generation that they will produce will have an opportunity to become a great body of self-respecting, constructive citizenry," Adamic declared, "and that, with the diverse racial and cultural backgrounds they inherited from their immigrant parents, they will enrich the civilization and deepen the culture of this New World."[17] Werner Sollors elucidates this simultaneously critical and redemptive view of a declining second generation (i.e., one written from the vantage point of the first generation):

> The pattern is familiar from countless similar expressions of fear that the next generation will become one of little fascists, brain-washed communists, hypnotized rock fans, Moonies, zombies, androids, *them* . . . On a deeper level, however, the metaphor of a declining second generation— perhaps, because it was such a prominent focus for the migrants' fears— strengthened the sense of common peoplehood and destiny: by scolding different people as a degenerate second generation one may in fact be molding a family.[18]

The dynamic Sollors describes here is particularly true of the Issei and Nisei, especially in the period before the evacuation and internment. After the complete evacuation forced people from different regions, classes, or levels of Americanization to live side by side in camp, the generational tensions became magnified exponentially. In the setting of Kikuchi's camp, the Gila Relocation Center, one will painfully and perhaps viscerally appreciate the burdensome weight of intergenerational expectations, disappointments, and conflicts within Japanese America at an especially heightened tension. Examined further in chapter 4, the "scolding" mentioned by Sollors occurred, but it was also transformed from rhetoric into perilously violent acts within the crucible of an already pressurized internment camp.

In the less intense world of letters between Kikuchi and Adamic, the older man well understood that "the problem [of second-generation Americans] is closely tied up with the socio-economic system under which we live . . . and that the cure for most of the second-generation ills lies, ultimately in the solution of our socio-economic problem."[19] Once again, the pupil would sing the tune of his teacher, as Kikuchi writes:

> Personally, I believe the Japanese Americans overstress their problems and do little towards remedial actions. In other words, there is too much talk about the plight of the "suffering Nisei." After all, the Japanese are a small drop in the bucket of the total population and most of the problems are common to all, i.e. economic rather than racial.[20]

This is an entirely understandable claim by Kikuchi, since the country was still dealing with the lingering effects of the Depression, and "proletarian Kikuchi," in particular, was feeling the strain of either working hard labor or anxiously not working at all during this period.

In the later months of 1940, as briefly mentioned earlier, Kikuchi's perspective on the intersection of race and class changed significantly after Japanese Americans were explicitly racialized and marked for internment. Here, perhaps, is where Adamic and Kikuchi's experiences and viewpoints diverged. As early as May 1940, when Japan was reportedly on the brink of claiming the Dutch East Indies, Kikuchi understood that if the United States ever went to war against Japan, many U.S. citizens would simply see race in conflict, not the potential for a class-based alliance. Presciently, he wrote of the Nisei during this moment: "The only thing that bothers them is that they might be thrown into 'concentration camps' in case of war involving the U.S., even though they [are] very pro-America."[21] A year later, in June 1941, Kikuchi conceded to Adamic that race was having even more effect on his thinking. The following remarks came exactly a month before Roosevelt's freezing of Japan's (and China's) assets in the United States on July 25. The comments also followed Kikuchi's news that he had been rejected for another job in the Mare Island shipyards, which employed more than two hundred Chinese Americans but not one Nisei ("I suppose they don't wish to take any chances of possible sabotage, but I do wish they would review my case as an <u>individual</u> and not as a 'Japanese.'"). He appears simultaneously disappointed and resigned:

> It is possible that our country will enter the war and perhaps fight Japan. This puts the Nisei in a "spot," and from what I have told you of my personal experiences, you can see that already there is an increasing feeling against us. It doesn't affect my feelings towards America because I am a part of it and nothing that happens will take this away. It's rooted too deeply within me.[22]

In his highly introspective manner, Kikuchi attempts to weigh these two opposing thoughts: even though Americans were categorically rejecting him and other citizens of Japanese ancestry, he still maintained a steadfast, "rooted" faith in Americanism: why? Proceeding with the letter, Kikuchi allows his thoughts to momentarily run and scatter. Most notably, "free association" leads him to the issue of race, and a fascinating elision of the Nisei predicament with that of African Americans.

> The other day I saw some "cops" beat up a Negro in Sacramento and it just made my blood boil. But this is also an aspect of America. Perhaps I am seeing too much of the soiled side of America, but they just can't be overlooked.[23]

Specifically in the last sentence, Kikuchi groups the supposed "Negro problem" with that of the current "Oriental problem." More accurately, he turns the two "problems" on their heads, demonstrating that, in fact, it is not the Negroes or Orientals who are causing any trouble, but rather it is the white majority's discrimination (rejection at the naval base) and violence (Sacramento police) against Asians and Blacks that is "the soiled side of America," as Kikuchi puts it. This would be one of the first, but certainly not the last, moments when Kikuchi would keenly see a direct connection between his predicament and that of African Americans.

"And Then the War Came"

With the bombing of Pearl Harbor, everything changed. In the immediate aftermath of December 7, a frenzy of suspicion, anger, and fear afflicted the West Coast and the nation at large. On the back of a typewritten letter, Kikuchi offered his mentor the following handwritten notes:

> Radio announces: Don't patronize Japanese stores.
> Boycott of store operated by Nisei.
> A Filipino swings at a Nisei in the Japanese district.
> Police officer sneers at a storeowner: "You ask me to be decent after what you 'Japs' did to Hawaii?"
> Crowd in Montana attempts to lynch a "Jap."
> Illegal to give money to Japanese nationals. Son can't give money to parents.
> Grant Ave. art goods store mostly failing.
> Chinese up and down coast wearing Chinese flags so they won't be mistaken for Japanese.
> Unions boycotting Japanese laundries in the name of patriotism.

He ends the note, saying, "This is the pessimistic side. It can't last. Or will it?"[24] Unfortunately, circumstances persisted and worsened. On the day war was declared, the rounding-up of potentially subversive enemy aliens and the raiding of Issei homes commenced. Between the 7th and the date of Kikuchi's letter to Adamic above (December 11), the number of enemy aliens detained rose from 800 to 1,400. The FBI incarcerated Issei newspaper owners and editors as well as business, community, and religious leaders, including Japanese-language teachers and Shinto and Buddhist priests. Simultaneously, close to 900 Japanese were picked up by the military in Hawai'i and held until they could be moved to mainland detention camps. Moreover, as Sucheng Chan has pointed out, Japanese as far south as Peru were arrested and extradited to the United States, while Greg Robinson has similarly reported on the Canadian government's removal of Japanese nationals from British Columbia.[25]

As events deteriorated in the Pacific theater over the next month, violence escalated against Issei and Nisei throughout the West Coast. A letter from Kikuchi to Adamic on December 20th captures the deep-seated anxiety of the moment:

> So many things are going on here that I just don't have time to sit down
> and write. I am still rejected from the army and Mare Island is not in-
> clined to give me a job even if I quit college to work there as a laborer.

His next observation reveals that events beyond his control were inevitably stigmatizing the Japanese as a monolithic race. "The seed of racial hysteria seems to
be growing," he laments,

> and I do not like the way the newspapers are running in front of this
> hysteria with stupid allegations about the Nisei loyalty . . . The native pa-
> triotic groups would even want to send all of the Nisei to concentration
> camps. This sounds crazy and I hope it does not go further than the talk
> stage, but is a most dangerous possibility and I am pessimistic about the
> outcome.[26]

Kikuchi had reason to be nervous, for it was not the American Legion alone that
was stirring up the paranoia.

Roger Daniels, for example, has emphasized that "Roosevelt harbored deeply
felt anti-Japanese prejudices," and was clearly the impetus behind Executive Order 9066, even beyond the nativists and the civilian heads of the War Department.[27] Furthermore, he argued, Roosevelt considered the act expedient, rousing
the support of Congress and the nation at large and avoiding conflict with es-
tablishment Republicans like Secretary of War Stimson. Of greatest significance,
however, Roosevelt simply believed that the Japanese, citizen or not, were a legitimate threat to national security. He had long felt the Hawai'ian Japanese should
be interned en masse (in spite of the military's strenuous disagreement), and
he remained easily susceptible to innuendo regarding the mainland Japanese.[28]
Robinson, for example, specifically cites notes from a Cabinet meeting in March
1942, wherein "Roosevelt told his Cabinet that 'friends of his' who had explored
the lower California region of Mexico some time previously had uncovered numerous secret Japanese air bases, which could be mobilized for work in concert with Japanese aircraft carriers on bombing raids into southern California."[29]
Thus, if the president was so easily moved to spread false rumors, it was no great
surprise that Hearst newspapermen and well-organized nativist groups would
indulge in the same type of racialized disinformation campaigns.

The danger, of course, was that citizens already fearful of the Japanese threat
and believing such rumors would simply take matters into their own hands. Indeed, as Tom Shibutani would later cite in *The Salvage*, the violence committed
against Japanese Americans by Filipino Americans in the immediate aftermath of
Pearl Harbor alone was cause for alarm, as well as bloody confirmation of the racial hysteria Kikuchi noted earlier. "Shibs" catalogues the Filipino crimes at length:

> A 31-year-old Nisei was stabbed to death on the sidewalks of Los An-
> geles on December 23; on Christmas day in Stockton, gangs broke the
> windows of numerous business houses, manhandled numerous Japanese,
> and killed a garage attendant. On December 29, a 57-year-old alien was

shot in Sacramento. On January 3, [1942,] fifty shots were fired into a Gilroy [CA] home, and two Japanese were seriously wounded . . . State and local officials responded promptly to this "reign of terror," and set up heavy patrols wherever Japanese were congregated, and picked up and disarmed numbers of Filipinos.[30]

Many of these stateside actions came at the same time as Japan's December 1941 invasion of the Philippines. While on the one hand, many Filipino Americans strongly believed that violence against Japanese Americans was justified in the name of American patriotism (despite their own ineligibility to be U.S. citizens and despite most Nisei being citizens by birth), others vehemently felt that their actions reflected their Filipino patriotism, a kind of proto-transnational resistance against the imperialist Japanese.

As Kikuchi's anecdote about Manuel and the relationship between Japanese farmers and Filipino workers demonstrated in chapter 1, or as Carlos Bulosan recounts in his "semi-autobiography" *America Is in the Heart* (1946), tensions stemming from socioeconomic inequality additionally fueled the bloodlust. One of the most celebrated proletarian writers of the cultural front, Bulosan recalls a Stockton strike by Filipino asparagus workers led by his friend "Claro," a character based on the activist Chris Mensalvas. The latter holds up a sign, demanding: "PAISANOS! DON'T PATRONIZE JAP STORES! IT MEANS HUNGER!" Later, Bulosan asks his friend why the walkout only included Filipinos and why, much to his chagrin, it was not simply a general strike, inclusive of all races. Bulosan recounts the following:

> "Yes, it is!" [Claro] shouted with anger. "But a Japanese woman is breaking it. She is supplying laborers." He walked on, looking from side to side, shouting greetings to friends watching from doorways. When he saw a Japanese face he became furious.[31]

Tragically, all the possible motivations for interracial confrontation were extremely misguided, and the outcomes—for Filipinos and Japanese alike—were catastrophic.

The irony is that at the war's conclusion, both minorities were lumped together once more by white America and vilified in equal measure. For example, in the July 28, 1945, edition of the *Nation*, the editors bemoaned the fact that the bloom was already off the rose: white Americans' views of Filipino Americans had darkened yet again. During the war, in the midst of collective agonies over the fall of Manila and the death march in Bataan, white Americans had temporarily embraced their "little brown brothers," especially those demonstrating loyalty in the States. Near the end of the war, though, after a strike in the Santa Maria Valley by Filipino field laborers, the niceties were done away with. The *Nation* cited an advertisement by Santa Maria's Economic Council, warning:

> At best, Filipinos are guests in the United States . . . While Americans are dying to free their countrymen from Japanese slavery, the lavish expen-

ditures of money by Filipinos on white women instead of assisting their countrymen is not promoting good-will among Americans . . . Filipinos want America to build up their homeland and protect them, while their people conduct themselves as strikers are doing in Santa Maria Valley . . . If these Filipinos act as they have recently, they should be classified with the Japanese; denied renting of land and such, as the Japanese were who also did not act properly as guests in America.[32]

Of particular note is the conflation of Filipino Americans with Japanese Americans at the end of the ad, with the ominous (thinly veiled) threat that Filipinos should face the same severe penalties meted out to their Japanese American counterparts (read: eventual forced incarceration). Of equal concern was the council's racially tinged rhetoric, which stereotyped Filipino men as lustful, hypersexualized, and threatening to white women (or, at least, confounding white women's obedience to white men), much in the same way that African Americans had been slandered as stereotypically hypersexualized ogres. Finally, the hubris with which the council treats the Filipino—presuming that all Filipinos "guests" wanted America "to build up their homeland and protect them"—signified the overdeveloped superiority complex and ignorance of America's own imperial history that informed most nativists. The tenuous honeymoon afforded by shared wartime suffering unequivocally ended when the war did.

During the wartime period and beyond, Adamic ensured that through all the noise of hysterical rhetoric, the voices of the Nisei would be heard in *Common Ground*. According to Ichioka, it was another young American writer with a Japanese face, Oyama, who was responsible for introducing Adamic to so many members of the Nisei community.[33] The two shared mutual friends, like Carey McWilliams, then the editor of the *Nation* (who also wrote *Louis Adamic and Shadow America*, as well as an introduction to Bulosan's autobiography), and John Fante, the author of *Ask the Dust* (1939).[34] When Adamic decided that he was going to include Japanese Americans in his proposed "Nation of Nations" series in late 1939, Oyama introduced him to James Sakamoto, publisher of the *Japanese American Courier*, and Tajiri, at the time the English editor of the *Japanese American News*. In return, Adamic published Oyama's "After Pearl Harbor: Los Angeles" in the second volume of *Common Ground*. Even without formal introductions, though, many Nisei knew of Adamic, in large part because of the cross-pollination that existed between *Common Ground* and *Current Life*, the magazine edited by Omura. For example, Kikuchi contributed to *Current Life* and wrote "A Young American" for Adamic, while Oyama also published in both periodicals. Kikuchi and she knew one another in the Bay, while Toshio Mori, another Nisei contributor to *Common Ground*, briefly interacted with Kikuchi at Tanforan.[35] Omura, for his part, advertised Adamic's books in his magazine and even invited Adamic to contribute on occasion. In one unsurprising coincidence (in January 1941), an article by Kikuchi—"Joe Nisei Looks for a Job"—was juxtaposed with Adamic's "The Nisei's Problem Is Difficult but

Natural" in *Current Life*. Quizzically, Adamic would simply state: "Mr. Omura, the editor of this magazine, asks me to write for him a brief article or editorial. I can do no better than quote the hero of my story 'A Young American with a Japanese Face' in my last book." He then lazily excerpts six short paragraphs from Kikuchi's narrative![36]

The preceding catalogue of multilayered and interwoven anecdotes underscores how the Nisei intellectual circle overlapped with both a West Coast intelligentsia and an "American ethnic" cohort. Additionally noteworthy is that Kikuchi was not the only common denominator for these networks and counterpublics. Oyama played an equally, maybe even more, critical role in this whirlwind of intellectual exchange, strategically introducing Nisei to sympathetic, high-profile (and mostly white male) activists.

In January 1942, however, *Current Life* folded under the pressures of post–Pearl Harbor fearmongering and governmental action; meanwhile, in February 1942, Kikuchi was typing one of his last letters to Adamic before internment. Writing in the immediate wake of 9066 but still living in San Francisco, Kikuchi expresses his deepest concerns:

> If we protest about civil liberties, we are disloyal and not cooperating; if we do protest, that proves that we are fifth columnists. You should see some of the amusing letters written into the papers about why the Nisei should all be put into concentration camps or thrown into the Bay. Sometimes I wonder whether they know what Democracy is about. To me, all of the things we, as Americans, are fighting for—Liberty, etc.—are a means and not an end in themselves. Yet we seem to persist in making them an end in themselves.[37]

At this point, one catches a telling glimpse of Kikuchi's early but evolving thoughts about the meaning of democracy. Rounding up and incarcerating loyal American citizens to ensure the freedom and liberty of other citizens was contradictory to established democratic principles, a hypocritical, irrational, probably absurd act. For Kikuchi, American democracy was as yet unformed, itself an evolving process—the means, not an end, as he astutely claims. Citizens wrapping themselves in the flag, or misusing "life, liberty, and the pursuit of happiness" as reasons for Japanese internment—these paradoxes confounded Kikuchi. Continuing in the same vein, he writes:

> There is a general recognition that defense measures are vitally necessary and the Nisei as a whole are ready for sacrifice, although measures aimed principally at them does not seem consistent [with] the beliefs which we today are fighting for in this war . . . If the orders are carried out in such a way that it is made to appear that all Nisei are disloyal and fifth columnists and not Americans, it will be a grand witch hunt for politicians and the so-called Americans who love to gang up in groups (Hitler set a nice example for them in his Jewish pogroms).[38]

Indeed, it was difficult for Japanese Americans to blithely accept their sentences, especially when public officials provided little or no support; the *San Francisco News*, for example, reported that nine out of fifteen governors in states west of the Mississippi wholeheartedly agreed: "No Japanese wanted—except in concentration camps."[39]

Columnists (or calumnists) were churning out just as many hysteria-driven pieces in newspapers as the "amusing" (in Kikuchi's words) "letter-to-the-editor" writers in their audiences. One feature writer, Arthur Caylor, took the opportunity to raise his readers' awareness of potentially dangerous interracial alliances forged during this period: "My story is that, whatever the philosophy involved, the enemy's agents in our town are not neglecting an attempt to create a Japanese-Negro anti-white-race fifth column." His conspiracy theory gained momentum:

> The Japanese colony and the Negro colony in San Francisco are close enough neighbors to provide many contacts. They share some things in common. The color-line is not so noticeable as it is elsewhere. This had made it possible, my agents learn from loyal Negro sources, for Japanese to spread racial propaganda.[40]

The fifth column nightmare of a Black and Japanese alliance was a familiar nativist threat. For decades, the FBI had been closely monitoring African American organizations, such as the Negro Alliance and the National Negro Congress, to root out Japanese influence and infiltration (in the Cold War years, this was done to disrupt and severely limit anticolonial movements led by African Americans). As Marc Gallicchio points out, the bureau and military intelligence should not have taken the phenomenon of African American sympathy for Japan lightly, but they completely misdiagnosed the source of antiwhite protest in Black communities as external, not internal. "In attributing black unrest and low morale to Japanese agents and propaganda," he writes, "they fell back on a time-worn tradition of defenders of the racial status quo by blaming outside agitators."[41] In other words, white-supremacist action at home could not possibly have been the cause of Black civil unrest. Nearly pathological in their willful denial of culpability, the agencies stoked not only worst-case-scenario fears, but also those of Caylor and other West Coast nativists zealously seeking any reason to persecute or expel whole communities based on race. In 1944, Gunnar Myrdal offered a diagnosis:

> During the present war crisis there have been rumors about various "fifth column" groups among American Negroes. For several years there have been attempts to disseminate Japanese propaganda to Negroes, but with minor success. Individual Negroes of the type who have been active in the small groups which are the remnants of the [Marcus] Garvey movement have given response, but their influence on the Negro opinion is small.[42]

Gallicchio and Reginald Kearney have recently mapped out how certain Black intellectuals and leaders—dubbed "Black internationalists," but perhaps more accurately, a forerunning strain of "extranationalists"—privileged Japan as "the champion of the darker races," but in the haze of early 1942, rumors of Black-Japanese fifth column activity were but one of a whole panoply of fears engendered by racialized hysteria.[43] For his part, Kikuchi's only interaction with African Americans during this period was unexpectedly dramatic and quite treacherous, the diametric opposite of most of his experiences with African Americans in later years in Chicago and New York. He starts by providing Adamic with some context:

> You really have to be out here [in Berkeley] to appreciate the tension that is in the air. Even now it would be a little foolhardy to venture out into the streets at night in certain areas as people have a difficult time distinguishing "spies" from the American-born Nisei. They act first and ask questions later—and a lot of them carry weapons.

Kikuchi was still enrolled at Cal as a graduate student in social work, so he had continued to work at a local welfare office, a requirement of his degree. "In one of my relief cases," he recounts,

> I had a big Negro start after me with a shaving knife. I didn't stop to explain that I was not a Jap, but beat a hasty retreat, you can bet! He said he was going to slit my throat and drain all of the yellow blood out of me, but I wasn't willing to wait around to let him find out that I had perfectly good red American corpuscles running through my veins![44]

"A Great Ideological Reawakening"

Without question, the immediate period covering Pearl Harbor, Executive Order 9066, and evacuation proved to be a challenging, anxious, and frustrating time for public intellectuals, writers, or journalists invested in race and ethnicity. Many of these individuals gave voice to the fears, emotions, and opinions of a growing minority in the nation—especially as the war progressed and the senseless internment crested. Initially, however, panicked by any unpatriotic backlash, a large proportion of figures on the Left cautiously bit their tongues. Two usual suspects—the Communist Party (active in minority rights since Scottsboro) and the American Civil Liberties Union (ACLU)—remained silent. As Daniels has previously exposed, the national ACLU was fairly consistent in its inaction throughout the war, only filing an amicus curiae brief for Fred Korematsu, but otherwise reneging on its offer to help Gordon Hirabayashi's challenge to De-Witt's curfew regulations, and politely (but first, publicly) declining to aid the draft resisters at the Heart Mountain Relocation Center in Wyoming.

Not all stood idly by, of course. As previously noted, Norman Thomas, the most prominent socialist in the United States, penned his protest of the evacuation with supporting signatures from Du Bois, the pacifist A. J. Muste, and Catholic Worker Movement founder Dorothy Day, among others (while the Socialist Party, for example, took no action as a group). The Quakers—who would serve an indispensable role in the resettlement of internees—also lodged a protest, as did a few Protestant denominations. Daniels points out, however, that even Carey McWilliams, Adamic's friend and the champion of Japanese Americans by war's end, in his role "as California's Commissioner of Immigration and Housing initially supported mass evacuation of Japanese aliens and was ambivalent about citizens."[45] With the CP and ACLU AWOL, and lefties like McWilliams slow to come around, to say that protest and dissent against internment was difficult to elicit during this ultranationalist moment is a terrible, unexpected understatement.

Yet even in the darkest of days, courageous words of support came from unsurprising but bravely principled sources. Writing in the *Pittsburgh Courier* only a month after the attack, for example, the conservative columnist George Schuyler made the argument that the bellicose actions of the Japanese in the Pacific was a case of "the chickens coming home to roost." He begins with a tantalizing provocation: "The boomerang is working in Hawaii." For decades, he explains, white planters growing sugar cane and pineapple on the islands of Hawaiʻi had, in effect, indentured Filipinos, Chinese, Koreans, indigenous Hawaiʻians, and Japanese immigrants as servants and wage chattel on their plantations. Profits soared, but so too did the population of American-born Asians, and now, Schuyler noted,

> The whites out here are scared to death. They don't trust those citizens
> of Japanese ancestry who are too numerous to be interned. Whites are
> quietly arming while pretending they believe in the loyalty of their brown
> fellow-citizens whom they once despised and now fear.

Best known for his satirical novel *Black No More* (1931), which tweaks the noses of the NAACP and the Ku Klux Klan simultaneously, Schuyler can almost be heard snickering as he pens the conclusion: "A reporter from the Mainland was told the Japs 'cannot be assimilated racially.' Had the white minority sought through the years to do so, it would not be so frightened now."[46] Granted, his caveat concerned the one state that could not intern its large Japanese American population for fear that those same planters Schuyler derides would lose their workforce and, by extension, their money. The economics of plantation elites trumped any racialized fears about national security—in the setting of the only Japanese attack on U.S. "soil" (Hawaiʻi did not become the fiftieth state until 1959). Nonetheless, Schuyler's message of solidarity appeared in one of the most widely circulated Black newspapers in the country and was most likely picked up on the wire by other weeklies, so the great satirist's point about white fear was well taken.

A month later at the *Courier*, Horace Cayton inveighed against "the white man's war" and reinforced the Double V campaign by pushing for the elimination of Jim Crow in the military as well as on the home front. Not entirely a direct response to Roosevelt's executive order, Cayton's piece nevertheless resonated with the evacuation and the need for vigilance in an interdependent, racialized world:

> The Negro is engaged in a struggle to make this a peoples' war for democracy, not just a white man's war. In this . . . task, it seems to me, Negroes are acting in the most patriotic fashion possible . . . This war effort must include black Negroes, yellow Chinese, and all of the non-white races of the world and be a war for democratic principles and ideas.[47]

Cayton was imploring his readers to notice the unique window of opportunity afforded all Americans, but African Americans specifically, to alter the trajectory of their own democracy, to force the nation to make good on its creed.

Two weeks later, the paper featured a photo of a Japanese American prisoner (in county jail for kidnapping) giving blood for the war effort, under a headline in twenty-point block letters that subtly asked, "IS JAP BLOOD OKAY FOR FIGHTING FORCES?" The convict-donor patriotically exclaims, "If my blood helps save the life of any American fighter, I'll be satisfied." After the article states that the criminal willingly volunteered to give blood every eight weeks, the author wonders, "Will his blood be put in a separate bank?" The reporter's rhetorical question was an incredulous follow-up to the initial news reported in the piece: "After months of bickering, the Red Cross finally accepted blood from Negroes for a separate bank."[48] As recently as November 1941, the Red Cross had abided by a policy of not accepting blood plasma donations from African Americans: complete exclusion. As more African Americans literally offered their blood (sweat, and tears) to support the war effort, the Red Cross relented in January 1942 and accepted Black donations, but as the *Courier* article highlights with frustration, the blood received would still have to be segregated from white blood, a policy that would officially remain in place until war's end and beyond. (Unofficially, on the front lines, wounded soldiers and medics increasingly disregarded the distinction, opting to save lives rather than preserve some impractical, nefariously eugenic status quo.) But the photograph of the Japanese American criminal appeared in more than one Black weekly and other national dailies (like *Picture Magazine,* or *PM*) that month. Clearly, it was not lost on many civil rights organizations or the Black community as a whole that if one were a prisoner or racially not Black, one could donate blood to the Red Cross with little fuss, while African American blood became a metonym for the entire Jim Crow system of policing of Black bodies.[49]

These examples from the African American press point toward a much larger historical phenomenon at work. During this era, multiracial and multiethnic networks of left-leaning, progressive intellectuals, activists, and authors faced the complex intersection of racialization processes (e.g., internment, de jure and de facto Jim and Jane Crow) with shifting elements of American democracy (creeds, principles, practices, pluralism, antifascism, citizenship, and inclusion). The Black press was therefore one reliable outlet for such individuals, groups, or counterpublics, while it additionally and simultaneously functioned as one of the most important institutional vehicles for moving and circulating the democratic discourse back and forth from its pages to other newspapers, magazines, and book publishers. Ottley stated as much in *Common Ground*: "The urgent need of extending democracy to the American Negro, and the profoundly positive effect it would have upon the colored peoples elsewhere in the world, is in brief the editorial line of the Negro press today."[50]

Hence, a critical mass of progressive intellectuals was feverishly discussing and redefining democracy: who or what comprised it, and how it could actualize the multipronged vision of its ideal. Philip Gleason further argues that the war produced at least two significant effects in regard to the phenomenon presented above. First, in the context of Nazism and talk of racial purity in both Asia and Europe, American rhetoric about national unity "intensified the efforts already under way to cut down prejudice, improve intergroup relations, and promote greater tolerance of diversity."[51] Second, Gleason continues, the "most crucial result of the war was that it stimulated a great ideological reawakening," adding that "it was in the context of this revival that activities in the sphere of intergroup relations took place." Using *An American Dilemma* as his exemplar, Gleason concludes:

> [Myrdal's] principal theme was the contradiction between American racial practice and the "American Creed"—the system of values which Myrdal believed Americans were genuinely committed to. He predicted that the war would hasten the resolution of the dilemma posed by this contradiction because the ideological nature of the conflict made it increasingly glaring and intolerable.[52]

While I question Gleason's overreliance on Myrdal and find debatable his subsequent declaration that Myrdal's prediction of "resolution" was "quite right," the two major points he makes in toto about the timing and context of this "reawakening" accurately identify the general foundational elements of this particular historical phenomenon. The period indeed witnessed an intellectual ferment in the American public sphere, and in many ways, one may consider the discourse a public debate on the importance and value of racial and immigrant equality within the central sphere of democratic ideology (through articles, papers, speeches, and books).

Yet Gleason points to the contradictory nature in, say, Adamic's theory of "unity within diversity":

> The ideological revival had a powerful, but somewhat paradoxical, effect on thinking about intergroup relations, ethnocultural affairs, and national identity. The substance of its message, and its practical effect, was strongly assimilationist in tendency. That is, what was actually being urged—indeed, required—was ideological consensus as the basis for harmonious intergroup relations.[53]

On the face of it, Gleason's reading seems correct: groups of "difference" would be tolerated at the same time that they would necessarily have to learn (or be taught) how to assimilate into Adamic's Old American culture. Even Gleason admits, however, that his is a general treatment of the period, acknowledging, for instance, that the Japanese American internment clearly ran against his larger argument that this period generally fostered a unified philosophy against prejudice and an increasing appreciation of diversity. He goes further by remarking that many of the intellectuals calling for a redefinition of American democratic culture possessed a cosmopolitanism that "enabled them to appreciate the good things to be found in the ways of life of the peoples they studied as [social scientists], and disposed them to urge their fellow citizens still locked within the ethnocentric confines of their own traditional culture to be more broad-minded and tolerant."[54]

Consequently, he states, it is not paradoxical to claim that "tolerance of diversity is a function of assimilation, since it comes easiest to those who have detached themselves from a specific . . . ethnic tradition, and have learned to get along with others whose background differs from their own."[55] Again, sweeping generalities mark Gleason's (nonetheless) helpful analysis; he deliberately tacks on an endpoint that the ability and strong desire of these intellectuals to critique American culture—one that marginalized and oppressed its own people—was another motivational arrow in these intellectuals' quiver. Finally, he identifies "cultural pluralism" (originally, Horace Kallen's term) as the "crucial legacy" of World War II with regard to American identity, but wisely provides the caveat that one cosmopolitan's definition of "cultural pluralism"—which, again, calls for an awakening to other cultures and a loosening grip on one's own possibly intolerant traditions—is another person's ethnocentrism, "a highly particularistic vision when appealed to by persons who care little about the overall design of American society," but heavily invest in the preservation of their own group's traditions.[56] Lillian Smith, the fearless editor of South Today and a lifelong Georgian, reckoned with this kind of ethnocentrism in the form of southern white supremacy. During the white gubernatorial primary in Georgia in 1942, Jim and Jane Crow were celebrated as the unabashed governing philosophy and party platform. Smith called for a second Reconstruction, a wholesale reform of southern white culture in the name of racial equality. But she notes the halting response:

> This isn't the right time, the southern liberals, the "decent" people of the South say. This isn't the right time . . . It is a sound that clangs on the Negro's eardrums. He has heard it since he was born. Now the whole world is hearing it.[57]

A southern white woman (and therefore a symbol of racial purity whose honor had to be protected by any means necessary), Smith used her bully pulpit to make sure everyone heard the grating dissonance of America's "white problem." "Wake up, America," Smith seemingly instructs, "because a new world's a-coming."

Uncommon Intellectuals, Common Sense

Given the intricate theoretical framework Gleason lays out, we must return to the empirical evidence and the various participants in this democratic "reawakening." As earlier sections of this narrative have established, whether edited by Adamic and Anderson or just by Anderson, *Common Ground* played a crucial role in the publication of ethnic, racial, immigrant, leftist, and progressive writers—whether veteran authors or just neophytes, like many of the Nisei. Along with African American weeklies, organizational mouthpieces like the *Crisis* or (at times) the *Pacific Citizen*, progressive publications such as *PM*, the *Nation*, the *Christian Century*, and *South Today*, as well as earlier discontinued efforts like Omura's *Current Life*, the pages and "space" of *Common Ground* represented an indispensable public sphere, one of several venues where writers could engage in debate with other progressive thinkers. It was a worthy private-sector analogue to the earlier Federal Writers' Project (1935–1943) in the deep benches of talent both called upon. Collectively, these intellectuals enjoyed a print culture and counterpublic that provided the common ground for intergroup relations, interracial interactions, and democratic discourse throughout this crucial decade. These writers—who all fall very loosely under my retroactive umbrella term the "Common Ground School" (or CGS, in the tradition of New Deal–era acronyms)—ignited and subsequently spread "the great ideological awakening" Gleason identified until they gradually dispersed during the Cold War era.

Furthermore, just as the term remains loose, the criteria for inclusion in the CGS is equally informal: namely, the list of authors who wrote for *Common Ground* itself; the circle of Adamic's friends who did not write for the magazine but nonetheless actively participated in the discussion (like Kikuchi); and those who were wrestling with similar intellectual challenges and contributing to the cluster of progressive, ethnic, and racial publications mentioned above. One might additionally consider the CCAU's statement of purposes (which was published on page 2 of every issue of *Common Ground*) as another reasonable guide for "membership" criteria. Sufficiently representative of the statement's spirit, its first aim was

> to help create among the American people the unity and mutual under-
> standing resulting from a common citizenship, a common belief in de-
> mocracy and the ideals of liberty, the placing of the common good before
> the interests of any group, and the acceptance, in fact as well as in law, of
> all citizens, whatever their national or racial origins, as equal partners in
> society.

What is noteworthy in the statement is the separate mention of "national" (bringing to mind "ethnicity" and "immigrant") and "racial" origins, an implicit caution against the slippage of treating racialized Americans as only slight variants of ethnic immigrant groups. On the one hand, Sollors reminds us that Adamic scolded new immigrants for not embracing their Americanness and instead persisting in their parochial identities: "Immigration created confusing uses of personal pronouns and Adamic wanted immigrants to be entitled to think 'we' when they heard the word 'Americans.'"[58] On the other hand, as previously stated, racialized groups like American Indians, Mexican Americans, African Americans, and Asian Americans did not fit easily into the ethnic template that worked for immigrants from Poland, Italy, or Slovenia. When they heard "we Americans," they knew that meant something or someone else. Since the term "race" was such a loaded term in this era of prewar and wartime fascism (e.g., negative associations with the term "Aryan race"), "multiculturalism" stood in for it, Sollors explains, and gained currency as the countermeasure to terms like "racism," "genocide," and "totalitarianism."[59] Thus, ethnic and multicultural minorities faced difficult but different tasks of defining their place and American identities within a sprawling and lively discourse. With the help of the CGS counterpublic and its outlets, though, their voices were amplified.

A Greek (American?) Chorus

After the evacuation began in March 1942 and the majority of internees had moved into assembly centers, and as it became apparent that not one citizen of Japanese descent or "enemy alien" had committed any act of treason or sabotage, the cautious silence that afflicted most forward-thinking writers between Pearl Harbor and the signing of 9066 began to dissipate. Much like Cayton above, for example, the future leader of the NAACP, Roy Wilkins, attacked the government's racialized fears and unconstitutional policy of interning American citizens.[60] In his column for the *New York Amsterdam Star-News*, appropriately entitled "Watchtower," he vigilantly observes:

> Our white people are acting strangely and dangerously in the evacuation of Japanese from cities on the Pacific Coast. Our country must be protected . . . but the steps which have been taken to move thousands of Japanese American citizens from their homes into virtual concentration camps do not reassure thoughtful Americans who love this democratic ideal of ours above all else.

After calling his readers' attention to the slippery slope of "internment for Japanese now, internment for African Americans later," he once again queries, but this time without any sarcasm, "Does it mean anything to be an American citizen?"[61]

The moment truly was a collapse of rational judgment and an irrevocable failure of national conscience. To place it in even sharper relief, Alain Locke, the father of the Harlem Renaissance and author of *The New Negro* (1925), had stated only months before: "Democracy has encountered a fighting antithesis, and has awakened from considerable lethargy and decadence to a sharpened realization of its own basic values."[62] Locke's personification of democracy here denotes its extreme vulnerability, its soft targets, so to speak, and though he was stigmatizing international fascism as democracy's likewise personified "antithesis," domestic fascism and racism collectively posed just as great a threat to the attenuated corpus of democratic values, a point Norman Thomas was consistently making. Additionally, anticipating Lillian Smith's alarm the following year in *Common Ground*, Locke purposefully uses "lethargy and decadence" to paint the picture of a slumbering giant, one spoiled by an era of profligacy and its consequences (the Roaring Twenties and its antithesis, the Depression) and one lulled into complacency through decades of imperialism abroad (the Philippines and Puerto Rico) and colonialism within (chattel and wage slavery, as well as indigenous genocide).

Approximately eight months later, in March 1943, Thomas commented on the internment, directly addressing McWilliams, who had inadequately spoken to the poor working conditions and unfair wages in the internment camps, two factors (among many others, like intergenerational tension) that gave rise to the riots at Manzanar (where two internees died) and Tule Lake. Thomas responded to the incidents: "Part of the price of the policy we have followed, a policy for which popular race feeling is probably more responsible than the Government's initiative in severity, is a vicious circle in which what we have done invites demonstrations which in turn encourage American intolerance and make more likely drastic actions against the minority group which will long outlive the war." Even though he gives the government too much credit in his last sentence, the committed socialist knew what the consequences of such actions, large (evacuation) and small (unfair wages), would portend for the United States on the world stage. He identified America as its own worst enemy: "No possible danger of sabotage could so menace our own cause as has Japanese propaganda in Asia describing our discriminatory treatment of Asiatics." And with a stinging dismissal of any national claim to the ideological high ground, he lamented the intellectually lazy approach taken by many participants in the discourse: "It is the failure of most American liberals to understand and to discuss openly these facts which warrants grave doubts concerning the success of our struggle now and in the post-war reaction against our own brand of totalitarianism and racism."[63] Getting one's house in order, Thomas and Locke seemingly argued, would be a prerequisite for any attempt at new world order.

Another New Yorker, Roi Ottley, took up a related line in "A White Folks' War?" for *Common Ground* in the spring of 1942. He then published his sociocultural study (and Peabody Award winner) *New World A-Coming: Inside Black America* in 1943, after five years as a social worker in Harlem and a columnist for the *Amsterdam News*. The oldest son of immigrants from Grenada and a Harlem native, Ottley was perfectly suited to contribute to Adamic's quarterly and to shape the discourse on race and immigrants in general. From his early college days at St. Bonaventure (and a short stint at Michigan), through the war as a commissioned officer and correspondent for *Liberty* and *PM* (the first African American war correspondent for a national paper), to his later work for the *Tribune* and *Defender* in Chicago, Ottley was considered the consummate journalist. In his article for *Common Ground*, he contextualized the tense relationship between Black and white, revealing that he thought the Japanese had so assimilated Black communities that "Negroes bear no *prejudice* against the Japanese people," since "the 'yellow Aryans' drew no color line."[64] As a reassuring counterpoint to these potentially caustic remarks (and more fifth column chatter from "white Aryans"), Ottley affirmed African Americans' loyalty and patriotism: Japan would not lead the darker races anywhere. But in citing Wilkins's and Du Bois's constant vigilance, Ottley encouraged his readers to gauge the war's outcome carefully—if the result benefits only the British and Americans at the expense of nations and peoples of color, then the imperialist white "folks" should expect cross-racial alliances and resistance, "for the black man, like all oppressed peoples, has a long memory."[65]

Likewise, in *New World A-Coming*, he picks up on Norman Thomas's theme of the internal fascism and racism suffered by American citizens, discussing the internment and the close relationship formed between Nisei and Blacks on the West Coast. Providing a primer on this region-specific interracial relationship, Ottley praises the neighborliness between the younger generation of working-class Japanese Americans and Blacks, the reasonable employment record of African Americans by Japanese farmers and vendors, and finally, the close friendships that ended up in "frequent intermarriage."[66] He decries the racist camp policy initially imposed on intermarried Japanese, which clearly pointed up white America's hypocrisy and its emphasis on racial hierarchy, sexual chauvinism, and hypodescent (i.e., the practice of classifying a mixed-race baby by its ostensibly "inferior" racial half). Officials did not like the possibility of the "white part" of a mixed-race child learning devious Japanese traits in camp. Therefore, they looked for ways "to save the children," so to speak, and reward more Americanized children (and parents). The early policy went as follows: if Japanese American men were married to white women with children, they could avoid camp but were banned from the West Coast; Japanese American women married to white men with children could avoid camp altogether. The only exception made for childless intermarried couples was for a Japanese American woman married to an American serviceman. Mentioning that the ACLU had finally deigned to help evacuees subjected to this policy, Ottley highlights, by contrast, the consistent level of Black support: "A friend of mine who visited the main evacuation center in Los Angeles frankly reports that he was amazed to see that almost a fourth of the visitors were Negroes."[67]

Not coincidentally, several of these CGS writers appear in Kikuchi's diaries, either because he had met or known them (e.g., the Adamic and Nisei networks), or was in the process of reading them, as he recorded in his diary (like Wright or Charles Spurgeon Johnson). This all-star list included Adamic, McWilliams, Fante, Saroyan, Wright, Drake, Cayton, Mori, and Oyama, among others. One other author from the "school" who makes a cameo in Kikuchi's diary is Bucklin Moon and his novel *The Darker Brother* (1943), a title alluding to the second stanza of Langston Hughes's "I, Too":

I am the darker brother.
They send me to eat in the kitchen
When company comes,
But I laugh,
And eat well,
And grow strong.[68]

Hardly Whitman's vision of America enthralled in song, Hughes's poetry reflected his pugnacity quite well. Picking up on this critical tone in Moon's book,
however, Kikuchi explains:

It is a story of frustration and bitterness on the part of the Negro youth.
Compared to the Negro problems, the Niseis are very well off because
they are more accepted. The reason I bought the book was to get Emiko
and Bette to read it since they are very much interested in social problems
right now.[69]

The novel tells the tale of a southern transplant to Harlem, his struggling lover,
and the difficulties Ben and Bessie face amid war and rapid urbanization. Aes-
thetically wanting (particularly on the tortured use of dialect), the book still tries
to elucidate challenges specific to African Americans (e.g., "last hired, first fired,"
or a Jim Crow military). And Darker Brother reached a wide audience when the
Book-of-the-Month Club made it an alternate selection. But Moon's stronger
work would come later in his career: an anthology by and about African Americans (Primer for White Folks, 1945); and a diagnostic sociological study called
The High Cost of Prejudice (1947). In the latter, sounding more like Kikuchi than
Myrdal, he concludes: "The Negro has been called the barometer of democracy,
but he is far more than that. So long as we have no solution for the Negro problem, we have no solution for any minority problem."[70] Dubbed "the Carl Van
Vechten of the bebop era" by Lawrence Jackson, Moon invested in many Black
writers as an editor at Doubleday, championing Himes and Ann Petry as well as
substituting for his close friend Cayton in his Courier column.[71]

Long before his career ended in 1953 amid accusations of pro-communist
activity, Moon visited with Zora Neale Hurston, a reviewer for Common Ground,
while he was a student at Rollins College in Winter Park, Florida. Hurston, of
course, was no stranger to the South. Born in Notasulga, Alabama, and the most
famous resident of Eatonville, Florida, only ten minutes from Rollins, she had
reportedly worked part-time at the college, often dropping in on a creative writing class and staging versions of her folk plays in the school's theater. During this
period, coincidentally, Rollins's president was none other than Hamilton Holt,
noted in the introduction as the respected author of the remarkably comprehensive and forward-looking Undistinguished Americans in 1906. Other kinds of
curious or coincidental overlappings and interconnections took place around the
humming center of activity at Common Ground. For example, in 1941, Adamic
featured a profile on his friend the novelist John Fante, written by Fante's con-

troversial collaborator Ross Wills, with whom he would eventually break, and for the same issue Fante penned a laconic essay on his and Adamic's common friend, the verbose Saroyan.[72] Although the group could seem like nothing more than a mutual admiration society, these writers and thinkers, in person and in the pages of CGS publications, behaved as if they were enjoying the twentieth-century version of an eighteenth-century European literary salon. Los Angeles, in particular, boasted a physical location closely analogous to a salon: the Stanley Rose Bookshop on Hollywood Boulevard. Adamic, McWilliams, Saroyan, Fante, and Bulosan were the core circle of West Coast literary leftists who often met in the back room of the bookstore, where other writers, such as Raymond Chandler and Nathanael West, also confabbed.

One of Michael Denning's darlings of the cultural front, Bulosan appears often in Kikuchi's diary and papers. In a letter to Yuriko in May 1946, Kikuchi shares: "I'm in the process of reading America is in the Heart, about Filipino life in America, and it reveals them as human beings, as they are, and not a bunch of sadistic rapists as so many Nisei believe."[73] Instead of caving into the customary, transnational backbiting between Japanese and Filipinos, Kikuchi reasserts the positive impression of the Filipinos he first really got to know: fellow migratory laborers with whom he worked and bunked back in the San Joaquin Valley, led by the college-educated Manuel. Kikuchi acknowledges the figures in Bulosan's "autobiography" as individuals, as humans, and as workers he may have known, rather than as an oversexed, dirty, and uncivilized mass. More than sixty years later, Kikuchi's best friend purposefully informed me: "By the way, I believe it was Charlie who suggested that I read Carlos Bulosan's America is in the Heart." In a characteristically exacting and self-reflective manner, Tsuneishi elaborated: "It struck a chord with both of us, and I know it was seminal in my own thinking of who I was as an American of Asian descent."[74]

An appealing tale to many Asian contemporaries and readers familiar with the "ghetto pastoral," exemplified by Henry Roth's Call It Sleep (1934), or Native Son, America Is in the Heart conveyed Bulosan's own proletarian sensibility as much as it established his representative otherness as an Asian immigrant. But Denning cautions against oversimplifying the commonalities between these writers:

> It is a mistake, however, to see these writers and the ghetto pastoral itself simply as "ethnic," that is, as the national literature of distinct ethnic groups . . . The plebeian writers [like Wright, Bulosan, and Roth] were united by a common historical situation that was not a common ethnicity but a common ethnic formation: the restructuring of the American peoples by the labor migrations of the early twentieth century from Southern and Eastern Europe and the sharecropping South.[75]

One might also insert "Asia" into the last sentence above, but exclusion acts and the 1924 Immigration Act had severely curbed Asian immigration by 1930, while U.S. nationals like Bulosan still trickled in from the colonial outpost as bachelor laborers. Denning elaborates further on his argument of commonality:

Though the forms—the rituals and emblems—of ethnic cultures differed, the content had much in common: it was the content of working-class tenements, sweatshop and factory labor, and cheap mass entertainments. The invention of ethnicity was a central form of class consciousness.[76]

Such a description would have fit Kikuchi for most of his young adulthood until Pearl Harbor: his racialized identity began to outweigh his class-based identity after that point, even though both were inextricably tied the rest of his life. He would never shirk these politically weighty identities the way some other post-war Nisei would shake off the old skin or don the cloak of denial. Old Ganbatte, on the other hand—Yoneda—proved to be a more compatible model for Denning's argument here, but his writing, like Kikuchi's, never went the way of truly proletarian literature, in the manner of Bulosan or the Chinese American novelist and dramatist H. T. Tsiang, whose *And China Has Hands* (1937) describes the life of a New York laundryman.[77] (However, Yoneda's politics would forever remain red, and he himself would live the proletarian life until his death).

America Is in the Heart enjoyed a revival in the 1970s, leading to its regular inclusion in college classes as a "foundational" text in Asian American studies. In 1973, the University of Washington Press reprinted the "autobiography" with a new introduction by Bulosan's good friend McWilliams. A year later, Frank Chin, Jeffrey Paul Chan, and Lawson Fusao Inada excerpted the work in their groundbreaking compilation *Aiiieeeee! An Anthology of Asian American Writers* (Howard University Press). Although the republished edition of *America* came seventeen years after Bulosan's death, McWilliams wrote so generously and lovingly of his old friend that Bulosan comes alive in the introduction, only to step effortlessly into the first page of his "autobiography." At the time of Bulosan's original publication (1946), Denning correctly points out that "for Popular Front writers on race and ethnicity, and over the next several years, its guiding spirit shifted from Adamic, whose attention was always primarily focused on the 'new Americans,' to Carey McWilliams, one of the leading voices of Popular Front anti-racism."[78] In this context, much has appropriately been made of McWilliams's controversial role as director of immigration and housing for California during the evacuation of Japanese Americans, a post he secured under the Popular Front governor Culbert Olson after McWilliams had published his exposé of migratory farm labor, *Factories in the Field* (1939).[79] McWilliams's initial support of the internment came as a tremendous surprise and disappointment to many, but after a fervent turnabout on the subject, he mounted a lawyerly defense of Japanese Americans in several publications, most especially in *Prejudice: Japanese-Americans, Symbol of Racial Intolerance* (1944).[80]

The literary scholar Colleen Lye offers the best explication of McWilliams's unexpected decision and justification, correctly defending him from venal attack by the likes of the conservative William Petersen, as well as persuasively contextualizing his choice within McWilliams's vision of assimilation and the naïve trust he placed, at the time, in a type of social engineering or "federally managed process of racial integration," as well as in the WRA's rationale of "conserving" Japanese American lives.[81] What confounded contemporary observers and subsequent scholars of Japanese America was that McWilliams accepted at face value the government's reasoning that internment was a military necessity. In McWilliams's rationalization, challenging the evacuation was moot because once the military had made its decision, the choice (i.e., evacuation) became ipso facto an incontrovertible reality. This extremely strained tautology stood out in his paper "Japanese Evacuation: Interim Report," delivered at the Institute of Pacific Relations in December 1942, wherein he repeatedly used the passive voice to avoid blaming the government, the military, or any other entity: "Suspicious aliens were to be rounded up and brought to . . ." By whom, exactly? Did they willingly incarcerate themselves? It was an absurd defense and a low moment in McWilliams's career. In his hearing before the House Un-American Activities Committee (HUAC) the following year, he volunteered that the military brass had approved his September 1942 article for *Harper's*, "Moving the West Coast Japanese": both the article and his admission of cooperation with military personnel reflected his decision not to hold military or civilian leadership responsible for the internment. In fact, in *Harper's*, he emptily argued:

> In the long run, the Japanese will probably profit by this painful and distressing experience. They had made a satisfactory adjustment to American life prior to December 7th; and through the unforeseen exigencies of the war it is possible that they can win for themselves a far more satisfactory position in American life than they have enjoyed in the past.[82]

In his 1979 memoir *The Education of Carey McWilliams*, a titular and intellectual homage to Henry Adams, he admitted to the grave misstep the government had taken while also explaining why he did not speak out publicly against the internment when he was still in the immigration and housing office: "I was drawn into the controversy that raged around the issue; in fact, I became an active participant. It was not a matter of choice; I was co-opted."[83] While startling in its directness, his admission of "active" participation was somewhat weak because of the statement that he had been "co-opted." His ambivalent tone almost forty years later reflected a deep-seated complex of contradictory emotions that he had not yet entirely resolved. To be fair, McWilliams's statements cast an undeserving shadow on the number of books and articles he wrote in stirring defense of Japanese Americans subsequent to the *Harper's* article and HUAC hearing. Like Adamic, McWilliams in the end was one of the most loyal allies to the Nikkei cause.

Interesting as further exploration of McWilliams's errant starting position and consequent mea culpa might be, I would rather focus on Denning's heralding of McWilliams as Adamic's successor, and the implications of McWilliams's subsequent ideological trajectory. Among a number of excellent points he makes in differentiating between the two friends' specific orientations, Denning particularly finds purchase with two assertions. First, "[McWilliams] insisted that the central issue was not the drama of 'old-stock American' and European 'new immigrant'; rather, it was the color lines between white Americans and various peoples of color." As evidence, Denning points toward the organization of McWilliams's 1943 study *Brothers under the Skin*. Instead of Adamic's *Nation of Nations* (1945), which focused mostly on European immigrant groups, or contemporary social scientists' predominant fascination with the black-white dyad and caste segregation, McWilliams privileged the question of "race relations" as his central issue. One gains a sense of this emphasis on "the race question" when looking at the table of contents of McWilliams's book, whose chapter titles include "The Hostage Japanese," "The Little Brown Brother" (Filipinos), and " 'The Negro Problem': A Case History." Denning goes on to credit him "as one of the earliest US figures to see race through California eyes," i.e., to broaden his definition of race and widen his lens to encompass South and Central America and the Pacific.[84] The intellectual move McWilliams executes here also allows for interrogating the paradoxical connection of an American empire's struggle to recover the basic principles of American democracy. If one wants a fully synthetic analysis of race relations in the United States, McWilliams seemingly argues, then the imperialism lorded over Puerto Rico, the Pacific Islands, and the Philippines historically signifies as much a racialized precedent as the sins of internal colonialism, genocide, and the legacy of slavery.

Next, Denning recognizes McWilliams's reperiodization of this particular history, wherein he considers 1876 a meaningful flash point: the government forced all American Indians onto reservations by January 31, 1876; in 1877, the end of Radical Reconstruction led to the federal abandonment of African Americans in the South; and in six years, the Chinese Exclusion Policy (1880) would graduate to the Exclusion Act of 1882. Of equal or more importance, claims Denning, was McWilliams's admission that his books written in the 1940s were unplanned reactions to what he termed the "racial revolution" of that decade. McWilliams explains: "The fact is—and it deserves emphasis—that the civil-rights movement of a later period is to be understood only in terms of what happened from 1941 to 1945 . . . Catastrophe initiates social change; it was the war that set the racial revolution in motion."[85] While this notion of the 1940s as a critical factor in the history of the long civil rights movement (built on the racialized origins of that flash point period of the 1870s) has been roundly accepted by most twenty-first-century U.S. historians of race, McWilliams's stating this in 1979 was quite a refreshing intervention at the time. Denning intervenes further by assigning 1942 the same kind of watershed status for racial and ethnic formation that McWilliams attributes to 1876. He marks the war with Japan as the beginning of thirty-five years of U.S. involvement in wars in Asia. For example, all the following began in 1942: the Japanese American evacuation; the bracero program, in which the federal government imported Mexican laborers for agribusiness; and the second Great Migration of African Americans from the South to wartime jobs in the Midwest, Northeast, and West Coast. By including additional events from the bookend years, like the 1941 March on

Washington, or the 1943 zoot suit riots in LA, Denning certainly makes a case for 1942 as a significant marker within the historically exceptional decade of McWilliams's "racial revolution."

In McWilliams's introduction and conclusion to the 1951 revision of *Brothers under the Skin*, he demonstrated that, in the course of eight years (since the original edition was published), he had not only done much soul-searching about the evacuation, its consequences, and his role in it, but also surveyed the intellectual landscape and taken note of the Chicago School's second generation of race-relations theoreticians. McWilliams heavily borrowed from theories propounded by the sociologist Everett M. Hughes—an acolyte of Robert Park's, a later advisor to Tom Shibutani, and the author of *Where Peoples Meet: Racial and Ethnic Frontiers* (1952). He applied Hughes's theory of labor and ethnicity to explain "strategies of dominance" in workplace hierarchies (bosses, middlemen, and workers) in which race or ethnicity determined positions on the pecking order. Hughes had theorized: "There grows up a body of belief about the special working qualities of various ethnic groups. These stereotypes, which may or may not correspond to the facts, act to limit the vision of those who select help and who initiate sponsorship."[86] Examining the process of imposing dominance on these stereotyped groups, McWilliams worked through the comparative problems of the sharecropping American South and the apartheid society of colonial South Africa. Hughes and the Chicago School became McWilliams's intellectual interlocutors at the time; coincidentally, these were some of the same social scientists who heavily influenced Kikuchi and the radical Nisei with JERS during the postwar era. In this context, then, McWilliams would assert: "In the last decade, science has forced a substitution of the social for the biological view of the racial question and this substitution has opened the way for social action."[87] He then mentions "the Thomas theorem," crafted by Kikuchi's next set of mentors, Dorothy Swaine Thomas and her husband, to advance his point:

> "If men define situations as real," wrote W.I. Thomas, "they are real in their consequences." A change in the public's definition of the nature of the problem, therefore, has always been the first condition to any improvement in race relations in the United States. That change has now taken place and it is, beyond any doubt, the most significant development in race relations since the Civil War.[88]

It was a bold conclusion, but after a decade of war, ethnic and racial genocide, domestic internment camps, race riots, Jap Crow fighting forces, desegregated armed forces, braceros, Filipino independence, the end of Chinese Exclusion, a march on Washington, among other similarly historic developments, McWilliams might have been entitled to such grand statements.

In the end, however, Adamic's words serve as the most appropriate conclusion to this picaresque odyssey through the work of various writers in the CGS, its web of connections, its ideological common ground, and its stimulating discourse. In his Antinian essay "Plymouth Rock and Ellis Island," Adamic avers,

The future, ours as the world's, is in unity within diversity. Our various backgrounds are important and valuable, but, in the long run, not in themselves, not as something perfect and final. They are important and valuable only as material for our future American culture.[89]

Sadly, that future would not include Adamic for much longer.

Giving Thanks

After Kikuchi entered the camps, his correspondence with his old friend and mentor appreciably slowed. Not only was Charlie preoccupied by his work with JERS, he was also faced with the reuniting of his family, the death of his father in camp, and his assumption of the head of an imprisoned and unfamiliar household. As diary excerpts from camp will demonstrate in the remaining chapters, Kikuchi certainly never forgot what Adamic had initially taught and shared with him. Expectedly, though, Charlie matured, took what he needed from Adamic's ideology, combined it with that of the Thomases, listened to friends and colleagues, and ultimately shaped his own vision and interpretation of American democracy.

At one point, in November 1943, having already relocated to Chicago for nearly half a year, Kikuchi exchanged pleasantries with Adamic, who had offered his former charge an opportunity to edit a book on Japanese Americans in his new series entitled The Peoples of America. Neck-deep in researching and writing reports for Thomas, Kikuchi politely declined, but offered Adamic a long list of other eminently qualified Nisei as possible alternatives. The list included Oyama, Omura, Tajiri, Shibutani, his JERS colleague Frank Miyamoto, and the newspaperman Hosokawa. He even included the controversial S. I. Hayakawa, a Canadian Nisei who wrote for the Chicago Defender during the war.[90] Two more years passed, and on the eve of Charlie's induction into the army, he contacted his old friend once more. After giving Adamic an update on his family and his work with JERS, he spoke of his postwar plans and his hope "to work in some phase of race relations." Toward the end of the letter, his writing reveals the markings of Adamic's indelible influence.

The past five years have been crammed with interesting experiences, and I think that I have learned considerably. One thing that it has done is that it has convinced me that it is possible for minority groups in this country to become integrated into the American way of life, and that it is not an impossible dream to achieve such a goal even though the process may be difficult. The evacuation in itself gave the Nisei the impetus in this direction, and it was not completely in vain, even though certain of our democratic principles were strained during the hysteria following Pearl Harbor.[91]

Adamic, uncharacteristically, responded promptly. In spots, he spoke with his typically terse and preoccupied tone, but his overall remarks this time were much less mannered and guarded, showing his genuine affection for Kikuchi.

> Awfully nice to hear from you after all these years, and to learn that you are in the main satisfied with what you and your family and the whole Nisei group have gone through. I think you're a great bunch, and I'm not thinking primarily of the 442nd Combat Team. What you tell me is all very interesting . . . I shall send [Stella] your letter, and I know she will be happy to have all the news of the Kikuchis . . . If you come this way as a soldier or otherwise, please be sure to look us up.[92]

The young Nisei took Adamic up on his offer three months later, joining the scholar, his wife, and, astoundingly, McWilliams for Thanksgiving dinner. The army had sent Kikuchi to the army hospital at Fort Hancock, New Jersey, to gain experience as a psychiatric social worker (dealing primarily with AWOL cases). Therefore, he was not too far from Adamic's Milford, New Jersey, farmhouse. He spent two engaging evenings with the trio, documenting the entire experience in his November 1945 diary. Kikuchi went into great detail about his visit: dissecting the personalities of Adamic's two dogs, revealing the fact that Adamic unexpectedly helped Stella with the dishes and housework, and remarking that McWilliams was a late sleeper. Of greater substance, Kikuchi simply enjoyed the highly energized conversations at the dinner table. The topics ranged widely, from Adamic's support of Marshal Tito's communist leadership in Yugoslavia, to McWilliams's latest books on Mexicans and African Americans in California, to the Adamics' trip to Guatemala, to their collective and prescient fear of the U.S. conflict with Russia. When combined with those seemingly mundane observations about the Adamics and McWilliams's circadian rhythms, the banter and company gave Kikuchi a deep appreciation for this makeshift, surrogate family on a holiday that he had rarely celebrated with his biological family. This is relatively unsurprising, given how many beliefs, objectives, and sensibilities the four of them shared, most notably their concern for racial and ethnic minorities at home and abroad. Consider the following recollection by Kikuchi:

> McWilliams said that it was a dynamite situation in California because the evacuation of the Japanese had set a precedent for action and it might be applied to the Mexicans. Adamic believed that the government should give the evacuees an indemnity just to guarantee that our constitution should not be violated again . . . It was encouraging to hear them say things about integration [of the Nisei] which I have always believed in, but which the bulk of Nisei will resist because of racial sensitivity. Mc-Williams felt that now was the time for the Nisei to keep moving forward despite individual bumps as the pattern would take shape from what was accomplished now.[93]

Adamic and McWilliams even took a fraternal (or quasi-paternal) interest in the young Nisei, encouraging him in his future endeavors. "[They] think I should write a book," he notes,

> but I said that this was a preposterous idea as I had no inclination in that direction, and certain limitations in writing ability had to be considered. [Note: This despite his having written more than eight thousand pages of diary entries in less than four years]. They put me on the spot when they asked me what I planned to do after I got out of the Army, because I really have no definite ideas on that . . . I told them that I was interested in working with some group which dealt with minority problems, but not to be restricted to any one group.

Once again, like a kind, avuncular figure, Adamic reassured Kikuchi: "[He] said to keep him in mind as he may have a suggestion along this line when I get out."[94]

This was not the first time that Adamic—in enlisting help from literati or intellectuals in his network—had encouraged Kikuchi to pursue a life of writing. In prewar San Francisco in 1941, as you may recall, Adamic arranged for Kikuchi to meet Saroyan, who then gave a riveting "pep talk" that ultimately led to Kikuchi's failed attempt to join the Merchant Marines (see chapter 1). Joining the two that night, however, were two other well-known authors: Fante, who had just come off a rousing response to *Ask the Dust*, and the popular *San Francisco Chronicle* columnist Herb Caen. In his interview with Hansen in 1988, Kikuchi reconstructed a wonderfully farcical evening in which Caen did nothing but drink, Saroyan borrowed $20 from Kikuchi for cocktails but never paid him back, and Fante came and went within a five-minute span. "Just Herb Caen, Saroyan, and myself," he remembered. "We all ran out of money." Even though the get-together turned informal quite quickly, Kikuchi understood Adamic's aim in uniting these diverse personalities:

> I think the point that Adamic was trying to make was that Americans are of all different groups. [That] I should meet this young Armenian American writer [Saroyan], Italian American writer [Fante], and Caen was Jewish American . . . The whole idea was that there are many, many individuals in the same boat that I was in: they just happened to be of different ethnic groups.[95]

All of them, like Adamic and McWilliams, also generously encouraged Kikuchi to at least try writing about his experience. Each writer had previously demonstrated genuine interest in the work and lives of Japanese Americans: Saroyan had already written the preface to Toshio Mori's collection (though it would not be published until after the war); Fante was a professional acquaintance of Oyama; and in his "It's News to Me" column, Caen had shared sympathetic accounts of Japanese Americans, even more so during the evacuation years.[96] As an index of their close friendships, Adamic, McWilliams, and Fante had all contributed often to H. L. Mencken's *American Mercury*, and they socialized with one another when Adamic revisited Southern California (he had lived in San Pedro long before moving to the East Coast). In *City of Quartz* (1990), Mike Davis goes so far as to dub Fante, Adamic, and McWilliams part of a group called "the debunkers," alongside "noirists" in Stanley Rose's bookstore, like Chandler and West. Not entirely a compliment or an insult, "debunker" was meant to describe someone who bemoaned the philistinism of Los Angeles "and skewered its apologists with Mencken-like sarcasm."[97] If the many interwoven networks and webs of intellectuals were not enough evidence, surely this extra anecdote proves how intimate (even incestuous?) the CGS group really was.

The night of authorial drinking also gave Kikuchi a synoptic history of the Armenian genocide (Saroyan) and Jewish American strife with Italian Americans in New York (Caen). "That's how I learned about the Armenians down in Fresno," Kikuchi asserted. "And subsequently I did go down to Fresno and I worked with some Armenians picking grapes. I never really followed through on the writing." He further explained:

> I was going to go into the country and work, and I was supposed to write about the different people that I'd met: the Filipinos and the Mexicans. And I never did it. I was too tired to begin with, and I didn't know what I could write about it.[98]

Notwithstanding the reasonable excuse of exhaustion, this pattern of denying his ability to write anything of import would mark his self-confidence for the rest of his life, despite, again, what would turn out to be more than one hundred thousand pages of daily writing. This insecurity did not cloud his mind completely, though, as he circled back to Adamic's lesson:

> I guess what he wanted me to do was to break out of this "Japanese American solution," which I was seeing as the only problem [and] to put it into its proper perspective in terms of what's going on in the U.S. Of course, I didn't understand at that time his [point] . . . But it did give me some appreciation of the fact that there were other minority groups in this country that were having many problems, including Blacks, Indians, and other groups.[99]

He was a mere twenty-five in San Francisco when he met and drank with this circle of literary luminaries. A month before his death at seventy-two, he was asked by Hansen whether his younger self knew that Saroyan was considered such a "great writer" by his contemporaries. "No," Kikuchi replies. "That I didn't know. Because I only met Saroyan that one time, and I guess I was upset with him because he didn't return the money [I lent him] and I needed that money. I was broke." He chuckles and feigns indignation for his interviewer, "So I had a more limited view of him: How dare he borrow my money when I needed it more than he did?"[100]

Thanksgiving 1945 marked the last time that Kikuchi saw his potential king-maker, Adamic, despite another invitation from Louis and Stella to return to their New Jersey home with his new bride, Yuriko (they married the following autumn). Nearly six years passed before Kikuchi would comment on Adamic at great length, this time after being "tremendously shocked" by the news of Adamic's suicide on September 4, 1951. Foul play was considered: the *New York Post* alleged that Adamic had been threatened on four separate occasions since 1949 and had been "kicked unconscious by men who warned him not to continue with the book he was writing favoring Tito" [a reference to *The Eagle and the Roots*, posthumously published in 1952].[101] Thus, rumors circulated that the Soviets, aggravated by Adamic's support of Tito's resistance to Stalin, had engineered the plot to kill him. At the same time, speculation abounded that given his red activity and notoriety with HUAC, the witch hunters ultimately responsible for Moon's downfall, Adamic was an easy target of the right wing. Other details raised suspicion: for example, the alleged suicide was from a bullet to the temple, but Adamic was discovered with his rifle resting comfortably and inexplicably across his lap. In addition, his large farmhouse and garage were set ablaze, but the local fire chief remained unconvinced, judging by the extent of the blaze, that Adamic could have acted alone. No suicide note was found, but an article describing his alleged Soviet spy activity was found on his body. Although all these pieces of evidence raised eyebrows, Stella Adamic publicly accepted the ruling that it was a suicide.[102]

McWilliams eulogized his friend in the September 21, 1951, issue of the *Nation*, sixteen years after he had written of Adamic's staying power and influence in *Louis Adamic and Shadow America*. Referring to clashing American traditions forged before and after the HUAC hearings and the rise of the Red Scare, McWilliams wrote:

> An eager and enthusiastic immigrant, "bewitched and bewildered by America," he wanted to be Americanized but on his terms; he did not want to accept both American traditions . . . His Americanization was complete from the moment he realized—which must have been shortly before his death—that he had surrendered more of himself to America than he had ever intended to surrender. There was, in fact, nothing more to surrender; he could no longer be detached; the social and the personal tragedy were one.[103]

McWilliams frames his colleague's death as a synecdoche, diagnosing Adamic's fatal wounds as the selfsame ills affecting the nation as a whole. Nativist and communist witch hunting, like uncontrollable bleeding, would likewise prove America's downfall, McWilliams argued.

In his diary, Kikuchi penned a more personal elegy for Adamic: "I feel a personal loss which is stronger than anything I ever felt before. He was a symbol to me of how an immigrant could achieve real success and he contributed a lot to the country in ideas."[104] This is a remarkably bold and telling admission on Kikuchi's part, given that he had lost his father in camp eight years earlier and had commented on his passing in only very brief terms: "At a time like this there isn't much we can do. All I can feel is that 'Pop was a good guy.' I didn't know him too well, but I feel keenly about [the death]."[105] What is more, he credits Adamic with being the symbol of the successful first-generation immigrant, in implicit contrast to his own first-generation father, a modestly successful barber and veteran who grew bitter as the years passed before his stroke and paralysis. The relative absence of his father in the diary relegated him to a ghostlike figure in Kikuchi's mind. Adamic, on the other hand, was, in Kikuchi's words, a "robust, vigorous man who enjoyed life fully," and the true father figure who helped jump-start his interest in the interaction between races and working with others, the eventual hallmarks of his career as a social worker.[106]

Admittedly, as cited earlier, Kikuchi eventually outgrew Adamic's influence, as his experiences in camp and in Chicago will show. He never lost track, however, of the formative experience he enjoyed with Adamic, an early apprenticeship in race-relations work. In his essay of remembrance, he recalled specific lessons learned: "At the time I was in Chicago, my idea was that the Nisei should discard everything from Japanese culture because I identified it completely with political, ideological beliefs. But Adamic's writings enabled me to modify my viewpoint and gain a greater perspective."[107] This advice contributed to Kikuchi's evolving understanding of what an American could be: not simply a homogenized, deracinated individual adhering to a false, Anglicized norm. "In his way," Kikuchi concluded, "Adamic was a great public figure who contributed more than his share of ideas to America, and this will not be lost."

What remained unresolved for Kikuchi, however, were questions he had posed to Adamic ten years earlier in the tense aftermath of Pearl Harbor: "What of the future? Are we rushing back to barbarism, or is there hope for reconstruction of a new social order which really will have democracy? Is this vision possible?" He attempted to answer his own query, albeit with an understandable pinch of uncertainty: "Democracy must win, a real democracy, I mean, if we are to avoid the old order of national greed and selfishness. America is the only country . . . in a position to lead the world to a new future. Will we bungle it? I hope not."[108]

Between Adamic's correspondence, his "school" of intellectuals, and Dorothy Thomas's hands-on guidance, Kikuchi learned much about the experience and formal study of race relations, but this dichotomy of lingering doubt and eternal hope regarding democracy would gain more prominence in his thoughts as the years passed. The next chapter traces the steps of Kikuchi's evolution under the Thomases, highlighting his diaries written behind barbed wire.

Chapter 4

"Participating and Observing": Dorothy Swaine Thomas, W. I. Thomas, and JERS

In September 1942, after being corralled at the Tanforan Assembly Center for four months, Kikuchi began the second phase of his internment in the desolate and arid environs of the Gila River Relocation Center, fifty miles southeast of Phoenix.[1] He received a letter of concern toward the end of the month, which began, "Thanks for writing to me in one of my roles other than that of college professor. I have been awfully worried about the situation at Gila but you are obviously adjusting so well that I feel a good deal better about it."[2] Writing from the relative comfort of Cal's Giannini Hall, the demographer Dorothy Swaine Thomas felt compelled to send Kikuchi a note to build up his confidence. Five days earlier, the young researcher had expressed doubts about his ability to contribute to a study Thomas was conducting. "I am intensely interested in the study," he wrote,

> but I feel inadequate when I think of the reams of material which your other observers are no doubt sending in. In other words, do you think that my work justifies a full time assistanceship? It's not that I lack confidence in myself, but I do feel guilty.[3]

This pair of letters accurately depicts the lengthy, honest, and mutually respectful nature of the correspondence between Kikuchi and Thomas, especially during the period of 1942 to 1945, when Kikuchi officially kept his personal diary for the Japanese American Evacuation and Resettlement Study (JERS), which Thomas led. Introduced to Thomas at Cal by Shibutani and Sakoda, who were already researchers in her employ, Kikuchi had been keeping his diary as part of the project since the beginning of his incarceration at Tanforan and would continue to do so until his induction into the U.S. Army in August 1945. As previously noted, Kikuchi would write for his personal use well past this end date, and he maintained informal communication with Thomas until her death in 1977. Thomas had initially asked Kikuchi to keep a diary in the hope that she would gain greater insight into the "normal" workings of camp life and the readjustment processes of an individual resettler after camp. She did not give him formal directions or strict guidelines, but simply asked that he write. But as his comments above make plain, Kikuchi thought very little of his contribution to the study back in 1942. Musing on the subject thirty years later, he remained consistently self-deprecating in his views: "I never thought of doing my diaries as more than a kind of source material for myself."[4]

Part of his insecurity stemmed from the fact that his friends Shibutani and Sakoda had already begun their training in sociology at Cal long before the evacuation. Having chosen social work as his future career, Kikuchi felt his writing might fall short of the academic mark. "I don't think I came up to your expectations at Tanforan," he would confide in Thomas, "but I am just not a Shibutani or Sakoda. My approach is different and I am in doubt whether it meets with your approval."[5] Thomas—in her infinite patience and wisdom that (in Kikuchi) she had something quite valuable and unique—allayed his fears.

> I don't want you to be another Shibutani or Sakoda . . . I feel that Charlie Kikuchi is a valuable addition to the study, and I am enormously pleased that he is willing to participate. I think of your relationship to the study as a continuing one, and I am confident of your ability to follow through on assignments that will be made from time to time.[6]

In truth, Kikuchi knew much more than he let on, revealing his natural instincts when it came to social scientific research. In the same September 1942 letter, he exclaims,

> You see, Dr. Thomas, in order to get the right tempo of the community I will have to enter life here actively. I just can't sit off to a side in a passive role. This means that I must donate my time to my job here, and time is so limited.[7]

Playing the part of a trusting and reaffirming mentor, Thomas assured her charge: "I agree with you thoroughly about full participation in community life. This sort of thing cannot be done by 'sitting off to the side in a passive role.'"[8]

Of course, Thomas herself was no stranger to the methods of participant observation and life histories, given her intimate connection to one of the most accomplished practitioners (and originators) of the forms: her husband, William Isaac Thomas. A graduate of the University of Chicago, he became a full professor in 1910 and was responsible for luring Robert Park away from Tuskegee in 1913 (as well as influencing Park's famous "race relations cycle").[9] In 1918, however, a highly publicized sexual indiscretion with the wife of a lieutenant serving in France torpedoed his career at Chicago, and one of his later studies—*Old World Traits Transplanted* (1921)—had to be published under the names of Park and Herbert Miller: the Carnegie Corporation, which underwrote the study, forbade its name from being connected in any way to Thomas. Nonetheless, long before he and Dorothy met in 1926 (they eventually wed in 1935), "W. I.," as he was known, had already challenged the conventional use of statistics in sociology, advocating a more subjective "life history" approach, most notably with Florian Znaniecki in the five-volume *Polish Peasant in Europe and America*

(1918–1920). Regarding merely empirical approaches to the study of sociology, Thomas warned:

> Taken in themselves statistics are nothing more than symptoms of un-
> known causal processes. A social institution can be understood and
> modified only if we do not limit ourselves to the study of its formal orga-
> nization but analyze the way in which it appears in the personal experi-
> ence of various members of the group and follow the influence which it
> has on their lives.[10]

To that end, Thomas and Znaniecki's research heavily relied on (and pioneered the use of) life histories and letters of immigrants—in this case, Poles—examining how they made the adjustment from the rural villages of the Old World to cit-ies at the center of the New World. Applying these same methods of analysis to deviant women in *The Unadjusted Girl* (1923), Thomas wrote: "The 'human document,' prepared by the subject on the basis of the memory is one means of measuring social influence. It is capable of presenting life as a connected whole and of showing the interplay of influences, the action of values on attitudes."[11] Carla Cappetti summarized his philosophy thus: "The first-person document, in the diverse literary forms it takes, emerges as the ideal sociological source."[12] In many ways, this approach unceremoniously questioned the holy grail of social-scientific objectivity in interpreting data. As one scholar of the Chicago School put it, Thomas stressed that "the sociologist must always remember that 'reality' lay just as much in the participants' *understanding* of any particular situation, as in the 'objective' measurable factors."[13] What is more, as far as who (and whose understanding) should be studied, Thomas was indiscriminate: "Ordinary and extraordinary personalities should be included, the dull and the criminal, the philistine and the bohemian. Scientifically the history of dull lives is quite as sig-nificant as that of brilliant ones."[14] This, of course, was extremely appropriate to Kikuchi's case, since he not only kept his own diary—as a self-described "regular guy"—but also recorded the life histories of sixty-four "ordinary" resettlers af-ter internment. In this context, then, the Kikuchi diary proved a worthy source, simultaneously plumbing the depths of a participant's understanding (in W. I.'s terms), and serving as "an extremely valuable document" (in Dorothy's words).

Ironically, though, Thomas herself seemed an unlikely midwife for a project based on life histories. A demographer by training, Thomas had spent most of her academic life privileging the use of statistics in studying patterns of popula-tion and migration. As an undergraduate at Barnard, she had apprenticed under William Fielding Ogburn, a leading proponent of quantitative sociology who joined the faculty of Chicago's Sociology Department in 1927. Her doctoral the-sis, written at the London School of Economics, correlated the fluctuations in marriage, poverty, and crime rates with changes in the business cycles of the United States and Britain. After earning her PhD in 1924, she accepted a job as her future husband's research assistant, and in 1928, they coauthored *The Child in America*, a study of behavioral problems in children. The volume included what came to be known as the "Thomas theorem": "If men define situations as real, they are real in their consequences."[15] Rationalizing the use of life histories, case studies, and psychoanalytic confessions, the theorem argued that the difference between how an individual ("subjective appreciation") and how others ("objective reality") perceived the same situation could explain "overt behavior difficulty" in an individual. While credit for the theorem should go to both husband and wife, W. I. thought that this concept of "defining the situation" was "his most significant contribution to the socio-psychological understanding of the formation of social personality and character."[16]

Perhaps of more pertinence at this juncture is the noteworthy migration by Dorothy Thomas away from her mentor Ogburn's statistical—and putatively objective—approach and toward the subjective analysis (and focus on behavior) offered by W. I.'s life histories. As further evidence of this shift, in a 1929 article in *The American Journal of Sociology*, she would write: "There is no magic in the use of statistical methods . . . The greater part of the statistical work that has been done in the social sciences is, from this point of view, of little value."[17] This struck many as a stunning statement, given Thomas's previously faithful reliance on numbers. But she was not advocating wholesale abandonment of the method:

> Statistics . . . can never completely exclude other methods of analysis used in sociology . . . The case-study, in fact, serves the same fundamental purpose for the sociologist that introspection does for the behaviorist. From the case-study he gets his "hunches" which will lead to the formulation of hypotheses to be tested out by scientific techniques or statistical analysis.[18]

It should come as no surprise that Thomas made room in her calculus for the approach of her husband. One scholar confirms as much, quoting Thomas years later as conceding: "W.I. Thomas . . . convinced me of the importance of the 'behavior document' in social research."[19] Moreover, while working with Yale's Institute of Human Relations in 1935, she would describe herself to a colleague: "Philosophically, I tend to fall in with the [Charles] Cooley–W.I. Thomas point of view rather than either the extreme biological or the extreme materialistic views."[20] The last half of this statement revealed that Thomas had already slain her scholarly father figure, Ogburn, whom she described in the same letter as having "developed an extremely mechanistic hypothesis," in contrast to the Cooley-Thomas focus on the individuals behind (or ahead of) Ogburn's statistics.

Around this time, Thomas synthesized the methods of case study and statistics in a major research project on migration in Sweden. Both Thomases had developed their interest in the Scandinavian country after meeting with Gunnar and Alva Myrdal in 1929, both of whom held Rockefeller Fellowships in the United States. The couples subsequently developed a significant friendship, and the Thomases frequently visited Sweden throughout the 1930s. In the meantime, Dorothy began her affiliation with the University of Stockholm in 1936, and over the next five years, published two volumes on the country's declining population,

Research Memorandum on Migration Differentials (1938) and *Social and Economic Aspects of Swedish Population Movements, 1750–1933* (1941). During this period, Swedes were engaging in an animated debate over the causes of such a decline. Conservatives used the opportunity to call for women's withdrawal from the workforce, anticontraception laws, and a more stringent immigration policy to defend against foreigners' weakening of the hearty Swedish stock. By contrast, the nation's Social Democrats, including, most notably, the Myrdals, saw the issue as one that should prompt discussion of national economic planning, reorganization of the family unit based on gender equity, income redistribution, and expanded social responsibility, among others. With Gunnar appointed to the Population Commission, some of these reforms were passed (with the noteworthy exceptions of family reorganization and income redistribution). Myrdal—much as his galvanizing work in America would prove—thus consciously integrated his scholarship with his politics. Dorothy Thomas, by contrast, would address few if any of these hot-button issues in her two studies of Sweden. Reviewers of the works most frequently remarked upon the volume of data in her sixty-five-page appendix, entitled "Memorandum," but hardly cited much more. This aversion to addressing the politically charged aspect of a study would crop up later in her work on the Japanese American "problem" as well. In this same window of time, a collaborative project planned by the two couples (although, in truth, Dorothy and Gunnar did most of the heavy lifting) fell by the wayside.[21]

Nonetheless, the Thomases and Myrdals maintained their friendship until W. I.'s death in 1947. Along the way, Myrdal credited W. I. for providing one of the theoretical cornerstones for *An American Dilemma* (1944).[22] In his introduction, he promised, "We want to follow through W. I. Thomas's theme, namely, that when people define situations as real, they *are* real . . . The interrelations between the material facts and people's valuations of and beliefs about these facts are precisely what make the Negro a social problem."[23] Later in the first volume, his analysis certainly made good on that promise, bearing identifiable traces of W. I.'s philosophy: "The Negro has to be defined according to social usage, [as] his African ancestry and physical characteristics are fixed to his person much more ineffaceably than the yellow star is fixed to the Jew during the Nazi regime."[24] Myrdal would additionally include Dorothy (appointed professor of rural sociology at Berkeley in 1941) among the constellation of scholarly contributors to his two-volume, landmark study of African Americans and the Achilles' heel of American democracy.[25] The friendship cooled somewhat, however; two years later, in 1946, Dorothy admitted to Myrdal that "communication has been cut off for too long a period, war or no war." She then proceeded to bemoan the "lost generation" of young American sociologists, their training interrupted by the chaos of war, and teased Myrdal over rumors that Cal was trying to recruit him to lead its nascent sociology department. Toward the end of her missive, she noted that, among her current students, she had only one to recommend to Myrdal for hire ("one cub but a lion"). "He is too young and inexperienced for a professorship," she writes, "and it would be a mistake to pull him out of his groove now, but he is someone to watch for the future."[26] Alas, the young intellectual of whom she so highly spoke was not our diarist, Charlie Kikuchi, but a budding Middle Eastern scholar named Georges Sabagh.[27] Unfortunately, Thomas never introduced Kikuchi to Myrdal, even though both men ostensibly shared similar concerns about the "Negro problem."[28] More immediate problems, however, would obviously keep Charlie preoccupied.

Thomas's Vision of JERS

While seemingly a departure from her previous work, particularly given the highly charged political implications of the internment domestically, JERS remained within the general framework of Thomas's studies of populations and mass migrations. Ambitious in scope, the study set out to analyze the causes and effects of a forced migration into internment camps as well as the adjustment processes of internees to life after camp. Interdisciplinary in design, the study ambitiously took on multiple approaches: sociology, anthropology, political science, social psychology, and economics.[29] As the war intensified, however, most of Thomas's collaborators (almost all of them men), such as the anthropologist Robert Lowie and the political scientist Charles Aikin, were called to work in other governmental efforts, so Thomas was left shouldering much of the administrative burden for the study. She could have delayed it, but given the uncharacteristically prompt response from the Rockefeller Foundation with a grant of $100,000, Thomas felt compelled to complete the work as initially planned.

These factors, however, coupled with the fact that the War Relocation Authority (WRA)—the civilian body established by Roosevelt in March 1942 to oversee camp administration—closely monitored her researchers, made for a very haphazard study. In fact, one of her sociologists in training, Shibutani, made his disappointment extremely apparent: the study lacked a theoretical framework, and consequently, the researchers in the field felt that they were receiving little or no guidance from the director. For most of these young men and women—who were internees themselves—the difficulties of how to achieve objectivity in their analyses or even to interview other internees without raising suspicions about spying for the government were overwhelming. On this latter point, internees could not be blamed for being confused about whom they were speaking to: other institutions were concurrently carrying out two other studies. The anthropologists John Embree and Edward Spicer led the WRA's Community Analysis Section in all ten camps, and the anthropologist-psychiatrist Alexander Leighton directed a study by the Bureau of Sociological Research, which focused on the Poston, Arizona, camp and came under the umbrella of the Bureau of Indian Affairs.[30] These two studies, though, focused exclusively on improving camp administration.

Thomas's study resulted in the publication of two official volumes. The first, entitled *The Spoilage* (1946) and coauthored by Richard Nishimoto, focused on the 18,700 evacuees who responded negatively to the "loyalty question" or failed to give an answer and were subsequently removed to the Tule Lake Segregation Center in California.[31] The second volume, *The Salvage* (1952), examined evacuees who were permitted to leave camp in 1943 and resettle, principally in the Midwest. A third volume, entitled *The Residue*, was initially conceived as a study of those Japanese unable to leave or who chose to remain in the centers, but this capstone was never published, because of disagreements between its lead researcher, Sakoda, and Thomas.[32] Instead, Jacobus tenBroek's *Prejudice, War, and the Constitution* (1954) unofficially filled this particular void, chronicling the history of anti-Asian discrimination in the West and debating the constitutional issues raised by the internment.

Since Thomas was most responsible for the first two studies, discussion of their findings and the reaction to these volumes will be of greatest concern here. In essence, *The Spoilage* found that certain background characteristics marked a higher percentage of those evacuees segregated at Tule Lake than did others. Those who chose segregation were more likely to be Kibei (than Issei or Nisei), Buddhists (than Christians), Californians (than Pacific northwesterners), farmers (than urban workers), and males (than females). Thomas's second data set measured the characteristics of those who chose to resettle (or out-migrate), and she found the same pattern, but only in reverse. Thus, she concluded that segregation was the choice of the least assimilated, while resettlement the selection of the most assimilated. Frank Miyamoto, a JERS researcher, emphasizes, however, that the study's "significance is more clearly brought out by interpreting the results in terms of discrimination and segregation [rather] than assimilation. . . . The data indicate that those who chose segregation at Tule Lake were those who had experienced the greatest amount of discrimination and segregation before the war."[33]

This particular volume brought mixed reviews. Many reviewers were simply pleased that the text (published in 1946) highlighted the wartime plight of Japanese Americans, bringing immediate recognition and possible redress. One wrote of the text: "The American public cannot afford to allow it to escape the attention of the executive branches of the government, if the survival of democracy is one of its ambitions."[34] Others were quite critical of the methodology of the study, correctly citing the fact that Thomas relied on only one researcher's data from which to draw her conclusions.[35] One of these critics, Marvin Opler, formerly the WRA Community Analyst at Tule Lake, was especially hostile, faulting Thomas for stressing the more sensational, strife-torn aspects of life at the center rather than what he considered the genuine community built there. "The 19,000 men, women and children cramped in a square mile of tar-papered 'theater of operations' barracks do not emerge as people," he claimed.[36]

The Salvage fared slightly better with reviewers, although its conclusions about those who chose resettlement did not differ greatly from those drawn about segregants in the first volume. In short, Thomas found, Kibei had the most difficult time acclimating to resettlement in cities like Chicago and Minneapolis, while Nisei navigated the adjustment process most successfully, and Japanese from urban backgrounds managed better than their rural counterparts. Additionally, the second half of the two-part volume comprised fifteen of Kikuchi's case histories, or interviews with Nisei resettlers. These were, however, straight transcriptions without any analysis, a shortcoming identified by many of the volume's scholarly reviewers. Forrest LaViolette, for example, opined:

> In fact as far as the two parts are concerned, they could have been published separately. The influence of W. I. Thomas is recognized and readily observable . . . but there is no analysis.[37]

Nevertheless, prominent scholars of American civilization such as Oscar Handlin thought highly of the study as a whole, and the life histories in particular: "These are illuminating, not only for the light they throw on the problems of evacuation, detention and resettlement, but also for the information they supply on the experience of the whole group, and in fact, for the general reflections they contain on the culture of the Pacific coast through the years involved."[38] Another reviewer went so far as to praise the budding social scientist in the group:

> Mr. Kikuchi deserves much praise for his excellent reporting. His material is apt, illuminating and recorded with a fine grasp of the language differences arising out of the social groups from which his subjects came.[39]

This was a welcome compliment for someone who, in his weakest moments, thought his writing and reporting inferior and unscholarly.

Years later, after convening a conference at Cal to mark the internment experience in 1987, Yuji Ichioka compiled an anthology of the proceedings, entitled *Views from Within*, which both criticized and celebrated the accomplishments of the JERS researchers. Having raised his own suspicions about the study, and conscious of the criticism retrospectively launched at Thomas and her methods, Ichioka was one of the first scholars to call for a reevaluation of JERS.[40] "Today, with the benefit of hindsight combined with a political perspective derived from the 1960s," he writes,

> some may condemn JERS out of hand as an unethical research project with no redeeming value . . . Those who reaped the benefits were Dorothy Thomas and those JERS staff members who were able to advance professionally . . . On the other hand, Japanese-Americans, the objects of JERS research, gained nothing—JERS neither improved their condition or status, nor promoted their political interests.

But Ichioka cautioned against dismissing the study too easily.

> It goes without saying that JERS was not a research project in the service of a political cause on behalf of Japanese-Americans. To say that it should have been is to engage in wishful thinking; to criticize it for not having been is to be naïve . . . To recognize and admit that does not mean

> JERS has no redeeming value. The JERS sources, especially those in the form of daily journals, diaries, life histories, and field reports, [expressly] produced at Thomas' insistence . . . , retain an enduring value because they lend themselves to the writing of a social history of concentration camp life.[41]

Ichioka was addressing a legitimate complaint by modern scholars that JERS, along with the two other loosely related studies, merely treated Japanese Americans as objects, anthropological curiosities viewed from an academic distance. To these critics, the JERS researchers and the study itself were apolitical, an unforgivable shortcoming given the circumstances. While not entirely unsympathetic to the critics' arguments, my work tries—as Ichioka has encouraged—to view the Kikuchi diary (one of many archival sources in the JERS collection) as a worthy example of a subject writing not only himself but also his entire people into history. Read very closely, in fact, the diary may demonstrate, to critics and sympathizers alike, that not all JERS researchers and documents were created equal. Some of them, like Kikuchi and his cadre of Nisei intelligentsia, could not help but be political in their views.

" A Good Outlet"

Initially, however, Kikuchi vacillated over whether to join the Cal study at all. His friend Shibutani had brokered the offer from Thomas, but Kikuchi resisted: "I told him that I would not want to make a full-time job of it, because I wanted to work right during the process and reflect back and analyze it because I don't have the training for such work." He considered doing the "academic" study part-time because he preferred gaining practical, real-world experience through the camp's social-work office. "It looks like girls will be doing this [social] work," he says, "but it shouldn't bother me too much."[42] As noted above, Kikuchi did not harbor any reservations about doing what some of his friends in other social sciences deemed "sissy work," because his ultimate aspiration was to be an activist, not an academic. In some ways, though, after accepting the offer to participate in JERS in the spring of 1942, Kikuchi blended the best of both worlds: the activist's interpersonal skill (through social work) with the keen observational eye and critical orientation (of the sociologist).

He considered his note taking, reports, and official record keeping in Tanforan and Gila as the primary task assigned to him by Thomas. His diary, meanwhile, was of secondary importance—in his mind, a mere work in progress. Before his death in 1988, he assessed the benefit of the diary he kept in camp:

> My diary assisted me in dealing with much of my confusion about being a Nisei and with pressures created by stress. Its main value during the 1940s was to help me sort out problems in research methods, in recording life histories, and in evaluating interview techniques.[43]

He had given a similar appraisal in 1944:

> I have a mania for doing a lot of worrying about the dumbest things. Most of the time, I keep it to myself though and a diary entry is a good outlet. The only trouble is that the Boss [Thomas] reads it. But I decided a long time ago not to pull any punches and write my thoughts of the moment even though I may get fired as a result . . . Behind the "Japanese Mask"![44]

In many predictable ways, then, the diary was a deeply personal and therapeutic outlet for Kikuchi.

Thomas did not want to disabuse him of this notion either. In fact, oftentimes she encouraged Kikuchi's unadorned, straightforward, and uncensored prose. For example, in January 1943, in another attempt to convince Kikuchi of the merit of his work, she wrote:

> I assure you that I consider you one of the most valuable people on the whole Study and that what you are doing is of the utmost importance to us. Aside from the value of your data, as bearing on the life in the project, you are producing a unique human document.

Not unlike Adamic's fatherly manner, described in the previous chapter, Thomas assumed (along with W. I.) a parental role for Kikuchi at this stage of his life— ironically, at a time when Kikuchi himself had reunited with his biological parents but had also unexpectedly assumed the head of household in camp. Thomas persisted in buoying her young charge's spirits:

> I hate to say too much about this for fear you will become self-conscious, but I trust you to be sufficiently objective to realize what I mean, and not let it affect your style of reporting. W. I., who is after all an expert on documents, agrees with me that the history of the Kikuchi family's adjustments is perhaps the best family history from the sociological standpoint that we have seen, and that your own observations and reactions to the changes that are going on represent an equally important contribution. So please continue just as you have in the past.[45]

Essentially, Kikuchi did just that. In his diaries written between 1942 and 1945— the years in which Thomas "supervised" Kikuchi's writing—one rarely detects any reservations or obfuscations on Kikuchi's part; in other words, he infrequently pulled any punches in his narrative. If one were to compare the set of diaries written under Thomas's watch to the volumes that came after it (from August 1945 onward), one would discover that tone, subject matter, and writing style all remain consistent. To be clear, however, Kikuchi's diary was not a self-consciously crafted autobiography, made to appeal to as many readers as possible, or provocatively planned for a hundred-year embargo like Mark Twain's. On most days, Kikuchi provided simple observations and systematic analysis based on his social-scientific training, generally pondering camp life, group behavior, and adjustments to the city, among several topics. Other days, he offered personal musings and observations about interactions with workmates, meaningful conversations with friends, or passing exchanges with strangers. Much like his narrative, then, the substance of Kikuchi's life and ideas resists simple and neat categorization. As diaries tend to do, these volumes expose Kikuchi's ideals and prejudices, triumphs and blemishes, and, most importantly, his simplicities and complexities of thought.

Kikuchi's Role in Camp

Looking back on his work for the study forty years later, Kikuchi remembered the concerns raised by his journal keeping, and the sorting out of his exact role in the study. "As a single Nisei interested in social interaction," he reminisced,

> there were occasions when I had conflicts over whether I should record some of my own unorthodox social activities. I was concerned from the beginning about issues of confidentiality and research needs.

Over time, Kikuchi noted, he realized that the research focus was of paramount importance, and the diary assumed a more objective tone. But he conceded, "Complete detachment and objectivity was the ideal goal, but not always completely possible." Thus, as his responsibility for the study grew and as he took on more research-oriented tasks, like taking notes on camp activity and, later in Chicago, the recording of sixty-four life histories, the diary slid back toward subjectivity, serving the purpose of providing an outlet for his truer feelings. "Since I was also a participant in the evacuation and resettlement," he recalled,

> I was always very much aware of how my own personal orientation could influence the research process. For this reason, I later often expressed my personal orientation about the role of the Nisei in my diary in order to consciously prevent these sentiments from entering the framework [of my research].[46]

In the early portions of the diary, Kikuchi did not have much trouble expressing himself. At the end of April 1942, for example, before reuniting with his family and entering Tanforan, Kikuchi's emotions were running high, and the diary perfectly captured the anxiety he was feeling. "Today [the 30th] is the day that we are going to get kicked out of Berkeley. It certainly is degrading," he wrote.

> I'm supposed to see my family at Tanforan as [my brother] Jack told me to give the same family number [to be grouped with them]. I wonder how it is going to be living with them as I haven't done this for years and years.

He then sprinkles a few of his frustrations through the rest of his nightly entry: "That General DeWitt certainly gripes my ass because he has been listening to the Associated Farmers too much"; "Some of those old Issei men must have gone on a binge last night because they smell like *sake*"; and ending with "God, what a prospect to look forward to living among all those Japs!"[47] Seemingly random comments, these three specific references suggest Kikuchi's unease with the prospect of seeing his father again. Ever since suffering abuse at the hands of his father, Kikuchi had kept his defenses up against figures of authority (with the notable "professionalized" exceptions of Adamic and the Thomases): hence, his unsurprising swipe at DeWitt, the top military officer in charge of the internment, who rationalized the mass incarceration by habitually quipping, "A Jap is a Jap." Kikuchi had also never forgotten his father's drinking, which led to regular beatings: in the second excerpt listed above, Kikuchi may be thinking of his first-generation father when observing the drunken Issei. Lastly, he spews the epithet "Japs," just as DeWitt does, a term he would repeatedly use during this period. This perhaps could be interpreted superficially as Kikuchi's attempt to ironically distance himself from the group as a whole, as a confirmation of his marginal status, an argument made by Ichioka and other scholars who deemed Kikuchi not loyal enough to the group and too much of a self-hater.[48] A more persuasive reading, however, points toward Kikuchi's imbuing the term with all of the anger he felt toward his father. The epithet then comes to represent his specific disavowal of the father and everything he had come to symbolize: (undeserving) authority, backwardness, violence, and intemperance. "Japs" meant the Issei, which in turn meant "father." It was not fair to project his volatile emotions surrounding Nakajiro onto older Japanese he did not even know, but the psyche is never that compliant. With the reunion of father and son inevitably close, frustrations born out of personal history were bound to unexpectedly resurface, and his writing simply reflected this mélange of emotions. What is more, Kikuchi's experience in Gila dramatically changed his view of Issei as "Japs," softening his antagonism toward the group, but not toward his father.

Simultaneously, profound sadness lurked beneath his deep-seated anger about his relationship with Nakajiro. This was most evident after the reunion took place and the father and son were living together again, this time in extremely close quarters. On top of this stress, the elder Kikuchi, a former barber, had poorly aged and was on the verge of losing a battle with diabetes. After only a few days in camp, the son admitted:

> Made me feel sort of sorry for Pop tonight. He has his three electric clippers hung up on the wall and Tom [one of Kikuchi's younger brothers] has built him a barrel chair for the barber seat. It's a bit pathetic when he so tenderly cleans off the clippers after using them; oiling, brushing, and wrapping them up so carefully.

Kikuchi appears nearly incredulous at the disconnect between the images of his father then and now:

> He probably realizes that he no longer controls the family group and rarely exerts himself so that there is little family conflict as far as he is concerned. What a difference from about 15 years ago when I was a kid. He used to be a perfect terror and dictator.[49]

At the same time, even in his old age (or despite it), Nakajiro still managed to raise Charlie's ire:

> Pop thinks Hitler is a sourfish and distrusts the Germans; Koreans are not the same as Japanese. A Jew is a cheating kike, a Filipino goes around raping women, and the Japanese in the U.S. are cutthroats (only when I am not arguing with him). Pop is a mixture of past fears and frustrations.[50]

It was difficult for Kikuchi to fully express his anger or sadness to any family member: he simply did not know any of them well enough to confide in them. His irritability and melancholy were thus directed outward, past the immediate circle of family members, and once again struck a familiar target. A mere day after offering his wistful observation about "Pop," he recorded:

> I was up in the Grandstands and had a good view of the outside; maybe I was depressed, but a funny feeling of loneliness and of being out of place swept over me. Perhaps this was due to the fact that I walked through the men's dormitory where all those Japanese old men were jabbering away in their conversations about the war.[51]

Again, some readers of the diary might interpret Kikuchi's unmitigated disdain of the Issei as incontrovertible proof of his rejection of a Japanese identity and his "outsider" status in the community. After all, he reports being depressed and "out of place." One must, however, keep in mind that he had just spent seven intense days with a family he never knew, with a father he never knew, after nearly eighteen years on his own. Additionally, remember that Kikuchi was not exactly a stranger to the Japanese American community: he had worked with them on farms; studied and lived with the network of radical Nisei at Cal; and written a report on their job opportunities for the NYA. His depression and loneliness at this moment derived less from not being an integral part of a Japanese community, and more from being forced to confront the family and father that never wanted him. This does not even take into consideration the glaring fact of his internment, a rejection of his entire race by "the American family."

The grandstand at Tanforan affected other internees quite similarly, offering a glimpse of the "outside world" and a voyeuristic, bird's-eye view of the camp. Miné Okubo, for one, recalls,

> Every time a group arrived I went out to the grandstand to watch them go through the induction steps I had gone through a couple weeks earlier. From the grandstand balcony I watched the coming and going of the baggage trucks.

For the young artist, these views from the perch profoundly influenced her, to the point that she admitted: "The humor and pathos of the scenes made me decide to keep a record of camp life in sketches and drawings."[52] The grandstand provided a necessary outlet to the outside world: every day, from 10 to 12 noon and 1 to 4 p.m., inmates received visitors in a room on top of the grandstand specifically designated for such occasions. Shows, pageants, and dances also took place in the grandstand, while personal quiet time was also possible there, as both Kikuchi and Okubo demonstrated. She concludes:

> The panorama from there reminded [residents] of the hills of home. One had a whole view of the racetrack and the surrounding country. Trains passed back and forth in the distance and airplanes skimmed overhead.[53]

Connected in some small measure to the world beyond, the internees could warm up in the sun, sleep, or meditate in this ostensibly grand space.

Needless to say, Kikuchi's grandstand perspectives and maladjustments to his family situation were only a fraction of the topics he covered in his voluminous diary. Ironically, he would remark: "I realized a long time ago that I can't write; it's too much of an effort on my part." His follow-up was less surprising: "I don't think I would like research so much because that is reflecting back on a thing after it has happened and I am more interested in being in the thick of things while it is going on with some social view of the future."[54] Indeed, Kikuchi's observations of his cloistered surroundings gave him serious pause, reenergizing his activist impulse and the desire to understand the larger meaning of the incarceration. Without any irony, he stated: "I saw a soldier in a tall guardhouse near the barbed wire fence and did not like it because it reminds me of a concentration camp."

> I am just wondering what the effects will be on the Japanese so cut off from the world like this . . . I hardly know how the war is going now, and it is so significant that the Allied forces win even though that will not mean that democracy will by any means be perfect or even justified. The whole postwar period is going to be something terrific.[55]

A few days later, in a bull session with Tsuneishi, Sakoda, and his brother Jack, Kikuchi renewed a debate on the aims of the war and the possibilities it held for the downtrodden in the United States and all over the globe. "All of us agreed that Fascism was not the answer," he reported,

> but there was a difference of opinions on whether an Allied victory would be any solution to the whole mess . . . Would the solution only include the white races, or will we be in a position to tackle the problem of India, China, and the other millions of "exploited" peoples?[56]

Taken up in more detail below, Kikuchi's internationalist perspective and his linkage of people of color at home and abroad were clearly not exclusively his own opinions. Other Japanese Americans—not all of them necessarily "radical"—felt an allegiance toward other nonwhite peoples. Ten days after "celebrating" the Fourth of July inside camp, for example, he and four friends (along with brother Jack) once again disputed the relationship between democracy and race.

> [Sakoda] suggested that the colored races of the world had reason to feel despair and mistrust the white man because of the past experiences . . .

Jack thought this was the reason why so many minority groups did not feel for democracy, because they have never had it . . . Marie said this feeling of hopelessness was one of the reasons why many Nisei were rejecting patriotism.[57]

These were animated late-night discussions, consciously out of earshot of the camp's administration and security forces, as well as far removed from the eavesdropping of disapproving or suspicious internees. Prescient in their predictions and incisive in their analysis, these discussants were anticipating the larger discourse of the later 1940s and the 1950s surrounding race, civil rights, the Cold War, and the agreement signed by African and Asian nations at Bandung, Indonesia, in 1955 (a precursor to the Non-Aligned Movement). But these were conversations unquestionably held under the radar—exposing the "darker," night side of American democracy, revealing what truly boiled beneath the surface of things.

Masking, Staging, and Performing

Kikuchi and his mates knew very well by July 1942 that such exchanges had to be surreptitious. Barely a month into incarceration, Kikuchi had already learned this lesson. The entire camp community—and the way in which he described it in his diary—seemed to come out of a traditional Japanese Noh play. Like the wooden masks worn by Noh's main characters, surface appearances concealed an underlying emotional reality. Kikuchi simultaneously picked up on and became susceptible to this superficiality:

It was nice and sunny today and everyone was out in their best Sunday clothes. I even got the urge to see how it was to wear my slacks again. The flag raising ceremony for the official opening of Tanforan was held in the infield and several thousand people were in attendance. A surprising number of Issei were in the group, and they gave the pledge of allegiance with the rest. The Boy Scouts raised the flag . . . Newspaper photographers were also around to take pictures. But flag waving alone will not solve the problem.[58]

The tableau he describes has a remarkably "staged" feeling to it: photographers from the outside world transmitting patriotic images to the rest of the country; savvy first-generation Japanese Americans saluting the flag, knowing full well that their constantly questioned allegiance would publicly be affirmed; Boy Scouts in their familiar costumes handling the ceremony; and all of the internees wearing their own costumes, or their "Sunday best," including Kikuchi in his best pair of slacks. Like Myrdal's description of America's failure to fulfill its creed, this scene speaks to another disjuncture in America's democracy: U.S. citizens, wrongly imprisoned, were paying fealty to a country that had explicitly marked, segregated, and rejected them. Keeping this in mind, Kikuchi cuts against the surreal and sunny imagery of the event with the warning of his final sentence: flag waving will not solve anything.

He then persists with this theme of surface imagery versus substance, turning his attention back toward the reality of camp life, away from the ephemeral and ultimately unsatisfying display of "patriotism":

> Things look calm enough on the surface, but there seems to be a grow-
> ing conflict between parents and children over minor things. The Issei
> haven't adjusted themselves and consequently are more touchy . . . Ru-
> mors are rife that there are some cases gone "batty" in the Hospital, but
> the Hospital will not release any information.[59]

Contrasted against the flag-waving imagery, this rendering of camp life reveals a more realistic and more complicated portrait of the internment experience. Per-forming patriotism, as it were, could hide only so much. But this "masking over" and "saving face" did not apply only to internees observed by Kikuchi at Tanfo-ran. The comment above on "batty" patients in the hospital especially brings to mind the tale, albeit fictional, of a Poston inmate who went mad. In "The Legend of Miss Sasagawara," by Hisaye Yamamoto, the title character is an elegant and accomplished dancer whose mother passed away before she and her father were evacuated to "this unlikely place of wind, sand, and heat."[60] To cope with the loss of his wife, the Reverend Sasagawara, a Buddhist priest, pursues nirvana, "that saintly state of moral purity and universal wisdom," completely turning inward and forgetting about his daughter.[61] Miss Sasagawara, meanwhile, gradually falls prey not only to the madness of her father's otherworldly devotion, but also to her own mental illness, resulting in her institutionalization by the end of the story. Although many other camp residents, like the narrator, saw the daughter's madness, they did not see—behind the mask of her eccentricity—the "monstrous sort" of madness inflicted upon her by the perfection-seeking father, quietly but religiously, every day "within the selfsame room."[62]

For Kikuchi, this reflex of keeping things on the surface and hiding or not seeing what was underneath afflicted not only individuals in the camps, but the community's collective national leadership, as well. The frustratingly ineffectual JACL had been established in 1929, primarily operating in California, to combat anti-Asian exclusionary laws aimed at both aliens and immigrants in the 1920s and 1930s. But as it advocated on behalf of its 120,000 interned constituents dur-ing the hysteria and suspicion after Pearl Harbor, progressives like Kikuchi faulted the JACL for its moderate and accommodationist stance. Founded by business-men and other middle-class professionals, the group in its early years, according to one historian, "believed that the best way . . . to prove their worthiness in the eyes of Euro-Americans was to be totally loyal to American ideals, which they understood to be individualism, free enterprise, and the ownership of private property."[63] Additionally, "As loyal Americans, they *never* criticized racism, al-though they worked hard to challenge discriminatory laws." During internment, however, this philosophy strained the relationship between the leadership and its members. The organization not only encouraged complete cooperation with the government and unqualified acceptance of the terms of internment, but was also rumored to have harbored informers for the WRA within camp. By contrast, as Greg Robinson has emphasized, writers for the organizational newspaper *Pacific Citizen*, like Ina Sugihara and Larry Tajiri, played very much against type. Radical in their orientation, the two protested the internment, and even went so far as to link the Japanese American predicament with the struggle of African Americans and other minorities in the wartime and postwar periods.[64] These two intellectuals, however, were far from representative of the rest of the image-conscious JACL leadership.

At Tanforan, Kikuchi picked up on the topic of the JACL and its shortsighted style of governance. "There are many Nisei around here who belong to the JACL and they are doing a lot of kow-towing," he noted.

> They will get far with the [camp] administration, but they are only getting at the surface of things . . . The JACL people are good as individuals, but they don't have the background. A doctor, an insurance salesman, a laundry owner, etc., cannot and should not be expected to be good administrators. Yet they will be given the leadership because they want to "cooperate."

He then bemoaned the fact that the local JACL stifled debate, quieting any open complaint about camp conditions or the very fact of being incarcerated. Invoking the long tradition of protest in the United States, he queried:

> But if we are American citizens, I see no reason why we should not do it the American way instead of taking everything. I think this is the issue on which the JACL leadership missed the boat . . . Those in camp here are more concerned with keeping the streets clean than analyzing the reasons why we are here and discussing our future role and what we do about it.[65]

Based in Salt Lake City, just outside the evacuation zone, the national JACL—like any umbrella organization—tried to speak with one voice, but the group failed to realize how trenchantly the pain and trauma of internment had affected its members, and it did not acknowledge how much dissonance existed in its ranks. Thus, the national JACL purposely spoke with a voice quiescent, hushed, and stereotypically Oriental. People within the community, like Kikuchi, certainly dissented, speaking truthfully about the injustice of the situation and thereby challenging the racist image of the timid, hyperfeminized, and submissive Japanese. In this sense, the most earnest sentiments and opinions of the ostensible JACL constituency were best expressed through alternative outlets, like Kikuchi's diary, his bull sessions, and the letters he sent to those he deemed true friends. Ironically, however, as the next chapter will demonstrate, Kikuchi attempted to co-opt the JACL at Gila as a vehicle for progressive unity, but the institution's safely moderate position proved too entrenched to budge.

One other potential outlet for Kikuchi was his writing for the assembly center's newspaper, the *Tanforan Totalizer*. The Wartime Civilian Control Agency (WCCA) administrators kept the editors, including Kikuchi, on a very tight leash; subsequently, although vignettes of the business and organizational politics of the *Totalizer* appear throughout the diary, reading the sixteen issues (May 15–September 12, 1942) of the paper yields little in the way of substantive reporting or provocative editorializing. For such a liberal, or even radical, group of *Nisei* (who completely dominated the paper, to the Issei's great displeasure), the publication afforded them no space for dissent, no oppositional "counterpublic," and no alternative. Of course, this was by design, but the furthest the paper could go resembled a mild form of jingoistic propaganda. For example, the July 4 issue, according to Kikuchi, initially had two potentially hard-hitting stories: one on the camp's constitution, and the other on scrip books, fairly innocuous subjects. For unknown reasons, Frank Davis, the camp manager, wanted the pieces revised, recalling all copies of the paper and forcing the staff to unstaple 2,400 copies. At the end of July 1942, Kikuchi oozed pure frustration:

> We have to fight for every inch and never received much cooperation from the administration. We take the censorship in stride, feeling that there is not much use in trying to buck [camp leaders] with their Fascist ideas. The work has fallen into a routine and some of the old zip is gone.[66]

As Arthur Hansen has remarked, the *Totalizer* remained "quintessentially Nisei, in composition and form," albeit without the unbridled content found in papers and magazines listed in chapter 1.[67] Kikuchi surrounded himself in the *Totalizer*'s office with some members of his clique from Cal, like Warren Tsuneishi and Lillian Ota, as well as other liberal Nisei, including editor in chief Taro Katayama, Bob Tsuda, Bill Hata, and Jimmy Yamada. He would augment this circle of journalist friends with other sympathetic liberals, such as Mitch and Ann Kunitani, his brother Jack, and his friend Shibutani. As early as June 1942, Kikuchi wrote:

> Taro and the rest of us are disgusted with the whole setup. We were thinking of starting some sort of magazine, but we would have to work against too many handicaps so have given it up for the present.

Additionally, he noted off-handedly, "There are a number of Nisei in camp that have the ability to write," naming Yamada, Tsuneishi, Ota, Katayama, Tsuda, Kay Nishida, Alex Yorichi, and the poet Toyo Suyemoto. Another name mentioned is that of Toshio Mori.[68] Widely regarded as a pioneer in Asian American studies, Mori would go on to a successful writing career, publishing three story collections before his death in 1980.

Another talented Nisei whom Kikuchi admiringly recalled at a later stage in his diary is the aforementioned power broker Mary "Molly" Oyama.[69]

Each had become a major hub around which different networks of intellectuals, writers, and activists—Nisei or white—hovered. While Kikuchi was best known in the community for his role as Adamic's anonymous subject, Oyama undertook the daunting task of publicizing her family's traumatic resettling experience so that larger, perhaps white liberal, mainstream audiences would know exactly what the Nikkei had endured. Having already written for Adamic's quarterly, Oyama shared her story "My Only Crime is My Face" in *Liberty*, a popular magazine (along the lines of the *Saturday Evening Post*) whose contributors included P. G. Wodehouse, F. Scott Fitzgerald, and the infamous Sax Rohmer, whose Fu Manchu series helped sow the racist seeds of the "Yellow Peril." Oyama recounted her family's solemn journey out of Heart Mountain Relocation Center, sounding eerily similar to her friend Kikuchi:

> On the train my [son] Richard and his brother played with some towheaded, blue-eyed children who were in our coach. (I couldn't help but reflect that the only true democracy there is, is the democracy of childhood—before a child's mind is contaminated by the prejudices of adults.) A kindly soldier offered his coat "in case they're cold," when the children napped.[70]

Arriving at her final destination, Denver, she unconvincingly conceded, "We are living in poorer circumstances compared to our pre-evacuation status, but we are not unhappy."

Despite the fact that this sizable group of Nisei writers did not ultimately produce a magazine, as Kikuchi desired, he managed to forge ahead on the camp paper, developing his own column, "Your Opinion, Please!"—a variation of "the man on the street" reporting (taking opinion polls of residents) and benign commentary. He privately confessed, however: "I don't see much future in a center newspaper so will try to get into something more along the line of my interests and ability, if any."[71] True to his word, Kikuchi abandoned newspaper work once he reached Gila, opting for a career-building "apprenticeship" in the social welfare unit. Leaving Tanforan, though, also meant saying farewell to a remarkable collection of Nisei who formed a critical mass of dissent and a familial counterpublic of forward-thinking intellectuals.

The Kikuchi-Thomas Correspondence

Counting only those letters between 1942 and 1945, the span of the JERS, Kikuchi wrote to Thomas nearly fifty times, while in turn, she responded on roughly thirty occasions. This was, of course, largely due to the fact that Kikuchi worked under Thomas and reported to her whenever he sent along copies of his diaries. But over time it became quite clear that both were also developing a friendship, a point confirmed not only by their continued correspondence until Thomas's death in 1977, but also by the tone and content of their letters to each other. During the early years of Kikuchi's work on JERS, 1942 to early 1943, their exchanges took on the expected quality of a student-teacher relationship, one that was not unlike Adamic's mentoring of Kikuchi. In the summer of 1942, for example, Kikuchi wrote Thomas a now-familiar refrain:

> I am very much interested in this whole study, but I realize the subjectiveness of what I write. It is almost impossible to analyze a given situation now because it is so close to me. This will have to be done at a later date when I get a better perspective of the whole process. I would feel much better if you would criticize me roundly and let me know how I can improve my observations.[72]

Thomas was quite clever with her replies. Instead of dwelling on Kikuchi's self-perceived shortcomings, she responded immediately and directly with a laundry list of assignments, requesting case histories of the JERS staff, the "opposition" groups, and the newspaper staff. She treated him as if he had always belonged to her group of researchers, leaving little doubt whether he was worthy enough. This, of course, was a taut tightrope to walk. Kikuchi's traumatic childhood abandonment and life as an orphan always raised questions later in his life—and in his own mind, really—about whether he was good enough for a particular task, no matter what the context. To his way of thinking, after all, his own parents had deemed him unworthy of keeping at home. Therefore, Thomas also recognized the effect her positive reinforcement had had on Kikuchi in the last few months, and consistent with this approach, offered:

> I want you to know how valuable I think your diary is. It is really a mine of information, insights, and valuable interpretations. And a wonderful record of a remarkable family.[73]

Increasingly, the two correspondents began to shift away from the mentor-student dynamic. The first turning point came during Kikuchi's years in Chicago, starting in the spring of 1943, when he was charged with taking care of two younger sisters—Bette and Emiko—while working on the life histories of Nisei resettlers for JERS. At this transitional stage, both Dorothy and W. I. approached Kikuchi with avuncular sympathy, sending Bette a coat for the brisk Midwest winter and simultaneously helping Jack (Kikuchi's brother in San Francisco) gain entry into medical school (a task, incidentally, left unfinished by Stella and Louis Adamic).[74] When the Thomases visited Chicago during this time, they took the whole Kikuchi clan out to dinner, and in 1944, they encouraged Bette to apply to Bennington College, even offering to help her find a scholarship. Much as Adamic had lent a fatherly or brotherly ear to Kikuchi's troubles, the Thomases temporarily took on the mantle of surrogate parents not only for Charlie but for many of the Kikuchi siblings as well.

In early 1945, Kikuchi took a month-long trip to the Bay Area to work further on JERS, but also to revisit some of his old haunts around Berkeley and
San Francisco. He often dined at the Thomases' home during this period, and
the accompanying set of diary entries provides telling evidence of the evolving
relationship between Kikuchi and Dorothy (and W. I., for that matter). Kikuchi's
description of the Thomases' house and his attention to the details of their lives—
when read in concert with the observations he made when visiting Louis and
Stella Adamic at Thanksgiving in 1945 (discussed in the previous chapter)—once
again demonstrate his growing friendship with the couple, but also, significantly,
his persistent attempt to find and re-create a surrogate family, in this case with a
pair of academic parents.

During his first visit with them, he noted how "roomy and comfortable" their
home was, how spacious W. I.'s study was, and how their dining-room table was
made from a door. "After relaxing in such a comfortable home," he stated, "I
felt the California people were very lucky to have such good housing." After fill-
ing himself with three servings of Dorothy's salmon salad, he shared "a cocktail
which almost knocked me on a loop" with W. I., who "was looking as spry as
ever . . . [and who] never seems to age at all." Concluding this initial stay, he
emphasized how comfortable he had been, "It really feels like a home there."[75] A
few weeks later, he enjoyed an even more intimate time with the two, "relaxing
around a real fireplace with pine wood burning in it." He mentioned having a few
more drinks with W. I. this time—"cocktails before dinner, beer, and a highball
after dinner," to be exact—and he recognized that a good drink was one of the
older man's favorite pastimes: "W. I. has good whiskey . . . He can remember
when Canadian Club whiskey only cost .95 a quart." The thought leads W.I. to
reminisce about his own youth, when in "the days after the Civil War in the
South . . . twenty-five cents was a good wage for a day's work." He informed Kikuchi that he used to be "a crack shot with the rifle," so much so that his brother
would confidently hold pennies between his fingers for W. I. to shoot out: "He
said that dimes were too scarce in those days to waste in this manner."[76] Whether
or not these were tall tales inspired by the warmth of the alcohol or the fireplace,
the anecdotes go a long way in reflecting Thomas's comfort level with Kikuchi,
a kind of warmth and closeness that Kikuchi seldom felt around his own family.

Dorothy, for her part, mirrored W. I.'s affection, sitting down with Kikuchi to
look over family albums and tell him of her own personal history. She shared the
fact that when she was an undergraduate at Barnard, classmates marked her as "a
radical because she smoked and bobbed her hair." When she graduated, they drew
a bomb under her yearbook photo, making it plain that she was a "Bolshevik."
Thomas then showed Kikuchi her baby pictures and described how her mother
had been a secretary for a branch of the Bonaparte family: hence, Dorothy had
Bonaparte crown silverware, andirons, and other such belongings in her home.
In this vein, Kikuchi picked up on many fine details regarding the Thomases and
their home. He noticed their Seth Thomas antique clock, their custom of always

eating chocolate with coffee after dinner, and, finally, the fact that "W.I. relaxes by reading western stories, while Dorothy's tastes run more to good detective stories." With this last observation, Kikuchi felt vindicated: "I guess it's okay for me to read funny [i.e., comic] books."[77] Taken as whole, these observations come across as somewhat scattershot, but in the context of Kikuchi's experience, the attention to home décor and the eccentricities of the homeowners hint at Kikuchi's desire to have a real home (and metonymically, a family) to which he could return and around which he could repeatedly feel "comfortable" (a descriptive that frequently came up in his writing during these occasional visits). At moments, his remarks resembled those of a son-in-law trying to acquaint himself with his new "parents." His last comment regarding comic books even sounded like the relief of a little child who discovers that his hobbies do not greatly differ from (or fall short of) those of his parents.

On March 7, 1945, Kikuchi spent his only remaining evening in San Francisco with the Thomases, who had agreed to throw him a fitting bon voyage party. Dorothy even played the role of matchmaker, purposely seating Kikuchi between two young female researchers. Kikuchi remembered it being like a holiday dinner with family:

> W. I. plays the host in a magnificent manner, and we all thought he was the life of the party . . . full of repartee and quick on the draw . . . It was a most enjoyable meal—turkey, tomatoes, pie, etc. I made the rice! . . . W. I. served his special cocktails, and we also had wine for dinner and highballs later in the evening.[78]

Returning to Chicago to be with his sisters, Kikuchi noted, "It makes me feel sad to be leaving here after getting to know everyone so well."[79] Once again he seemed to be leaving his desired family unit with a wistful yearning that at least allowed him to process his sadness.

But the final test whether Kikuchi and Thomas had cultivated a friendship, not just a working relationship, came in the summer of 1945, when he was facing induction into the U.S. Army. For months, Thomas wrote the draft board on Kikuchi's behalf, admittedly fearful of losing one of her best researchers, but more desperately concerned for the welfare of a young man who had grown to be her close friend. As early as 1944, she had lobbied on his behalf. "I know that this must be very upsetting to you," Thomas wrote in an authoritative, maternal tone.

> You are of great value to the Study, and I shall make a strong case for deferment on this basis . . . I know that you are a chronic worrier, but I wish that you would try to be a little less fatalistic in this case, and leave the burden of worrying up to me until we really get some sort of decision.[80]

In time, of course, the deferral requests reached their limit, and Kikuchi entered the army in mid-August. Thomas bade him an appropriate farewell. "So at last you are 'in,' or very near," she began.

Now a new era begins for you, and we are all wishing that it will be a
happy and successful one—not the interlude in the Army, but your long-
time future in the postwar world. You have certainly shown that you've
got what it takes.[81]

It was a generous gesture, written before either of them knew the bombs would
drop on Japan and effectively end the war in another week. In other words,
Thomas could not have been sure that Kikuchi would not see action on the bat-
tlefront. As she always had, she bucked up his confidence and made sure that he
knew she had great faith in him.

In return, Kikuchi's initial letters out of boot camp were all addressed to
Thomas. Writing on stationery emblazoned with the United Service Organizations flag, Kikuchi reported:

I'm finally settled down in a regular company here [Camp Lee, Virginia]
so I can start to receive mail. It's a pretty rugged life but I have no com-
plaints so far . . . There are no other Nisei in our company so I guess I
won't be able to get any notes on them for the Study.

Nonetheless, like the budding social scientist Thomas had groomed, Kikuchi
kept his well-trained eye on an area of his expertise:

I don't like what I have seen of the South—in social conduct. For the first
time in my life, I have seen the Negro segregation on streetcars and in
public places—in Richmond, VA.[82]

Just as he would grow to appreciate and sympathize with African Americans in
the Windy City, Kikuchi here demonstrated that exposure in the army to Jim
Crow helped him understand his own segregated internment experience much
more clearly. In this context, the "Negro problem" and the "Oriental problem"
did not seem so dissimilar.

At the same time, despite drawing unsettling connections between past and
present, he attempted to communicate some levity to Thomas:

In spite of some dumb propaganda with which we are indoctrinated, my
morale is fairly high—and I think I'm even enjoying some of it! It's all in
the mind, I suppose. We have a nice bunch of fellows in our barracks,
along with some very dumb ones, and I rather enjoy talking with them.[83]

At this point, the war had come to its conclusion, and it was apparent that Kikuchi would be able to find a more manageable army assignment in a psychiatric
social welfare unit in New Jersey. As a result, Thomas picked up on the lighthearted banter Kikuchi offered:

You certainly picked a swell time to be drafted. My hope now is that they
will keep you in at least ninety days so that you will get the G.I. benefits.
Then I would really like them to demobilize you so that you could do
some work for us.[84]

Clearly, some of the anxiety over Kikuchi's wartime fate had subsided; two successive letters in September 1945 informed Kikuchi of her plans for publication of part of his research material in the second volume of the study. Thomas also appeared quite preoccupied, keeping her letters uncharacteristically short and businesslike. However, she still managed to include traces of her usual concern and warmth: "I look forward to getting your diary, when I assume I will not only read everything that has happened to you, but will also find out how Bette and the other members of the family are getting along."[85]

The two would keep up their correspondence over the next thirty years, particularly in the late 1960s and early 1970s, when Charlie collaborated with Modell to publish the first nine months of the Kikuchi diary. Thomas had been the one to introduce Modell to the diary in 1970. The letters exchanged between Thomas and Kikuchi took on a much more adult, collegial tone as Charlie updated his former mentor on the progress of his work, his wife's exciting dance career, and the signal events of his children's lives. A testament to how much Kikuchi felt influenced by Thomas, however, may best be captured in a single fact: when Charlie and Yuriko were expecting their first child, a daughter named Susan, his first choice of a name for her was "Dorothy."[86]

W. I. Thomas and Bridging Theories of Race Relations

Frank Miyamoto, a leading JERS researcher, was a friend of both Kikuchi and the Thomases. After earning his PhD from Chicago in 1950, he went on to teach sociology at the University of Washington for thirty-five years.[87] Miyamoto admitted that he had no specific knowledge of W. I. Thomas's official contributions to JERS, but felt confident in saying that W. I. strongly influenced how Dorothy conceived and ultimately shaped the study. Citing the theoretical underpinning of W. I.'s "definition of the situation," Miyamoto stated:

> The Thomases acknowledged that subjective definitions play a critical role in determining adjustmental behavior. This way of approaching social research produced a pragmatic open-mindedness that precluded the use of any particular theory of human behavior as the underlying scheme.

Given this understanding, Miyamoto asserted:

> I believe it was this very general formula that guided the JERS fieldwork. Inasmuch as these ideas derived from W. I. Thomas' theory of research, I believe that he exerted a fundamental influence on the project.[88]

Robert Spencer, an anthropology student under Robert Lowie at Cal, was a JERS researcher from 1942 to 1943, and partnered with Kikuchi at Gila. After JERS, he wrote a dissertation on Japanese Buddhism in the United States and became a professor of anthropology at the University of Minnesota. In addition to being research partners and peers, Charlie credited "Bob" with leading him "to participate in Japanese cultural activities" that he had previously avoided.

> As a result, I learned about sumo, go, mochi pounding at New Year's, Zen ceremonies, Japanese kinship, and many other aspects of culture in the seven months that we worked together. My view of Japanese culture moved from negative to tentative.[89]

Kikuchi also recognized Spencer for changing his approach to life histories, putting less emphasis on the goal-oriented approach that social work had encouraged in Kikuchi. Spencer also affirmed Miyamoto's claims about W. I.'s sway:

> It is worth stressing that Dorothy S. Thomas owed to his influence her perception of the Japanese-American problem. Throughout the years of research, W. I. Thomas remained in the background, not contributing directly perhaps, but making his theoretical position felt both by his wife as well as by her assistants. The compilation of life histories, those to be found in the second volume of the JERS summary, *The Salvage*, finds a parallel in the case studies of Polish peasants.[90]

Kikuchi unambiguously credited W. I. for persuading Dorothy that the life histories had to play a more substantive role in JERS at this particularly crucial stage.[91] He even remembered W.I. dispensing explicit advice later that year:

> W.I.'s words of advice which sounded logical to me were that we should collect all the data we could first. He said that it would be a crime for me to change my approach in the case documents by trying to apply preconceived theories, amen. He felt that we should emphasize the following of the individual careers [i.e., life histories] without trying to dig out any psychological interpretations as we go along as that would limit our work.[92]

Now, to be clear, it would be patently false to assume that Dorothy Swaine Thomas was a mere front woman for W. I.'s puppetry and theorizing. After all, as mentioned above, when the original architects of JERS pulled out in early spring 1942, because of wartime commitments to the government, Dorothy was left to bear the weighty work of at least four other men (Lowie, Aikin, Milton Chernin [social welfare], and Frank Kidner [economics]). Robert Merton has reminded scholars of the equal contributions Dorothy and W. I. made to "the Thomas theorem."[93] However, I would like to emphasize W. I.'s influence at this point in order to place him in a role of intermediary, bridging the work of his older Chicago School colleagues, like Park, and those of JERS researchers like Kikuchi. This does not signify a privileging of Park's theories in reading the Kikuchi diaries. Rather, it should give readers a sense of, and a context for, the race-relations theories contemporaneous with and familiar to Kikuchi and other JERS researchers. In other words, how did Kikuchi understand interactions between the races at this particular time (1942–1943)? How had scholars like Park conceptualized and established theories of race relations in the period leading up to this historical moment? The common factor in the answers to both of these questions is W. I. Thomas.

In his study of the Chicago School, Fred Matthews explicitly identifies the connection between Thomas's Polish peasants and Park's "Negro and Oriental problems." He begins by showing how this school of thought recast the analytical lens: "The essential approach of the 'Chicago school' in psychology and social psychology was . . . important in shifting scholarly attention away from the biological roots to the cultural and environmental determinants of personality, and, on the level of psychological concepts, the replacement of 'instincts' by 'attitudes,' which were products of experience and interaction, and therefore changeable to a degree." Matthews then cites the source for this transformation: "In particular, W. I. Thomas' discussion of the Polish peasant in America in terms of the disorganizing impact of a new environment upon traditional attitudes was to have considerable impact upon Robert Park's own work both on the adjustment of European immigrants and on the relations between black and white."[94] Park himself would say that *The Polish Peasant* demonstrated that "social attitudes . . . could be used in characterizing local cultures as well as in measuring, in some fashion, cultural and institutional changes," additionally calling "attention to the fact that the situation of the European immigrant in the United States can be defined in terms that imply its logical relation to that of the Negro."[95] Matthews concluded: "This perception formed the framework of all Park's work in the field of race relations and ethnic adjustment: the relations between Negroes and whites in the South, Orientals and whites on the West Coast, Poles and Anglo-Saxons in Chicago, were all to be seen in interactional terms, as examples of the contact and collision of culture, a process which was one of the most important energizing forces in human history."[96]

Since his days at the Tuskegee Institute as press secretary and ghostwriter for Booker T. Washington, Park had long been concerned with the "Negro problem." But Park first expressed his deep interest in the conundrum of the Oriental when he led a team of researchers, recruited by Christian missionaries, to conduct the Survey of Race Relations (1924–1926) on the Pacific Coast, during a period that saw the most exclusionary anti-Asian immigration laws put on the books. The survey primarily defined "Oriental" as Chinese and Japanese, with East Indians and Filipinos getting short shrift, and its simple objective was to scientifically explain the nature of race relations and the impact of immigration on the West Coast. As Henry Yu has persuasively argued, Park saw this research as an incredible opportunity: "As both immigrants and a 'nonwhite' race," Yu writes,

> Orientals provided the ideal link between the Polish peasant and the Negro problem. All three of these research interests—race relations between Negroes and whites, the adjustment experiences of European immigrants, and race relations between Orientals and whites—were linked by one foundational theory.[97]

Yu then points to the interaction cycle, or race-relations cycle, as the operating principle behind the survey, identifying it as "the most important concept within the Oriental Problem for the next forty years."

In the *Introduction to the Science of Sociology* (1921), Park and Ernest Burgess established the four stages of the interaction cycle: competition, conflict, accommodation, and assimilation.[98] According to Park and Burgess, whenever two groups come in contact with each other, they inevitably compete over territory and jobs.[99] Made aware of their differences, or brought to "self-consciousness," the two groups then enter a stage of conflict, which is highly politicized and marked by increasing hostility. The third stage, accommodation, reflects the agreement, whether by force or compromise, either that one group will accept subordinate status or that the groups can coexist. Assimilation, the final and most stable stage of the cycle, is "a process of interpenetration and fusion in which persons and groups acquire the memories and sentiments and attitudes of other persons and groups, and, by sharing their experience and history, are incorporated with them in a common cultural life."[100] Yu, however, picks up on potential exceptions to the rule: "The main aspect of what Park saw as the Oriental Problem was the inability of Orientals to achieve the last step of the assimilation cycle because of 'race consciousness' among whites."[101] This did not necessarily mean that the interaction (or assimilation) cycle was inaccurate in theory, for "just because Negroes and Orientals had not yet been assimilated into American society [this] did not mean that they could not or would not be assimilated."

Matthews attempts to clarify further by stating that Park "made the crucial assumption that relations between black and white, or Anglo-Saxon and Chinese, must be studied not solely in the historically unique context of contemporary race relations in America but in the context of sociological process and comparability," namely, in the context of the race-relations cycle. "What is important," Matthews continues, "is less the innate qualities of the different racial groups than the terms and stages of their interaction and the attitudes which are produced therein."[102] Park, unfortunately, put a great deal of faith in people's ability to choose freely and wisely at these different stages, thereby failing to acknowledge "the constraints inherent in the environment in which individuals and groups construct their activities."[103] In other words, he focused so intently on the interactions themselves that he insufficiently factored in the role of outside forces, like white resistance, or fully considered the importance of social class in such interactions.[104] Park's own students, like St. Clair Drake, Horace Cayton, and E. Franklin Frazier, certainly picked up on this shortcoming, and over time "each pointed out that the fate of the black community was overwhelmingly determined by decisions made by whites and upon events occurring outside the black ghetto."[105] Park's theory simply did not hold up well in practice. Additionally, as Yu asserts, Park operated from a belief that cosmopolitan whites would lead the charge, willingly recognizing differences and allowing for a common cultural life. But, as Yu cautions, "this should not blind us to the fact that, at the time, Park's analysis and his pride in association with African Americans [and Asians] were not widely shared among white Americans."[106] More specifically, not only were most contemporary whites not cosmopolitan in orientation, but even those who were did not necessarily agree with Park's tack. Thus, it became increasingly apparent that Park's belief in the inevitable "interpenetration and fusion" of markedly different groups at the assimilation stage was naïve. Whites wielded the most power and influence, and their interactions with Blacks and Asians were based on inherent bias and the imbalance of power and resources. The dynamic of nonwhite assimilation would prove to be exceptionally complicated.

Shifting the Lens

While—as Park's work suggests—white reactions to Asians and white interactions with African Americans are both fruitful paths of inquiry to pursue, my greater interest lies in following the less worn path. It is of equal, perhaps greater, significance to understand how African Americans intersected with and viewed their Asian neighbors and coworkers. The chain reaction of internment and postwar resettlement filled cities with intermixing and competing Blacks and Japanese (and other Asians), as succeeding chapters will demonstrate. And Kikuchi, his head swimming with freshly absorbed concepts of social science and theories of interaction, provided a running commentary and analysis.

In the end, aside from anecdotal evidence that Kikuchi and JERS researchers used Park's office at Chicago's Social Science Research Building, north of the Midway on 59th Street, as a base for a short time, Kikuchi never met Park in person. Nonetheless, it may be assumed that Park's race-relations cycle was not entirely unfamiliar to Kikuchi and his colleagues, given the popularity of the theory at the time in (theirs and other) social-scientific circles.[107] Additionally, both Park and Kikuchi admitted to being heavily influenced by Thomas's life-history approach; hence, their work shared similar foundations. If nothing else, Kikuchi became intensely aware of the stages of the interaction cycle (with all of its strengths and weaknesses) not only in theory, but—by the time he had spent a year in the Windy City—in practice as well.

Consequently, Kikuchi was substantially exposed to the ideas, practices, legacies, and lives of three of the most preeminent scholars of his day: Adamic, Dorothy Thomas, and W. I. Thomas. How Kikuchi understood and experienced race relations in light of such acquired knowledge would grow clearer in Chicagoland during resettlement. First, however, he still had more time to bide and more patience to lose in a San Bruno horse stall and the scorching desert of Pinal County, Arizona.

Chapter 5

The Tanforan and Gila Diaries: Becoming Nikkei

Stable 10. Stall 5. That was where the Kikuchi family spent its first four months (May–August 1942) of incarceration at Tanforan Racetrack. As previously noted, Kikuchi cautiously, even if not reluctantly, had decided to rejoin his family during the initial phase of the internment. Before evacuation, he had occasionally interacted with his siblings but rarely visited his parents. In fact, the period of the internment and resettlement represented the most time Kikuchi would ever spend with his family of origin. Even though they would survive the trauma of internment together, including Kikuchi père's death, it did not appear to be a bonding experience that Kikuchi could build upon in the postwar years. It surely was not for lack of trying. As early as July 1942, Kikuchi infused the connection to his family with the greatest significance: as an index of his Americanism, a sign of his loyalty to the nation. The following excerpt lays bare how closely Kikuchi aligned success within his own family with his ideal of the American family.

> Here all of my life I have identified my every act with America but when the war broke out I suddenly find that I won't be allowed to become an integral part of the whole in these times of national danger. I find I am put aside and viewed suspiciously . . . Americanism is my only solution and I may even get fanatic about it if I'm thwarted. To retain my loyalty to my country I must also retain family loyalty or what else have I to build upon?[1]

Kikuchi's intertwining of his two aspirational families is striking. Filiopietism translated into patriotism or, to use his term, Americanism. The two wrenching traumas of his life up to that point—abandonment at the orphanage at eight years old and the roundup of Japanese Americans (abandonment by America) at twenty-six—seemed to slip back and forth into one another as his senses (both literally and figuratively) started to falter: "I keep saying to myself that I must view everything intellectually and rationally, but sometimes I feel sentiments compounded of blind feelings and irrationality . . . My set of values gets twisted; I don't know what I think."[2] "Blind" and "twisted": Kikuchi's better judgment is impaired, rationality giving way to sentiment. The source of his Hamlet-like vacillating was the news that Tanforan residents (of which there were nearly 8,000 at maximum capacity) would have to evacuate either as family units or as individuals to one of the ten relocation centers.

The Kikuchis were deciding between Tule Lake, California, and Gila in Rivers, Arizona, the latter of which they ultimately chose. However, in the confusion of this transitional period, Kikuchi was truly wrestling with issues that had wracked him emotionally for most of his life. His next observation shows just how discombobulated he felt as he allowed undeserved guilt to engulf him.

> If I am to be in camp for the duration, I may as well have the stabilizing influence of the family. If I go my own way again at this time, it will be the end as far as the family is concerned and they may feel that I ran out on them in a time of crisis. If they were holding me back, it would be another matter; but actually they are shoving me forward. The family setting gives this whole thing a more normal balance.[3]

Desperate to have one of the older siblings take over in light of the father's failing health, and fearful of an unknown future in the camps, the Kikuchis were pushing "head of household" on Charles, again despite his having been a relative stranger to all of them. Instead of their collective guilt, or at least the parents' guilt and irresponsibility over Charles's neglect, the Kikuchis allowed the oldest son, their oldest brother, to feel as if he were at fault, as if he had made a choice at eight years old to leave his abusive father and ambivalent mother, as if he had abandoned them to go "[his] own way," when the truth was starkly the opposite. "It will be the end" and "they may feel that I ran out on them" are poignant reminders that even at the age of twenty-six, Charles Kikuchi still felt very deeply like that orphan left in Healdsburg eighteen years before. On the one hand, who could blame him for wanting to be with his family, especially after nearly two decades apart from them and now in the midst of an unprecedented crisis? On the other hand, he was well within his right—legally, morally, and emotionally—to go his own way. But he did not. Feeling their "shove," he sought the family unit, no matter how dysfunctional it had proved and would still prove to be in the future; he even inexplicably perceived his family's presence as providing "normal balance."

Immediately before the family's departure for Gila, Kikuchi reiterated this newfound optimism on August 31:

> In reviewing the four months here, the chief value I got out of this forced evacuation was the strengthening of the family bonds. I never knew my family before this and this was the first chance that I have had to really get acquainted. There is something wholesome about it and with the unity which it presents, one does not feel alone, knowing that there are some who will back one up in moments of crisis.[4]

Kikuchi is careful, however, to qualify his musings by the end of his daily entry: "Of course, we have only had four months of this life and things may be different after we have been in camp for a much longer period."[5] He assumes a willful amnesia about the previous months in Tanforan, running the risk of greater disappointment in the months ahead at Gila. Only six weeks earlier, for example, the entire family unit almost unraveled in one fell swoop over the aforementioned issue of establishing a "head of household." On July 11, Kikuchi reported that the family's debate over who should lead the family onto Gila came to a head. The father, already suffering from physical and mental infirmity (and a year away from his stroke), had exclaimed that he wanted both Charlie and the second son, Jack, to take over family matters. The mother objected, singing the praises of Alice, the sister who had been keeping things together ever since the oldest sister, Mariko, had left the family and fled to Chicago. Different siblings took opposite sides, but in the end, the father's decision still won out. In the midst of all of the heated discussion, however, Nakajiro resented Alice's defense of her mother, Shizuko, to the point that he admitted to Charles that he was going to hit his daughter for what he considered her insolence.

Worse, resentment had festered for so long between the parents that Nakajiro had taken a paranoid, stubborn attitude toward his wife, thinking that she was constantly cheating on him, that she believed being a barber was low class, and that "she was too proud to walk with him in public because he looked like an old man."[6] Seventeen years his wife's senior, Nakajiro could not control his growing dementia and jealousy. Kikuchi provides a chilling example:

> He said that at one time when Mom went to S.F. for a divorce he almost killed the four [youngest] children and planned to commit suicide. That was one of the reasons why he never lived among the Japanese—because he feared that the men would try to steal his wife.

Of course, with the benefit of hindsight, Kikuchi wrote about the animated argument with an adult's calm but also a detached emotional immaturity: "This was one chance in which I had an opportunity to practice social case work." For eighteen years, this family had been developing its own dynamic, its own choreography of arguing, and its own way of being without Charlie. And before he was ultimately appointed paterfamilias, half wanted him to take charge, while the other half still did not quite know who he was. In this larger, more realistic context, rereading Kikuchi's August 31 entry above ("strengthening of the family bonds" into a "wholesome . . . unity") raises the question of how much he was willing to deny in order to finally have his family.

"A Process of Education"

When the Kikuchis left the Tanforan horse stalls behind at the beginning of September 1942, they were also leaving behind a more cosmopolitan group of evacuees, all of whom had lived in the Bay Area. The Gila River Relocation Center, on the other hand, housed a cross-section of diverse groups of Japanese descent from the West Coast: rural and urban, older Issei bachelors and Nisei families, Kibei, some Hawai'ian Nisei, worldly Angelenos, Berkeley academics, and San Joaquin Valley farmers, among many others. The center was located on land belonging to the Gila River Indian Community, comprising the Pima and Maricopa tribes. The reservation never authorized the building of a prison camp on its sacred land, but the federal government never asked for permission: Milton Eisenhower, the head of the WRA, did not want to relinquish control of the center to the Office of Indian Affairs, because of the camp's potential for profitable agricultural production. Hence, the Office of Indian Affairs simply gave the WRA a five-year lease on 16,500 acres of land (as a quid pro quo, many of the camp's administrators were Indian Affairs employees). The center opened on July 20, 1942, and closed on November 10, 1945. Two different camps existed at the center, three and a half miles apart—Butte and Canal—housing 13,348 internees at their peak. Two camp factories completed projects for the military: one made camouflage nets and the other, model warships; the latter produced eight hundred models for the U.S. Navy. Although summer temperatures averaged an unforgiving one hundred degrees, two other features distinguished Gila from the other nine camps: internees tilled and cultivated seven thousand "profitable" acres of crops through a vast, labor-intensive agricultural program; and Butte touted the best baseball diamond in all the camps, designed by "the Father of Japanese American Baseball" and Fresno internee Kenichi Zenimura.

The Kikuchis ended up in Butte, the "more cosmopolitan" of the camps, according to Robert Spencer, who had already been in camp for JERS and helped the family move in. Sharing unit 65-9-B with a Nisei couple, the family took their time getting used to the cramped and dusty barrack in the desert. For his part, Kikuchi not only continued his diary keeping for Thomas's study, but also took a position with the camp's social welfare unit, a job that fit his graduate work and exposed him to the lives of all types of Japanese living in camp. As he describes it, Gila was much more a "process of education" than Tanforan had been.

> Up until that time, the Nisei to me was in a category that was more intellectual and academic. That started in the prewar situation and then also on the campus. Then making labels, "Nisei is *this*," you know? And I think I continued some of that broad definition of categorizing *Nisei, Japanese, country people* . . . and it wasn't until I got to Gila that I began to separate [out that] "*this* is an *individual*."[7]

Instead of abstractions or theories about mainstream Nisei, Issei bachelors, or "hicks" from the country, Kikuchi could finally put much of what he had learned at Cal into practice and take a hands-on approach to people's problems in the privacy of his welfare office. In the process of intimately getting to know these internees as individuals, he had to learn to forgo seeing groups or cliques within the camp as monolithic, and as a consequence, he began to soften and reconsider his previously less informed and less empathetic attitudes toward all of these discrete groups. Reflecting on this period decades later, Kikuchi conceded that Gila indeed had been a formative moment in his own process of becoming Nisei.

> If I hadn't gone through that experience [in the social welfare unit], I probably would have gotten out of camp very rapidly. I would have had this brief exposure to the Japanese American society and that's the end of it. But because I stayed for those seven months or so I suddenly became a *Nisei* although I did not take on all of the outward appendages of a *Nisei*.[8]

Fortunately for Kikuchi, his maturity relative to the rest of the Nisei population (the average age was twenty-two in Gila, seventeen in all camps) served as an anchor for the myriad changes he faced:

> I had my own particular adjustments to make. But I saw that as part of the process of being Japanese American so that I didn't have to fight it so much.

Furthermore, unlike many others in his position (e.g., Ichiro, the fictional protagonist of John Okada's *No-No Boy* [1957]) who were dealing with double or triple kinds of consciousness, Kikuchi stressed that he had gained enough perspective and had cultivated indispensable coping mechanisms before arriving at Gila. He concludes, "The fight was not internalized to that extent that I became immobilized or angry or confused." Hindsight once again affected Kikuchi's recollection of that evolution, since I would argue that, on the contrary, he had internalized the struggle for identity, as many young people in their midtwenties are wont to do (especially those with unconventional childhoods), while confronting a series of extreme external pressures. On the other hand, Kikuchi did at least offer substantive evidence for his claim of calm objectivity.

For example, he vividly recalled the case of an Issei farmer on whom the entire unit of social workers had given up. The older man faced inoperable stomach cancer, colostomy bag and all, and most likely suffered from encephalopathy—an inflammation of the brain common to end-stage cancer patients, which can cause hallucinatory spells. In his spiraling decline, the man had taken mercurochrome used for doctoring wounds, painted his bed sheet to look like a Japanese flag, and then stood on his bed and waved the flag, asserting his love of Japan and yelling at anyone who came into his hospital room. At one point, the staff attempted to send in a social worker—under Kikuchi's charge—who could speak Japanese, in hopes of settling the addled man; instead, he threw a shoe at her and told her to leave. "So I decided I'd go see him," Kikuchi remembers.

> I had nothing to lose. At that point, when I entered his barracks room, I didn't see him as a Japanese nationalist with a Japanese flag . . . I saw a dying individual who had to have something to justify his life. He felt that being a Japanese was something he could strongly identify with.[9]

Kikuchi's intervention allowed the staff to get some food into the older man, and in time, the Issei calmed down enough to just sit and talk with Kikuchi during his final days. "I didn't understand what he was saying," recalled Kikuchi.

Yet there was some kind of communication going on. I couldn't put it into words. The man ultimately died and I was with him.

Kikuchi recognized that this was a significant turn in his thinking about the Japanese in America. As suggested above, he did not see the sick older man as a "nationalist," but rather as an individual with a specific personality in a specific cultural context: a dying man who had farmed for all of his life without recognition and who now felt he had little connection to anything—except to his original home. Those particularities were what moved Kikuchi with regard to this case and pushed him further away from stereotyping, grouping, and "categorizing," as he might put it. "I was able to accept it," he says.

> I didn't see him as Japanese, whereas if he had been a well person and put up a Japanese flag, I would have reacted . . . "Well, he's not being American enough. Why isn't he speaking English to me?" This kind of behavior.

But the context was quite different, and Kikuchi's knee-jerk impulse to derisively call all Japanese "Japs" was altered dramatically by intimate exposure to people with real-world problems and individual personalities. In his interview with Arthur Hansen, Kikuchi haltingly offered, "I think that whole experience of working with these individuals . . ." He paused in midsentence, took a moment, and resumed with redirected certainty: "I learned *a lot* in terms of the cultural factor in case work."[10]

Contrast these observations with some of the first impressions recorded by Kikuchi when he first arrived with his siblings in Gila and scouted the available housing. While it is unsurprising for people to express trepidation under new circumstances, and groups or families tend to turn inward, territorial, and isolationist under extreme pressure—like moving into a barbed-wire camp with military overseers—Kikuchi's commentary is still quite cutting, markedly condescending in its tone. On September 2, 1942, he wrote:

> The next place we went to, there were some old Issei in the place. "Old Frog Voice" raised great objections to anybody moving into his domain . . . The old lady in there was one of those rural, Japanese types— very crude and rude.[11]

Emiko and Bette, the two youngest sisters did not like it there and, "made many disparaging remarks about the Japanese 'hicks.' "[12] After two days in camp, Kikuchi had already seen enough of the rural Japanese to say:

> I know I don't like their messhall manners. They come in all sloppy and sit down and gobble up their food without saying one word all throughout the meal. There seems to be a very large percentage of the Issei group eating at our messhall. They don't even ask for anything— just reach right over your plate and grab it. Some of the waitresses are Issei women and there is much more Japanese spoken here than in the Tanforan group.[13]

Even in the microcosm of the dining hall, many different elements blur in Kikuchi's mind at this early point, mostly descriptors with a negative connotation: Issei, rural, working class (waitresses and farmers), and the Japanese language. With little sense of irony, the family longs for Tanforan—the horse-stall barracks—because of its Bay Area cosmopolitanism. Their conflation of disparate elements of the Japanese—as monolithically "Jap" or as the singular Other—is troubling but not necessarily unexpected; nor is it a type of chauvinism exclusive to the Nisei.

The historian Evelyn Brooks Higginbotham, for example, defines "the politics of respectability" as a forceful dynamic sprung from the tensions felt by middle-class Blacks, established in cities like Chicago when southern working-class migrants arrived to take advantage of industrial job opportunities. Although Higginbotham's analytical model referred specifically to the women's movement in the Black Baptist church (1900–1920), it nevertheless provides a useful precedent for the phenomenon the Kikuchis experienced a generation later. She writes:

> Respectability demanded that every individual in the black community assume responsibility for behavioral self-regulation and self-improvement along moral, educational, and economic lines. The goal was to distance oneself as far as possible from images perpetuated by racist stereotypes. Individual behavior, the black Baptist women contended, determined the collective fate of African Americans.[14]

Unquestionably, this type of strained relationship and high set of expectations informed Kikuchi's view of his rustic campmates:

> They have very few college people and the leaders are the doctors and church people . . . The rural element can be seen in all of these mothers sitting out in the porch, breast feeding their babies. Nobody pays any attention to them.[15]

With a petulant flourish, Kikuchi insists: "In Tanforan, I did not see one baby being breast fed in the open."

For all of the family's insecure classism and judgment, however, one can still detect a minor shift in Kikuchi's thinking as he spent more time in Gila. As described above, acknowledging his fellow internees as individuals within certain cultural contexts laid a sturdy foundation. A handful of factors helped weaken his biting rhetoric and boorish behavior. First, Kikuchi began to take his role as the oldest brother more seriously; early in their Gila experience, the only family members present were Charles and three younger siblings—Emiko, Bette, and Tom. Especially at that point, he realized how important his influence could be. At one point, he berated himself: "I am afraid that Tom is reflecting some of my attitudes as he makes remarks about those 'Japs' [who] don't know how to speak English at all."[16] After confessing this in his diary, as if in penance, he immediately went on to describe the "clever" rock garden an older Japanese had begun building, as well as "a beautiful baby crib" the former carpenter put together with some extra lumber. To provide shade, other neighbors had constructed "real fancy" extensions for their barracks, "porches . . . done with an Oriental type of architecture." His observations then turned even more attentively to the agricultural prowess of the "country people":

> A large percentage look like they have been used to manual labor all of their lives and they are pretty healthy. I see them in the shower rooms in the evenings and they look all muscles and are tanned from the outdoor life—although many of them are gnarled and almost bent over. So far I have seen very few of the soft fat type of man who has lived an easy life.

Perhaps unconsciously feeling guilty about what he had said about these "Japs" to his younger brother, Kikuchi expressed a genuine respect for these hard-working people he initially deemed "hicks." He continued:

> Even the women around here look as if they have been used to hard work all of their lives . . . They wear the simplest hair dresses and no makeup. In this camp, many of these farm women will no doubt live a much easier existence.

His admiration does not seem at all canned at this point; in fact, Kikuchi sounds as if the sun-drenched images of these lean, unadorned workers remind him that not too long ago he too was stooping to pick vegetables in the valley and migrating from summer job to summer job just so he could pay his college tuition. In comparison, these country folk labored year-round. Kikuchi understood the dignity of that reality: "6,975 acres of this land has already been used for alfalfa for the past 5 years." He then intimated that the vast acreage will pose little challenge for these skilled rural folk: "There is a large percentage of the farming people in this camp so that they will not lack for experienced hands."[17]

At Cal, Kikuchi had consciously avoided the so-called mainstream Nisei, those who might have formed the Nisei Club and stayed within the self-segregating circle of Nisei. He took pride, as well as great comfort, in being on the margin of that mainstream group, largely because he could safely critique the parochialism he attributed to those by-the-book Nisei from a distance. The radical Nisei—Kikuchi, Tsuneishi, Shibutani, Murase, Ota et al.—clung to a highly intellectualized, nearly self-abnegating discourse. As budding sociologists and social workers, they believed that integration (unlike assimilation, which seemed like a capitulation to exclusively white, middle-class values) was the proper course for Japanese Americans of the younger generation. Kikuchi therefore appeared more a radical reformer from the edge of the mainstream group (but still within its orbit) than any kind of expatriate revolutionary from outside the sociocultural group. In many ways, then, Kikuchi's evolving self-identification as a Nisei at Gila was not entirely surprising. As was the case with many Nisei during the internment, a surplus of external enemies provided easy targets toward whom all the Nikkei community could direct its collective anger—including the internal security chief W. E. Williamson, who conducted a witch hunt for disloyal internees;

the ill-prepared WRA administration; and the feckless head of Kikuchi's welfare unit, William Tuttle.

For example, when Tuttle took over the social welfare unit, he arrived in the winter of 1942–1943, just as the desert weather quickly worsened. During this time, Kikuchi was in charge of basic amenities like housing and clothing; he would dispense it to the neediest or most indigent in the camp community. However, the WRA employed a strict means test—whether an internee qualified for welfare based on a predetermined maximum of money—before assigning housing or giving out staples like blankets or winter clothing. Completely oblivious of the season's conditions, Tuttle followed strict protocol, expecting those working under him to check internees' bank accounts (if they had one) to determine who qualified for winter clothing and who did not. This struck inmates as the height of absurdity, just as it did one of the unit's own employees, Kikuchi. He recalled:

> I felt that that was not really the function of the welfare department: to be involved in determining whether the evacuee had sufficient funds for clothing or whatever. I thought you should just give it to them. And *that* was not the function of the social worker: to decide whether that person deserved it or not. That was not the role. The role of the worker was to help in every possible way. And I guess I felt that if you had to bend the rules, you bent the rules.[18]

Therefore, Kikuchi gave evacuees blankets or whatever necessity they requested, obviating the humiliation and impracticality of applying a means test to a people already disenfranchised. This particular situation—an inane, cut-rate bureaucracy laced with explicit racism—helped close the gap between Kikuchi's cartoon definitions of Nisei, Issei, Kibei, rural, or single, and reality. "Even though it might have been very dishonest from someone else's criteria," he remembered,

> I did not see that as dishonest. I just looked at it as a need on the part of the individuals. And whether I had feelings about that person being Americanized or not had nothing to do with it. He needed it. That, in the end, proved to be part of my education in accepting people as individuals.[19]

Changing Lenses: "The Hansen Thesis"

Kikuchi's every move, his every thought was recorded, whether he achieved success or suffered failure. The uncertainty, the ambivalence, and the angst felt by the rest of us in agonizing experiences usually go unnoticed and thankfully undocumented for scores of people to see and judge. For Kikuchi, however, his life was and remains an open book to any reader. All of us are cracked vessels, free to make errors in the privacy of our own lives. In many ways, though, like most "public" intellectuals (admittedly, a loose term for Kikuchi), he did not have that luxury; his limitations and blind spots stand up on the page as much as his val-iant ideas and courageous acts. In this context, then, what I term "the Hansen thesis" (after the scholar Arthur A. Hansen) provides clarity and another helpful road map through this intellectual's peripatetic life.[20]

Most importantly, Hansen convincingly makes the case that Kikuchi under-went three distinct stages of identity formation. First, from his time as a child growing up in the multiethnic orphanage (1924–1934) at Lytton Springs through his tenure with the Yamato Garage Gang and his concurrent four years at racially and economically diverse San Francisco State (1935–1939), Kikuchi was exposed to an unusual but nurturing set of multiracial milieus. Therefore, by 1940, Kiku-chi had established a strong, foundational multiracial identity. Second, through his NYA study of the Nisei and especially during his time at Cal, Kikuchi took a genuine interest in the Nisei "genus." Granted, Kikuchi also wore it as a badge of honor that along with the era's phenomenal cadre of budding Nisei intellec-tuals, he was still on the margin of the mainstream Nisei, those "squares" who flocked to the Nisei Club, the Berkeley Fellowship, and Nisei churches. Even if he considered himself a radical on that margin, though, Kikuchi was nonethe-less within the larger group's orbit and understood clearly what it meant to be identified as Nisei. Furthermore, his incarceration at Tanforan and his dedicated (but ultimately censored) commitment to the *Totalizer* was another sign of his growing political consciousness as a Nisei, while the numerous bull sessions he enjoyed with left-leaning cosmopolitan liberals like the Korematsu brothers, Tsuda, and the Kunitanis only solidified his credentials as a Nisei leader by the time he reached Gila.

Third, what he described to Hansen as "becoming Nisei" might more accu-rately be translated as his "becoming Nikkei." The "cracked vessel" analogy comes back into play here, since Kikuchi was simultaneously guilty of bald-faced chau-vinist and elitist views toward Issei bachelors, the farmers, and the porch women who breast-fed in broad daylight while also feeling deep respect for the bent but unbroken bodies of the Issei farmers and doling out clothing and cold-weather supplies to poor families who would not have passed the WRA's means test. His Nikkei identity, then, augmented the layered foundation of his multiracial Ni-sei identity. It should also be noted that various factors during his incarceration at Gila finally opened Kikuchi up to the possibility of identifying himself, with qualification, as Nikkei: his frustration with the WRA; his contentious position in the Gila JACL; his connection to this intergenerational community through the social welfare unit; and his wading into the violent Issei-Nisei political maelstrom in camp. Kikuchi realized that the cultural markers did not matter as much any-more: he needed to see each person as an individual (including himself), even if he or she had different cultural politics. Recognizing his own Nisei-ness, or his own Nikkei-ness, within this uniquely experiential context, he could feel part of an even larger body, like a member of another "family," with all of its challenging complexities and global networks: that is, of a piece with the Japanese diaspora.

A War within the War: Kikuchi, the JACL, and Issei Political Will

The irony here is that Kikuchi's American or democratic urge toward individualism (and toward seeing his fellow evacuees as individuals) belied the deep tension among the multiple groups at Gila that grew out of cultural expectations of abiding by a generational hierarchy. As Arthur Hansen and Paul Spickard have previously demonstrated, cultural politics and institutional politics (in the form of camp councils or the JACL) were in contested flux throughout the war. Using a wide lens, Spickard correctly asserts that Pearl Harbor brought about the diminishing role of the Issei in Japanese American communities before evacuation:

> Whole Japanese communities were paralyzed by the FBI raids. They were left leaderless. The Issei who remained did not have the skills of leadership, or they refused to risk being arrested themselves . . . The institutional processes of the Japanese American communities nearly ground to a halt. The only Japanese American organization in a position to deal with the crisis was the JACL.[21]

Under the new leadership of its executive secretary, Mike Masaoka, a Nisei, the JACL trumpeted the notion that the second generation, "not the Issei of the Japanese Associations, were the true leaders of their communities."[22] Furthermore, as seen in *Common Ground*, Masaoka had written the "Japanese American Creed," an explicit pro-U.S. manifesto, which he paired with a movement to completely dissociate the JACL from the Issei. When FDR issued Executive Order 9066, however, the JACL offered little resistance, appearing passive and complicit. Many of the groups in camp, regardless of affiliation, believed that the league had identified the radical and dangerous elements of the communities to the authorities before evacuation. As rumor and resentment spread, then, Masaoka and the accommodationist JACL looked like the Nisei version of Uncle Tom. Hansen adds:

> So great, in fact, was the animosity toward the JACL by the time of the community's incarceration in assembly centers that they tagged many of the leaders with the pernicious label of *inu* (dog; informer) and threatened them with, or administered, beatings. Accordingly, the WCCA administration prudently adopted a policy disallowing formal organization of JACL chapters.[23]

Kikuchi, for his part, could not stand the JACL before his arrival in Gila. Along with other progressive Nisei intellectuals at Cal and in the state college system, he vociferously opposed their jingoistic cheerleading before the war and continued to express his distaste for the organization throughout his Tanforan stint. For example, during community elections in the summer of 1942, Kikuchi said of one JACL leader at Tanforan: "He dominates the present council and bootlicks like hell for personal advancement." He continues, "These God damn JACL's . . . They are not even aware of the problem as a whole and yet they profess to be the leaders of the Nisei."[24] Spickard elaborates on this oppositional group of progressive intellectuals: "Like the JACL, they were intensely patriotic; but they had more concern for the maintenance of civil liberties." After citing Gordon Hirabayashi's conscientious stand against the evacuation (for which he spent ninety days in prison and whose case came before the Supreme Court), he points out:

> Their education and political liberalism cut them off from the people in their communities, for few Issei had been past grammar school and most Japanese Americans were relatively conservative. These liberals were talented but unorganized. They could oppose the JACL as individuals, but they could do little to unseat it.[25]

In the end, Spickard argues, the mainstream Nisei assumed leadership of the JACL, assiduously attempting to speak for all Japanese Americans during the internment and serving as the liaison between governmental agencies and the communities.

The Issei, generally speaking, saw the wisdom of stepping back from leadership roles that might attract too much unwanted attention during the war. But in Gila River, Hansen argues, the Issei in Canal camp put up a fight for less public but culturally important (and ultimately powerful) leadership positions, resulting in the blacklisting and beating of prominently positioned Nisei or other Japanese sympathetic to those camp leaders. The WRA wanted the Nisei in positions of public leadership because, compared to the Issei, they were more Americanized, spoke English fluently (thereby facilitating the transaction of any official camp business), and appeared less hostile toward the WRA. Additionally, the power structure established by the WRA prioritized Temporary Community Councils, which could be made up only of Nisei or American-born Kibei citizens, explicitly leaving the alien Issei without representation. This form of governance profoundly offended the Issei, especially those in Canal who were largely from rural areas in the Sacramento Valley delta and the San Joaquin Valley (Butte, where Kikuchi lived, contained a better cross-section of urban, rural, and suburban internees). Disgruntled evacuees expected the administration and the younger generation to observe a particular hierarchy with deep roots in Japanese cultural norms, a practice rarely obeyed by the quickly Americanizing Nisei (with the exception of the rural, valley Nisei).

By November 1942, things came to a head when the Issei acted upon their frustration over deteriorating camp conditions. Hansen states:

> Living quarters were inadequate, stoves had not arrived, the food lacked quality, clothing allowances were short, and toilet and washing facilities were abominable . . . The Issei blamed camp conditions on a system whereby the government, army, WRA, and camp authorities had ignored the natural leaders of the Japanese American community, and leaned on an artificial "leadership" of inexperienced, incompetent, and misguided citizen appointees.[26]

Forming an oppositional force under the aegis of the Ken-Kyu-Kai ("study group"), the Issei took on much more actual power in Canal. Its membership "overlapped and interpenetrated a medley of formal and informal internee groups emphasizing Japanese cultural forms and practices," including the Kibei Club, the Sumo Club, the drama and literary clubs, the Zen Buddhists, and the Judo Club, among others.[27] While it theoretically was a group organized to study the poor conditions of the camp, the Ken-Kyu-Kai instead met to target certain camp leaders who sympathized with the WRA-appointed Nisei or the administration itself, as well as other high-profile positions, like the editors of the camp newspaper or the wardens appointed to police their own people. Fed up with what they perceived as favoritism and sycophancy, five members of this informal Issei-led coalition attacked and severely beat Takeo Tada, a Kibei-Nisei, on November 30.

Tada's crime? He appeared to be too close to the administrations of his assembly center (Turlock) and relocation center (Gila). Tada had been in charge of clothing and coupons for the Turlock store when shortages seriously affected Issei and Kibei bachelors, leaving them without clothing allotments or any coupons with which to buy supplies at the camp store. Even though Tada was not responsible for the shortage, many of his fellow Turlock campmates still carried a lingering resentment against him when they all relocated to Arizona. Appointed to the Temporary Community Council and the Community Activities Section at Gila, Tada did little to assuage any of the Ken-Kyu-Kai's concerns when, because of circumstances beyond his control, he failed to procure enough equipment and supplies for the camp's numerous recreational clubs. To add insult to perceived injury, Tada—in his capacity as liaison and spokesperson for the camp administration—denied recognition to the Kibei Club and would not provide it with any meeting space. That was the last straw for the Ken-Kyu-Kai crew. Tada seemingly represented everything they detested about the Nisei leadership: he was a self-promoting university graduate who was cozy with white administration leaders, a JACL supporter who was a member of the WRA-handpicked Community Council. At Canal, therefore, a line was drawn in the sand: you were either with the Issei or against them.

Meanwhile, over at Butte camp, contrary to all his normal instincts, Kikuchi was considering membership in the Gila chapter of the JACL (notably, the only chapter established at any of the relocation centers). On November 4, he was elected secretary. As a consequence, and given his role in community affairs (as part of the housing and social welfare unit) and his associations with prominent Nisei, Kikuchi was beat up by unknown assailants on December 23, an event that understandably frightened him and fueled his desire to leave camp as soon as possible and resettle. More surprising than his being assaulted, however, was his puzzling about-face on the JACL. Consider Kikuchi's own reaction to his election. Calling himself a "hypocrite," he wrote:

> I almost fell over when they announced that I was elected. I had just gone
> to the meeting to "observe" and I never had been a member and was op-

posed to the group. I'm not even a paid-up member! What a joke! When Shibs, Mitch, and some of my other "radical" friends hear of this, they will roar with laughter.[28]

Kidding aside, two legitimate factors influenced Kikuchi to take the risk of joining this "targeted" group. First, Kikuchi's partner and confidant on JERS, Spencer, convinced Kikuchi to attend the meetings, if for no other reason than to gather data for their field reports to Thomas. Kikuchi had already begun speaking with members of the Kibei Club, so Spencer thought coverage of more "groups" in camp would make for a thorough accounting. As mentioned above, Spencer was an anthropologist by trade, one who had studied many of the traditional elements of Japanese culture, and throughout his partnership, he encouraged Kikuchi to view particular events as cultural practices rather than as overtly political acts of Japanese nationalism. "I wouldn't have done it otherwise," Kikuchi recalled.

But Bob said, "Go to the sumo matches," and all these little festivals that he dragged me to. So I learned a lot. [I thought,] "It's funny, I'm learning about Japanese culture."[29]

As noted above, his attitude toward "all things Japanese" correspondingly improved from negative to comically "tentative" (what would pass for "positive" for any other person).

Second, what started out as an intellectual exercise for him evolved into a potential reform movement:

Maybe I can help them push the program of Americanization even to the point of the parting of the ways with the Issei, if necessary. The leaders of the JACL here are the leaders in the community. The group is the closest thing to a liberal group that I will find here. Shouting from without won't do much good. It also does place me in a position where I may get to know the leaders well.[30]

He concludes the entry by joking, "I can just hear Warren [Tsuneishi] saying: 'Alas, poor Charles, I knew him well, / Before he joined the Stuffy JACL!'" Perhaps exceedingly naïve, Kikuchi thought the JACL—as the "most liberal" of groups at Gila and the bane of Canal's Issei population—could provide the vehicle (or even just a conduit) for the kind of Americanizing that Kikuchi envisioned: integration rather than assimilation; a break with overtly Japanese practices; and a strong national voice through intellectual journalists, like Tajiri, the editor of the *Pacific Citizen*, who always wrote opinions as if he were solidly to the left of the entire JACL.

What appears remarkable is that forty-six years later, Kikuchi remembered his written rationale above almost word for word (with no checking of his diary during the interview), confirming many friends' claims that he possessed a photographic memory:

I had early on arrived at a decision that, "Well, if you can't beat them, join them and see what you can do from within." I honestly believed that maybe if the JACL chapter in Gila could get well organized that they could do a lot of things in terms of the goals that I myself believed in . . . The JACL leaders that I had met in Gila seemed to be of a much more liberal personality . . . I really thought that by pushing JACL membership that I might be able to affect its policy to some extent and to help it to develop as a strong force in the community.[31]

He remained well aware that the league's larger reputation was overwhelmingly negative, and he underestimated the staying power of its historical standing: his dream of transforming it was noble but, frankly, naïve. The older members of the community had already taken so much from hostile parties (the government, the WCCA, and some Nisei) that they were not going to remain passive any longer, especially toward those who were supposed to be representing their interests and rights. One of Kikuchi's closest friends in Gila was an older like-minded Nisei named Ken Tashiro, an editor for the *Gila News-Courier* and an officer in the JACL. Given how much he respected Tashiro, their friendship alone might have been the major reason for Kikuchi's joining the Gila chapter. However, the friendship also stigmatized Kikuchi in the eyes of the more conservative elements in camp, including the Ken-Kyu-Kai in Canal. To these Issei, Tashiro's leadership in the JACL was offense enough, but his close ties to Tajiri through the national newspaper put him over the top. Therefore, guilty by association, Kikuchi was considered inu, a possible informant to the camp administration. And near the end of December, he literally and physically absorbed their message.

Before that fateful night, though, Kikuchi kept his word and aggressively conducted a recruitment drive for the JACL, especially among the youngest generation of Nisei, even when confronted with widespread Issei parental disapproval. He enjoyed some success: the Gila chapter of the league ultimately boasted nearly a thousand members. In the process of recruitment, however, he gained a strong sense of the generational divide among the Nikkei as a whole, but this time, instead of simply dismissing the Issei, as he would have only months before in Tanforan, he genuinely tried to understand their motivations for such staunch opposition. For example, the federal government had given Gila the camouflage-net project for internees to work on and explicitly demonstrate their contribution to the war effort. Kikuchi reported that the evacuee head of the net project was having trouble garnering enough community support for the job, and, worse, this leader had already received threats from the older groups. "As usual," Kikuchi opined,

some Kibei and Issei are opposed to the net project because they do not want the evacuees to help the government in any way. There has been a deliberate rumor started that the J.A.C.L. got the net project here in an effort to discredit the organization. As if the J.A.C.L. has that much influence![32]

A little further along in that day's entry, he tempered his frustration toward the anti-JACL Issei and Kibei by emphasizing an anecdote from his day in housing and welfare. Sixty-nine-year-old Mr. Ikeda (an Issei) was desperately looking for a job so that he could provide clothing and sundry essentials for himself and his elderly wife. Unfortunately, most employment was already spoken for: in the mess halls, Issei women filled the majority of positions, and Nisei workers almost exclusively filled spots on the camouflage-net project. What is more, Ikeda was much too old to exert himself in any open slot. Kikuchi noted that Ikeda

> had a slip from the doctor saying that he wasn't strong enough to work and [that] he recommended welfare assistance. But Ikeda wanted to work. Because of his needs, he had to accept the welfare.

After muscling a grant of five dollars for Ikeda from the unit, Kikuchi then declared with sympathy: "This was quite a blow to his pride."[33] As he returned to his barrack, Kikuchi found a package from the old man, a gift. His reaction is a striking measure of just how far Kikuchi had come in his conscious efforts to understand the Issei as individuals rather than as one large collective opposing the Nisei. Kikuchi observed:

> I was extremely angry. At first I thought that it may have been a bribe on his part. Then I stopped to think of his past actions and I realized that this gift was an expression . . . of an independent attitude. It made him feel good to show me that he still had money left which he could spend as he pleased. His motives were of the best.[34]

Being a man of strong "independent attitude" himself, Kikuchi could appreciate Ikeda's generous gesture, one born out of cultural and personal pride as well as the custom of "saving face." Whereas Kikuchi would previously have skewered Ikeda for being too "Japanese-y" and traditional, or not "Americanized enough" and a "Jap," he now distinguished the man behind sixty-nine years of labor, the individual struggling in the middle of an Arizona desert, and the husband and wife just trying to do their best under the worst of circumstances. Kikuchi was not only doing his job as a social worker in the welfare unit, but also performing the morally appropriate duty of serving "the least of these." Ironically, through his commitment to seeing and valuing individuals in the community, Kikuchi was slowly, surely becoming a member of the entire Nikkei family.

Slipping Inside the Breaks and Looking Around

That same winter of 1942, Kikuchi recounted an afternoon's passing conversation. "I was walking over by the Butte this afternoon and I stopped to talk about the camp with a Negro workman who was digging postholes for the fence which is going around the place," he writes. The young African American asked Kikuchi about the loyalty of Japanese Americans, and disappointed to discover that the majority of Nisei (including Kikuchi) pledged allegiance to the United States, the workman responded:

> Boy, you are making a mistake. Why should you be loyal to a country that don't want you? . . . This is a white man's country and all the colored peoples of this world has got to change this so that I can get a good job just like a white man and I don't have to dig post holes to lock you Japanese up who are born in California. You help this country out and they will turn around and give you a kick in the pants afterwards.

Kikuchi responded:

> I suggested that maybe these things would be changed with a democratic victory, but he thought I was crazy. "Man, you read too many books. Too much education make you believe something that don't come true. The white man don't ever give you a chance. I should know that."

Kikuchi reflected on this dialogue:

> What a joke! Here I am, a person conceited enough to think that I am just as good an American as anybody, but I have to be put behind a fence dug by a black man who doesn't even feel that this is his country . . . It just doesn't make any sense. In wartime, nothing is ever rational.[35]

Both the exasperation of the anonymous workman and the subsequent surprise expressed by Kikuchi represent only a fraction of the emotions involved in a number of interactions between Japanese Americans and African Americans during this period. Issues regarding political alliance, military segregation, common legal battles, intercultural "exchange," housing, and intermarriage gained more prominence as the two minorities met each other more frequently in neighborhoods, at work, on the street, and even within the confines of a concentration camp. Kikuchi systematically recorded and analyzed such newfound and complicated interactions in his diary, providing persuasive firsthand knowledge of and evidence for arguably *the* watershed era in relations between African Americans and Japanese Americans.

While Blacks and Japanese had interacted before this time, they had never previously been forced—in such large numbers and with such regularity—to share urban spaces so intimately, compete for similar jobs so intensely, or agitate for civil rights with such collective might. In the wake of the evacuation in the winter of 1942, abandoned homes and apartments in "Little Tokyos" were quickly rented to African Americans, Mexican Americans, and Filipino Americans. By the end of the war, in 1945, the government permitted Japanese Americans to return to their former neighborhoods, filled now with a host of other minorities. Both relieved at their regained freedom and fearful of nativist violence, Issei and Nisei clustered once again in Nihonmachi (San Francisco), Little Tokyo–Bronzeville (Los Angeles), and Yesler Way (Seattle). Others joined small but established communities in Chicago (as the Kikuchis would), New York, and New

Jersey, in cities that also housed significant Black populations. Hence, this deliberate relocation left African Americans and Japanese Americans in the city little choice but to interact in both public and intimate spaces. The next decade, however, would witness substantial "yellow flight" out of the so-called ghetto, and by 1970, as mentioned in the introduction, the number of mainland communities where two Japanese American families lived next to each other barely registered demographically.[36] To take one specific and relevant case: between 1942 and 1950, approximately thirty thousand Japanese Americans settled in Chicago; by 1960, only fifteen thousand remained.[37] Given these statistics, the 1940s proved crucial in the historically significant interaction between Nisei and African Americans.

Kikuchi's narrative fills the interstices between conventional African American and Asian American history, demonstrating that both are more complicated and more interconnected than we have been led to believe.[38] The lineages of these allegedly "discrete" histories are not pure and unmixed. In fact, there was much cross-pollination between the races—either for political advantage, ideological exchange, strategic organizing, or even for love, in the form of intermarriage; for example, as mentioned earlier, Kikuchi's younger sister Bette married an African American postal worker named Gene Orro. Japanese Americans did not always choose whiteness, and sometimes inhabited what Craig Wilder has previously termed "a situational Blackness," a type of active resistance to the status quo and a refusal to be imprisoned by what would eventually be called "the model minority myth."[39] These individual rebellions, like that of Kikuchi, contributed to a culture of dissent, social reform, and individual agency: a type of interracial counterpublic. The histories and conversations embedded within that culture reveal what ultimately limited those individuals or what limited their society in the quest for long-lasting interracial alliances. Their history also reveals what was possible.

Kikuchi's understanding of the relationship of the local to the global helped him contextualize the Japanese American predicament within a larger racialized framework that had dismissively elided the "problems" of the Negro, the Oriental, and the immigrant. In many ways, the experience of racially driven, institutionalized internment simply reinforced his belief in the necessity of multiracial and multiethnic alliances and in the insidious interconnectedness of racism on many fronts. Kikuchi rejected the false comparisons between Blacks and Asians imposed by white America, unequivocally refusing to play a game of racial competition—pitting protest minority against model minority—thereby allowing for his principled appeal for interracial coalitions.[40] Much like the wartime slogan of African Americans—"Double Victory"—Kikuchi dreamt of tyranny overcome abroad and democracy achieved at home.

For him, assimilation was not simply a stamping out of Old World cultures, customs, and languages. Rather, it required both the genuine acceptance of New Americans by Old Americans, and the nation's full commitment to integration—not erasure—of the diversity of its minority and immigrant cultures (in a nod to his mentor Adamic). What is more, Kikuchi felt that the stories of Nisei and other minorities had to be shared and their situations defined (much in the way

W. I. had encouraged). Given his varied experiences as a migratory farm laborer, an internee, and an active social worker with minorities before and after camp, Kikuchi envisioned a democracy that was truly multiracial and multiethnic, one that could address both racial and socioeconomic dilemmas in more expansive terms. American democracy, as he knew it, had consciously enslaved and interned its own people—making it no different from the fascism bleeding Europe and Asia.[41]

As evidence, Kikuchi observed the following in the autumn of 1942, after his arrival at Gila:

> It does seem a little inconsistent that our war aims conflict with what is carried on in this country in many states. Evacuation of the Japanese is just one small, but important part of it. The problem of our 13 million Negro population is much larger.

He then cited greater implications:

> Treatment of colored people in this country is directly connected to our "aim" to free the colored people abroad . . . If the ideals of the Atlantic Charter are carried through it certainly will make a difference to the Negroes, Mexican, Japanese, Chinese, and other non-caucasian groups living in this country.[42]

He situates the "Negro problem" within a larger wartime and global context, prefiguring the efforts of participants in the Bandung Conference of 1955, including Carlos Romulo (Philippines), Jawaharlal Nehru (India), and Kwame Nkrumah (Ghana).[43] Kikuchi thus represented a notable departure from the Asian American intellectual tradition. A progressive, he steadfastly adhered to the primary organizing principle of his philosophy: genuine acceptance of and equality for African Americans was not only the crucial starting point but also the key to a successful democracy in America and globally. Other racial and ethnic minorities should not only follow in the footsteps of African American freedom fighters but also support them in the midst of their ongoing struggle.

Kikuchi, it must be remembered, was a victim of child abuse. After his parents had placed him in an orphanage in Healdsburg, he created a surrogate family of his own among "brothers" who were African American, Native American, Mexican, Chinese, and white. As the discussion of "the Hansen thesis" above suggests, this unique situation prepared Kikuchi for numerous interracial and interethnic relationships later in life, and made multiracial environments seem natural, familiar. The childhood period of abuse and abandonment not only fueled his disdain for his father, but also made Kikuchi particularly aware and protective of African Americans, the most severely abused members of the American family. Their "problem" was his problem. Once again, when African Americans fully achieved the rights of citizenship, the breakthrough would serve as a hard-won catalyst for other marginalized groups seeking their rightful turn in the democratic debate: this signified his one and only article of faith.

To demonstrate the broadly constructed lens Kikuchi used in viewing the "problems" of all people of color, consider the following conversation he had with an American Indian inside Gila in the fall of 1942. The young Arizonan delivered evacuees' mail from camp to the local post office beyond the confines of Gila, driving approximately 125 miles every day for his route. "He was very sympathetic to the people here," Kikuchi recalled,

> and thought it was a shame that such discrimination goes on. He asked if the MP's [military police] ever beat up any of the people. Some of the Indians in his village think that this is the case and they feel very sorry for us.[44]

The man told Kikuchi that he would like to visit during one of the holidays so that he could witness Japanese customs, but Kikuchi told him that they "did not celebrate any Japanese holidays," because they were "mostly Americans." He cautioned Kikuchi about the postwar period:

> If I were in your place, I would be afraid of going out for private jobs because of all the white people around here [who] hate you people for starting the war. I don't think you are to blame at all.

In a fascinating glimpse of the obstacles that lie in the way of interracial alliances, the man admitted that the local Native Americans also hated Japanese Americans immediately after Pearl Harbor, but after "many of them got jobs around the place and became acquainted with the people, they changed their minds and thought the evacuees were all right." Additionally, noted Kikuchi,

> He thought that we got treated worse than the Negroes, so I had to explain to him that we were making very good progress in California and the other coast states.

After the young Native expressed the opinion that "Indians were probably Asiatics and related to the Japanese," Kikuchi repeated his own call for solidarity: "I told him to be on guard against racial propaganda, because all of the minority groups should work together to see if we could solve the whole minority problem in this country instead of looking to Asia or Hitler." In a final statement particularly fitting given the setting, the young man "said that he was a good American, but sometimes he did not get treated as one." Kikuchi understood this sentiment completely.

Diagnosing the Problem

In 1944, Myrdal pinpointed American's dilemma, arguing that the nation had utterly failed to live up to its creed—generally defined as the lofty ideals of freedom, equality, and opportunity for all—by consistently and often violently depriving African Americans of participation in the democratic process:

In principle the Negro problem was settled long ago; in practice the solution is not effectuated. The Negro in America has not yet been given the elemental civil and political rights of formal democracy, including a fair opportunity to earn his living, upon which a general accord was already won when the American Creed was first taking form.[45]

Kikuchi's own lifelong quest to solve, or at least, address, this dilemma necessitated an expansive vision of what America was. While he certainly demonstrated his loyalty to the nation (e.g., by enlisting in the army), Kikuchi was not blinded by any notion of American exceptionalism. Rather, he expressed a greater loyalty to the ideal of democracy, looking forward to substantially transforming the definition of "Americanism" in the postwar years.[46] In examining the diaries written between 1942 and 1945, one finds that this struggle required a highly critical, sometimes contradictory, but invariably persistent scrutiny of America's democracy and its potential to be a multiracial one. Like Myrdal, or Cayton and Drake, Kikuchi believed the most crucial element for fulfilling the democratic creed lay deep within Black America.

Although he often called for a banding together of "the colored races," at other points in his diary Kikuchi acknowledges the difficulty in forming such "colored" alliances. In particular, he recognizes the challenges unique to African Americans, especially those posed by his fellow Japanese Americans. From Gila, he wrote:

Some funny fellow put a sign in our latrine today: "For Japs only. Niggers use the ditch!" I tore it down. I have seen little outward race prejudice among the residents here so far, but they definitely hold bias against certain colored groups.[47]

Kikuchi had gained firsthand knowledge of Japanese prejudice toward African Americans before his arrival in camp. In his diary for November 1942, Kikuchi remembered a prewar incident at Berkeley:

[Last] semester I took a Negro friend to a Nisei dance and the reception was horrible. He was ignored completely; there was an obvious reaction of disdain. Afterwards he said to me: "I feel like I was isolated. Why should the Japanese girls have such an arrogant contempt?"

Kikuchi ends the entry quizzically: "Could it be that these Nisei are compensating through projection—blaming others for their own failures?"[48] Despite looking for therapeutic explanations, he could not find easy, definitive answers.

He himself was not completely innocent of falling prey to simplistic theories of race when considering questions of inferiority. "Race prejudice works two ways," he postulated at Gila.

If a group feels superior and another minority group acts submissive, the feeling is bound to become more intensified and accepted. I doubt if the Nisei around here will get that submissive attitude which I have noticed among the Negro workers here.[49]

On the other hand, Kikuchi made no claim about the innate inferiority of Mexicans and Blacks (as Myrdal later would), but rather focused on the economic straitjacket imposed on both minorities from without. Class still intersected with race much more prominently in Kikuchi's incomplete calculus at this point:

> Prejudice against the Japanese arose in large part from economic competition. The Japanese arose beyond the level of a ready available labor force to be exploited, whereas the Mexicans and Negroes in this state are still in a submerged status.[50]

Two years later, in 1944, highlighting what he similarly considered the more difficult task lying ahead for African Americans, Myrdal stated:

> The Negroes do not, like the Japanese and the Chinese, have a politically organized nation and an accepted culture of their own outside of America to fall back upon. Unlike the Oriental, there attaches to the Negro an historical memory of slavery and inferiority. It is more difficult for them to answer prejudice with prejudice, and, as the Orientals may do, to consider themselves and their history superior to the white Americans and their recent cultural achievements. The Negroes do not have these fortifications for self-respect.[51]

As far as a commonly shared, traditional "outside culture" serving as a protective shield or touchstone for Asians, Myrdal's assumption may have held up if he had been strictly speaking of the older generation, the Issei, but with each successive generation of Japanese in America, ties to the old country surely wore thinner and thinner. In the postwar era, Nisei who had experienced internment especially deemphasized any common, older culture and tried to avoid looking too clannish, because they knew all too well the consequences.

The issue of language provides an instructive example: even though many Nisei attended Japanese-language schools, in addition to their full days at conventional American public schools, language retention remained weak. According to Hosokawa,

> In the early days of World War II, the U.S. Army interviewed 3,700 Nisei in a search for men to be recruited for intelligence work. Only 10 percent were sufficiently fluent in Japanese to be useful to their country.[52]

Certainly, failure of language retention alone does not signify complete abandonment of Japanese culture, but as Miyamoto notes, something was lost in translation:

> Nisei spoke poor Japanese. We could only talk about everyday things with our parents. While Nisei picked up some Japanese culture, they didn't understand Japanese concepts the way the way Issei understood them.[53]

Kikuchi recognized this particular tension, but took the opposite tack, encouraging his parents to study English classes in camp "because the young kids are growing up and soon they will not be able to talk to them in Japanese." His brother Jack added: "[Pop] should study it hard because the Issei may be given a chance for citizenship after the war . . . if they show that they are being Americanized enough."[54] Mixed into this dilution of cultural tradition was Kikuchi's initial distrust of the Issei and their potential disloyalty. At one point he wrote:

> Sometimes when I hear Japanese being spoken I have an urge to shut the whole thing out as if I were in a nightmare experience. I don't hate the Japanese here, but their conventional ways get me sometimes . . . They should really let themselves go occasionally, but you can't tell what is going on behind the Oriental mask.[55]

With that suggestive last sentence, hinting at the stereotype of Asians as inscrutable, shifty eyed, and the "yellow peril" incarnate, Kikuchi made plain the fact that, contrary to Myrdal's claim, he put little faith in a fall-back culture "outside America" for Nisei or, alternately, a poverty of culture for African Americans.[56]

Therefore, in the vast majority of his reflections on the challenge facing Black America, Kikuchi disregarded assertions of innate inferiority (or inability to retain culture) and instead drew attention to the systemic lack of recognition for African Americans, their agency, and their status as "people with problems," rather than as "problem people."[57] For example, in March 1943, still in camp, Kikuchi recorded a discussion with an ex-serviceman, also Japanese American, who discouraged him from enlisting:

> Another Negro I know in Pennsylvania. He work for a white woman. For 10 years after the [Great] war, he sleep with her. She like it. But one day a white man find them in the basement. So she scream "rape." They take the Negro out and lynch him. They say a white man's word is better than a black man . . . What is American? I tell you—it is man with white skin who think all other colors is low class and only fit for slaves.[58]

Earlier, the same man had exclaimed:

> I fight for this bullshit Democracy. They pat me on the back. But after the war, I get kicked in the face. I tried to get a job one time in an iron factory. They tell me: "We don't want no Japs!" I go all over the country and they say the same thing. Some Americans nice, but they don't like you behind the back . . . I don't have the democracy.[59]

In juxtaposing these two experiences, Kikuchi acknowledged the frustrations commonly shared by African Americans and Japanese Americans in their struggles to achieve freedom in the face of hypocritical white supremacy: both the Black Pennsylvanian and the Issei veteran were actively denied their rights (in the former case, his life) as citizens. Kikuchi emphasized the veteran's last sentence, not for its grammatical miscue, but for its literal, active-voice expression: the veteran wants, strives, and struggles for democracy ("I fight for this bullshit Democracy"). He does not simply wait for it, passively, to be handed to him. But "this country" does not "keep the promises," actively, often violently preventing others from possessing, from "*having* the democracy."

In the following excerpt, Kikuchi went further by endorsing the activist model set by African Americans during the last postwar period, seeing the potential for like-minded Japanese Americans to follow suit. He wrote, "[Bill Sasagawa] said that the Negroes only get things because they fought for their rights and we should do the same." Kikuchi's friend cited World War I and the intense racial climate generated by white resentment of Black migrants' coming north to fill wartime jobs. He remembered that Black soldiers returned from their tours of duty, having fought for democracy abroad, with little evidence of it at home. Kikuchi continued:

> After the war the Caucasians made a determined effort to drive all Negroes out. The returning Negroes refused to turn in their guns, but used them instead to stand for their rights. Bill did not mean to say that we should use guns, but that we should fight for what was ours and we would, if we really felt like Americans and believed in the democratic principles.[60]

As Nisei looked to the Black model of oppositional politics and resistance, African Americans likewise began to feel incipient solidarity with their recently incarcerated fellow citizens. For example, the satirist Schuyler—never known to shy away from controversy—repeatedly expressed his support of Japanese Americans in his *Pittsburgh Courier* columns, going so far as to predict their internment the day after Pearl Harbor, based on his intimate understanding of how American racism operated.[61] Writing just as the evacuation was under way, he opined that the incarceration "may be a prelude to our own fate. Who knows?"[62] Marc Gallicchio, however, reminds us of the precarious nature of this unified sentiment: "Despite general agreement on the injustice of the relocation, blacks faced with overcrowding in Los Angeles and San Francisco moved into the abandoned houses of the cities' 'Little Tokyos' and worried about the original inhabitants' return."[63] African American organizations waded into the issue, but with expected caution. As Allison Varzally's history of interracial California points out, only one official release came from the NAACP during a chapter conference in LA.[64] While a few individuals within those organizations protested the incarceration from the start, David Levering Lewis characterizes Walter White and other civil rights leaders as fearful of being collectively "tarred with the brush of anti-patriotism."[65] Given such precedent and context, Kikuchi's interactions with African Americans—during internment and relocation—demonstrate similar ambiguity and contradiction. On balance, though, Kikuchi faced slightly less conflict and more cooperation. For example, early during internment, amid a number of African American visitors to camp, Melvin Stewart, a classmate of Kikuchi's from SF State who was also planning to enter social work, spent time with his friend. Kikuchi had already expressed how upset he felt about Tanforan administrators formally recording the names of these suspicious African American friends and neighbors, as if a fifth column were forming right then and there in San Bruno.

> When [Stewart] saw all the Negroes around he said, "You know who are your real friends now. A lot of us are behind any movements that will fight this thing because we have had to face a lot ourselves and so are opposed to anything so un-American . . . We know you Nisei are just as loyal as we are. The color of the skin is no indication of loyalty—we can testify to that."[66]

Thankfully, however, the two racialized groups shared much more than oppression at the hands of a fearful, tin-eared majority.

Commenting on another development that same day, Kikuchi wrote:

> The Negroes are coming down in increasing numbers. Peter Ray, a well known dancer who used to perform with Duke Ellington's band, came to see Mornii and the other jive boys, and he drew a great crowd by his dancing exhibition.

Kikuchi then remarked on the "Afro-Americanization" of the camp's youth culture:

> The jitterbug craze is still strong with the young kids and for them nothing else exists . . . Last night at the dance they were all dressed up in their draped pants and bright shirts. These boys are really extrovert and many of them speak the same jitterbug language with the facial expressions which they copy from the Negroes.[67]

Around the same time, he wrote to a friend:

> The little girls and young kids still think this is a picnic and they spend all their time putting on "face stuff" and dressing up in their best slacks and then strolling around the tracks to draw admiring ohs and ahs from the sharp boys—some of whom are now under the S.F. Negro "Club Alabam" influence. They wear these pants that come way up to their necks and drop down to choke the circulation at the ankles.[68]

Both Catherine S. Ramírez and Luis Alvarez have recently reexamined the history of the zoot suit, wartime youth culture, and the riots of 1943, noting the multiracial use of the suit (by both genders) and the countercultural symbol it came to represent within younger communities of color. Undoubtedly, these oppositional practices, like wearing the zoot or club hopping around taxi dance halls, violated the time-honored customs of respectability and deference expected by whites in many major cities. Nonetheless, Alvarez adds: "Like Mexican American and African American zoot-suiters who clashed ideologically with the Mexican American and African American middle classes, Japanese American zoot-suiters articulated a cultural politics that rejected their inferiority and were skeptical of the desire to be like the rest of U.S. society."[69] Writing in his regular column "From Here to Yonder," Langston Hughes weighed in on the LA zoot suit riots of 1943, condemning the white mobs that invaded communities of color, targeting zoot-suiters but beating up by-standing war workers and students in equal measure. Conveying to his readers of various colors that "we're all in the same boat," he cautioned that the mob mentality could easily lead rioters down the slippery slope:

> From the saffron-skinned Japanese-American citizens of Los Angeles to brown-skinned Mexican-American citizens is only a step . . . From the brown Mexicans to the vari-colored Negroes is only a step, too . . . Logically speaking, color has nothing to do with citizenship or democracy. But prejudice and the mob-spirit pay logic no mind. The zoot-suits on a handful of kids are a nice excuse for reactionaries . . . to start a campaign of big headlines in the [LA] press against the Negro and the Mexican people.[70]

In contrast to the wartime and postwar expectation that only tension would mark the interactions between communities of color living cheek by jowl in ever-changing cities, a fair number did not at all feel hostile toward their new neighbors but rather acknowledged that they shared common threads of history.

Chapter 6

From "Jap Crow" to "Jim and Jane Crow": Black and Blue (and Yellow) in Chicago and the Bay Area

In 1940, only 390 Americans of Japanese descent called Chicago "home." Despite taking place nearly 5,000 miles away, the attack on Pearl Harbor would immediately affect those midwesterners' lives. Law enforcement quickly canvassed the small area of twenty-five Japanese lunchrooms and caterers and, at Mayor Edward Kelly's order, shut them down. The *Chicago Tribune* ran the headline "CHICAGO JAPS GLOOMY, HIDE BEHIND DOORS" for an article reporting on "a group of Japanese huddled in a rear room . . . in the Tokyo lunch, one of the largest restaurants, at 551 South State street."[1] Angry residents took matters into their own hands, smashing windows in businesses like the Oriental Trading Company on Madison Street, where "the proprietor's wife was slightly injured when hit by a heavy ball bearing."[2]

According to the Chicago biographer Dominic A. Pacyga, Japanese Chicagoans harbored no illusions about the imminent upheaval facing their community. "Goro Tsuchida, a thirty-year resident of the United States, and his Kentucky-born Japanese American wife sat gloomily in their lunchroom at 1130 North Clark Street as their two sons waited to be drafted," Pacyga writes. "Madame Shintani's Restaurant at 743 North Rush sat darkened as anti-Japanese sentiment ran throughout the city."[3] A letter to the editor of the Black weekly, the *Chicago Defender*, captured the heightened tension of the moment: "Judging them by their attitude toward Koreans, Chinese and other Asiatics . . . too many thoughtless Negroes have too much blind sympathy for the Japanese, never observing their silent contempt."[4] Certainly, additional incidents, accompanied by the general tenor of fear and rumor in the city after the initial attack, revealed the palpable and growing distrust of Japanese Americans or ostensibly similar-looking residents in the Chicagoland area. For example, the *Tribune* trumpeted:

> Chicago's Filipinos want the rest of us to know they're not Japs. That's the reason they pinned to their lapels yesterday buttons reading 'USA-Philippines' against a background of both [national] flags . . . The action had been decided upon after numerous Filipinos complained they were being mistaken for Japanese.[5]

For all of the chest-thumping and fear-filled bleating, though, a surprising amount of support for Chicago's tiny Japanese population tended to dominate the news coverage in the first few days after Pearl Harbor. Beulah Barker wrote to the *Tribune* editor: "It shall not be the American way to behave hastily or like hoodlums merely because the person is of the Japanese race—nor indeed behave like hoodlums in any case!" She concluded: "Any way, since brother fought brother in our Civil war, we should know not all Japanese are in agreement with the militarist party of Japan."[6] A former American consul to Honduras, Samuel McClintock, weighed in: "Japanese cherry trees in Washington hacked down by some fanatical patriot! How silly! . . . I know more than one Japanese living in our midst who has no more sympathy with the war lords in Japan than has the most ardent American."[7]

The resettlement of West Coast Japanese Americans in the Midwest and Northeast after internment irrevocably transformed the population of Japanese Chicagoans. As both Allan Austin and Gary Okihiro have amply demonstrated, many young Nisei managed to leave the camps earlier than expected by filing education waivers.[8] They matriculated predominantly at midwestern and East Coast schools, and some of their campmates were recruited for Japanese-language immersion at the Military Intelligence Service Language School, based at Camp Savage, Minnesota. Some were recruited to industrial centers like Chicago to shore up labor shortages in munitions and other war-related factories. Others, like Kikuchi and two of his younger sisters, were permitted to leave Gila for Chicago so that Bette and Emiko could finish school. For Kikuchi, it also did not hurt that Dorothy Thomas had moved her JERS operation to her husband's old stomping ground, the University of Chicago, and its well-regarded School of Sociology; and she still required Kikuchi's help on the project. All in all, approximately twenty thousand Japanese Americans "resettled" in the Chicagoland area, starting in 1943. When the West Coast reopened after the war's end, many families returned to their former homes and warmer climes, but a significant proportion decided to stay in the "flinty" city of Chicago, which at midcentury was no longer "Nature's Metropolis," nor completely a "Black Metropolis" alone.

For those Japanese Americans who came to Chicago in 1943, housing covenants that had long restricted African Americans and unwanted immigrants to particular districts forced Nikkei settlement into two main areas: the intersection of Division and Clark Streets in the Near North Side area, and the Oakland/Kenwood and Woodlawn areas of Hyde Park near the University of Chicago on the South Side. Alice Murata, the chronicler of Japanese Chicago, and the historian Charlotte Brooks have both accurately described the neighborhoods into which most Nisei moved as "buffers" or "transition zones" between Black and white neighborhoods.[9] The WRA—the government agency responsible for the placement of resettlers and ominously renamed the War Agency Liquidation Unit—noted that the "depressed transition area" on the North Side had always been a kind of way station for newly arrived minorities before their movement into other parts of the city. Because of this historical precedent and the gradual deterioration of the area, a "pattern of entrance of new minority groups has been established, and as a result, opposition to new groups is at a minimum." In addition, the Clark/Division area was made up largely of "rundown rooming houses, hotels, and a large number of cheap night clubs and bars," an environment deemed suitable for the large number of Nisei bachelors who came to Chicago in the first wave of resettlers.[10] The WRA report confirms the squalor:

> The majority of apartments in this area are located in small buildings which originally were not designed for such purposes and the apartments that have resulted tend to be makeshift affairs. In rooming houses, rooms rent from $5 to $10 per week, depending on location and type of room. In most of the rooming houses, the rooms are small and dirty, there is one bath to the floor, and as many as 10 to 12 individuals use it.[11]

For a group that had recently been confined to makeshift horse stalls (at assembly centers) and spartan-like barracks in relocation centers, these "accommodations" were hardly shocking.

In the same WRA update, the government uncritically bemoaned increased delinquency among these single men, citing "fourteen babies, probably more, born out of wedlock," a high number of gambling arrests, "a sex maniac still at large, accused in at least seven instances of having raped young Japanese women," and in general, "numerous frustrated individuals on the margin of neurotic and psychopathic behavior."[12] The Liquidation Unit strongly recommended parental supervision of these young men (assuming their parents were still alive) or "wholesome recreational facilities in areas like this." In time, however, Nisei established a stable, even if only temporary, community of shops, clubs, and restaurants that catered specifically to the Japanese American community. By 1950, Murata notes, Clark and Division had developed as far north as Goethe Street (most notably marked by the Nisei Tavern, Don Noro Veterans Club, and Woolworth's) and as far south as Oak Street near the Newberry Library (with the Yamato Café, Gila River Restaurant, and the Corregidor Barber Shop). What is more, the community formed a number of recreational facilities—the Chicago Nisei Sports Association, Citywide Recreation, and the Girls Club Council, among others—at the intersection of Maple and LaSalle Streets.[13]

Yet residual delinquency among Nisei bachelors and the lack of children's playgrounds still made the North Side area less than appealing to Nisei families; hence, another critical mass of Japanese Americans congregated on the South Side. The WRA once again summarized:

> The south side area tends to be one of small unit apartments, the University of Chicago area especially so. Apartments around the Cottage Grove–39th to 43rd Street area, tend to be a little bigger and it is here that many of the south side family groups have settled.[14]

The area west of Cottage Grove Avenue had seen better days, particularly during World War I, when midwestern factories finally opened their doors to Black workers, many of whom had flocked to Chicago during the first major wave of the Great Migration from the American South. World War II witnessed a second large wave of Black migrants into Chicago, but as mentioned above, restrictive housing covenants reigned supreme, consigning African Americans to the area known as Bronzeville (or as the title of Horace Cayton and St. Clair Drake's groundbreaking study of Chicago termed it, the Black Metropolis).[15] Made up of overcrowded and dilapidated tenement houses in a small, seven-mile strip (between 22nd and 63rd Streets), Bronzeville nonetheless enjoyed a reputation as the center of African American commerce and art. Its most notable hubs of activity—35th and State Streets and 47th and South Parkway (later, Martin Luther King, Jr. Boulevard)—hummed during the day with a rush of Black professionals, shoppers, job seekers, picketers, and newspaper reporters, while at night this "city within a city" buzzed with citizens and celebrities hitting dance halls, the historic Regal Theater, and nightclubs featuring the best of jazz and blues performers.

As Drake and Cayton vividly describe it:

> Stand in the center of the Black Belt—at Chicago's 47th St. and South Parkway. Around you swirls a continuous eddy of faces—black, brown, olive, yellow, and white. Soon you will realize that this is not "just another neighborhood" of Midwest Metropolis.[16]

Within a half-mile radius, they point out, Black-run institutions lined the thoroughfares: Provident Hospital, the George Cleveland Hall Library, the YWCA, the nation's largest Black Catholic church, and Cayton's Parkway Community House, among many others. The historian Adam Green correctly cautions, however, against overly romanticizing the self-sufficient and self-governing nature of Depression-era Bronzeville, pointing, as an example, to Baliban and Katz Management, the Regal Theater's white owners and the same partnership that ran the Savoy in Harlem. Their desire to build the Regal right at the future crossroads of the area (47th Street and South Parkway) drew business away from existing Black-run theaters and redirected foot traffic away from Black-owned institutions like Binga Bank on State Street, all of which had been mainstays of Bronzeville before the Regal's arrival. "What seemed to Cayton and Drake a vital self-governing locus of community life, then, is open to a different reading in light of actual institutional history," writes Green.[17] Something existed within Bronzeville, however, that was unavailable, even "unthinkable," as Green puts it, elsewhere in Chicagoland: upward mobility, especially for figures like Ken Blewett, the first African American manager of the Regal (who had begun as an usher) and Dinah Washington, initially a washroom attendant, who then performed for Lionel Hampton and signed with him in 1943.[18] Green asserts: "While it is an exaggeration to describe black-owned or run clubs during the 1940s as egalitarian spaces, it is clear the class and status lines were permeable."[19]

While the collective wattage of star power, activity, and sheer excitement shone brightly in the hubs of Bronzeville, that light could not possibly counterbalance the darkness of the tenement houses surrounding those satellites. Before the U.S. entry into World War II, one of Chicago's native, even favorite, sons— Richard Wright—returned to this northern Black Belt with the photographer Edwin Rosskam in tow. Wright wrote a searing narrative to accompany Farm Security Administration photographs that captured both the rural and urban plight of millions of African Americans during the Depression, the dreams deferred and false starts of many migrants in the promised land. Entitled *12 Million Black Voices* (1941), the collection displays both the despair and the dignity of those Americans who were last hired and first fired, particularly in the direst of economic times. Wright gives voice to everyday people, demonstrating how Black oppression and Black agency went hand in hand. The tenement apartments, or "kitchenettes"—dilapidated, crowded, unlit, and bald-facedly exploitative—glow as a vessel for Wright's fury:

> The kitchenette is our prison, our death sentence without a trial, the new form of mob violence that assaults not only the lone individual, but all of us, in its ceaseless attacks . . .
>
> The kitchenette is the funnel through which our pulverized lives flow to ruin and death on the city pavements, at a profit.[20]

As if in response to Wright's indignant but truth-filled call, Gwendolyn Brooks, the doyenne of American poetry and lifetime South Side resident, assumes the collective first person "we" introduced by Wright and offers but fleeting hope in "kitchenette building" (1945).

> We are things of dry hours and the involuntary plan,
> Grayed in, and gray. "Dream" makes a giddy sound, not strong
> Like "rent," "feeding a wife," "satisfying a man."
>
> . . . .
>
> We wonder. But not well! not for a minute!
> Since Number Five is out of the bathroom now,
> We think of lukewarm water, hope to get in it.[21]

This is what lay west of Cottage Grove. This is what the aptly named South Side looked, sounded, and felt like: a version of the American South grafted onto the metropole of the Midwest like a cattle branding. This is what the Black metropolis had come to signify by 1943. For many, living in the industrial North proved no different from the experience of the hellish South; in Wright's terminology, Lords of the Land simply traded places with the Bosses of the Buildings. For others, Chicago was a destination, an endpoint, and a sigh of resignation. For yet even more, though, Chicago represented just the beginning. For the Nisei coming out of concentration camps, Chicago was absolutely an opportunity to begin again, but for some, like Kikuchi, the city would take some getting used to.

African Americans and Japanese Americans could not help but interact and bump into one another at that increasingly hectic but unique moment in Chicago's history. The practices of white institutions toward both groups appeared nearly identical, effecting a shared present: cemeteries would not allow the burial of Japanese Americans in their hallowed grounds; hospitals often denied them service; and although labor shortages necessitated the reluctant hiring of Nisei, most unions remained steadfastly opposed to nonwhite membership.[22] Other unions merely seemed to be taking advantage of the newly arrived. As one of Kikuchi's subjects, a welder, shared:

> Some of the boochie [Japanese] guys I know pay union dues but they don't have full membership [in the American Federation of Labor] like I do. That's the craps because it shows that there *is* that discrimination feeling against them.[23]

He later remarked that one white coworker at the plant—"sort of educated and one of them broad-minded guys"—a fellow appropriately nicknamed "Red," wanted "to get the Negro guys into the union but the rest of the guys won't allow them either."

This particular young Nisei appears to have been very impressionable, since at one point he informed Red that he did not like working with African Americans, citing their laziness. Red immediately chastised his coworker, whom "he looked on . . . as an individual," adding that if all workers would do that, "there would be less of this racial stuff getting [them] in trouble."[24] Just moments earlier in his interview with Kikuchi, this same young laborer had asserted his solidarity with his fellow workers of color, blithely commenting:

> The Negroes are swell to us and we get along with them the best. [My roommate] is always telling me that we are underdogs just like them. One Negro worker said to me that the Japs had been kicked around as much as them, so that he knew what it was like.

He ended his reverie by stating: "It makes you feel good when you know that a bunch of guys like to stick together after going through the same thing as you do."[25] This confusion on the part of the young welder exposed his youth and impetuous, inconsistent behavior, but it also revealed the kind of manic mindset that perhaps affected so many different people in these close environs within the context of a war and racialized hysteria. One day, this young man met a welcoming and reassuring Black worker, so therefore he believed that he liked all Blacks. Then, on another day, he saw one Black worker perhaps loafing at the plant, and the young man indicted the entire race of African Americans for being lazy. Red, his allegedly enlightened white coworker, at least deployed the appropriate rhetoric by insisting on the Nisei's need to treat everyone individually, to see each coworker as an individual rather than as an undifferentiated instance of a repeated pattern. Through his own example, Red demonstrated this kind of "educated, open-minded" behavior by interacting with the Nisei as an individual, as an equal.

By contrast, however, most Chicago landlords saw nothing but undifferentiated masses of black and yellow, making housing discrimination a shared matter of agitation and concern for Blacks and Nisei. Many of the Nisei bachelors who resettled and attempted to live in apartments on the Near North Side found long-standing redlining practices that mirrored the patterns segregating African Americans throughout the city. One of Kikuchi's subjects for his case histories was a young agricultural student from California who had been interned at the Rohwer Relocation Center in Arkansas, a site quite accustomed to the rules of Jim and Jane Crow. He told Kikuchi that after quitting jobs a couple times in Chicago, he "started working at the garage," and in the meantime, he added,

> Our apartment house got a new manager and he didn't want any boochies there. He said that we had to get out. We didn't know about OPA [the Office of Price Administration] or anything so I started looking around for a new apartment since I had the most free time.[26]

The OPA could have helped the Nisei by protesting the unfair housing practices or by appealing to extant price controls, but this young man chose a different route, experiencing many rejections to his housing inquiries, with one memorable interaction. "In one place," he offered,

> the [white] lady was not so nice. She acted nice until she asked me if I was a Jap. I said "yes" and then she just closed the door in my face and said she didn't want me around.

Eventually, he landed a place for himself among twelve other Nisei in a tiny one-bedroom, noting: "We are paying above the ceiling rent but we don't say nothing." While hardly the decrepit kitchenettes so ubiquitous throughout the Black Belt, these sardine-can bachelor pads afforded little more comfort than a fraction of floor or mattress to sleep on; landlords were having a field day. The young student recalled:

> It was pretty crowded for us but we would take turns sleeping on the couch. We had to get a small reserve room later on in order to put our friends up and one of them sleeps there now as he is the only one of us who is immune to the bedbugs . . . Sometimes I would come home and find a stranger in my bed and I would just tell him to move over as I figured he was my pal's friend.

Kikuchi similarly experienced the ignorant, anxious, and awkward interactions in the search for housing. After he and his sisters had been settled in their South Side apartment for more than two months, their landlord, a "Mrs. Blumenthal," suddenly reversed her stance toward the family. Even though Bette also worked for Blumenthal during the afternoon by cleaning her apartment (the landlord lived just above the Kikuchis), neighbors allegedly reported Blumenthal to the area's Better Business Bureau. A supposed representative of the bureau phoned and warned her that neither "Chinese" nor any other nonwhites were allowed on Drexel Boulevard, and subsequently,

> Mrs. B got worried and said that she did not want any trouble in her house . . . that we were "first class" people . . . but she thought that things may become unpleasant for us and perhaps it would be better to leave.[27]

Steaming, Kikuchi sought an explanation, eventually speaking with a man in the Swan-Lorsch Real Estate office. The man put it plainly to the young Nisei:

> He said that the color line was drawn most sharply against the Negroes who were not allowed beyond Cottage Grove. "That's the way it is. People think that way and we can't do much about it. I know that you may be 'O.K.,' but the other people don't think that way and I can't change them." He was under the impression that I was Chinese and I did not correct him.

Kikuchi ultimately settled the issue with local officials, clearly demonstrating that his landlord had been duped and called by one of her neighbors. With a sigh of disbelief, he concluded, "It is a mystery to me that a Jewish person [Mrs. Blumenthal] could fall for this sort of line after what their group has gone through." In her role as maternal surrogate, an incredulous Thomas interceded, lobbying vehemently on Kikuchi's behalf. Writing to Blumenthal on June 26, 1943, she assumed a stern, scolding tone:

> Mr. Charles Kikuchi informs me that some questions have been raised about permitting orientals [sic] to live in your house. I trust that you will take a firm stand in allowing the Kikuchis to keep their apartment. I think you will agree with me that the Kikuchis are as American as all of us and that there is nothing oriental about them except their faces. They are people of extremely fine character and are, of course, completely loyal to this country.[28]

Hoping for some racialized, perhaps even "underdog status," solidarity, Kikuchi quickly discovered that color—most prominently green and nonwhite—mattered a great deal in Chicago, drawing strict boundaries around its people and contested topography.

Poet, author, and columnist for the *Defender*, Langston Hughes was no stranger to either balkanized Chicago or the struggles of exclusion facing Kikuchi and his sisters on the South Side. He took great pride in reaching wide audiences, mostly through his *Defender* character Jesse B. Semple, or "Simple," an everyman figure whose comic exterior belied a critically serious interior discourse of sociopolitical issues affecting Hughes and his readership. But his most trenchant, engaging, and rhetorically devastating work appeared in his column, "From Here to Yonder" (as well as in concurrent pieces in *Common Ground*). For example, in the spring of 1943, just as Japanese American resettlers were about to arrive in Chicagoland, he penned a satirical but scathing indictment of America and its empty, or at the very least, "deferred" promises. As a wish list for the postwar era, he wrote:

> American citizens of Japanese parentage will be released from their con-centration camps—non-citizen Germans or Italians were not so treated. Chinese in Mississippi won't have to go to separate schools, nor will Negroes.
>
> Mexicans, in the Southwest, will receive the same courtesy in public places, parks and swimming pools as do any other citizens. Color won't matter anymore. It's really going to be fine all over America when every-body will be decent to everybody else after the war.
>
> Am I dreaming? Well, isn't it better for a person to be dreaming than to have a nightmare? Huh?[29]

Hughes reminded readers not to invest too deeply in the democratic rhetoric spewed by government agencies like the Office of War Information, which aimed to persuade both international and domestic audiences of the benign aims of the American war effort. Hardly an incorrigible naysayer, Hughes nonetheless rang the alarm in an attempt to shake any naïve idealists out of their collective reverie. No matter a minority's color, Hughes asserted, he or she would face Jim Crow, its cousin Jap Crow, and many more dehumanizing versions of segrega-tion. The same poet who had spoken of "many rivers" and "dreams deferred" needed to give his readers a reality check: even in the fervor and possibility of achieving true democracy, domestic fascism would undoubtedly stake its claim, and for progressive people of all colors, the war would not end when Hirohito surrendered.

"A Windy and Dirty City"

For thirty-five dollars a month, Kikuchi lived with his younger sisters in the base-ment apartment at 4743 Drexel Boulevard: a kitchenette, one large bedroom, one small bedroom, and a shared toilet. Only a boulevard away from Bronzeville and about eight blocks north of campus, he enjoyed a unique and proximate perspec-tive on the fault lines between Black and white Chicago. Accompanied by Emiko and Bette, Kikuchi was thus reunited with his older sisters Mariko and Alice, the former who had been living in the Midwest before evacuation, the latter just recently out of camp; in Chicago, the two eldest sisters lived in the downtown Loop. "Mariko and Alice have a basement apartment in the downtown loop area among a very poor type of people," Kikuchi wrote.

> They look like immigrants the way they dress. The houses in that neighbor-hood are very old and dirty. Their room is dingy, but furnished with good, sturdy, old-fashioned items. Mariko calls it "Bohemian;" I call it a dump.[30]

The government had included Kikuchi and his sisters among the forty-three thousand or so "loyal" Japanese Americans permitted to leave camp and find work or study in locations cleared by the military. Of course, this meant leaving behind much of his family still at camp in Arizona, but Kikuchi had been granted this pass to resettlement because of his work with Thomas's JERS. Settling into the study's new headquarters in the Sociology Department at the University of Chicago (while taking classes with the distinguished professor Edith Abbott at the School of Social Service Administration, a Quaker with great interest in helping Nisei during resettlement), Kikuchi was charged with amassing and writing up numerous interviews with resettlers, of which nearly twenty thousand came to the city in the time he was there (1943–1945). Ultimately he completed sixty-four interviews, fifteen of which were included in *The Salvage*. In the meantime, Kikuchi continued his disciplined and daily habit of writing in his journals. One of the first entries of his "Chicago diary" resumed his wrestling with the question of race. During his first Sunday stroll across Cottage Grove through a section of Bronzeville, he observed its overcrowded and restrictive nature:

> Going through the Negro section was a little depressing . . . The Negro area is dirty and we passed by the back ends of the houses which were filthy beyond description. Nobody can ever convince me that the Negroes are happy to remain cooped up in this area.

He then added a commentary that was striking for someone who had just been released from an internment camp: "The thousands of people who pass through this Negro area must become callous to these horrible sights or else they must feel that the Negroes are animals. A sight like this is enough to turn one's stomach and it certainly is a black eye to Chicago."

Kikuchi then alluded to the American Friends Service Committee, the Quaker social organization that (along with organizations like the Church of the Brethren and the Salvation Army) volunteered to aid Japanese Americans relocating to Chicago. "The Friends are not seeking housing for Nisei in this area because it may cause racial tension & the FBI are suspicious of the Japs and Negroes getting together," he writes.

> Could this be a tacit acknowledgment that the whites fear the fraternizing of two minority American groups that have been grossly mistreated? This is a hell of a way to solve a problem. Suppression by force only breeds fraud and greater barriers.[31]

His suspicions about governmental paranoia would be confirmed only two months later, during the Detroit race riots. Thirty-six hours of rioting began on June 20, 1943, culminating in the deaths of twenty-five African Americans and nine whites. Seventeen of the twenty-five African Americans died at the hands of police officers. Rep. Martin Dies of Texas, the chairman of HUAC, went so far as to blame recently arrived Japanese Americans for stirring up the Black population in a shared hatred of the white population. The day after, Kikuchi offered:

It's a national disgrace and there is no doubt that the Axis will make the most out of it for propaganda purposes. The race tension in Detroit must really be bad. It is a problem and the Negro won't be kept down by force forever.[32]

As he predicted, the Axis powers made great hay out of the riots, proclaiming on German-controlled Vichy radio that the Detroit riots demonstrated "the internal disorganization of a country torn by social injustice, race hatreds, regional disputes, the violence of an irritated proletariat, and the gangsterism of a capitalistic police."[33]

On the heels of the violence in Detroit, Mayor Kelly established a Committee on Race Relations (which would become the Commission on Human Relations by 1945) in the hope of forestalling, and preferably avoiding, similar racialized violence in Chicago. Headed by the Rosenwald Fund's Edwin Embree, the committee boasted some influential figures: Charles S. Johnson, who had written the report on the last Chicago riot (1919); the Chicago School sociologists Wirth and Cayton; and the Northwestern anthropologist Melville J. Herskovits. Unfortunately, the committee was not able to fulfill its original aim of evaluating race relations and public policy and addressing the community's concerns. Occupied by crisis management, it spent its time identifying the areas with the most potential for conflict instead of proposing solutions for the horribly unacceptable conditions on the South Side or the plight of its segregated schools. By the time the committee became the commission, it had turned toward planning and hosting a series of conferences on home front unity, a development welcomed by many national figures concerned with race, including Carey McWilliams and *Common Ground's* Margaret Anderson, who was helping "intercultural education" programs develop curricula in schools nationwide. At one of these conferences, Kikuchi heard one of his old acquaintances, Setsuko Matsunaga Nishi, who worked closely under Cayton as the Parkway Community House's education chairperson. Like Kikuchi, she believed deeply in interracial alliances:

I'm supposed to be here to represent 110,000 Japanese Americans but I work in the Negro community and my attitude is that I am working for the common cause of democracy . . . I can honestly say that the Nisei here do not think apart from the Negroes and the Jews . . . The Nisei have gone through an experience which makes them realize more than ever that a united effort among all racial groups is necessary for their self-preservation.[34]

In the midst of this immersion, and for the first couple of weeks of his stay in the city, Kikuchi maintained an observational, nearly scientific, distance from African Americans, demonstrating a great deal of innocence and, possibly, ignorance. While in one breath he expressed his sympathy and alliance with African Americans, in another he offered contradictory but honest moments of confusion. Late in April he mused:

The Negro area is interesting. There were a number of drunk young fellows roaming the streets. I wonder what they have to look forward to. I heard one of them say that he was going to dodge the draft because he had nothing to fight for and that Democracy was a bunch of bull----.

Reflecting on the scene, Kikuchi concluded:

I suppose the Negroes do have a funny psychological twist of mind due to the way that they have been suppressed for so many years. They all wear such extreme clothes. I suppose it is an outward expression of their inner frustrations.

Unconvinced, he ended with a list of free associations:

The Negro problem is far from solved and it is one of the most important issues of the War. The color question won't be solved very easily.[35]

As was the case with Issei and rural Japanese at Gila, it was not until Kikuchi engaged African American Chicagoans individually that he gained subtler understanding of his interactions and a reassuring confirmation of his initial, progressive instincts about African Americans. In August 1943, for example, he enjoyed the privilege of accompanying his friend George Yasukochi to Bronzeville to meet with the Reverend J. C. Austin, Sr., of the historic Pilgrim Baptist Church at East 33rd Street and Indiana Avenue. Joined by his recently arrived younger brother Tom, Kikuchi recalled:

As I was waiting out in front a couple of Negro boys came by. They were very curious to see an Oriental face in an area where all the faces are black so that they asked me if I were a Chinese man. Some of the older Negro fellows acted very friendly as they walked by, several of them saying "Whatcha say, Buddy" or similar greetings.[36]

Kikuchi then met with the reverend before the service, engaging him on questions of Black nationalism and segregation. He admitted:

I was surprised to hear his views. The Reverend calmly accepts conditions as they are and he feels that nothing can be done about it. In time these misunderstandings will be swept away, but in the meanwhile the best should be made of things as they are, the reverend said. I did not agree with this view.

Pressing the reverend a little further, Kikuchi found that the man favored Booker T. Washington's compromise of remaining separate but equal:

If the reverend were a Japanese, I would be opposed to him because he believes in the segregated unit. I suppose it is different with the Negro because of the past traditions and history of the group. It is an immeasurably harder task for them to assimilate than the Nisei.[37]

After meeting with the Reverend Austin, his friend Yasukochi addressed the parishioners on the Nisei predicament (sounding much like Myrdal would a year later): "The Negro problem, the Polish problem, the Japanese problem, the Mexican problem—they are all American problems."[38] In a fitting end to his visit, Kikuchi related:

> The reverend asked us to come to the services and invited us to become a member of the congregation if we cared to. He said that even a heathen of Oriental extraction could be made into a Baptist of the black race since we were all the same in God's eyes. We enjoyed talking to them and meeting the people very much.[39]

This conversation reflected how much Kikuchi desired to get to know African Americans on a personal level, to affirm that the Nisei shared much in common with African Americans, but at the same time, to mindfully acknowledge that some challenges and struggles remained unique to each group. The interaction typified many of the exchanges Kikuchi experienced in Black Chicago: personal, dialogic, and open-minded.

This was a terribly difficult path to tread: even those whom Kikuchi respected acquiesced in the status quo when it came to the "Negro problem." After a meeting with the Thomases and William Ogburn, Dorothy's former mentor at Barnard and, at the time, a faculty member in sociology at Chicago, Kikuchi recorded an unsettling discussion. Apparently, Ogburn had tried to convince the Thomases that the recent appointment of Allison Davis, an African American social anthropologist with a PhD from Harvard, would blight the Chicago campus. Originally from Georgia, Ogburn was most concerned that the university's image would be tarnished among its alumni and prospective applicants from the South. Kikuchi remembered, "As I sat there, a feeling of disappointment, resentment swept over me. To think that a Liberal Sociologist was susceptible to such prejudices!" He disguised his true feelings and tried to understand what lay beneath Ogburn's "concern":

> It's all too common and sometimes I get discouraged and feel that the Negroes are in a hopeless situation. The Nisei should feel grateful that they do not have such barriers. The prejudice against Negroes is so deep rooted that it almost seems inherent. There seems to be a psychological revulsion towards the black man—as if he were the symbol of all filth, dirt, crime, and evil.[40]

Having learned very quickly about the racial and psychological divide in the city, Kikuchi avoided such barriers at all costs, consciously choosing to view African Americans as human, as fully realized individuals, and not as one unrecognizable mass. Quite often he persuaded other Nisei, including those in his family, to consider the social and historical contexts under which African Americans labored before judging them. At one point, he recalled:

Even [my sister] had the idea that the Negroes "smell." She rides home on the crowded "L" every night and she says that the odor almost suffocates her. I explained to her that this was more due to the fact that these Negroes were on a low rung of the economic ladder and that they had to do hard physical labor. I even said that a Caucasian doing similar work would have a heavy odor. [She] got the point very well.[41]

He concluded with a prematurely Adamic-like, willfully hopeful inflection:

Fortunately [my sisters] do not have the intolerant racial prejudices like a great majority of the Nisei—aimed at Negroes, Filipinos, and Jews. They have lived among the second generation of these groups and they know that they are not so different.

Accompanied by one of those sisters, Bette, on another stroll through the city, Kikuchi chanced to meet an off-duty laborer who had worked for the Manhattan Pickle Company for twenty-five years. He offered Kikuchi help in finding a job in the factory, as well as his own thoughts about an impending "race war." Kikuchi remembered the man's first words: "Say, please don't get mad, but are you a Jap or a Chinaman?" Bette replied, "We are Americans." The man then qualified his query: "I know that. I'm an American too, but also a Negro. What I mean is: are you of Chinese or Japanese ancestry?" The man apologized to Kikuchi and then told him:

I'm an American, but I was for Ethiopia. You are an American and you are for Japan. Don't think that I'm going to tell the police on you. I'm for you. The Negroes, my people, are 100% with you people. We are going to show the white man a thing or two. They won't strut so much when they find out how strong the dark people are. You just let them kick you around and put you in a concentration camp but your time will come, wait and see.[42]

Kikuchi responded:

I don't think that you are taking a very healthy attitude. This is not a race war. I want the Negroes and the Yellow man to be equal with the white man, that's what we are fighting for. But I don't think that Japan will give such a thing to the world. You had better hope that Democracy wins because that's your only hope.

The exchange accurately captures what Gallicchio describes as a genuine flirtation by some African Americans in the first half of the twentieth century with the thought of Japan as "the champion of the darker races." Since Japan's defeat of Russia in 1905, notes Gallicchio,

Black intellectuals, journalists and editors, leaders of radical mass movements, and mainstream civil rights organizations wrote and spoke admiringly of Japan. They frequently viewed international events from a Japanese perspective, convinced that what benefited the nation would improve the condition of the world's darker races.[43]

Ironically, given their own "internal colonialism" in the United States, these intellectuals failed to notice the blind spot of Japan's imperial machinations in Manchuria and Korea. Although, as previously noted, Pearl Harbor compelled many of those same Black intellectuals to restrain their enthusiasm for Japan and to consequently affirm their patriotism (through silence on the question of Japanese American internment), others maintained their respect for Japan through later stages of the war, albeit in relatively hushed tones. For example, after atomic bombs were dropped on Hiroshima and Nagasaki, Cayton remembered telling a friend:

> I'm torn a dozen ways. I didn't want the Japanese to win; after all, I'm an American. But the mighty white man was being humiliated, and by the little yellow bastards he had nothing but contempt for. It gave me a sense of satisfaction, a feeling that white wasn't always right, not always able to enforce its will on everyone who was colored.[44]

When companions rationalized the bomb's use as an effective way to avoid more U.S. casualties, Cayton withdrew from the conversation, saying, "My sympathies right then were with the Japanese, and strangely . . . with myself. The Japanese at least tried to break the color line."

Although not a public intellectual like Cayton, the workman quoted above certainly championed hopes of the darker races on an Ellisonian "lower frequency," proudly carrying the ideas of a Black internationalist on the street. But this particular interaction also revealed the awkward assumption by the young African American (and other internationalists) that the Kikuchis would naturally be Japanese nationalists. Black internationalists could discuss the impact of Japan, the nation, on Black America with detachment, but they betrayed marked unease when thinking of Black and Japanese America mixed together. In abstraction, as a nation far removed from American shores, Japan seemed like a fair and vaguely familiar fighter to back. In reality, however, when faced with returning citizens in Little Tokyos on the West Coast—on the ground and in their neighborhoods—African Americans may have been less eager to show their support (although, in fairness, the workman above does affirm his allegiance). What is more, as Kikuchi's incredulous reaction demonstrated, Japanese Americans may also have been caught off guard, not envisioning a "race war" as Black internationalists were.

This curious conversation marked another necessary step for Kikuchi in his informal education about race relations, in person and on a practical level. Reflecting upon the repartee, he tried to gather his thoughts: "That Negro man is like the frustrated Kibei who turns to Japan only he hasn't got a country to turn to so he identifies himself with another 'colored' nation which he thinks will give the Negro a chance in this white man's world."[45] Whenever nationalism came up, Kikuchi always voiced skepticism. Admittedly, America held the greatest promise in Kikuchi's eyes, not so much as a nation strictly defined, but almost as a vessel or conduit for his overflowing ideal of a fully integrated, multiracial democracy. The historian Gary Gerstle taps into this notion in *American Crucible* (2001), identifying the risk of too fully embracing an imagined nationalism: "Throughout its history . . . American civic nationalism has contended with another potent ideological inheritance, a racial nationalism that conceives of America in ethnoracial terms, as a people held together by common blood and skin color and by an inherited fitness for self-government." Of course, this racialized ideal left no room for Africans, Asians, and Latinas/os, or in the 1920s, southern and eastern Europeans, all of whom were simply excluded, expelled, segregated, or subordinated. Gerstle concludes: "The hold that this tradition exercised over the national imagination helps us to understand the conviction that periodically has surfaced among racial minorities, and especially among African Americans, that America would never accept them as the equals of whites."[46] In this context, then, it is understandable that Kikuchi made fine distinctions between nation and democracy in his conversation with the laborer above. Whereas his sister asserted simply, "We are Americans," his message was more nuanced and more urgent: "You had better hope that Democracy wins because that's your only hope."

As 1943 gave way to 1944, Kikuchi found himself much more at home in Chicago, working on JERS and raising his younger siblings, now joined by Jack, the oldest of his brothers. Kikuchi's writing at the time reflects a continued sense of maturing and an increasing eagerness to engage various strands of the American racial dilemma. In the spring of 1944, he gleefully reported: "When [Jack, Bette and Emiko] came back from the skating rink, they said that they had a swell time. The Savoy rink is in the middle of the Negro district and only colored people were skating." He awkwardly joked: "Jack said that Emiko and Bette caused quite a commotion and all of the young Negro wolves cut in to skate with them." More seriously he noted:

> They said that these people were quite friendly and informal and one of
> the colored boys gave them a ride home. They said that everyone down
> there skated to boogie woogie music. We are planning to go to one of
> the large Negro Baptist churches soon in order to hear the Negro choir.[47]

In another moment of pause, Kikuchi retold the conversation he had with a fifty-three-year-old World War I veteran named Bowdre, a Pullman porter for twenty-one years who lived only half a block from the family's apartment. Born in Texas to a mother who had been a slave, "Bowdre has a very pessimistic outlook on life and he thinks the Nisei are much better off than the Negroes." He shared with Kikuchi that he could never make more than $140 a month in his labor-intensive job, while "the conductor makes $300 a month and he has an easy job." Ironically sounding a great deal like "Joe Nisei" looking for a job two years earlier in the Bay Area, Kikuchi is forced to comment:

What inequalities the color of a person's face will bring. It just isn't right, but I don't see how the existing society is going to change for a long time. I just hope the Nisei don't ever get placed in a segregated caste system like the Negroes. I don't think so, but it could happen.[48]

Many other Nisei, intellectual or otherwise, felt similarly about African Americans during this wartime era. Some expressed their views in print, either in the Japanese American or Black press. For instance, the short-story writer Hisaye Yamamoto and the linguist S. I. Hayakawa wrote for, respectively, the *L.A. Tribune* and the *Chicago Defender*, two Black weeklies that largely encouraged their readership to embrace interracial cooperation during the wartime and postwar eras (after the initial "patriotic" silence regarding internment). As discussed earlier, more radical members of the JACL communicated their unmitigated support of Blacks in the *Pacific Citizen* and in the NAACP's *Crisis*.[49] In comparison with these figures, then, Kikuchi represented a difference of degree, not kind. That is to say, he enjoyed an intimate, highly experiential, face-to-face relationship with Blacks unmatched by any of his peers. Moreover, no Nisei wrote about Blacks with such frequency or passion, locating them at the epicenter of the global struggle for democracy, the vanguard in a formidable battle to define America's future. The Nisei had much to learn from their example. In many ways, he unapologetically privileged the experience of African Americans over that of his own race. For example, after reading *Patterns of Negro Segregation* (1943) by Charles S. Johnson, Kikuchi asserted, "The Nisei have nothing to complain about when compared to the status of the Negro. I can't blame the Negroes for being so resentful when so much crazy prejudice is imposed upon them. It is not a rational thing at all, but emotional." His indignation took in all of white society: "It seems that even the ministers and the other professional people of the South accept that the Negro is inferior."[50] Coming home from Bronzeville in a similar frame of mind, he observed:

> I saw a blind Negro selling pencils on the streets and there were flies all over the sores he had on his face. Not many [Nikkei] evacuees were ever so miserably treated as that beggar, I thought. It was a pitiful sight.[51]

It was apparent that Kikuchi had quickly but decisively chosen where he stood on the critical questions of "the Negro" and "the Oriental" at midcentury.

Part of his more daunting challenge, however, continued to be to convince other, less progressive-minded Nisei of the virtue of crossing racial lines to find solidarity. As Blacks and Japanese competed for scarce wartime jobs and shared contentious workspaces, unavoidable tensions arose. In October 1944, one Nisei acquaintance told Kikuchi about his wallet being stolen by an African American coworker at a manufacturing plant for cosmetics. After moronically remarking that he bore only partial responsibility for leaving the wallet unattended in the men's dressing room, the young man reported:

> When I told the boss he said that a lot of things had been missing in that place ever since he hired the last three Negroes. He said the other one

who had brought my wallet back was an old employee and he was okay. This Negro sounded so sorry that one of his race had pulled a dirty trick on me. The boss said not to trust anyone in the place. I sure lost faith in the Negroes though. Those guys work sloppy and they make a bad reputation for all the rest, just like the Nisei zoot suiters.[52]

This specific incident sheds light on the difficult but achievable task of avoiding generalizing or stereotyping an entire group based on the acts of one or two of its members. As the above sequence of events demonstrates, not all of the Black employees engaged in the theft of the wallet; in fact, one Black employee found and returned the empty wallet and even apologized on behalf of his entire race. Nevertheless, the Nisei victim (like his white employer) held the entire group responsible, and then, unaware of his own irony, compared them unfavorably to "Nisei zoot suiters." Clearly, this young man was able to differentiate among Nisei—some good, some bad, without claims about all Japanese—but he failed to apply the same standard to African Americans, assigning guilt to the whole race for the crime of one.

Some working-class Nisei harbored extremely conflicted views of their Black brethren, clouding any opportunity for either class or racial solidarity. In May 1945, a laboring friend of Kikuchi's who was working in an automotive parts company found himself on the short end of a housing crisis. His use of a racial epithet reflected an inherent bias toward African Americans. He told Kikuchi:

A lot of niggers have been moving across from Cottage Grove Ave. A nigger bought [our] place [through a white intermediary who put the place in the Black man's name], and told us to get out by the 25th. Now the real estate company is raising hell about it, and I think that the sale was canceled, but we have to move anyway.

Surprisingly, Kikuchi's friend then changed his tune, drawing attention to the unstable, highly complicated, and frustratingly contradictory nature of American race relations:

About a week ago, some hakujin [white] guys tried to burn up the home of a Negro minister who was only a few doors down from us. We saw the guys running after they started the fire. It was about 3 in the morning, and we were just coming home. It was a hell of a thing to do. The guy paid for the house so why in the hell should he be chased out?[53]

This last reaction provides an opening into a broader discussion about the white-imposed housing covenants that afflicted both Blacks and Japanese resettlers. Simply put, this marked a critical issue upon which both minorities could have found (and in some cases, did find) common cause. Togo Tanaka, a like-minded friend of Kikuchi and a former JERS analyst at Manzanar, reported to him on the racial tension surrounding a housing crisis from 38th to 41st Streets in June 1945:

The [white] property owners down there believe that their property values will decrease if the area gets Negro residents in it. A lot of the [Ni-
sei] resettlers are living in that district, and if any racial flareups occur, it
could be turned against them too. It shows just how serious the housing
situation is. The Negroes are having a much more difficult time than the
Japanese out here.[54]

Despite the (theoretically) insurmountable obstacle it presented, Kikuchi nonetheless attempted to address the problem on a very personal basis. For example,
when his family needed to relocate within Chicago after two years, he sought
the aid of the Salvation Army. The brigadier in charge informed Kikuchi that
the district council would have no problem with Nisei moving into a particular neighborhood, but it would definitely prevent Blacks from doing so because
they drove property values down. A debate ensued, with Kikuchi emphatically
asserting:

"I wasn't aware that Negroes or any racial group actually deteriorated
property values. That is a fallacy. The fact that Negroes are confined into
a compressed and segregated area, usually the poorest parts of town, is
what actually causes the neighborhood to deteriorate."
The "Brig" replies, "If the Negroes were allowed to come into the
district, they would push everyone else out, and then the church value
would fall to $20,000. They will have been the direct cause for it."

His effort at "reeducating" the brigadier proved genuine, but ultimately useless:
"Jesus Christ, that guy is a religious man and he is supposed to preach tolerance
and understanding, and yet he can say such stupid things."[55] Even in this failure,
though, Kikuchi's attempt at lobbying on behalf of African Americans and forcing the issue of their plight still signified an important moment. Some might
consider such interactions to be only symbolic gestures, limited and ineffective
against a more massive institutional racism. On the contrary, this incident—
aggregated with other similar occurrences in Kikuchi's life—underscores the
point that Kikuchi (and others) represented, both through his writing and
through his activism, the possibility of what could be in American race relations
and, by extension, in American democracy.

"The Talented Tenth" in Brown, Black, and Yellow

It is equally important to note that this was not an unrequited, one-way relationship between Kikuchi and African Americans. A number of his African American acquaintances and close friends—despite occasional disagreements and
debate—corroborated Kikuchi's views, largely endorsing his vision for a multiracial American democracy. These engaging conversations, however, did not take
place solely in Chicago, but in San Francisco, as well, where Kikuchi made his

critical six-week visit to the Thomases' home in early 1945. For a portion of his stay, Kikuchi spent time with his brother Jack and his Filipino fiancée, Dolores, and her family. He also revisited some Black friends, an elderly couple named Mr. Camba and Mrs. Butler, who ran a funeral home in Kikuchi's old prewar neighborhood. And finally, he matched wits with a few new friends—in particular, a young African American intellectual and future civil rights lawyer named Doug Greer—while staying at the International House on Berkeley's campus.[56]

During his first week back "home," Kikuchi wandered the streets of Nihon-machi, or at least what used to be the old Japanese district. "The Japanese signs on the stores are still up," he wrote,

> but the faces of the people in this district are all black. There are about 17,000 Negroes in this district now, whereas there were only 4,000 before the war. This is one of the most perplexing problems of the Bay Area since there is no housing available for this group.[57]

As in Chicago and Los Angeles, the realities of housing competition between African Americans and Japanese Americans severely challenged San Francisco. But in speaking with Mr. Yngojo, Jack's future father-in-law, Kikuchi realized that it was not simply a two-horse race in the former Japanese district. A storeowner and landlord who had benefited from the rapid influx of Black migrants during internment, the elderly Filipino "said that at the time of evacuation, he tried to get some of the Filipinos to take over Japanese businesses but they didn't have the initiative to do this," adding, "the Negroes then moved into the places and they were doing very well."[58] Mr. Yngojo presumptuously blamed the preponderance of single Filipino men for their lack of ambition and weak intellectual drive. Having come from nothing, Yngojo immigrated to the United States as an agricultural laborer after Japanese and Chinese workers were excluded by the 1924 Immigration Act.[59] Over time, he saved enough money to start a business with one of his brothers, while he sent a third brother on to college and an officer's rank in the Filipino battalion of the U.S. Army. Furthermore, he and his wife encouraged their children to embrace "the American way of life," primarily emphasizing education; as a result, their daughter (and Charlie's future sister-in-law) was finishing up at Stanford, where she studied nursing. Although he had respect for Mr. Yngojo, Kikuchi was not too enamored of Dolores. He considered her extremely spoiled and could not stomach the fact that she refused to wait on African Americans in her father's store "because she has a false feeling of belonging to a superior social class."[60] Nonetheless, Kikuchi expressed deep admiration for the Yngojos and their hard-won middle-class status: "It is amazing how typically American the second-generation Filipino is. They are way ahead of the Nisei in this respect."[61]

Sharing this set of exchanges between the Yngojos and Kikuchi demonstrates that the struggles and negotiations taking place in these former Little Tokyos included more than just Blacks and Japanese: third (Filipinos) and fourth parties (like Mexicans, Chinese, or Jews) complicated these interracial relationships—at times strengthening them, while at other times problematizing them to no end. The overarching point here is that the simplistic black-white paradigm of U.S. race relations does not and should not suffice for an examination of the 1940s, as Kikuchi's observations make clear. The boundaries of this dichotomy stretch and eventually snap, allowing for a more accurate and more "colorful" analysis to emerge. With black-white or even yellow-white dyads rendered insufficient, it can thus be argued that a significant number of minorities interacted during this wartime and postwar period. Indisputably, the groups ran into conflict with one another, particularly when seeking the same job, the same apartment, or the same political space (however small). But in these communities, as Kikuchi proved, many individuals also sought one another out, finding common cause, maintaining open dialogues, and seeing one another as human.

This could not have been truer than in the conversation between Kikuchi and his two elderly African American friends a few days later. Charlie had met Mr. Camba and Mrs. Butler five years earlier when his sister Mariko celebrated her birthday at an African American nightclub. Kikuchi, Camba, and Butler were introduced that evening by a common friend named George Clark, an African American married to a Chinese American, Helen Wong.[62] Kikuchi characterized Camba and Butler as "examples of the fine type of educated Negroes." As he described it, Butler belonged to "the upper class in Negro society," a woman who knew many of the artists and professionals around the country—those Franklin Frazier dubbed "the Black bourgeoisie."[63] She told Kikuchi of her recent conversation with the famed contralto Marian Anderson, while he took note of her extensive library collection on African American history. Butler worried over the heavy migration of southern Blacks into the Bay Area, fretting, "We are not getting the more stable type of Negroes or whites into S.F. Many of them are of the extreme lower classes and these Negroes have a chip on their shoulder so that they are very aggressive." Concerned with the "politics of respectability" described by Evelyn Higginbotham, Butler claimed, "It is this group which might be incited into riots against any of the returning Japanese if they feel that it is a threat to their 'insecure' security in housing now." By contrast, she asserted, "The more intelligent Negroes that I know are extremely sympathetic towards the Japanese evacuees because we know what it is to suffer because of the accident of race . . . We Negroes are very concerned about democracy because we certainly know what happens when there is a lack of it."[64]

For his part, Mr. Camba, in addition to helping run the funeral home, moonlighted as a bookkeeper for Italian and Black nightclubs in the area. His interaction, noticeably marked by his recent need to be wheelchair bound, was tinged with a wistful kind of sadness. He told Kikuchi: "Your citizenship, my citizenship, and Franklin Roosevelt's citizenship are all the same thing. If your citizenship rights are violated, then mine is bound to suffer and also Franklin D. Roosevelt's." In a further sign of solidarity, he proclaimed: "My people deeply sympathize with all of the Japanese evacuees, and we certainly want to do everything possible to help them get back here." With that goal in mind, Camba was trying to recruit a

Nisei girl out of the camps to assist him with the bookkeeping, to encourage her resettlement there. He ended on a blue note, however: "I often sit by the front window and think about all of my former Nisei friends and I miss the sight of them walking down Post Street."[65] Kikuchi remarked before he left: "Mr. Camba is certainly an amazing person."[66]

Kikuchi found that this sentiment of interracial alliance was not unique to the older generation of African Americans. His most spirited discussions of the trip took place among young intellectuals at Cal's International House. Kikuchi's sparring partner during these debates was a young African American named Douglas Robinson Greer. They proved to be a fitting pair, given that Greer's background and career—in a broad sense—mirrored Kikuchi's. Born in LA on January 27, 1916, only nine days after Kikuchi, Greer grew up in Sacramento and went on to serve two years (Kikuchi spent seventeen months) in the U.S. Army at the Tuskegee Institute, home of the famed "Tuskegee Airmen." He then attended Berkeley (where Kikuchi had previously been a graduate student) as an undergraduate on the GI Bill and matriculated at the University of San Francisco School of Law, graduating in 1952. Motivated by his desire to combat housing discrimination and unfair employment practices, Greer moved back to Sacramento and opened his own office, becoming only the second African American to establish a full-time law practice in the city. In the course of his career, he tested public-accommodation laws and other discriminatory acts, taking on corporate entities like Harrah's Casino and Greyhound Bus Lines. When a Sacramento couple was denied the purchase of a home in the late 1950s, Greer filed a malicious interference suit on the basis of race, the first of its kind in California. His championing of civil rights earned him the presidency of the Sacramento chapter of the NAACP from 1953 to 1957, a long-standing relationship with the Southern Poverty Law Center, and in 2003, a Medallion of Honor for his life's work from the *Sacramento Observer*, which simply labeled him "Pioneer. Hero. Legend."[67] Coincidentally, on September 8, 2004, three months after Greer's death, the late congressman Robert Matsui, Democrat from California's fifth district (which includes Sacramento), and a Japanese American internee, formally paid tribute to Greer on the floor of the House of Representatives, proclaiming, "It was truly a privilege for me to count Douglas Greer as a friend."[68] Martin Dies must have been rolling over in his grave.

Describing his newfound friend back in 1945 at International (or "I") House, Kikuchi made a point of acknowledging that Doug represented "the intellectual Negro's point of view," and so was not representative of "the group who will be threatened economically, especially in housing." Kikuchi nonetheless remained riveted by Greer's intellect, carefully listening to him as he commented on the repeal of the ban on Japanese Americans' return to the West Coast and the housing crisis facing minorities nationwide:

> I'm very glad that the restriction was lifted because I think that we Negroes looked upon this from a very selfish point of view. We were always

opposed to the evacuation, because it meant that a denial of free rights to any one minority group is also a threat to us.

Greer caught himself, however, and conceded: "Of course, there are some Negro groups on the lower economic level who sort of resent the possibility of the Japanese returning, but I am sure that they will vacate the Japanese homes even though it will be hard on them to find other housing." His greater concern was a familiar one: "I think that we Negroes do not resent the Japanese so much as we resent the Caucasians who impose restrictive housing covenants on us." Therefore, Greer, as much as Kikuchi, hoped for the avoidance of racial competition, pitting black or brown against Japanese, and encouraged an embrace of their political and moral imperatives to unite against a common adversary. He even revealed to Kikuchi, "I was up in Sacramento last weekend and I mentioned that I had met you. Most of my friends were very glad that loyal Japanese had finally been justified."[69]

Greer and Kikuchi enjoyed a spirited debate one evening with another budding intellectual, a Chinese American named James Wong from Minot, North Dakota. All three expressed concern at the self-segregating tendencies of the Chinese students at I House. Wong was especially confused, since back home he (and his other Asian friends) had always been integrated into the community. Surprised by how "race conscious" these California Chinese were, he mentioned:

It was a long time before I found out that most of them had never been to China. The way they talked, I was almost sure they were foreign students. They feel much more Chinesy than I ever have.

Nonetheless, Wong confessed, "But I find myself being drawn into this sort of thing and getting conscious of China more than ever before in my life." He asked Kikuchi: "Isn't that one of the things the Japanese Americans were condemned for?"[70]

Kikuchi answered affirmatively, emphasizing his belief that "such a segregated pattern [should] not ever develop again even though it seemed to be an idealistic goal." Greer chimed in as well, explaining that more liberal African American groups were equally interested in integration, but not to the extent of breaking up Black communities entirely. He also addressed Wong's question about segregated tables at I House, pointing out that African Americans never sat together at an all-Black table, for fear that other students would have an easy excuse for avoiding them. Greer conceded that African American women on campus criticized him for not socializing with their group enough, but, as Kikuchi remembered, "he was most interested in seeing the Negroes advance out of their segregated status." Greer then gestured toward greater implications:

I am not fooling myself about Democracy . . . We don't have it now, but this doesn't mean that we never will have it. But I think that the gradual process method is too slow. It has to be a revolutionary sort of thing.[71]

Wong replied in kind, addressing both men:

> I don't know if it is possible for the Chinese to ever become dispersed
> throughout this country because the family solidarity is strong and we
> believe in it firmly . . . This is the sort of thing [for] which the Japanese
> were evacuated and it is just a trick of international fortunes that I was
> not evacuated instead of you [Charlie].

He concluded:

> I am only glad that I am not in a position of the Nisei who had to make
> a sudden decision [as to] where he stood [with] the war. Such a thing
> would twist me all up and I might even consider myself more Chinese.[72]

Greer offered a response:

> But I don't think that this is a matter of patriotism. It is natural for any
> group to protest against the social order if [it] is getting pressed down and
> not allowed to draw a fresh lung of air. In the case of the Negro, this bit-
> terness against the social order is very strong and yet they consider them-
> selves as Americans . . . That is why the Negro is determined to have a
> change now by peaceful means if possible and violent means if necessary.

Following this protonationalist flourish, he emphasized the fact that African
Americans made provisional advancements during the war—earning eight times
as much in defense plants than in their prewar jobs—but that they all knew that
once the war ended, the pink slips would come to them first. "The Negro has
never had his fair share of this country's wealth," he commented, "and if democracy means anything at all, now is the time for them to get it. I've often felt that
all of the minority groups should stick together on this issue." Turning to Kikuchi
(and sounding a great deal like him), he opined,

> Maybe the Japanese Americans can get integrated gradually since there is
> such a small number, but I am rather doubtful. I think they have to come
> along with the wave of minority groups who rise to assert themselves and
> it may come within a few years after the war. But most of the minority
> groups fail to see that their success or failure of obtaining the real fruits
> of democratic life will depend upon close cooperation.[73]

Building on this positive outlook on interracial coalition building, Greer viewed
it as a key to cultivating a genuine democracy. Pointing to his military service, he
said, "That is why I fought for democracy and I don't want to feel cheated." Given
his thoughtful and wide-ranging answers, Greer ended with a bit of an understatement, looking to Kikuchi and saying, "I sympathize with the Nisei because I
know some of the things you have been going through."[74] Relaying this provocative and highly intense conversation to his sister by letter the next day, Kikuchi
conveyed his impression of Greer accurately and concisely: "Brilliant fellow."[75]

Regrettably, this is the only set of conversations recorded between Greer and Kikuchi in the diaries, and there is no external evidence that the two corresponded. Both men would go on to travel separate paths, but based on the conversations they enjoyed in Berkeley, the blueprint for their journeys was seemingly a shared one. While Kikuchi graduated to a career practicing psychiatric social work with veterans, many of whom were African American, Greer became a freedom fighter of a different sort, helping Blacks and other minorities navigate a legal system largely set up against them. Even though their dialogue back at Cal remained on the intellectualized, theoretical plane, their activism in the postwar years and beyond proved that they could practice what they preached. Kindred spirits, Kikuchi and Greer were ultimately both "brilliant fellows."

Back to the Midway

In her exceptional study of Japanese American resettlement in Chicago from 1942 to 1945, Charlotte Brooks makes a compelling argument that "Japanese Americans, like members of many other ethnic groups, accepted the prevailing myth of black inferiority and chose to work for white approval." It was completely understandable, in other words, that a minority group just recently stigmatized and segregated on the basis of race would likewise reproduce the abuse that had been heaped upon them, and subsequently find a convenient (and equally racialized) victim. As Brooks puts it,

> Many Nisei avoided or ridiculed African Americans, whose supposed inferiority seemed to place them beyond hope of movement in Chicago's racial hierarchy. Rather than potential allies, blacks were the group from whom the Nisei fought to distance themselves as they climbed the racial ladder. The benefits of avoidance and separation appeared to far outweigh those of acknowledging a common predicament.[76]

While I do not necessarily question the main thrust of her argument—that the majority of mainstream Nisei over time chose, in effect, whiteness over blackness—I would strongly urge scholars of race relations to broaden the scope of their investigations and consider the choices made by other mainstream, radical, or progressive Nisei—like Kikuchi—who did not distance themselves from Black Chicago, who acknowledged a common predicament, and who tirelessly fought for Japanese American *and* African American equality. Some of these radicals, like Kikuchi, Yamamoto, Tajiri, Sugihara, and in later years, Yuri Kochiyama (the follower of Malcolm X's who cradled the bloodied head of her assassinated mentor in the Audubon Ballroom in 1965), or Guy Kurose and Richard Aoki of the Black Panther Party, would in fact choose a situational Blackness over any form of whiteness: their allegiances would most clearly be pledged to a multicolored America. This line of argument does not wholly discount Brooks's interpretation by any means, but rather demonstrates that the arguments are not mutually exclusive. Even if only as a minority within a minority, a culture of dissent formed within the Japanese American community when it came to these questions of whiteness (assimilation) and blackness (protest and civil rights). Their very presence, amid the majority and the mainstream, remains historically significant. This sliver, this piece, this penumbra of dissent represents the possibility of ever-changing perspectives and the limits therein, as well as the redefinitions of (inter) racial identities and the limits therein. What cannot be dismissed, then, is the evidence for such dissent, the proof of such resistance against the status quo, and the confirmation of such iconoclasm.

In the next and final chapter, I raise the subject of "the derelicts of Company K," a Nisei unit documented by Tom Shibutani, who amply demonstrated the perceived similarities of poor performance between Black military units and Company K, especially considering the latter's demoralization and blatant distrust of the white military leadership (which had, after all, incarcerated them and their families not long before). These company men—unlike the highly decorated 442nd—were not poster boys for wartime newspapers, heralding the patriotic sacrifice of those Americans of Japanese descent. They represented the anti-type of "the fighting 442nd" and were not ashamed to inhabit that oppositional space of protest and antiheroism. Similarly in chapter 5, when I mentioned the 1943 riots in Los Angeles, and the role, albeit marginal, that Japanese American zoot-suiters (derogatorily termed *yogores*) would play in this stylized nightclub counterculture, I wanted to provide evidence of another oppositional group or network among the Nisei. Viewed as a much less unified and politically minded group (than even Company K), the zoot-suiters nonetheless borrowed styles and fashion first made famous by African American men, like young Malcolm X in Roxbury, Massachusetts. These zoot-suiters may not have had a formal platform or political aim, but as Luis Alvarez correctly asserts, they still perpetrated equally significant acts of protest and violated (white) norms:

> The phenomenon of interracial sex among hepcats and pachucos, especially when white women were involved, surely intensified the threat that zoot suit culture posed to dominant sexual mores and added to fears of miscegenation. When the perceived hypersexuality of male zoot suiters targeted white women in particular, it underscored their masculinity and sexuality as threats to the moral and social stability of the home front.[77]

Not coincidentally, Alvarez mentions one Nisei by the name of Blackie Najima, a pseudonym for one of the case histories recorded (but not published) by Kikuchi, and then taken up once more by the historian Paul Spickard. Both Alvarez and Spickard note the heavy emphasis that Najima placed on the enjoyable multiracial sex he experienced before and during resettlement in Chicago. Delineating the four major elements of what he appropriately terms "the Nisei underclass," Spickard analyzes sexual promiscuity, nightlife entertainment (especially jazz-influenced jitterbugging), gang life (as Kikuchi experienced in his youth), and a wholesale disrespect for straight-laced, mainstream Nisei. On the issue of sex,

Spickard makes astute observations that bind various actors as well as strands of this narrative more tightly:

> Many of [the Nisei] engaged in casual sex, sex-for-hire, and sometimes forcible sex as early as their young teenage years. By their own account, most of that was interethnic sex, with whites, blacks, Chicanos, and other Asians . . . The celebration of promiscuity by the Nisei underclass in these interviews [by Kikuchi] is in stark contrast to the other, more conventional Nisei whom Kikuchi interviewed. Those mainstream Nisei almost never mentioned sex, except when they whispered disapprovingly about people like . . . Blackie Najima.[78]

Undoubtedly, these kinds of narratives rankled the "respectable" Nisei in the resettlement community, whether it was LA, Chicago, or, as Kikuchi admitted before he left Gila for good, in the "red light district" of Block 51 back at camp. However, raising the issue of these apparently frowned-upon acts is not meant—either by Spickard or by me—to cast aspersions on the multiracial underclass, particularly the Nisei individuals, like Najima, who participated. Nor should this be interpreted as a facile conflation of hypersexuality among Blacks, Latinas/os, Japanese, or Filipinos, as if these pleasure seekers were simply subhuman.

On the contrary, without romanticizing the acts, or the abuse (physical and otherwise) of the power dynamics in these transactional relationships, I would argue that it is patently obvious, and historically significant, that these young hepcat, yogore, pachuco men and women (I am thinking here of zoot-suiters, as well), who might well be most accurately described as the era's underclass, purposely flouted the rules and conventions of their ethnic or racial groups' respectable, middle-class, mainstream rules. Furthermore, as a clear rejection of white mainstream culture, the actions, appearance, and social mores of this underclass proved not only oppositional, but also defiantly antiassimilationist. Spickard additionally points out:

> Previous writing has depicted the Nisei as inhabiting an ethnically discrete social world. But the underclass Nisei formed intimate relationships with whites, Chinese, Mexicans, blacks, and Filipinos, so perhaps other Nisei were not so isolated either.[79]

Regardless of whether this was a consciously collective move by the Nisei underclass, its very existence—as documented by Kikuchi himself—requires thorough consideration of what I would like to term "the Spickard thesis," the need to reconsider "the degree of openness for options that Nisei experienced in Chicago, especially during the war itself." Spickard emphasizes the divisions in the Nisei community (e.g., Hawai'ian Nisei versus San Joaquin Nisei) and the ways in which different people experienced their actions and decisions during resettlement in so many dissimilar ways.[80]

I raise Spickard's layered analysis of this diverse community of Japanese Americans in Chicago as a mild and respectful corrective to Brooks's argument in her article on the "in-betweenness" of Nisei resettlers. Again, I believe she makes a convincing overarching argument that Nisei followed white flight out of the city, in effect choosing whiteness over blackness over the long haul. Brooks's evidence, which includes some of Kikuchi's case histories, undoubtedly points the reader in that general direction. As Spickard has foreshadowed, however, my point is that the Chicagoland community of Japanese Americans comprised so many different types, from the Clark/Division bachelors, to the families near Kenwood, to those living on the border of Cottage Grove Avenue and the wonder of Bronzeville. Brooks and others have at least entertained the potential stance of Nisei "opposition," but for the most part, scholars dismiss it as a peculiar and temporary disruption of the American racial economy. But the same archives of evidence we share provide clear examples of such opposition—or at the very least, of the possibilities and multiple choices made by Nisei at that particular point and time. As Kikuchi's unpublished history of Najima and his rougher-edged friends suggest, flowing with the Nisei or white mainstream was a sure path to drowning; living on the edge, on that sliver of cultural geography of dissent, was Najima's modus operandi. It might not have been popular, or particularly shrewd, but it was possible. That was what mattered. Hence, the minority within the minority still found voice and relevance in Kikuchi's diary and case histories. Compared to Kikuchi himself, Blackie was nihilistic, confused, dangerous, and thrillingly alive all at the same time. Breaching the protocol of his participant-observer status, Kikuchi rarely kept enough distance from Blackie. On one occasion, however, the trust built up by Kikuchi allowed Najima to state:

> Sometimes I just walk around the Negro district by myself. [My roommate and I] have to get up so early that it's no use going out. Besides we don't know anybody. We just go to the Negro pool halls or else to the Regal Theatre (Negro). The Negroes don't look at us as much as the *hakujins* [whites].[81]

Najima finds qualified comfort among African Americans rather than whites, a seemingly Pyrrhic victory between two "underdogs," and the district provides him with a vague sense of home.

After more than a year of fraternizing with Kikuchi, Najima explained both the freedom and the curse of living in this alternative, oppositional, rebellious, and potentially empowering counterpublic. Like Marlon Brando in *The Wild One*, he bluntly testified:

> If I don't marry, then I guess I'll just be a gambler for the rest of my life. It's a good way to live and you don't have to have any damn haoles [whites] bossing over you all the time. That's one thing that burns me up. Every time, I feel like running a knife into one of those haole bastards who think their crap don't stink. I'm through taking all that stuff from any guy . . . I'd rather live the way I am.[82]

Hardly the "model minority" quiescence to be roundly celebrated two decades later, Najima's deeply combative, combustible, and restless nature echoes that of the main character in Wright's *Native Son* as well as that of the restless expatriate, existentialist writer himself. In one sense, Kikuchi provides his diary readers with a cautionary tale: that of the Nisei who could not find his way to sobriety and, by extension, the suburbs, but was deeply affected by both the upheaval of his evacuation from the West Coast and resettlement. In another sense, the diarist gives his audience an antihero, perhaps the one Kikuchi could never really be, despite his proclivity for questioning authority. Najima was not, of course, part of a greater whole, a member of an organization on the South Side that would bridge gaps between the races. Leave that to the academics like Shibutani and Miyamoto or the activists like Oyama and Kikuchi. Nor was he "in between," because his anger simply would not let him forgive the white government for putting his people in concentration camps. Even if those people included judgmental mainstream Nisei or backward "boochies," they were still his people. Here was a working-class Nisei with few friends, little work experience, poor English skills, and a melon-sized chip on his shoulder. Upward mobility was not a choice; Najima was the antithesis of the model minority.

"I didn't get home until 7:00 a.m.," Kikuchi wrote after one confab with Blackie. "And I slept until noon before I got up."[83] Participant observation definitely took its toll, but Kikuchi went to such great lengths to get to know these resettlers—ostensibly for fieldwork, but more accurately for the friendships and networks opened up to him. Vocation and avocation conveniently dovetailed. So much so that Spickard appropriately speculated: "Charlie Kikuchi probably understood all these things far better than any of us ever will."[84]

Soldiering On

We return to Chicagoland for a final conversation between Kikuchi and another member of the diverse Black population in the city, this time an officer in the air force. Kikuchi listened carefully as the young pilot, also segregated in the armed forces, expounded on the decorated 442nd. Kikuchi wrote:

> The fellow said that he had met some Nisei on the western front and that they had a fine record. He was very indignant about the evacuation . . . He said that it was a dirty racial discrimination trick to remove the Japanese from the coast, but that he believed strongly in Democracy and he felt that the lights would go on for the Nisei as well.[85]

The airman told Kikuchi: "You know, we are all fightin' to make it good for democracy in America as well as in Europe." This last dialogue serves as a fitting end to this chapter within Kikuchi's diary and life. A few months later, Kikuchi was inducted into the army at Fort Sheridan, Illinois, right around the days of infamy that would devastate Hiroshima and Nagasaki. As we turn to this stage in

Kikuchi's development, his scrutiny of race relations and democratic possibility persisted and deepened; conversations with fellow soldiers dominate the bulk of his army diary. He also compared notes, by letter, with two old friends from back in his days at Cal, both fulfilling their military service at different posts around the globe. One of them was his best friend, Warren.

It was Tsuneishi who offered a thoughtful paean to his fallen friend after Charlie succumbed to cancer in 1988. He wrote:

> As Nisei, Charlie and I had come a long way. From being outcasts in American society before and during the Second World War, we joined the American mainstream in the post-war era. We lived to see basic American attitudes transformed through the civil-rights movement, and we took a certain pride in the fact that we had been optimistic about American society changing and moving toward the ideals it espoused.

He conceded, however, that even though they had come a long way, "Charlie saw that we as a nation still had a long way to go in alleviating the plight of Afro-Americans and other minorities in finding their rightful place in American society."[86] For Charlie, then, the heady days of the 1940s on the edge of the Black Metropolis and multicultural San Francisco were only the beginning. The American dilemma had yet to truly be solved.

Chapter 7

"It Could Just as Well Be Me": Japanese American and African American GIs in the Army Diary

Barely a week had passed since the twin bombings of Hiroshima and Nagasaki violently hastened the end of World War II. On the other side of the world, at Fort Sheridan, Illinois, a recent inductee into the U.S. Army recorded the following incident in his diary on August 16, 1945:

> A Negro soldier came in, and he had a difficult time in printing his name so I did it for him. "Four-eyes" then commented after the colored boy departed, "You shouldn't have helped that damn booby." I asked why not, and he said that it was too dangerous to even touch a pencil that "a Nigger handles because half of them were rejected because they had the syph or flat feet."[1]

Kikuchi, now close to thirty years old, had entered the army only six days earlier. His tour of duty was split into two stages: three months of basic training as a foot soldier (August–October 1945) and more than a year's worth of training as a psychiatric social worker at military hospitals catering to veterans and soldiers under courts-martial (November 1945–December 1946). Having spent the two previous years living in Chicago, working on his master's degree in social work, and conducting research for JERS, Kikuchi found army life somewhat of a rude awakening. It proved to be as much a mental challenge as a physical one: the bureaucracy of the military hierarchy and its conservative ideology (relative to that of the general population) were most surprising to Kikuchi. He discovered that deep-seated racism directed toward African American soldiers and civilians pervaded the army ranks, a difficult pill to swallow given his own position as a recently imprisoned Nisei. Nevertheless, he managed to retain an intense faith and belief in the power and potential of America's democracy, hoping that his individual service would, in some small measure, reflect the commitment of the Nisei as a whole. Taking what he had learned from Adamic's circle, the Thomases, and Black Chicagoans, Kikuchi kept a watchful eye on his surroundings, absorbing a wide array of interpersonal experiences and continuing to build on his understanding of race relations in the particularly masculine crucible of the U.S. military.

Epistolary Bull Sessions

One must recall at this point that Kikuchi had especially enjoyed the late-night bull sessions he shared with Nisei buddies and roommates at Berkeley before the war began. Even in Tanforan, he managed to continue these discussions with his brother, a couple of his grad school pals, and other liberal Bay Area Nisei. But the army would take some of those friends away, hastening them off to training camps in the American South or to strategic outposts in the European or Pacific theater. This did not seem to deter Kikuchi, however: his diary includes a number of letters he exchanged before his induction with two of those closest friends from Cal—Warren Tsuneishi and Kenji Murase. Both men had been in the service long before Kikuchi received his induction papers, but they nonetheless kept up their correspondence with him, making sure that the bull sessions continued, even if only by military post. Their letters thus serve as a fascinating counterpoint to Kikuchi's diary at this time, drawing him out into a larger, globalized conversation while simultaneously showing how other young Nisei men were planning to face the brave new postwar world. They also prepared Kikuchi for his own experience in the army a few months later. Admittedly, it was an uncertain time for all three men, but the correspondence was a welcome reminder that friends would be waiting for one another's safe return home.

First, however, as a point of comparison, consider the following December 1941 diary entry from Kikuchi, in which he mentions both Tsuneishi ("Wang") and Murase, and contemplate how quickly these young men had to "grow up" within a period of two to three years of evacuation and war.

> Wang and the guys have a bull session every night, and they are going to organize the Nisei progressives on campus to make a statement to the *Daily Cal.* I am for that. Kenny and I are supposed to work on this letter, but I will let Kenny do the writing and I'll pretend that I'm giving him the idea. He is a hell of a writer. Wang can write, too, but he has an inferiority complex. He keeps pestering me to take him to San Francisco to a whorehouse because he says he may get drafted into the Army and be sent off to war; and he does not want to die a virgin. Kenny gets sore when we talk like that because he is a Christian deep down and very pure in heart, and he thinks that we should keep our minds on the war and think progressive thoughts. He says I am a bad influence on the guys . . . because I go chase girls every night.[2]

Tsuneishi was forced to part ways with Kikuchi after Tanforan, sent off to the Heart Mountain Relocation Center in Wyoming. With the help of the American Friends, he left camp for Syracuse University in early 1943, where he finished his senior year of college. After graduation, like the unlikely Karl Yoneda, he volunteered for the Military Intelligence Service Language School (MISLS). Because of security considerations, the MISLS was minimally publicized, but it had been established in the summer of 1941 as the threat of going to war with Japan seemed imminent. Meeting the need for Japanese linguists, the school primarily enrolled Nisei soldiers who already possessed a basic knowledge of the language. The school opened its doors in November 1941 at the Presidio in San Francisco, with sixty students (fifty-eight Nisei, two whites) and four Nisei instructors. When the United States entered the war, the demand for linguists increased, and the school moved to Camp Savage, Minnesota, and later to nearby Fort Snelling. White linguists who had trained separately at the University of Michigan eventually joined their Nisei comrades at Savage and Snelling. By the end of the war, the MISLS had graduated six thousand students, approximately three-quarters of whom were Nisei.[3] After joining the MISLS, Tsuneishi saw action with the 306th Headquarters Intelligence Detachment, Twenty-Fourth Corps, as General Douglas MacArthur made his famous "return" to the Philippines in October 1944.

While still training at Camp Savage in November 1943, Tsuneishi wrote to his good friend, explaining why he had decided to join the service. "Little boys constantly stopped me on the street and asked me "what I was," he recalled. After answering "American," they nonetheless persisted:

> "But what are you, really?" I began to wonder, and have doubts. I volunteered to prove to myself, to prove to others that I was American.

He continued:

> I had often questioned the sincerity of JA's [Japanese Americans] who waved the flag with all their might, called themselves Americans, were super-patriotic, and protected their complete innocence. Well . . . the shoe was on the other foot—my foot—now.[4]

This was a dilemma many Nisei men faced at this stage of the war, especially with news abounding of the successful 442nd Regiment/100th Battalion, the all-Nisei unit fighting in Europe (see discussion below): would Japanese Americans volunteer in resounding numbers and temporarily put to rest any doubts about their loyalty? Tsuneishi provided some rationale for why they would:

> Most JA's really love the country in which they were born and reared . . . But it's obviously a different kind of patriotism than is commonly held by most Americans. [Additionally,] I suppose most of the JA's have never lost faith in American democracy. In the end, most JA's feel that like a fairy tale, everyone will live happily ever after. I'm quite sure that the boys from Hawaii [the 442nd/100th] training at [Camp] Shelby and in Italy have never lost that faith.[5]

After a month with MacArthur, Tsuneishi contacted his best friend once more, in December 1944, providing some lighthearted comic relief:

> The Philippines is no Hawaii—not by a long shot. They have the same romantic palm groves edging up to the sea, like the one in which we are now encamped, but there the similarity ends abruptly. While Hawaii had

bright lights for the homesick soldier, here we have no bright lights save for those installed by Army engineers.[6]

He then, however, turns to more serious matters. Having trained at the MISLS, Tsuneishi was expected to help translate captured documents and radio intercepts. He mentions that volumes have been brought in for his colleagues and him to scan. "It all seems damned futile to me," he admits, "but then I suppose every bit of information we turn out does have its importance." Heavily, he notes, prisoners of war have come in for interrogation. "What a bunch of sad Japs they are," he writes. "Passive, not showing any emotions . . . Most have no fight left in them, accepting their fate with utter resignation." Despite the fact that he speaks their language and shares their ancestry, Tsuneishi cannot help thinking of these Japanese as extremely foreign to him. He describes the Japanese air raids, the lack of hesitation as kamikazes dive-bomb the U.S. ships or simply crash into the ocean:

> I've got to confess, Chas [Kikuchi], that this is one aspect of the Jap that I can't understand. Maybe it's because I love life a lot, but I can't fathom people who throw away their lives for nothing but the honor of being enshrined as clay gods in some damned little shrine.

After receiving Warren's letter, Kikuchi took the time in his diary to reflect on how different their lives had turned out to this point. "When we were living together on the campus 3 years ago," he writes,

> we had no idea that we would be out of the state in such strange ways. Here I am in Chicago living a fairly normal life and I sort of feel out of the war directly . . . At the same time Wang is on the other side of the world.

In a familiar refrain, he frets, "I have no doubt that the Study [JERS] as a whole will be a valuable contribution to minority problems and their solutions although I can't convince myself that I am contributing too much." By contrast, he lists all of Tsuneishi's wartime duties, and then deadpans: "He doesn't seem to be depressed by the fact that he may be killed at any moment."[7] The truth was that, of course, Tsuneishi was not entirely carefree and content with his lot, despite his admission that he and the other MIS soldiers were "living like kings compared to the guys in the front lines." With Christmas looming and thoughts turning toward home, he shared with Kikuchi: "It still looks like a long, tough war, and we look with anger, and perhaps with envious longing, at the people back home getting ready to celebrate V-E day and V-Asia day . . . It makes our lot harder to bear."[8]

Murase, at this time, had just been married and was living with his wife in New York City. After spending his evacuation at the Poston camp in Arizona, he continued his undergraduate work at Temple University in Philadelphia. He then moved on to the New York School of Social Work, which, he told Kikuchi in February 1945, was "a pretty stuck-up outfit—lousy with big money and people."[9] Worse yet, he said, "the emphasis is too much on maintaining 'professional standards' . . . You lose perspective, and pretty soon the clients aren't real human beings anymore, but just 'cases.'"[10] In later years, he would confess that the papers he had written in graduate school were simply "loaned" to Kikuchi to copy when the latter attended the School of Social Work a couple years later.[11] Despite the fact that he would also later reveal that his friendship with Kikuchi cooled over the next few decades, at this intense moment in the mid-1940s, Murase's letters to him still conveyed a keen sense of their friendship. "You're right when you say you are a hell of a correspondent," he told Kikuchi in another letter from February 1945, "but the redeeming thing is that whenever you do write, it's an altogether satisfying experience reading what you have to say."[12] The two would presumably have much to talk about, sharing stories of social work and the struggle against racial discrimination (which might explain why their friendship chilled as the years passed, i.e., because of competition on similar turf). At this stage, Murase was still unsure of his career path, telling Kikuchi, "The more I get to know about the whole field of social work, the more limited do I think possibilities are." Worried about his effectiveness and reach as a social worker, he connected this observation with his aggravation at the Republicans in both Congress and the New York state legislature for stymieing the passage of fair employment and antidiscrimination laws. "So damn much seems to rest on whether the public will follow or not," he writes, "and it's frustrating as hell to wait around until some geezers in Congress finally wake up and legislate what the public has been wanting for years."

After completing eight weeks of basic infantry training at Camp Blanding, Florida, Murase reconnected with Kikuchi in September, elaborating more extensively on his concerns about social work. His biggest fear was that social workers in the postwar world would not be able to get to "the real roots of economic and social difficulties" and would be left to "patching up the wreckage thrown up by a system that is wrong to begin with." The only means of achieving "desired social ends," he went on to say, was through legislation, which in turn depended on public support and skillful sponsorship. "To get this public backing," he theorized, "we have to organize public opinion—and this is essentially where I see myself as fitting in." He concluded his remarks by all but dismissing the field entirely: "I don't know what you think—I think you would argue that social case work, at least, is a pretty feeble and ineffectual method of coping with social problems." This was a strong assumption on Murase's part, and somewhat offensive, given that Kikuchi had been spending all of his recent professional life doing such casework (at Cal, as part of his MSW training, at Gila's social welfare unit, and in Chicago as part of JERS). Of course, Murase could not have known that Kikuchi would go on to spend a twenty-four-year career in social casework, but then again, Murase also did not know that he himself would later earn a doctorate in social work and teach it at San Francisco State for more than thirty years.

Murase also received letters from Tsuneishi during this time. Significantly, these particular missives, in comparison to those Tsuneishi sent Kikuchi, have a qualitatively different tone. With Charlie, "Wang" took on a much more fraternal, jocular disposition, even mentioning an occasional flirtation with local women. By contrast, with Kenny, Tsuneishi wrote as if he were speaking to a friendly, intellectual acquaintance, someone who might have taken a number of literature classes with him at school. For example, in November 1944, the description of his division's landing takes on a crafted, dramatic lyricism.

> Finally the time has come to load into our landing craft. We scramble down the nets, our full field packs heavy on our backs. While circling about the mother ship preparatory to heading into shore, our craft begins to rock and pitch. A sudden squall has come upon us. The seas are heavy. We are drenched by the downpour and by the salt water breaking over the bow. Soon only our rifles are dry.[13]

Murase seemed to recognize the nature of this relationship, for he sent Tsuneishi a book of poetry as a Christmas present. Tsuneishi wrote back appreciatively:

> People must think I'm a nut on poetry. Can you imagine me sitting in a foxhole with Japanese planes overhead and reading a verse that will soothe this savage breast? "Little lamb who made thee? Dost thou know who made thee?"[14]

Compare these passages to excerpts from Tsuneishi's letters to Kikuchi. Again, he speaks to Charlie as if he were an older brother (Kikuchi was five years his senior), joking around and maintaining an informal, chatty tone. In February 1945, he mused: "I'm finding plenty of time to catch up on my correspondence which I'd been neglecting for the past few weeks for a very good reason: Jap, he try get me; me, I try get Jap." He then launched into how he spent New Year's in the Philippines: "All in all, I think I had eight cans of ice-cold Pabst's Blue Ribbon, but after the long, parched period from Hawaii to New Year's during which my body had become almost completely desiccated, eight cans of 3.2 had absolutely no effect on my alcohol-starved system." The jocularity persists in the following passage as Tsuneishi describes a performance from the USO: "When the girls appeared on stage, a low moan went up from the crowd of starved GI's. All sorts of obscene remarks made the rounds, especially when the contortionist, a hefty piece of well rounded beef, began to contort and assumed all sorts of interesting positions."[15]

It would be disingenuous, however, to characterize all of Tsuneishi's letters to Kikuchi as bawdy or merely playful. The overarching point here is that he felt comfortable enough to engage in a genuine kind of male bonding (unpleasant sexism and chauvinism included) with Kikuchi that was not as apparent in his exchanges with Murase. Nonetheless, Tsuneishi was incredibly thoughtful, intelligent, and far-reaching in his communications with both men. Whenever he brings up the Japanese POWs, for example, his mood turns extremely serious. To Murase, he reports: "I went to the hospital to interrogate some wounded prisoners of war. Some are in great pain, some stink from their hitherto untreated wounds; all are singularly impassive. They are grateful for a cigarette or a drink of tepid water." Sounding a bit like the pre-Gila Kikuchi contemplating the Issei's mask, he queries, "What are they thinking about? What are their feelings behind those stolid faces? I can get only the facts."[16] With Kikuchi, he shares his disappointment over what he hears of the flagging Nisei morale in the relocation centers back home. "I must say they've developed self-pity to the highest possible degree," he writes. "I can understand how they feel, and if I'd stayed in a center, I'd probably be bitching with the worst of them . . . [But] there are GI's out here leading a hellish life that would make center life seem like paradise in comparison."[17]

Emphasizing the different tones and substances of these letter exchanges highlights a recurring theme in Kikuchi's life. Just as he had done with the orphans at Lytton, the Adamics, Dorothy Thomas and W. I. Thomas, African Americans in Chicago, or even with his Cal buddies before the war, Kikuchi was consistently able to re-create a family unit in any environment in which he found himself. Admittedly, in the months leading up to and including his induction, he was simply extending what had been established with Tsuneishi and Murase back in the Bay Area: a sense of brotherhood, a fraternity that would prepare him for experiencing boot camp and living in army barracks. As in any family of brothers, however, different dynamics characterized the relationship between any pair of them: jocularity, distance, mutual respect, strain, judgment, deep affection, and competition. Arthur Hansen has engagingly argued that for decades after the war, on some level, Kikuchi and Murase were acting out a variation of a sibling rivalry over Tsuneishi: hence, a possible reason why they infrequently spoke to one another after this period.[18]

The Tanforan diary from June 1942 already demonstrated cracks in the friendship. Kikuchi critically evaluated Murase: "To me, it appeared that he was compensating for frustrating situations by plunging away like 'a bull in a china shop' leading, as he sincerely believed, an 'intellectual' cause—the fight against racial discrimination." He explained that Murase's inferiority complex impelled him to seek out friends' gratuitous reassurance of his intelligence, including "pseudo-intellectuals," as Kikuchi put it, and some Cal communists. "He used to take me to the rooms of the fellow travelers who amused me with their almost religious fanaticism," he wrote. Pointedly finishing up his "diagnosis" of Murase, Kikuchi teasingly called him a "momma's boy," and then finally concluded: "K. is a very maladjusted young man, like all Nisei who have more than average brains. His immaturity is his salvation."[19] It is a genuinely searing indictment of Murase: at other points in the diary, Kikuchi expresses anger, but not with this intense tone of disapproval and air of condescension. Since it appears so uncharacteristic of Kikuchi's writing, this entry stands out, drawing attention to the potential underlying issues beneath such seething jealousy and petty name-calling. As Kikuchi observed, those Nisei with "more than average brains" are *all* maladjusted, so therefore he must also have been including himself in this diagnosis. It appears that the relationship with Murase was one onto which he projected a great deal of his own self-critique and, perhaps, self-loathing. In some ways—and this is not unprecedented for many people with siblings—he was closer to Murase (and Tsuneishi) than he was to his own blood brothers. In that intimacy, Charlie and Kenny were very similar: future social workers in the shadow of their intellectual buddies; activists deeply invested in African American equality, to the point that Murase wanted to attend all-Black Howard University in order "to plunge into the Negro problem"; and two talented Nisei "writers" championing progressive causes in a time of war.

Despite these shared interests, however, they most likely would not have been friends were it not for Tsuneishi, but therein lies the potential homosocial/homosexual competition. Hansen put this question directly to Murase in his 1999 interview. Murase could not pinpoint exactly why he and Kikuchi went their separate ways over the years, but Hansen proposed the idea that perhaps both men were in some way vying for Tsuneishi's best friendship, possibly with some understandable but latent homosexual overtones. Murase had roomed with Tsuneishi at Cal before Kikuchi entered their social circle, but relatively soon after meeting Kikuchi, Tsuneishi and Charlie became fast friends: someone was always the third wheel, so to speak. Even Kikuchi's nicknames for the two men were suggestive: "Wang" for Tsuneishi, a common Chinese American surname, in tribute to his sympathy for China after Japan's invasion; and "Pierre" for Murase, as in Robespierre, the French revolutionary who was considered, among many things, physically unimposing. For his part, nearly sixty years after the end of the war, Tsuneishi reiterated his deep regard for his late friend, perhaps with little or no knowledge of the "sibling rivalry" being played out over him. What is more, the passage of time can always obscure or color one's memory. He remembered: "The thing about Charlie was that he was extremely perceptive about basic attitudes, behavior, and how people tried to conceal their inner feelings, especially about their personal shortcomings and how they tried to compensate for them. But he was completely non-judgmental about human foibles."[20] Whatever the case may be, Murase ultimately handled the difficult question of his rivalry with Kikuchi graciously and diplomatically, saying that Kikuchi was fairly critical of a slew of people, adding, "So I felt he wasn't just necessarily taking out after me." At another point, he offered, "I had the sense that he had some reservations and never was really open with me."[21] Although this aspect of their friendship remains speculative, another aspect remains absolutely certain: all three men continued to build on a fellowship based on ideas and the vigorous debate of those ideas.

Appropriately, given the times, democracy was discussion topic number one. Equally fitting was the globalized context for the question, since Tsuneishi would soon ship off from the Philippines for Okinawa. Despite remaining stateside, both Murase and Kikuchi found their most immediate concerns related to the spread of democracy abroad. On V-E Day, for example, Kikuchi wrote to Tsuneishi:

> I am just thinking out loud now, but it does not seem conceivable that the fault is entirely one-sided. Chauvinisms, racialisms, and race prejudice were not invented by the Nazis and I am afraid that the Allies will allow

these things to survive if the present trends go on . . . I get the impression that anti-Semitism and other racial tensions are increasing rather than decreasing under the stress of the war.[22]

Kikuchi did not want to let any of the fascists off the hook and agreed that their violence had to be met with Allied violence, "but I would hate to see this continue after the war and have democracy sacrificed for the sake of economic imperialism." Specifically with regard to Germany and Japan, Kikuchi feared that the Allies would simply humiliate and subordinate them, without any hope of reconstruction. "If we enslave them," he wrote on this momentous date, "they will rant with hatreds and attempt to be the masters of the next generation and dream only of revolt and escape instead of getting 'democratized.' And when do we reach the point where they will become eligible to enter the 'family of nations'?"

Ten days earlier, Tsuneishi had shared with Kikuchi a story about Okinawan women hiding away in caves, fearful of the arrival of American soldiers. It was a cautionary tale, one that dovetailed with Kikuchi's observation that the victorious had a responsibility to bring promises of democracy, not fears linked with fascism, to the defeated. Tsuneishi recalled:

> The two women were crying while a young girl, her eyes darting about here and there like a trapped animal's, plainly showed terror. I think they feared with all their hearts that they would be tortured and killed. Even though I repeatedly assured them that they would come to no harm and the best they could do would be to put themselves under our care, still they were reluctant to leave their shelters.[23]

At the same time, Tsuneishi noticed that, given their own historical marginalization, the Okinawans were not entirely committed to the empire of the sun. "Some nurses told us that they had been warned by Japanese soldiers that they would be violated if they should happen to fall into our hands," he recalled. "The manner in which they spoke, when they were coherent, suggested that they resented the Japanese for their lies."

While Tsuneishi faced challenges on the ground while playing the liberator in the Pacific, Murase and Kikuchi continued to express their own fears and doubts about democratizing Japan from afar. A couple weeks after the emperor's surrender (September 2, 1945), Murase contacted Kikuchi once more: "Well, Charley, I hope this is the beginning of an active exchange of ideas." At this stage, Murase was still in his rifle company at Camp Blanding, while Kikuchi had been reassigned from Fort Sheridan to Camp Lee, Virginia, to continue his training. In response to a question Kikuchi had posed about the prospects of democracy in Asia, Murase offered a pessimistic analysis, based on the fact that he "did not expect much in the way of upsetting the status quo when MacArthur assumed Supreme Command—for he is known to be committed to the philosophy of economic conservatism." As evidence, he pointed to MacArthur's embrace of wealthy Filipino collaborators "at the expense of rejecting the guerilla forces that represented the Philippine people," adding that "of course, the State Department itself, has consistently gone along in the principle of expediency rather than principle." Exhibit B for Murase was MacArthur's strategy in Korea, where he allowed the Japanese to retain their regime, thereby flouting the terms of the Potsdam Proclamation (July 26, 1945) issued by the United States, Britain, and China, which mandated that Japan maintain sovereignty only over the islands of Honshu, Hokkaido, Kyushu, and Shikoku. Murase then drew a persuasive conclusion from this evidence, telling Kikuchi: "While we could say that the Atomic Bomb crushed Japan's resistance and led to its capitulation and a great Allied victory, on the other hand, in the subsequent developments, the Japs have won a political victory that may even overshadow their military loss, in terms of the future."[24] Murase further argued that the Japanese military would simply take the blame for the war, while the ruling oligarchy, in the form of the *Zaibatsu* (industrial and banking combines), would unflinchingly protect the emperor and his interests and continue with business as usual. Murase was not far off in his prediction: despite the Allies' attempts to break up the *Zaibatsu* during their occupation of Japan (1945–1952), the combines simply reemerged in the postwar as *keiretsu*, pooling all their resources to aid Japan's rise as an economic force in the postwar era. "In short, at the very outset," Murase complained, "by returning to the status quo, we are blocking off whatever democratic ferment there may exist from arising to the surface."[25] Finally, in regard to a question from Kikuchi about the possibility of Japanese communism, Murase presciently anticipated the chess moves of the impending Cold War.

> I would not be as confident as you are of a Communist rebirth in Japan—at least for the time being while MacArthur has any influence. I have a suspicion that MacArthur himself is motivated by a fear of Communism, and hence, is reluctant to reduce Japan to a third-rate power, but wants to keep Japan strong enough to serve as a "buffer" against Russian encroachments.[26]

In their exchanges, Tsuneishi and Kikuchi returned to domestic issues, focusing on the Japanese in America. At one point, Tsuneishi was quite concerned about evacuees being permitted to return to their homes after the WRA announced imminent closure of the camps. Initially, he had believed that the government would simply treat the camps like Native American reservations, keeping the Japanese Americans contained for an unspecified amount of time. "The 'residents' have had three long years to sit and brood," he told Kikuchi. "Their policy seems to be to 'sit tight' and I don't believe any threats of closure will move them into making hasty decisions." While, on the one hand, the closings meant freedom once again for Issei and Nisei, on the other hand, Tsuneishi thought that the evacuees would have a very difficult time making the transition out of the camps. "For example," he asked, "to what extent would evacuees be self-sustaining if they were thrown on their own resources again? How many could earn a decent living? How many have sons in the service who are unable to

Figure 2. Charlie Kikuchi's squad, Camp Lee, Virginia, September 15, 1945. Charlie is sitting in the center of the second row. Photo courtesy of Yuriko Amemiya Kikuchi and the Department of Special Collections, Charles E. Young Research Library, UCLA.

help except by monthly pittances?"[27] Unspoken but implicit was the concern of how these incarcerated citizens would be treated by their old and new neighbors once they left the camps. Kikuchi's mother, for one, had grown accustomed to her life in camp, especially after her husband had passed away in July 1943. She did eventually join her son and daughters in Chicago, but much as Tsuneishi feared, many Issei and Nisei found reentry into American life an unappealing and jarring prospect.

Kikuchi was worried that with the Nazis defeated and all attention turned toward Asia, the Nisei would once again feel the intimidating glare from the rest of America. This pivot toward "the Orient," he claimed (writing once again on V-E Day), "adds to their feeling of insecurity because they are on the defensive and they feel that they still are not accepted as real Americans." Some, he added, feel that the war would now shift contexts, becoming much more a "racial war," pitting the slant-eyed kamikazes against the (ironically) blue-eyed Aryans from America. "About the only guarantee of protection they have," he informed Tsuneishi, who was literally sitting by a cave in Okinawa, "is the 13,000 Nisei in the service now. I don't think their fears are entirely unjustified although I don't anticipate any of the violence which I have heard mentioned." He ended this train of thought with a mildly distant, nearly scientific observation: "It has been a hard struggle for the Nisei to grow up, but I think that they are making progress towards greater maturity."[28] Finally, in a statement rife with relevance (given his imminent induction into the army), he exclaimed,

> I have a strong distaste of any system which regiments people and I certainly hope this war is going to stamp out these things, but I am a little worried that it may not happen that way. It's not that I don't have a faith in democracy, but men are human and there is always that greed for power.[29]

Unfortunately for Kikuchi, this last statement would be sorely tested during his own military training. Admittedly, unlike the rigors of intelligence work and intense interactions with a familiar-looking enemy experienced by Tsuneishi in the Pacific theater, or the physically taxing infantry training endured by Murase, Kikuchi's time in training was relatively mild and confined to stateside installations, but he still had to reckon with the unique experience of being a soldier in the U.S. Army. All the correspondence and advice shared by Tsuneishi and Murase prepared Kikuchi to a degree, but as he would soon find out, he would have to engage anew with questions of race relations, discrimination, democracy, and manliness in an environment unused to his kind of cerebral freedom fighting.

In Between: A Racial No-Man's-Land

Earlier periods in Kikuchi's life—when he was living in San Francisco, attending Berkeley, and resettling in Chicago—afforded him numerous interactions with a variety of ethnic and racial groups: African Americans, Filipino Americans, Mexican Americans, Native Americans, Chinese Americans, other Japanese Americans, and ethnic whites. By contrast, during his time in the army, when he was assigned to a white company, his experience emphasized the view held of African Americans (and, to an extent, that of Japanese Americans) by white Americans. His observations regarding these matters are recorded in his Army Diary, which runs from August 1945 to December 1946. Fresh from the friendly confines of Chicago and his intense interactions with Nisei and African Americans in "the second city," Kikuchi had race on the brain. Hence, regarding the incident at Fort Sheridan that began this chapter—wherein a young Black soldier could not print his name—Kikuchi reflected with utter disappointment:

> The other fellows all started to condemn the Negroes, and it didn't make me feel very good even though they gave me the dubious honor of including me among the whites, and apparently it didn't occur to them to make a distinction. They just take on these biased attitudes without really trying to understand the Negro.[30]

Privileged with, but clearly ambivalent about, this "honorary white" status, Kikuchi would treat subsequent conversations with white soldiers as opportunities to interrogate his colleagues' views of African Americans, to map their prejudice, and possibly to stretch the boundaries of their (and, inextricably, his own) un-

derstanding of democracy. At the same time, although limited by the racial segregation of the armed forces, Kikuchi practiced what he preached, endeavoring
to meet and converse with as many African American soldiers as possible, to recognize them as individuals rather than as parts of an undifferentiated Black mass.
Arguably, he continued to bear firsthand witness to the "American dilemma" diagnosed a year earlier by Myrdal and other social scientists.

However, as evidenced by the intensity and substance of his correspondence
shown above, and his wide-ranging experience from the preceding four years,
Kikuchi was armed with a broader notion of this dilemma. As he told Tsuneishi:

> Internationalism seems to be a grand and mighty chorus right now, but
> our "peanut politicians" may defeat the will of the people and the efforts
> of the fighting soldiers on the front. Somehow I believe that this war will
> be followed by a great amount of human progress, but there are many
> obstacles standing in the way.[31]

With this idealism in mind, Kikuchi stood on high alert during his sixteen-
month tenure in the service, finely tuned into the first of many major "obstacles"
to the "human progress" he envisioned: the hypocritical treatment suffered by
his African American counterparts in the army. His experience in the military
further convinced him that the struggle of African Americans represented the
most challenging but most consequential battle for those fighting for freedom
and justice. During his second day of basic training, he observed:

> There [aren't] any Negroes in these "white" barracks. I wondered what
> had happened to them until I discovered that they were segregated into a
> separate unit. The army does it in a very efficient way.[32]

Sardonically, he ended his daily entry by saying: "I guess it feels that the colored
boys will be able to fight for democracy better if they are set apart!" Two weeks
later, commenting on his particular company, he wrote: "I'm the only Nisei in
the group and I seem to be 'acceptable.' But, if there were a larger batch of Nisei,
I know that the segregation process would start."[33]

Having experienced the separation and racialized stigma of internment, he
therefore sympathized acutely with the plight of segregated soldiers, making conscious efforts to seek out and converse with African American GIs. Kikuchi held
one such discussion on August 18 with a soldier who was a social worker before
the war; he keenly felt the discrimination in the army and argued that Jim Crow
had directly caused low morale among Black soldiers. There were more than seven
hundred Black men in the army, and this young man resented the fact that an in-
finitesimal amount (1 percent) of those soldiers was made up of commissioned
officers; he additionally made the argument that these officers were rarely chosen
over white junior officers for fear of causing embarrassment.[34] He told Kikuchi:

> That's why I don't think much of the Army propaganda that it is fighting
> for Democracy when there is such Jim Crowism . . . The Army should

have a guilty conscience because it should be fighting against these things. The contradictions between the principles and practices are so obvious that any simple person could see it. Yet it is tolerated.[35]

Specifically, the man cited the preferential treatment afforded German prisoners of war:

Even the PW's over there (pointing to the stockade) are treated better than we are and they are recognized with respect as human beings. The MP's would be more brutal to a Negro prisoner in the guardhouse than to a German PW. That doesn't make much sense.

This soldier's testimony corroborates other accounts of the military's uneven hand in race matters. In Studs Terkel's oral history of World War II, Dempsey Travis, a Black GI, recalls his days at Camp Shenango, Pennsylvania:

The army was an experience unlike anything I've had in my life. I think of two armies, one black, one white. I saw German prisoners free to move around camp, unlike black soldiers, who were restricted. The Germans walked right into the doggone places like any white American. We were wearin' the same uniform, but we were excluded.[36]

This hypocrisy, or "democratic disconnect," similarly affected Japanese American soldiers serving in the armed forces. Kaun Onodera, one of three brothers who volunteered for service all on the same day (without knowing the other two were likewise enlisting) remembers his all-Nisei regiment guarding German prisoners of war at Fort McClellan, Alabama:

We'd have these trucks, loaded with these handsome German soldiers . . . and here were these slant-eyed Orientals, a couple on each side and one at the end with rifles. The truck would go through industrial parts of Alabama that only employed women. So all these women, they'd come out of their factories. Man, they'd rave about the German soldiers 'cause there were no [white] men around; they're either working on farm or defense. That's what I'd say was rather ironic: They were cheering them, not us.[37]

Given the anecdotal evidence, clearly the American dilemma was not unique to African Americans. Seemingly, all nonwhite Americans faced similar discriminatory practices, to the point of absurdity whereby a Nazi prisoner of war could receive better treatment solely based on his whiteness. In short, America's global struggle to uphold "democratic principles," ironically, did not prioritize erasure of the color line domestically (or internationally, for that matter).

Kikuchi continued to witness this fact firsthand, since Fort Sheridan, in Illinois, proved just as steeped in Jim Crow customs as would Camp Lee, in Virginia. He observed:

The Dayroom here is a fairly cozy spot . . . [It] is located in the same block as the Negro barracks, but I haven't seen one Negro boy in here yet. I think they have to go to their own recreation room which usually looks very crowded and it is not furnished nearly as nicely as far as I could see. I bet the argument is that the colored boys feel more "comfortable" in a room of their own; but the soldier-loving public has forgotten to put as many recreational items into it as in this place.[38]

This unequal treatment would become even more apparent after his company departed the Midwest for its next stage of training in Virginia. Riding the rails and sharing a bunk with a white soldier, Kikuchi quickly learned of his colleague's paradoxical approach to American race relations. Carl was a twenty-nine-year-old bank supervisor from Chicago, described as "a serious, earnest fellow." After Kikuchi explained his racial background and the fact that he had spent nine months in an internment camp, Carl expressed the sentiment that "it was the rawest deal that any American citizen ever had to go through . . . and he hoped that it would be a lesson for this country never to violate constitutional rights again." However, when Kikuchi raised the question of African Americans, Carl could only demur, asserting that they were "doomed to an inferior position in this country," adding:

There is nothing much I can do about it. If I spoke up in protest, I would be called a "Nigger lover." I have nothing against them: I have nothing to do with them.[39]

Resigned and uninterested, Kikuchi's bunkmate did not recognize the contradiction in his reasoning: "constitutional rights" applied to Blacks as equally as they did to Japanese Americans. Frustrated and indignant, Kikuchi could only offer: "It's really so damn inconsistent how a man's mind works sometimes!"

During this same trip to the South, a group of thirty-four soldiers from various companies had to negotiate sleeping arrangements on one of the Pullman cars. With only fourteen upper bunks and fourteen lower bunks, larger soldiers were expected to have upper bunks by themselves, while smaller soldiers could double up in the lower bunks. Needless to say, not one white soldier wanted to sleep beside a Black soldier. To complicate matters, each of the Black GIs (of whom there were but four) had already chosen an upper bunk, despite their comparatively slighter frames. The commanding officer attempted to force the African American GIs into lower bunks by pairs, but they refused. In the meantime, all the white GIs groused, muttering under their breaths and blaming the African American soldiers for the delay. At this point, as Kikuchi comments: "The net result was that it created an impression that the colored boys were very selfish. It never occurred to any of them (Caucasians) that they could pair up with one of the Negro fellows." Kikuchi critiques both sets of participants:

The colored boys were angry about the whole thing. It was also a good example of their extreme sensitivity as they believed it was discrimination. I was in the washroom when they were talking about it and they believed that they were thrown out of their bunks because of their race. This was a silly idea because it was rather obvious that the largest boys should get the single bunks in order to be fair to everyone. It was just as silly for the white boys to assume that selfishness was a basic trait of the Negro race.[40]

Naïve in his reading of the situation or at least partially on the right track, he goes on to cite his unusual but awkward vantage point as neither black nor white:

I'm in a position where I can go from one group to the other so I got reactions on both sides! On the surface, everyone acted polite, but this little incident indicates the extreme difficulty in adjusting race differences. By this one situation, the Negro boys were looked upon as a racial group and not as individuals and I doubt if they will be able to break this barrier during the rest of this trip. It is so unfair on them.

At the very least, he recognized the racialization of these Black soldiers and the knee-jerk tendency of many nonblack individuals to treat African Americans as indistinguishable objects or as convenient stereotypes retrieved from memory or the zeitgeist.

Consistent with his personal philosophy, Kikuchi always took the time to acknowledge African Americans, even at the risk of being called a "nigger lover" or losing his honorary white status (an interesting category given his "situational Blackness" mentioned in previous chapters). Immediately before the train trip to Virginia, for example, Kikuchi made a point of introducing himself to the four Black soldiers:

[They] are only about 18 yrs. old. I was talking to one of them, and he was not very excited about the trip as he said that he would be placed in kitchen or other menial work. He seemed to be resigned to it.

Wistfully, Kikuchi concluded: "None of the colored boys knew each other when we started out, but they seemed to have withdrawn and been forced into their own group because of the unspoken social customs."[41] In breaking with such traditions and crossing such lines, Kikuchi hoped to set a modest example for his white company mates. In many ways, he was strongly motivated by his prewar and wartime experiences. From working on farms with Filipinos to suffering the indignity of incarceration with other Japanese, to his exposure to individual Issei at Gila, to living with African Americans in Chicago, Kikuchi had inevitably learned the value—however simple—of getting to know someone in order to dismantle racial and ethnic (and occasionally, generational) barriers. At one point he summed up his own "Kikuchi thesis":

As long as any one racial group in this country is discriminated against, no group is safe and it's the strongest barrier towards achieving Democracy. These [white] fellows won't change their minds until they get to know individual Negroes, and the whole group can't be "sold" to them without these personal contacts. The same goes for the Nisei, and any other minority group in this country. The war for Democracy didn't end on V-J day; it's a continuing process which may never end.[42]

He had in fact felt quite self-conscious about his own "difference" from the very first day in camp. Immediately upon induction, Kikuchi wrote:

> About 10 Nisei in the large group here and they all stick together. Negroes in great proportion and they stick together. I didn't like it when they put Jap after my name so the girl changed it to Japanese American. Technically, this is not my race at all, but I am sensitive.[43]

This was a far cry from the pre-camp Kikuchi, who indiscriminately used "Jap" with such unthinking disdain. The ugly truth was that most Japanese American volunteers for combat duty had already been similarly labeled and segregated. Immediately before Pearl Harbor, approximately five thousand Japanese Americans were serving in the armed forces. Soon after December 7, a majority of them were unfairly discharged, and the army suspended the drafting of any other Nisei. In May 1942, however, a group of Hawaiʻian Nisei and other Japanese Americans still in the army formed the 100th Infantry Battalion, quickly seeing combat the following year in North Africa and on the beaches of Salerno, Italy. At that point, the army resumed the drafting of Nisei, and in January 1943, the government approved the formation of the segregated 442nd Regimental Combat Team, which was composed of 4,500 volunteers from both Hawaiʻi and the mainland. The following year, the 442nd combined with the 100th Battalion (then known as "the Purple Heart Battalion" for its extremely high casualty rate), and took part in seven major campaigns, concluding the war as the most decorated unit in U.S. military history: 18,000 individual decorations, 9,500 Purple Hearts, and eight Presidential Unit Citations.[44] Such courageous service was magnified by the fact that these same young soldiers had *chosen* to volunteer for a government that had unconstitutionally imprisoned them only months before, much like the hundreds of thousands of Black soldiers asked to fight for a country that had lynched them, deprived them of equal rights, and Jim and Jane Crowed them for centuries. Undoubtedly, then, at least on the surface of things, Japanese American and African American soldiers shared much in common, not least of which was the struggle for progress even in the face of unrelenting violence and abuse.

Nisei soldiers themselves, however, were not uniformly accepting of African Americans. Only a year before his induction, for example, Kikuchi engaged a captain with the 100th Battalion who had won a Purple Heart in Italy. Approving of the segregation of his own unit, the Hawaiʻian Nisei told Kikuchi:

> I certainly wouldn't want to be placed with Negro troops. I worked with them in one of the Army camps for a while and they are bad soldiers. They are dirty and messy and the Army unit is only as strong as the weakest point. I certainly wouldn't feel confident if I were fighting side by side with the Negroes.[45]

In disappointment, Kikuchi reflected:

I had a very high opinion of Capt. Suzuki but it was jarred a little when he expressed his attitude towards Negro soldiers. I don't know where he picked up these ideas as there certainly aren't very many Negro soldiers in Hawaii and that place is supposed to be the perfect example of the melting pot.

Like their African American counterparts, Nisei soldiers faced harsh criticism for poor behavior in the armed forces. One such outfit was Company K, largely comprised of Nisei soldiers trained at the MISLS to serve in the Pacific as interrogators and interpreters. Company K pointed to the woeful treatment suffered by Black soldiers as a reason for its own insubordination (whether this was a justifiable excuse for its action is another question). Building on his doctoral work under sociological giants at Chicago (George Herbert Mead, Louis Wirth, Herbert Blumer, and Ernest Burgess), Kikuchi's friend Tamotsu Shibutani published a finely researched monograph on these men, provocatively entitled *The Derelicts of Company K: A Sociological Study of Demoralization*. He reports:

> Since Company K men had become so accustomed to lax enforcement of regulations, the strict discipline of the navy appeared unnecessarily repressive. They felt hounded by "chicken shit," and resentment against officers was magnified with the invidious distinctions aboard. Furthermore, the treatment of Negroes made respect for the system even more difficult.[46]

Unlike the media-friendly narrative regarding the sacrificial and patriotic 442nd, the boys of Company K were "black sheep" brothers, or diametric opposites of the model Nisei outfit. In a genuine and deliberate sense, they represented a latter-day version of Kikuchi's own prewar Yamato Garage Gangsters, the countercultural relatives of the wartime Nisei zoot-suiters, and the oppositional forerunners to the Nisei underclass so well documented by Kikuchi, and then Spickard, in postwar Chicago in the preceding chapter. "Shibs" continues his analysis of the "derelicts":

> Before long, reaction against authority crystallized, and patterns of insubordination first developed at Fort Meade were again instituted. No conscious planning was involved; the men simply lapsed into their old habits. Orders issued to Nisei soldiers were obeyed reluctantly, if at all. Frequently the men muttered "chicken shit" before the officer was out of hearing range—letting him know how they felt.

The company witnessed how often the military brass mistreated African American soldiers, to the point that—reality or rumor—white officers (and sailors) were in the crosshairs of every "derelict." For example, when fact and rumor blurred over the details of Black soldiers found sleeping on duty because of seasickness, the word spread that the delinquents were court-martialed, a consequence never suffered by white or Nisei sailors for a similar offense. However, as Company K grew more intolerant of the military's differential treatment, they spouted their venomous ire toward the *keto* (a derogatory term for "white," meaning "hairy") and saved their sympathies for Black comrades. Shibutani captures the emotional distress:

> Most Nisei accepted it as inevitable; after all, the navy had always refused to accept Nisei for service. Some noted that the Japanese prisoners of war were being treated with far more consideration than American soldiers who happened to be black.[47]

This last observation also reveals the soldiers' conscious remembrance of historical acts of discrimination against the Nikkei (not least of which was the concurrent internment of many of their family members and friends) and their experiential connection to antiblack racism. To be sure, they understood the differences of degree between the discriminatory practices, but that did not at all preclude the formation of interracial friendships based on shared histories and common domestic enemies.

In his situationally specific position of "in between" as the only Nisei of his cohort, Kikuchi continued to observe awkward interactions between white and Black colleagues in both military and civilian settings. One such incident took place in, of all places, Washington, D.C., the celebrated cradle of democracy. On a short leave from Camp Lee, his company had decided to dine together in the nation's capital. "An elderly colored man came in," he remembers,

> and the waiter stopped him and said that he could not be served as it was restricted for whites only. The man walked out very puzzled, muttering, "Well, I'm a United States citizen!" I felt pity and hot anger.

Frustrated, Kikuchi asserts:

> I was for walking out in protest, but the boys wanted their steaks so I didn't say anything else. It was pretty disillusioning to be a witness to such disgusting blind prejudice in the Nation's Capital. Blind intolerance like that bothers me and I go through a lot of emotions because it could just as well be me.[48]

Kikuchi does not simply compartmentalize the "Negro problem" apart from the "Nisei problem"; in fact, he collapses the distance between the African American man and himself, recognizing that the elderly man's experience could have well been his own. As has been previously argued, Kikuchi felt a deeply intense connection with African Americans, to a degree that most other Nisei, simply could not; some, however, like those in Company K, felt it all too keenly.

This identification with African Americans would be severely tested during Kikuchi's stay in the South. In another instance, while he was still stationed at Camp Lee, a group of white soldiers (who still included Kikuchi as problematically "honorary") invited a handful of Black soldiers to dine with them. Af-

ter breaking bread with one another, albeit awkwardly, the white and Black soldiers went their separate ways, and Kikuchi—by his own admission, somewhat
shamefully—accompanied the whites to Richmond. He recalls, "The Negro boys
went off alone afterwards while the rest of us headed for the downtown USO."
Initially, he felt relatively secure in the company of his white mates, but as the
night wore on, he feared that his difference stood out. "We passed a couple of
Chinese laundries on the way downtown and I was stared at curiously," he relates.
"I don't know whether it was the fact that I was in the South, but for a second,
I had the damndest feeling that I would be challenged as I entered the USO for
'whites.'" He pauses to reflect, "I guess I have been conditioned too much about
the racial biases in the South."[49] The personal pronouns he uses shift from "we"
to "I" very quickly and easily. It is additionally curious to note that when Kikuchi
is left as the only nonwhite in the group, even with his "near-white" status, his
thoughts inevitably gravitate back toward African Americans. His fear, both real
and imagined, that he is being watched and that he will be denied entry into the
USO based on his race immediately prompts associations that draw him closer
to African Americans. As proof, he directly follows up his thoughts above by
remembering a previous, jarring experience:

> It was in Richmond that I saw for the first time with my eyes the [Jim
> Crow] discrimination in practice. The Negroes all sit in the back of the
> cars. The boys with me felt it was very foolish even though they didn't
> particularly like Negroes.

The sequence of statements comes across as a collection of non sequiturs, but in
Kikuchi's mind, the anxieties stemmed from the same source: discrimination toward him was one and the same as the discrimination perpetrated against Black
trolley car passengers. His problem was their problem; their problem was his
problem.

Is Yellow Black or White?

Kikuchi was not the only Nisei to observe firsthand the strain of southern folk-
ways. Thomas Higa witnessed customary southern practices outside of Camp
Shelby (a third of a mile from Hattiesburg), where he would subsequently train
with the 100th Battalion. Although he did not comment directly on interaction
between soldiers of different races (as Kikuchi does), he remembered:

> I was surprised at the invisible wall that existed between blacks and
> whites. I learned about it traveling in the South. On buses, the front seats
> were reserved for whites and the rear seats were for blacks. Since I was
> neither white nor black, I could sit anywhere. When there was a seat in
> the white section, I sat there. No one complained . . .

> The bus stopped in a country town. While I was looking around for a restroom, a white gentleman came to my aid. As we were about to enter, a black man approached us and said, "no," and attempted to make me enter the one for blacks.[50]

This particular "neither-nor" category signified a no-man's-land in the South for these Nisei soldiers, "dis-Oriented" literally and figuratively. At the same time, much like Kikuchi, Higa recognized an implicit solidarity with Black southerners:

> Once, when I was waiting in the information line while trying to buy a bus ticket . . . the receptionist was black. He treated the whites in an unkind manner, failing to give them ample explanations . . . He completely changed his attitude when it was my turn. He took the time and gave me detailed explanations, despite the fact that there were many people in line behind me.

Higa and, to a greater extent, Kikuchi, made use of these kinds of interactions to question the integrity of the black-white binary. Uncertain of where they necessarily stood in these contexts (southern towns, army bases, military units in times of war), they nevertheless experienced moments of alliance with both groups, white and African American, temporarily rendering the exclusive and rigid membership in these groups meaningless.

Back in Virginia a month later, however, bunkmates reintroduced Kikuchi to the customary American approach to race relations and its comfortable reliance on the simplistic and historically entrenched black-white dyad. Compared to discussions at Cal and in the internment camps, this was a vastly different bull session than Kikuchi was used to, but he tried hard to make his voice heard among those of five other GIs. A young Turkish American named Ramey, one of these discussants, admitted that he harbored deep prejudices against Blacks because they "were trying to push themselves into acceptability and that was not the proper method to create race harmony." Another soldier, Thorburn, countered that Blacks needed to be aggressive to become socially acceptable, but Ramey nonetheless claimed that he could not shake his bias. He did concede that he understood the Nisei better through his conversations with Kikuchi, who, in turn, traded on his "honorary white" status in an effort to change some hearts and minds:

> I took this cue to inject my chief point that it was dangerous to bait one minority at the expense of another. I directed this at Trioco who is of Mexican ancestry and very prejudiced against Negroes. Rogers and Endicott's solution was to shoot all the black bastards.[51]

This was far from the high-minded conversations Kikuchi had enjoyed with Tsuneishi and Murase by letter. Even in this context, however, he was pushing the boundaries of the discussion and challenging the fallacy of racial competition. These discussants needed Kikuchi's challenge of mental lifting much more than Warren and Kenny did.

Making the Transition: Soldier to Social Worker

After nearly three months of basic training in the South, Kikuchi transferred to the army hospital at Fort Hancock, New Jersey, to continue his military service, albeit this time as a psychiatric social worker ministering to soldiers facing courts-martial.[52] At the time, there was an overwhelming need for psychiatric social workers and other health care professionals in both the military and Veterans Administration hospital systems. One contemporary study reported that the patient load for neuropsychiatric cases spiked from 5,000 in 1920 to approximately 33,000 in 1940.[53] The length of stay for more than two-fifths (42 percent) of psychotic World War II veterans was at least three years, and the average had only increased since war's end. "The Veterans Administration problem respecting veterans with psychotic disabilities is one of considerable magnitude," another study cites.

> There is a dearth of trained and experienced personnel qualified in treatment of psychiatric patients. Not only is there a shortage of psychiatrists, but of clinical psychologists and psychiatric social workers as well.[54]

"Unto the breach" stepped Kikuchi. Based on Sandy Hook and living with fellow soldiers and counselors, Kikuchi eventually earned the rank of sergeant. Thirteen months on the job afforded him numerous interactions with imprisoned soldiers, the vast majority of whom were African American, while his proximity to New York City provided another site for interracial exchanges to compare against those he had witnessed and experienced in San Francisco, Arizona, Chicago, and the South. With the war at an end, and assigned a more reasonable workday (compared to Murase's infantry duty or Tsuneishi's overseas counterintelligence operations), Kikuchi made the short commute to the hospital every day like a regular professional. Occasionally, he would take overnight passes into Manhattan to see friends and, in May 1946, to meet his future "better half," Yuriko. Thus, he occupied a uniquely liminal space between soldier and citizen and, consequently, witnessed race relations in their various forms and contexts. One remark in late October accurately sets the tone for many of the remaining entries in his Army Diary: "Race tension in this country cannot be ignored because it permeates all aspects of our living."[55] Kikuchi hence widened the lens of his scrutiny, becoming a "citizen soldier" contemplating the tensions inherent to the legal system and public accommodations.

For example, Kikuchi exposed the uneven justice delivered in courts-martial, criticizing the disproportionate punishment meted out to Black soldiers. "A white boy was given an 18 months sentence for cursing an officer and calling him a 'chicken shit bastard,'" he wrote in late 1945. "Another boy was given an 18 months sentence for being AWOL for 40 days. But in sharp contrast was the 10 years sentence given to a colored boy for being AWOL for one day." With severe understatement, he deduced, "An element of prejudice exists even in our Army courts of justice, a sad commentary."[56] Three days later, he compiled more evidence: "Two colored boys I interviewed this afternoon got 15 and 25 years for rape, while a white boy got only 7 1/2 years."[57] In searching for possible root causes of such institutional prejudice, Kikuchi repeatedly found that individual discrimination lay at the heart of a systemic problem. Much like the conversations he had held with fellow GIs during basic training, Kikuchi attempted—in incremental but significant gestures—to interrogate his colleagues' points of view, to offer alternative explanations and practicable solutions. In regard to the racialized assumptions surrounding rape, he notes:

> One of the interviewers under me mentioned that the Negroes were the ones to rape the girls the most, and he was inclined to be a bit harsh upon them so that I tried to explain a few things to him so that he wouldn't have a biased attitude in the cases he handled ... I also added that colored boys were not the only ones who have gone around and raped foreign girls.[58]

Superior officers aroused Kikuchi's frustrations as much as subordinates did:

> I got a little angry when Captain Bolton, the Psychologist, told one of my colored cases that he would get along better if he "realized his place" and "eventually your people will be recognized like George Washington Carver was." It was so stupid and condescending. I insisted upon minimum control for the boy and Bolton finally agreed after I explained the social background.[59]

At last recognizing the limitations of his relationship with these white colleagues (and implicitly acknowledging his closer affinity to African American ones), he wrote, "I get along well with them [the whites], but it is just by chance as it could be me," implying that he could just as easily have been the target of racist assumptions and condescension, once again echoing a refrain he had uttered in Washington, D.C., only months earlier.[60]

Kikuchi did in fact—unlike his white colleagues at the hospital—seem at ease when speaking with Black inmates. In an effort to understand the distinction, he mused:

> I suppose that psychologically it is difficult to get the Negro inmate to express his inner feelings because to many of our interviewers he acts as he is expected to act and he is afraid to express resentment or opposition for fear that it would go against them.[61]

Once again referring to the masks that minorities sometimes need to wear, or perhaps even to Burgess's theory of self-fulfilling stereotypes, Kikuchi drew on his own experience of having been judged by his eyes, his skin color, and his name. He speculated further:

> Maybe I have an advantage because the Negro inmate responds to the fact that I am "colored" too, but that can't explain the whole situation. Too

many of our staff are bored with the proceedings and they don't really try to understand the Negro inmate.

Kikuchi humbly underestimated the impact of his willingness to view Black patients as human (not subhuman), as real men with historically contingent problems (not childlike men without a past). If nothing else, his superiors took worrisome note of his approach. His supervising officer, Sless, "felt that I shouldn't probe so deeply on the causative factors and to tone a colored boy's story down because in the Army situation 'you can't do honest case work.'" Even worse, he warned Kikuchi that he would most likely have to answer to the review board at the hospital "because already I'm considered as 'that Jap nigger lover.'" Although instructed to desist "being sympathetic to the Negro inmates" and to simply label them with "personality defects," Kikuchi refused.[62]

He could hardly contain his anger when it came to dealing with such bald-faced prejudice and bureaucratic apathy. A far cry from the ostensibly objective social scientist or clinician, Kikuchi would lament the systemic, institutionalized shortcomings of his field: "It makes me so damn mad when the Negro inmates we process are methodically classified as 'psychoneurotics' and 'psychopathic personality' when so many of them are perfectly normal and only reacting in a way that any man would." The sum of his experiences in the preceding six years had sufficiently exposed him to injustices based on class and race. Working on farms and scaring up odd-end jobs, living alongside South Siders, and seeing firsthand the inequities of the Jim Crow South had made him particularly sensitive to the struggles waged by African Americans. The deck was perennially stacked against them, and no amount of military service to their country could trump historical practice. "How in the hell is a Negro expected to react," Kikuchi queried, "when he has less security; he is the first employee to be fired; he isn't generally accepted as a true GI; [and] he has to face the prospect of going back to a civilian life of crowded housing, prejudice, etc.?"[63] Outlining his mildly revised approach to case reports, Kikuchi demonstrated a strong grasp of the historical and social dynamics affecting his patients.

> The colored boys really let loose on all of their resentments after we get talking for a while, but I only give hints of these intense feelings in my case records . . . He is expected to act in a stereotyped humble manner and not show any spunk or it will go hard with him. Justice seems to be relative, and it correlates highly with the colored line.[64]

The Souls of Black Folk

Kikuchi's analysis here reflects traces of Du Bois's influence, confirming that the problem of the twentieth century—as true in 1946 as it was in 1903—remained that of the color line. Appropriately, then, Kikuchi shares an anecdote uncannily

reminiscent of an incident in Du Bois's "Of The Coming of John," the penulti-
mate, fictional chapter in *The Souls of Black Folk*. Du Bois's protagonist, John
Jones, a Black southerner temporarily transplanted to New York, takes in a performance of Wagner's *Lohengrin*. Unbeknownst to him, his former childhood
playmate—and white doppelgänger—attends the same event. Just as Black John
enters the opera house, white John impatiently follows behind him with his date,
patronizing her for not quite understanding the "cordial and intimate relations
between black and white as are everyday occurrences with us [southerners]." As
the white couple nears their seats, however,

> the man stopped short and flushed to the roots of his hair, for there di-
> rectly beside his reserved orchestra chairs sat the Negro he had stumbled
> over in the hallway. He hesitated and grew pale with anger, called the
> usher and gave him his card, with a few peremptory words, and slowly sat
> down. The lady deftly changed the subject.

As the opera progresses, and Black John becomes captivated by the music, remaining oblivious of the commotion caused by his presence.

> The infinite beauty of the wail lingered and swept through every muscle
> of his frame, and put it all a-tune. He closed his eyes and grasped the el-
> bows of the chair, touching unwittingly the lady's arm. And the lady drew
> away . . . It left John sitting so silent and rapt that he did not for some time
> notice the usher tapping him lightly on the shoulder and saying politely,
> "Will you step this way, please, sir?" . . . The manager was sorry, very, very
> sorry . . . he would refund the money, of course . . . [but] before he had
> finished John was gone, walking hurriedly across the square and down
> the broad streets, and as he passed the park he buttoned his coat and said,
> "John Jones, you're a natural-born fool."[65]

Although lacking Du Bois's lyricism, Kikuchi wrote of an episode with
strikingly similar markings: New York as backdrop, theater as venue, and awkward seating arrangements as precipitant. This time, however, the reader benefits from the witness of a third party, allowing for the triangulating of black,
white, and yellow. For many of his weekends away from Fort Hancock, Kikuchi
enjoyed attending plays in Manhattan. One Sunday evening in April 1946, he
remembered:

> At the play, which had an all-colored cast, there was a Negro GI sitting
> next to me. A couple had the two seats next to him, and the lady was
> seated by the colored boy . . . She made references about Negro bodily
> odor, and why Negroes should be seated in a segregated section. Her es-
> cort said that he would sit next to the Negro during the second act. Then
> the lady turned around and started to praise the cast of the play with such
> comments as "Aren't some of those colored girls so beautiful—almost like
> white girls."[66]

Kikuchi concluded his observation by stating: "The lady was perfectly willing to be acceptable of colored people and appreciate their talents as long as they were on the stage, but not willing when this application of equality was extended to the seating arrangement in the theater." In his exasperation, Kikuchi's last line could well have been a slight variation on the fictional John Jones's asserting: "Lady, *you're* a natural-born fool."

Both "stories" share the theme of recognizing others' humanity. In Du Bois's tale, John grows enraptured by the Wagnerian drama and the interplay between the damsel in distress, Elsa, and her mysterious knight in shining armor, Lohengrin. Despite her persistent pleas, Lohengrin resists identifying himself or his origins. Du Bois consciously chooses this opera for John to witness, using it metaphorically to point out that questions of origin or race are needless criteria for judging one's humanity. Both John and, by extension, Du Bois, remain wistfully hopeful of this goal. In the parallel reality of Kikuchi's experience, he appears confounded by the hypocrisy and outright racism expressed by the white woman. She seemingly approves of African Americans in their role as entertainers (or, worse, minstrels), but the physical separation ("the breach") afforded by a stage must remain in place. Clearly, the fact that her seated neighbor was a veteran of the war makes no difference to her. The only identity that matters is racialized, and she literally cannot "sit" with this discomfiting reality. By his reaction and his emphasis on the "application of equality," Kikuchi implies that he was unrealistically hoping—much like Du Bois—that the appreciation, however superficial, this woman felt for Black performers might be equally applied to her Black seatmate. By contrast, Kikuchi's passage provides a disturbing converse of the theme of *Lohengrin*: recognizing the humanity of an individual takes a backseat to identifying and, ultimately, stigmatizing him by his race.

Conclusion: Tatsuro, "Standing Man"

Unbeknownst to either principal, Charlie first saw his bride-to-be, Yuriko Amemiya, on Saturday, March 20, 1943, as she danced on a moonlit stage at Gila. The
two, of course, did not speak to each other that evening, or at any other time both
were in camp. Despite making a mess of her name in his diary, Kikuchi nonetheless wrote with clear admiration of the Kibei dancer's talent and artistry.

> This evening we went to a classical dance concert under the Arizona
> skies. The admission was five cents. Yuri Amariya used to be a profes-
> sional dancer in L.A. and she directed the show. All of the dances were
> created by her . . .
>
> The atmosphere was just perfect. About 5,000 people were present. It
> was not too cold. A full moon added to the setting . . . Yuri Amariya did
> the best dance.[1]

Three and a half years later, on September 14, 1946, the couple jointly performed
"the delicate dance," exchanging marriage vows in the chapel at Fort Hancock.
They had been dating for only three months, but Kikuchi was smitten by the San
Jose native. Being in her presence seemed to be the only time he was ever at a loss
for the right words: "I wish I were a true connoisseur of Beauty because then I
would be able to express myself with considerably more eloquence on the subject
of what a rare person you are but I feel so limited in saying what I mean in an
exact way."[2] Given the weekend off for their honeymoon, the couple took a ferry
across Sandy Hook Bay and celebrated their nuptials in Manhattan, their eventual home for the next forty-two years. Hearing the good news, Adamic sent the
couple a gift copy of his most recent publication, *Dinner at the White House*.[3] The
Thomases sent a letter from Berkeley, wishing Kikuchi well and saying, "Incidentally, we are unanimous in thinking that she is a very lucky girl, and we hope that
she appreciates the Charlie for whom we have such admiration and affection."[4]
Clearly, the surrogate parents approved.

Later that year, in December, the army gave Kikuchi his discharge and GI
Bill, which he immediately used to finish his master's degree at Columbia. In
September 1947, he submitted his thesis, based on his resettlement work with
Thomas, entitling it "The Social Adjustment Process of the Japanese American

Figure 3. "Family man": Kikuchi with his daughter, Susan, New York City, 1950. Photo courtesy of Yuriko Amemiya Kikuchi and the Department of Special Collections, Charles E. Young Research Library, UCLA.

Resettlers to Chicago during the Wartime Years." After receiving his MSW in the spring of 1948 and moving to Greenwich Village, Kikuchi relied on Yuriko's budding career as a dance teacher and, ultimately, star performer for the Martha Graham Company. In the fall of that year, they welcomed their first child, named Susan, creating their own close-knit family unit in the leafier confines of Brooklyn. In 1949, Charlie began working at the Veterans Administration Hospital, a post he would keep for the next twenty-four years (although he would move between sites in Brooklyn and the Bronx).

Meanwhile, in preparation for the publication of *The Salvage* in 1952, Kikuchi would often bring the family down to Philadelphia, where Thomas had moved to join the faculty at the University of Pennsylvania. Both Kikuchis would keep in contact with Thomas over the next two and a half decades, until her death in 1977. While W. I. passed away in 1947, and Kikuchi's other surrogate father, Adamic, would meet his ignoble end in 1951, the momentary void in the Kikuchi family circle would be joyfully filled in 1955 with the birth of their second child, a son named Lawrence.[5] As for Kikuchi's biological family, the ties he initially kept after the camp reunion frayed over time. Certainly, in that stretch of years, he corresponded and visited with siblings, as well as his mother, who would outlive him, dying at the age of 104.[6]

Although everyone in the family thought Charlie the most likely to intermarry, he obviously married within his race, while most of his siblings paired up with partners of different races. The one that caused the most hand-wringing, however, especially for Kikuchi's mother, was Bette's marriage to Gene Orro, an African American classmate from Roosevelt College. Just as the nation and world witnessed tectonic shifts in 1948, the year also stood out as the date when the Kikuchi family irrevocably changed, undergoing this final "crisis" together and then splintering for the rest of Charlie's life. The debate ultimately hinged on Orro's personality, despite Shizuko's adamant opposition based solely on his race. According to Miyako, Charlie's youngest sister, "I don't dislike Gene because he is a Negro. I dislike him as a person. He thinks that he's 'it.'"[7] Joining Miyako and the matriarch were Tom and Mariko, while Emiko and Charlie supported Bette (unsurprisingly, this was the trio that had spent all of their initial time together after resettling on the South Side). The issue came to a head when Bette confronted her mother. In a letter to Charlie, she frustratingly reported:

> I said that Mom should try to get to know him, and that she never invited him to dinner. Mom said very angrily that she would not sit at the same table as a "Nigger." Naturally, this made me furious as the real reasons for her objections came out into the open. I told her then that I loved Gene as a person, and furthermore, I was going to marry him.
>
> Then Mom got very hysterical and she slapped me and said that no daughter of hers was going to marry outside of her race.[8]

In the fall of that year, as the frequent arguments grew into ambient "white noise," Kikuchi considered the future possibilities for his own daughter Susan compared with those of Bette's stepchildren. "It probably will be a lot more difficult for Susan's new cousin, Terry Pamela," he theorized.

> Because society has made the racial label more rigidly for those with any touch of Negro background. Actually, Terry Pamela seems to have a rich heritage which springs from the sources of three continents: Europe, Africa, and Asia; and they have all blended together here even if we may have a rather imperfect country.[9]

He attempted a hopeful conclusion: "I don't think the parents of this generation are going to eliminate discrimination and prejudice, but maybe Susan's generation will do a lot better job." In the interim, Bette would go on to marry Orro the following year, with the full support of Charlie and Yuriko. Reflecting on the interracial drama that had played out within his family, Kikuchi expressed his disbelief:

> It is amazing how the stigma of intermarriage is used in keeping love apart. The minority group takes on the majority attitude in this respect, and it's a perfect weapon for a majority group to use in preserving social inequalities. I often wonder how people can be so stupid to think that this is the main problem in race relations.[10]

After this final period of family time together, Charlie escaped to New York and rarely looked back over the next three decades. As a final index of how estranged he felt toward the family, he permitted only his youngest brother, Tom, to see him on his deathbed in the fall of 1988. In many ways, the legacy of sadness, anger, and abandonment associated with his father never quite left Kikuchi, and his transference of feelings about Nakajiro to the rest of the family prevented him from getting too close to them. "It seems that the 'family' has drifted into its individual streams of adjustment," he noted scientifically, only a handful of years after their initial camp reunion.[11] As an alternative, he continued his quest to seek out connections with other, more "familiar" kinds of surrogates.

A Nation of Nations

The postwar period remained charged with democratic possibility, but ideological retrenchment lingered both domestically and internationally. In an attempt to build on the Fair Employment Practices Commission (FEPC) initiated by FDR and A. Philip Randolph in 1941, which made it a crime for any company with a government contract to discriminate based on race or religion, President Harry Truman commissioned a Committee on Civil Rights in 1946 to study the problem of race relations and civil rights. In the 1948 presidential election, Truman famously defeated the heavily favored Republican, Thomas Dewey, and Progressive Henry Wallace, while southern Democrats, angered by the inclusion of a civil rights plank in the Democratic platform, had stormed out of the convention in protest, forming their own party, the Dixiecrats, led by Strom Thurmond. Truman demonstrated how seriously he took the issue of civil rights by ordering the end of segregation in the federal workforce and the armed forces, two incredibly significant steps toward measurable progress and reform. Since he won back both houses of Congress in 1948 as well, Truman proposed the century's first civil rights bill (making the FEPC permanent, prohibiting poll taxes, providing federal protection of Black voting rights, and supporting a long-awaited bill to make lynching a federal crime) but southern Democrats filibustered, dashing the entire proposal. Truman remained undeterred, however, encouraging the Justice Department's aggressive approach in court battles against discriminatory statutes. Although Truman's efforts barely chipped the bulwark of segregation, they represented noticeable stirrings of a new era of federal efforts to deal with the "race problem."

Simultaneously, the Supreme Court played a crucial role in the late 1940s and early 1950s, with the climactic case *Brown v. Board of Education of Topeka* in 1954, a unanimous decision overturning the precedent of "separate but equal" established in *Plessy v. Ferguson* (1896) and prohibiting segregation in public schools.[12] In 1947, for example, in *Mendez v. Westminster*, the Supreme Court decided that Mexican American schoolchildren could not be separated from white students, because the law in question barred only the intermixture of white students and children of "Japanese, Chinese, or Mongolian" descent.[13] While the high court did not challenge *Plessy* as unconstitutional in that case (as it would in *Brown*), and while Mexican American civil rights organizations emphasized their eligibility as "white" citizens, downplaying amicus curiae briefs from both the NAACP and the JACL, and thus deemphasizing any discrimination based on race or ancestry, the case still signified an important precedent on the pathway to *Brown* and led to the statewide repeal of any remaining school segregation laws in California.[14] On the all-important question of housing discrimination, the Court ruled in *Shelley v. Kraemer* (1948) that the courts could not be used to enforce restrictive housing covenants against Blacks and other minorities.[15] On a related note, and in a remarkable display of Black agency, courage, and resilience, Jackie Robinson broke the color line in Major League Baseball in 1947 with the Brooklyn Dodgers, Kikuchi's favorite team.

Internationally, in 1946, the Philippines finally gained independence from the United States, while Britain relinquished its colonial hold over what would become India and Pakistan through a violence-laden partition in 1947. Anticolonial efforts spread throughout the world, and the first of many Arab-Israeli wars began in 1948 on the heels of Israel's declaration as an independent state and the subsequent displacement of Palestinians from disputed land. Formally established in October 1945, the United Nations was launched as a new international governing body, with common principles and objectives agreed to by the victors in World War II, led by the United States, the Soviet Union, China, Great Britain, and France. As Ottley had predicted, a new world order had indeed come, but as the destabilizing postwar events above demonstrated, the UN had more than its fair share to handle in its infancy. What is more, the chess match played by Truman and Stalin before war's end foreshadowed a long, cold winter. The Korean War (1950–1953) marked the first test of National Security Council Report 68, which outlined the government's new and expansive foreign policy of containment with regard to communist heavyweights, the USSR and China. A proxy war across the thirty-eighth parallel between communist North Korea and democratic South Korea, the confrontation essentially ended in stalemate. But it also had the unfortunate corollary effect of engendering stateside hysteria over communist spies, undue influence, and fifth column infiltration. HUAC and the FBI's "loyalty" investigations, among other factors, led an anxious and impressionable element of the general public to rally around the red-baiting figure of Senator Joseph McCarthy.

In one sense, of course, after such an all-encompassing, global event like the war, the landscape dramatically changed: Nazism and Italian Fascism defeated; rising decolonization movements in many African and Asian nations; the policy shift toward de jure segregation domestically; and a honeymoon of international cooperation and agreement for at least a year or two. In another sense, however, one could have asked, "Were things markedly better in 1950 than in 1940?" Even with prohibitory legislation, Jim and Jane Crow resumed their de facto positions in both North and South, and African Americans remained "first fired, last hired." The labor movement now faced a staggering uphill battle against management: the 1947 Taft-Hartley Act weakened unions' ability to strike while allowing states to implement "right to work" laws, effectively neutralizing unions. Additionally, as previously mentioned, Michael Denning pointed out that the war with Japan was only the beginning of nearly thirty-five years of American participation in wars fought in Asia, all in the name of anticommunist democracy. Therefore, one might say that in 1950, just as in 1940, instead of figuring out affirmatively what America was, the country persisted in defining itself negatively against what it certainly was not: that is, not communist; not pacifist; not integrationist; and not heterogeneous.

American exceptionalism had apparently survived the war.

It Don't Mean a Thing

The 1950s and 1960s were largely a period of acclimation and settlement for Kikuchi. He witnessed and enthusiastically encouraged his wife's burgeoning career as she parlayed her virtuoso talent into opportunities both on stage and in film, most notably in Jerome Robbins's production of *The King and I*. At the same time, Kikuchi settled into his job at the VA hospital, beginning what would be a lifelong struggle to convince administrators that they could not treat African American veterans like poor, neurotic stepchildren. Oftentimes, his work with these Black veterans dovetailed with the larger currents of American public life. For example, in June 1950, the Supreme Court had just issued its decisions in two cases—*Sweatt v. Painter* and *McLaurin v. Oklahoma State Regents*—upholding African Americans' rights to full educational benefits at public graduate schools.[16] After commenting on a suicidal Black patient in his care, Kikuchi made an immediate association with the court decisions: "It is an advance in race relationships and democracy, but I could not agree with the [N.Y.] Times editorial which felt that segregation should not be legislated out since the people [are] not ready for it, and it urged that leaders of both races continue to cooperate and 'educate' the public and some day we would have the millennium." Disappointed by this endorsement of an incrementalist approach, he concluded: "To say that both groups should 'cooperate' means for the Negro to keep his place and take what is given him. The case I handled today is one of the consequences of these stupid social attitudes towards the Negro by the majority."[17]

In the context of the Korean War and the Cold War, Kikuchi especially recognized the global significance of African American inequality. In March 1949, for example, he was reading Drake and Cayton's study, which prompted the following nexus of thoughts, including interracial possibility, the ever-present Cold War danger, and the prospect of true American democracy:

Right now I am browsing through "Black Metropolis" and I notice that [Brooklyn neighbor and Nisei artist] Bunji Tagawa downstairs did all of the illustrations for the book.

The book poses a lot of dilemmas and it concludes that we are rapidly coming to an explosive situation more dangerous than the atomic developments if the race question is not somehow solved . . . When I was down in the Puerto Rican barbershop this morning, I observed a lot of social mixing which I wish there were more of . . . Democracy in theory has as one of its fundamental tenets that we respect the natural dignity of Man, but this seems to exclude the Negro as biologically inferior.[18]

A year later, as the Korean Peninsula quaked, he lamented: "The whole war business seems so unreal and fantastic yet we are all drifting towards it relentlessly. It's gotten to the point where anyone who speaks up for peace or even desires it is labeled as a communist dupe!" In an echo of his experience in the army, he decried the blatant inequity faced by Black soldiers:

A lot of things don't make sense. Even in the fighting, I thought it was so ironic when the papers proclaimed that a segregated Negro outfit had stopped one unit of the North Koreans. Here these Negroes are fighting for democratic principles, but they have to be in a segregated unit to do it![19]

Ultimately, Kikuchi would be heartened by the 1954 *Brown* decision, moved to take part in civil rights demonstrations in the 1950s and 1960s, and brought to sympathize in the late 1960s with the Black Power Movement, despite his long-held belief in the power and force of integration.[20] "We were very conscious of what was going on in America," remembered Yuriko. "We went down for a march in Washington before King's speech, and we often talked politics after the kids went to bed."[21]

In their social circles during this era, the Kikuchis were surrounded by an eclectic and diverse set of people, appropriately heady company in Manhattan. In October 1950, Kikuchi offhandedly remarked:

The other day Ruth [James] took Yuriko down to the Paramount to meet her brother Duke Ellington, and they had a Chinese dinner backstage. Ruth hoped that her brother would keep Yuriko in mind if he did a Broadway show. Yuriko got all dressed up and looked glamorous. Now the [Jameses] would like us to find an apartment uptown so that our children will get together more often.[22]

A Columbia alumna, Ruth James was head of Tempo Music, her brother's music publishing company, and in the 1950s she hosted her own radio program on WLIB in New York and stayed thoroughly involved with the NAACP. Her husband, Daniel James, was the managing editor of the *New Leader*. At a later point in the diary, Kikuchi recalls attending a New Year's Eve party at the home of one of Yuriko's colleagues, a drummer in the orchestra for *The King and I*. In blasé fashion, Kikuchi mentions that he met Eartha Kitt there, the versatile singer and actress who won both a Tony and an Emmy Award and collaborated with Orson Welles, but may best be remembered as Catwoman, replacing Julie Newmar in the campy 1960s television series *Batman*. The diarist speaks highly of Kitt's talent, but ill of her personality, because she exuded "so little warmth, like Ramona, [the drummer's] wife."[23] Kikuchi did not appear too starstruck; in fact, he seemed quite comfortable, even somewhat amused, by Frazier's "Black bourgeoisie." It certainly provided him with a stark contrast to the struggling young soldiers and veterans he was counseling during the day. Once again, he was exposing himself to a noticeably diverse cross-section of African Americans in the city; they were neither monolithic and deracinated nor "invisible men and women." In an anecdote from 1951, he reports with a hint of his trademark wiseacre attitude:

> Sunday evening we went up to Harlem to have dinner at Ada Jones' apartment . . . Ada is one of the leading social lights in Harlem and she and her friends are always giving parties for the benefit of the NAACP and they get written up all the time in the Negro press. All of these wives are very light-skinned, and they are married to Harlem professional people. They live in a world of their own and they seem to get a lot of satisfaction out of it. We had quite a discussion on the role of the NAACP in Negro society.[24]

Little did Kikuchi know in March 1943 that the young Kibei dancer on the makeshift stage at Gila would later provide him with such highbrow entrée into the multiracial New York social scene—much less agree to marry him.

Redrawn Maps, Disconnecting Networks: The CG School and the Nisei Intelligentsia

The vibrant democratic discourse of the 1940s gave way to the chilling and Orwellian environment of the late 1940s and early 1950s. As Penny Von Eschen has suggestively argued, African American activists and intellectuals, like Robeson and Du Bois, managed to maintain their activity from the late 1930s and early 1940s into the later part of the decade, struggling for civil rights at home and anticolonial movements in Africa and Asia, but their voices grew increasingly distant and unheeded. She asserts:

> Anticolonial activists of the 1940s had advocated freedom for Africans and those of African descent within an antiimperialist, anticapitalist framework . . . But civil rights activists of the 1950s and 1960s negotiated in an international and national terrain dominated by the Cold War. Although civil rights leaders such as Martin Luther King, Jr. and Bayard Rustin were personally interested in anticolonialism, it was not a programmatic part of the civil rights movement.

Furthermore, the marginal gains made by the executive and judicial branches were an important but largely symbolic precedent of federal support: *Brown v. Board* was undoubtedly a major breakthrough in 1954, but the oxymoronic recommendation to desegregate schools "with all deliberate speed" a year later in *Brown II* was a reflection of the nation's self-contradictory approach to race.

In many ways, it was only window dressing for a global audience without substantive change on the ground that could be felt in the everyday lives of African Americans and other minorities. Von Eschen continues:

> The preoccupation of the Truman administration with America's 'Achilles' heel' had led instead to frenetic efforts to shape the world's perception of race in America and ultimately to the effective disruption of leftist anticolonial politics. It did not lead the administration to act decisively on civil rights.[25]

The events that would take place between the mass mobilization of African Americans in 1955 (the Montgomery bus boycott) and the all-important Freedom Rides of 1963 would eventually catalyze the federal government to enact actual, rather than symbolic, change in the form of the Civil Rights Act of 1964. Nonetheless, she contends:

> The fate of the 1940s politics of the African diaspora tells us much about the stakes involved in challenging economic exploitation and the fight for human rights. The collision of anticolonial politics with Cold War liberalism illuminates the political and economic conditions faced by later democratic projects [like those of the Nation of Islam's Malcolm X, Congolese independence leader Patrice Lumumba, and the anti-apartheid movement of the African National Congress] as well as the vulnerability of these projects to internationally organized state repression.[26]

Thomas Borstelmann similarly points out the necessities and the limits of America's democratic project in this Manichean context of Cold War "white hats" and "black hats." He observes:

> Competing with the Soviet Union in the postwar world meant, by definition, maximizing the amount that other peoples saw of American life. Hiding one's flaws was considered the telltale sign of a secretive, unfree country—precisely what American leaders in the late 1940s identified as the defining characteristic of a Communist nation.[27]

He continues:

> The Cold War focus on the ideals of democracy and freedom assured that racial exceptions to the American practice of those principles would receive careful attention . . . Acts of racial violence in obscure rural parts of Dixie changed almost overnight from events of mostly local interest to headlines splashed across newspapers around the world.[28]

To wit, consider the following reflection by Kikuchi in early 1949, after he had just commented on the outrage that a Texas undertaker would not bury a Mexican American GI for fear of offending fellow white Texans in town. He writes:

It is sickening that [this] is perpetuated in the name of Democracy, especially at a time when a world wide struggle with Communism is taking
place and the rallying cry for the democracies is that this is the best way
of life. It is with limitations, but we don't seem to be able to make enough
headway to get rid of these limitations.[29]

As Borstelmann asserted, the ordinarily localized nature of these racialized
events in Dixie turned national and international very quickly in this era, since
everyone waited to see what the federal government's next move would be in
explaining away the blatant duplicity of American democracy. Kikuchi's last line
also reinforces both Borstelmann and Von Eschen's trenchant point that the limits and, truly, weaknesses of the democratic project were far too apparent to any
onlooker. What might have been minimized in the *Dallas Morning News* as an
issue of states' rights and local custom (i.e., euphemisms for Jim Crow) was now
appropriately a black eye for the Truman administration in *Pravda*.

In self-regarding fashion, the nation was auditioning in front of a critical,
worldwide court, and Borstelmann emphasizes that these judges most wanted
to see how the white American majority reacted, especially in the democratic
metropoles of Washington, D.C., and New York City. I would offer that another
index of the democratic body's health was the extent to which such normative
stereotypes pervaded racial and ethnic minorities themselves. In this context,
Kikuchi explained one of his counseling sessions with a young soldier of color
in late 1948.

Antonio is a Puerto Rican with a terrific inferiority complex and he has
taken out a lot of his frustration against the Negro. He said that he didn't
want to be identified with Negroes because he had been in Washington,
D.C. during the war and he was forced to go to a segregated place once.
The curious thing about Antonio was that instead of getting angry about
the social situation which allowed such practices, he took out his hostility
on the Negroes. He lives in East Harlem, and hates the native Negroes of
West Harlem. He said that his hair got curly when some acid dropped on
his head.[30]

This young man's self-diagnosis was an inverted type of psychosomatic behavior. Instead of mental anguish translated into physical pain, Antonio claimed
that the curly hair on his head and, by extension, his appearance—all physically
external elements—were the source of his internal, psychological "maladjustments." He wanted to have his hair straightened in order to erase any vestige
of African descent on his person, or at the very least, to not look Black in any
way, shape, or form: he clearly understood the racialized hierarchy in America,
with the added burden of Puerto Ricans' being an imperial afterthought, living
as disenfranchised "citizens" in an "unincorporated territory," an appendage to
the American national body. He therefore projected his anger, unsurprisingly,
onto African American bodies, both in D.C. and New York, shamefully seeing

himself in the faces and follicles of his neighbors, or else quite simply knowing that to be a true American—even for the most recent arrival from Ellis or Angel Island—one needs only use the violent but upwardly mobile epithet: nigger. Kikuchi attempted to place Antonio within the structural context of the larger social forces and systematic racialized practices that led to his maladjustments, but Antonio believed what the majority discourse encouraged him to believe: that he was worthless, and African Americans even more so. This type of destructive internalization of American cultural norms and customs posed a more dangerous and immediate threat to American (or Puerto Rican) communities of color than any item of Soviet propaganda: one need only recall Kenneth and Mamie Clark's "doll test," cited in the *Brown* decision, to know that America had already inculcated its children of color with the notion that "white makes right."

In that vein, Kikuchi was well aware of the internal smear campaign America employed during the war. Now he was just as prepared to indict the press and the government for collectively propagandizing against leftist activists and painting all dissenters critical of Orwellian policies with the same red brush. When two congressmen tried to pass the Mundt-Nixon Bill, also known as the Communist Registration Bill, requiring all CP members to "register" with the attorney general, both Kikuchi and his sister Bette's hero, Paul Robeson, were up in arms. The diarist angrily commented:

> Radio reports state that the "communist mob which descended on Washington today" in protest to the Mundt Bill is very reminiscent of how Communists took over European countries. It was about the stupidest interpretation I have heard yet. One of the commentators added that the "motley mob was led by Paul Robeson, Negro singer." I think this was the same technique used by Fascists to spread race and political hatred in order to divert people away from the real issues.[31]

Despite Kikuchi's sympathies with Robeson and his stance against such extreme, un-American acts (registry of suspicious citizens and the press's uncritical propaganda was 1942 all over again), he could only watch from afar as Robeson was unceremoniously pushed to the side of the world stage. The government's watchful eye and the newest civil rights leaders, who branded him "an integrationist duped by communists," weighed heavily on him; increasingly isolated, he died unrecognized for his tireless championing of black (and yellow) rights around the world.[32]

The unofficial members of the Common Ground School were simultaneously dispersing, both with the end of the magazine's publication in 1949 and with Adamic's passing in 1951. These events did not signify the absolute end of all progressive, interracial activism or discourse; the continuing efforts of Du Bois, Rustin, McWilliams, Kikuchi, and many others persisted well into the 1960s. However, *Common Ground*'s last run did represent a changing of the guard to a younger generation of activists and intellectuals (who would move back and forth between racial nationalism and Third World internationalism), while it also signaled the arrival and staying power of a reactionary ideological consensus, among Democrats and Republicans alike. Hence, HUAC vanquished Bucklin Moon, for example, who was then fired by *Collier's* over charges of alleged communist sympathies in 1953; he consequently suffered from major depression, leading to an attempted suicide. He had also suffered a falling out with his close friend and fellow southerner Lillian Smith around this time in a dispute over her autobiography. Feisty to the end, Smith herself fought breast cancer from the early 1950s until her death in 1966.

In 1946, Richard Wright began his expatriate life in Paris to hobnob with the existentialists Jean-Paul Sartre and Simone de Beauvoir: while he would publish *The Outsider* (1953) and *White Man, Listen!* (1957), he would die prematurely at the age of fifty-two in 1960. His literary rival, Zora Neale Hurston, met with an equally tragic ending that same year, her genius unacknowledged, poor in health and finances, and working as a maid in Florida, where she was buried in an unmarked grave. A third giant to pass in 1960 was Ottley, whose last decade produced five successful books, including *Black Odyssey* (1948), a well-received history of African Americans.

After Carey McWilliams wrote *Witch Hunt* in 1950 as an early salvo against McCarthyism, his stock spiked as a high-value target of HUAC and the FBI; he finally left California, assuming the editorship of the *Nation* in New York the following year. Saroyan, dramatically, became embroiled in two divorces with the same wife, one in 1949, the other in 1952, while his friend John Fante—in what was expected to be the era of his most prolific work—was diagnosed with diabetes in 1955, which led to his going blind in the 1970s. During the height of McCarthyism, George Schuyler made his strongest turn toward conservatism, writing an article for the mouthpiece of the John Birch Society as well as publishing *The Communist Conspiracy Against Negroes* in 1947; the *Courier* would let him go after he protested the awarding of the Nobel Peace Prize to Martin Luther King, Jr. After years of marriage, Chester Himes separated from his first wife in 1952 and, like his friend Wright, set sail for Paris, where he struggled with alcohol until his first detective novel, *The Five-Cornered Square* (1957), met with both critical and financial success; as his European life settled, Himes remarried in 1962. Finally, blacklisted for his labor organizing, Carlos Bulosan was watched closely by the FBI in the early 1950s, only to experience a sudden death from malnutrition and tuberculosis at the age of forty-two in 1956.

For their part, Nisei thinkers traveled the route of further social science studies in an effort to understand exactly what it was they had just experienced, and perhaps to compartmentalize—through even more intellectualizing—what was clearly a deeply emotional trauma. One need only browse the list of dissertations from the University of Chicago written by or about Japanese Americans between 1947 and 1963 to gain a sense of how keenly the entire internment process affected a majority of the Nisei generation. Doctorates were earned by the WRA anthropologist and lifelong Nikkei ally Rachel Reese Sady (1947) as well as Shibutani (1948), Miyamoto (1950), Eugene Uyeki (1953), and Nishi (1963), among others. Furthermore, as Allan Austin reports, Ota managed to leave camp and study at Wellesley and Yale, the consummate "goodwill ambassador" for the council that began organizing the student relocation of five thousand internees in 1943.[33] After earning her PhD in history in 1951, Ota graduated to a storied career at the University of Connecticut and published two books: one a bibliography of Southeast Asian studies with noted anthropologist John Embree (who had, incidentally, led the training for the War Department's Japanese area studies at Chicago for officers billeted to Japan), and one with her fellow scholar and husband Floyd Dotson. A few years after earning his PhD in psychology, Sakoda joined Ota at Connecticut in 1952 until he landed at Brown, teaching for many years before retiring in 1981. By that time, he had also become quite the expert in origami, authoring *Modern Origami* in 1969. Popular in both his avocational and scholarly communities, he died in 2005 at eighty-nine.

After two years in the army, Shibutani drew on the GI Bill to complete his PhD with Wirth, Blumer, and Hughes at Chicago, where he earned an instructor's position in 1948. Returning to California, he taught at Cal and UC–Santa Barbara, publishing *Society and Personality* (1961), *Improvised News: A Sociological Study of Rumor* (1966), and *Social Processes* (1986). "Shibs" died in 2004 at the age of eighty-three. Like Kikuchi, Murase finished his master's at Columbia in 1947 and then a PhD in 1961. In 1952, he was the first American Fulbright Scholar to Japan. Very much true to his word, Murase remained deeply invested in the social welfare and mental health of communities of color, especially African Americans and Puerto Ricans in New York. At San Francisco State, where he spent thirty-three years, Murase trained scores of graduate students of all colors, while his focus shifted in later years to the plight of recent Southeast Asian refugees and Pacific Islander students. "Kenny" passed away at eighty-nine in 2009.

Mary Oyama Mittwer was much more of a cipher publicly after the war. In 1946, she wrote one last article for *Common Ground*, entitled "A Nisei Report from Home," which told of her family's return to their former LA house and neighborhood, and their necessary, awkward, but ultimately satisfying adjustment process.[34] Jean Johnson, Himes's first wife, greeted her after living in and taking care of the Mittwers' home during their three years of internment. She disappeared from the public record until 1991, presumably because of the full-time and unsung job of raising her family, when Valerie Matsumoto wrote a historic article on Nisei women writers of the 1930s, highlighting Oyama's prewar advice column, in which she used the pen name "Deirdre." Oyama wrote the column, which was along the lines of "Dear Abby," for the Japanese American *San Francisco New World–Sun*, emphasizing how Nisei women could strategically navigate the white world, and offering helpful tips on love and etiquette.[35] She passed in 1994.

Lastly, Tsuneishi continued to enjoy his days with his talented artist wife, Betty Takeuchi, in Bethesda, Maryland. After leaving MISLS in Okinawa in January 1946, he returned to the States, earning master's degrees at Columbia in 1948 and 1950, and his PhD in political science from Yale in 1961. He published the scholarly *Japanese Political Style* in 1966, and retired from the Library of Congress as chief of its Asian Division in 1993. Despite his diminishing eyesight (due to macular degeneration), Warren remained the keenly perceptive, last "witness" of this group of remarkable Nisei intellectuals and friends. He died on January 29, 2011, at the age of eighty-nine. The very next day, the legendary author Hisaye Yamamoto would also pass in LA at eighty-nine.

"What's Going On"

The most difficult time in Kikuchi's later years came in 1973, coincidentally just as Modell published the diary. Kikuchi chose to retire from the Veterans Administration, fed up with the Vietnam War and appalled by what he considered persistent discrimination against African American veterans returning from the conflict. Despite being trained in social-work theory, Kikuchi refused to rely on it, preferring the empirical method he had developed and been encouraged to use while working on JERS in Chicago. He said,

> I'm not anti-Freud, but there comes a time when you listen to others and you say "it doesn't work." And then the staff I was working with—God, they were making up fiction. They're taking these concepts and fitting the cases to the concepts. And I refused to do this.[36]

Additionally, he felt the need to challenge the entrenched and backward policies of the VA: "And for many years I was asking, 'How come we don't have any Black, Negro, social workers?' That was taboo." His reason for continually asking that question?

> I felt we were getting all these Black veterans coming back [from Vietnam] and they all come from fatherless families or divided families. I said, "These theories don't work. You've got to write up these case histories as if these people grew up in Vienna of 1890. It just doesn't work." And the people in charge refused to discuss it. So that is one of the reasons I decided after [twenty-four] years, that I'd given enough to social work.

As a result of his iconoclastic approach, Kikuchi never earned a promotion, but proudly held on to his status, telling his superiors,

> "I just want to be a social worker. I just want to be left alone." And, you know, there was a reward to that because they did leave me alone. I did many other things that social workers in our office never did.

He continued:

> I went out and I picketed against the Vietnam War right outside the hospital, the only social worker that did that. And then they were going to

arrest me for violating federal property, and I found out through a lawyer friend of mine that the government only owned [up] to the middle of the sidewalk. So I picketed on the other side. I'm a social rebel, let's face it.

Helped by some good fortune on the stock market, Kikuchi left the VA officially in the fall of 1973 and became Yuriko's manager until his death fifteen years later. In the meantime, he took frequent trips to their summer home on idyllic Block Island, off the coast of Rhode Island, a necessary refuge and "base" for the entire family, while maintaining an apartment in Manhattan. Both Charlie and Yuriko also took time to see the world during this period, thanks mainly to Yuriko's flourishing career, and these adventures brought them to spots as far-flung as eastern and western Europe, the Caribbean, Mexico, Cuba, Australia, Japan, China, India, North Africa, and Israel, among others. Unquestionably, then, both Kikuchis became "cross-cultural travelers" not only in America, but also around the globe. True to his nature, though, Charlie always kept a watchful eye on the state of race relations, no matter what the setting. Looking back on his formative youth, and the period that set the tone for the rest of his life, Kikuchi told Hansen just a month before his death: "All I wanted to do was to find out what's going on, and that's why I used so much energy in joining the so-called left-of-center groups." He explained why he shied away from a narrowly conceived academic focus and gravitated toward the activist impulse that was as lively in 1988 as it had been nearly fifty years earlier:

I was more interested in what happened to the longshoremen, and what happened to the unions, and how come unions didn't accept Asian Americans, and trying to get the Mexicans and Filipinos organized in country work. And I lost jobs because of those things. But that's been my pattern.[37]

Following this blueprint of protest, and faithful to the internationalist orientation he had adopted back in the 1940s, he wrote from Paris in 1976:

I am always amused when our French friends tend to minimize that Paris also has racial problems . . . From what I have observed, the Black North Africans are the low man and they clean the streets with those branch brooms. Then come the North African Arabs who seem to be in construction work . . . The few Indians get mistaken for Arabs so they don't like it when they are turned away from a bar which [forbids] North Africans . . . The Portuguese are next and they do the domestic work, and the Spanish are the waiters and the cooks. The Chinese seem to get by because they have the stores and most of them seem to be from Vietnam and they speak French . . . Yet, I still think it is better than most cities in the U.S.[38]

The Tocqueville of Japanese America had indeed gone global. And as the angle of his lens widened, Kikuchi's activism and penchant for freedom fighting seemed only to grow.

In a donation letter to the Detroit Chinese Welfare Council seven years later, he passionately remarked on the injustice of the verdict in the Vincent Chin murder trial. In June 1982, Chin was a twenty-seven-year-old Chinese American draftsman enjoying his bachelor party when a run-in with two white men at a Detroit nightclub ended with Chin's being bludgeoned to death with a baseball bat. Calling him "Chink" and "motherfucker," the two men, one of whom had been a foreman at a Chrysler plant, blamed Chin, and people who looked like him, for the loss of autoworkers' jobs. On their day in court, the judge issued a sentence of three years' probation and a fine of $3,000. Despite widespread protest, especially in Asian American communities, and a federal case brought against the men for civil rights violations, neither ever spent a day in jail. Proffering a modest sum to the American Citizens for Justice (the community group led by a former autoworker, Helen Zia, and Chin's courageous mother, Lily, who tirelessly lobbied to overturn the decisions), Kikuchi wrote,

> I read with a sense of outrage about the miscarriage of justice in the Vincent Chin case. It is beyond understanding why a judge would free the two men who beat Mr. Chin to death . . . It is this kind of racism which poisons our democratic system and the violation of Mr. Chin's rights should not be forgotten.[39]

Kikuchi's commitment to social justice intersected with his desire to be a part of something, to be part of a whole, to be part of a larger cause. His membership in a catalogue of organizations committed to such causes bears this out. Indeed, at the time of his death, he was a card-carrying member of the ACLU (ironic, given its noticeable failure during internment) as well as several left-leaning organizations, like the United Negro College Fund and the Committee in Solidarity with the People of El Salvador.[40] Fittingly, given the meaning of his middle name—Tatsuro, or standing man—Kikuchi always stood tall for social justice and firmly against xenophobic and racist assaults on individual liberties and group rights. While a deep emotional involvement with African Americans remained the constant baseline in his life, one can infer from his organizational affiliations that he broadened his interracial concerns over time: Japanese American internees from the 1940s had as much in common with African American freedom fighters of the 1960s, as they did with labor unionists in El Salvador in the 1980s. What is more—and again, befitting his distinguished Japanese name—Kikuchi met the end of his life in Russia while standing for yet another important cause: nuclear disarmament and peace.

In 1987, International Peace Walk, Inc. and the Soviet Peace Committee established the Soviet-American Walk as an exercise in citizen diplomacy. Over a six-week span in the summer of 1987, 230 Americans and 200 Soviets walked 455 miles between Moscow and Leningrad as a way to call for peace and the resolution of cross-cultural conflicts between the two superpowers. A year later, efforts were redoubled, and two separate walks took place in both the United States and the USSR. Kikuchi took part in the march from Odessa to Kiev in August and

September. Despite spending the months leading up to the event walking several miles a day on Block Island, Kikuchi could not shake stomach pains he had begun to experience early in the trip. By late August, he was in a Ukrainian hospital, diagnosed with terminal cancer. Yuriko and Lawrence eventually brought an ailing Charlie back to Mt. Sinai Hospital in Manhattan. He died on September 25, 1988.

Even in his last days, Kikuchi managed to keep writing letters to his family back home, and in those reports, it was evident that he still had some fight left in him. As an example, one of the highlights of his experience was an interview with a radio station in Kiev. The host at one point asked Kikuchi what he thought of Reagan's recent apology for the internment of Japanese Americans. His answer—like many of the thoughtful observations he had made over the past half century—struck an expansive, visionary tone, hinting at the possibility of a larger, globalized family.

> I made my point that most governments do not correct its errors in this way and it was a triumph for our democratic system that allowed our President to apologize . . . I will be asked about the Nisei many times on the trip and I don't mind answering . . . My thesis at the end of the Radio Kiev interview was that all countries have problems and we happen to believe that a democratic system solves them in time, but that the most important point is that it can only happen when people begin to trust one another.[41]

And when Tsuneishi eulogized his best friend in Riverside Church later that fall, he captured the spirit of the man, calling Charlie "an ardent advocate of social justice, a diarist, and a scholar." Recognizing that the "early estrangement from his family forged his choices," Tsuneishi emphasized that Kikuchi "insisted on his identity as an American and that America is a work in progress." And with a brother's love, he recalled: "He was never judgmental, always accepting, and said we must forgive those who abuse us, those who defeat us, those who rob us. Hatred is only conquered by love." Professing that ethic himself, Tsuneishi concluded, "I claim him as my best friend and the Soviet Peace March was Charlie's final 'witness.'"[42]

And truly, Kikuchi had borne witness to a great deal. As his diaries covering the period from Pearl Harbor to his first years in Manhattan prove, Kikuchi not only documented, but also actively participated in the most significant events of the period between 1940 and 1948, a most crucial stage in the history of American race relations. Undoubtedly, the signal events of that era—like the war and the internment—were transformative experiences for him. But it was in the ordinary moments of conversation, reflection, and writing that Kikuchi gained even greater insight into what it meant to be a Nisei, a democrat, and an American. Adamic and the Thomases had blessed him with an informal education about immigration history and the usefulness of social science when applied to race relations, but it was Kikuchi himself who gleaned what he could from these lessons and then deftly employed such knowledge in discussions with the talented (Nisei) tenth at Berkeley, "I House" intellectuals, everyday Chicagoans, and GIs of every stripe in the army. Based on the wealth of these interactions, Kikuchi reoriented, perhaps even exploded, the black-white paradigm of race relations in the United States. By occasionally embracing a situational Blackness, he demonstrated that the distances between racial groups were often merely "masks." At the same time, he intimately understood the historical barriers and systemic limits to forming a genuine multiracial democracy. His internment proved as much, temporarily occluding his vision for reform, but the segregation of and discrimination against his African American brothers and sisters remained the most shameful lie kept by the American family. True to his Japanese name, however, Tatsuro never backed down, standing tall even when his body (or nation) failed to live up to the strength of his spirit.

A Final Entry

Books line the walls of a sitting room in the Kikuchi apartment on Lexington Avenue: William Styron's *The Confessions of Nat Turner*; John Nance's *The Gentle Tasaday: A Stone Age People in the Philippine Rain Forest*; Johnson's *Patterns of Negro Segregation*; Myrdal's *An American Dilemma*; thick, dog-eared novels by James Michener; yellowed copies of Tolstoy; and psychoanalytic textbooks, amid rows of others. The living room reveals slender wooden beams and posts that frame a high ceiling and chalky walls, in the elegant style of a Japanese tea cottage. Photographs fill every room, tracing the narrative of a dancer's graceful career, a patriarch's undying love of fishing, a couple's limitless travels, and a family's rich celebration of a life together. One particular photo graces the entry to the living room, a color head shot of Charlie late in life: a regal lion's mane of white hair tucked back behind his ears; a wide, tanned mug lined from squints and smiles; and the collar of a pea-green army jacket framing his sideways glance. Proudly, one might say, an Old American with a Japanese Face.

Notes

Preface

1. The mother of modern dance, Martha Graham developed the counterbalancing movements of "contraction" and "release" as groundbreaking techniques in modern dance (Yuriko Amemiya Kikuchi, interview by the author, New York, N.Y., August 28, 2004).

Introduction: An Age of Possibility

1. Charles Kikuchi Papers (Collection 1259), Department of Special Collections, Charles E. Young Research Library, UCLA (hereafter cited as CKP), box 12, 4:1174. This entry, dated December 5, 1941, actually appears in the December 8, 1941, insert of his paper "Neurotic Tendencies Among the American Born Japanese," written for a psychiatry class at Cal.

2. Charles Kikuchi, *The Kikuchi Diary: Chronicle from an American Concentration Camp*, ed. John Modell (Urbana: Univ. of Illinois Press, 1973, 1993), 42–3 (entry dated December 7, 1941; page reference from the 1993 ed.); hereafter cited as Kikuchi, *Diary*.

3. See Greg Robinson, "Farewell to L'il Tokyo: Wartime Nisei Writers and the Ambiguities of Assimilation" (unpublished conference paper, American Studies Association, Hartford, Connecticut, October 19, 2003).

4. See Michael Denning, *The Cultural Front: The Laboring of American Culture in the Twentieth Century* (New York: Verso, 1997); Nikhil Singh, *Black Is a Country: Race and the Unfinished Struggle for Democracy* (Cambridge, Mass.: Harvard Univ. Press, 2004); Penny Von Eschen, *Race against Empire: Black Americans and Anti-Colonialism, 1937–1957* (Ithaca, N.Y.: Cornell Univ. Press, 1997); Thomas Borstelmann, *The Cold War and the Color Line: American Race Relations in the Global Arena* (Cambridge, Mass.: Harvard Univ. Press, 2001); Mary Dudziak, *Cold War Civil Rights: Race and the Image of American Democracy* (Princeton, N.J.: Princeton Univ. Press, 2000); and Colleen Lye, *America's Asia: Racial Form and Literature, 1893–1945* (Princeton, N.J.: Princeton Univ. Press, 2005).

5. Michael Warner, *Publics and Counterpublics* (Cambridge, Mass: MIT Press, 2002), 56.

6. Robert Park, "Human Migration and the Marginal Man" (1928), in *Theories of Ethnicity: A Classical Reader*, ed. Werner Sollors (New York: NYU Press, 1996); originally from "Racial Assimilation in Secondary Groups," *American Journal of Sociology* 19:5 (1914): 606–23.

7. On Black Chicago, see St. Clair Drake and Horace Cayton, *Black Metropolis: A Study of Negro Life in a Northern City* (New York: Harcourt, Brace, 1945); Allan H. Spear, *Black Chicago: The Making of a Negro Ghetto, 1890–1920* (Chicago: Univ. of Chicago Press, 1967); James Grossman, *Land of Hope: Chicago, Black Southerners, and the Great Migration* (Chicago: Univ. of Chicago Press, 1989); Adam Green, *Selling the Race: Culture, Community, and Black Chicago, 1940–1955* (Chicago: Univ. of Chicago Press, 2007).

8. Charles Kikuchi to Louis Adamic, n.d. [February 1940?], 21 (box 59, folder 7, "Japanese" Subject File, Louis Adamic Papers [C0246], Correspondence, Manuscripts Division, Department of Rare Books and Special Collections, Princeton University Library; hereafter cited as LAP).

9. See Charles Kikuchi, "A Young American with a Japanese Face," in *From Many Lands*, ed. Louis Adamic (New York: Harper and Bros., 1940), 183–234.

10. See Singh, *Black Is a Country*, 111–13.

11. Werner Sollors, "Americans All: 'Of Plymouth Rock and Jamestown and Ellis Island'; or, Ethnic Literature and Some Redefinitions of 'America'" (New York: NYU Press: n.d.), http://www.nyupress.org/americansall/americansall.html?$string.

12. For the most compelling examples, see Lane Ryo Hirabayashi, *The Politics of Fieldwork: Research in an American Concentration Camp* (Tucson: Univ. of Arizona Press, 1999) on the work conducted by one of Kikuchi's fellow researchers, Tamie Tsuchiyama; Brian Masaru Hayashi, *Democratizing the Enemy: The Japanese American Internment* (Princeton, N.J.: Princeton Univ. Press, 2004); David H. Price, *Anthropological Intelligence: The Deployment and Neglect of American Anthropology in the Second World War* (Durham, N.C.: Duke Univ. Press, 2008), which looks more closely at the WRA studies; and for a broad overview of the analysts, see Arthur A. Hansen, *Japanese American World War II Evacuation Oral History Project: Analysts (Part III)* (Munich: Saur, 1992); Hansen, "Cultural Politics in the Gila River Relocation Center, 1942–1943," *Arizona and the West* 27:4 (Winter 1985): 327–62; and Hansen, "'The Evacuation and Resettlement Study at the Gila River Relocation Center, 1942–1944," *Journal of the West* 38:2 (April 1999): 45–55.

13. W. I. Thomas lost his job and standing in the community in 1918 when he was caught having an affair with the wife of a naval officer serving in France.

14. This last grouping has been thoroughly documented and thoughtfully critiqued by Henry Yu, *Thinking Orientals: Migration, Contact, and Exoticism in Modern America* (Oxford: Oxford Univ. Press, 2002).

15. Craig Wilder, personal communication to the author, Dartmouth College, Hanover, New Hampshire, January 2005.

16. Charlotte Brooks, "In the Twilight Zone between Black and White: Japanese American Resettlement and Community in Chicago, 1942–1945," *Journal of American History* 86:4 (March 2000): 1655–87.

17. Paul Spickard, *Mixed Blood: Intermarriage and Ethnic Identity in Twentieth Century America* (Madison: Univ. of Wisconsin Press, 1989), 53, 55.

18. Louis Wirth, *The Ghetto* (Chicago: Univ. of Chicago Press, 1928; New Brunswick, N.J.: Transaction, 1998), 287 (page reference from the Transaction ed.).

19. See Carla Cappetti, "Sociology of an Existence: Richard Wright and the Chicago School," *MELUS* 12:2 (Summer 1985): 37.

20. David Brion Davis, "Some Recent Directions in American Cultural History," *American Historical Review* 73:3 (February 1968): 705. Thanks to John Stauffer for referring me to this indispensable work. See Stauffer, *The Black Hearts of Men: Radical Abolitionists and the Transformation of Race* (Cambridge, Mass.: Harvard Univ. Press, 2001).

21. Stauffer, *Black Hearts of Men*, 3.

22. Kikuchi, diary entry, March 22, 1943 (CKP, box 12, 5:2340–2).

23. See James W. Cook and Lawrence B. Glickman, "Twelve Propositions for a History of Cultural History," in *The Cultural Turn in U.S. History: Past, Present, and Future*, ed. James W. Cook, Lawrence B. Glickman, and Michael O'Malley (Chicago: Univ. of Chicago Press, 2008), 3–58.

Chapter 1: Before Pearl Harbor

1. See Kikuchi, "A Young American"; Dorothy Swaine Thomas *The Salvage*, with the assistance of Charles Kikuchi and James Sakoda (Berkeley and Los Angeles: Univ. of California Press, 1952). *The Salvage* is the second volume of the Japanese American Evacuation and Resettlement Study (JERS). The other two JERS volumes, also published by the University of California Press, are Dorothy Thomas and Richard Nishimoto, *The Spoilage* (1946), and Jacobus tenBroek, Edward N. Barnhart, and Floyd W. Matson, *Prejudice, War, and the Constitution* (1954). There was also an unofficial book from a former JERS researcher: Morton Grodzins, *Americans Betrayed: Politics and the Japanese Evacuation* (Chicago: Univ. of Chicago Press, 1949).

2. See Kikuchi, "Through the JERS Looking Glass: A Personal View from Within," in *Views from Within: The Japanese American Evacuation and Resettlement Project*, ed. Yuji Ichioka (Los Angeles: Asian American Studies Center, Univ. of California at Los Angeles), 179–96; Dana Y. Takagi, "Life History Analysis and JERS: Re-evaluating the Work of Charles Kikuchi," in Ichioka, *Views from Within*, 197–216; and Kikuchi, interview by Arthur Hansen, August 1–3, 1988, Japanese American Oral History Project, Oral History Program at California State University, Fullerton (hereafter cited as Kikuchi, Hansen interview), unpublished version in author's possession. Also see Hansen, "Political Ideology and Participant Observation: Nisei Social Scientists in the Evacuation and Resettlement Study, 1942–1945," in *Guilt by Association: Essays on Japanese Settlement, Internment, and Relocation in the Rocky Mountain West*, ed. Mike Mackey (Powell, Wyo.: Western History, 2001), 119–44.

3. See Modell, introduction to Kikuchi, *Diary*, 1–39.

4. Kikuchi, "A Young American," 187. Modell rightly asserts that this piece was "pseudo-autobiographical" (Kikuchi, *Diary*, 11).

5. Yuriko Amemiya Kikuchi confirmed this fact (also found in his birth certificate) and offered the enlightening translation as well (interview by the author, August 28, 2004).

6. Introduction to the unpublished manuscript "The Kikuchi Diary," edited by Donald P. Kent and Barbara K. Fitts, ca. 1951 (Modell file folder "Correspondence between Charles Kikuchi and John Modell," copy in author's possession [hereafter cited as Kent and Fitts, "Kikuchi Diary"]; all use of material in the Modell file folders is courtesy of John Modell, Brown University). Kent was a sociologist at the University of Connecticut, and Fitts was a collaborator of Thomas's from the days of JERS. Kent and Fitts edited and annotated versions of the Tanforan diary but never secured a press to publish their project.

7. Warren Tsuneishi to the author, June 1, 2004, 1.

8. Kikuchi to Barbara Fitts, September 7, 1955, 4–5 (JERS Records, folder W1.15, BANC MSS 67/14 c, Bancroft Library, University of California, Berkeley; hereafter cited as JERS Papers).

9. Kikuchi, Hansen interview, 34.

10. See Roger Daniels, *Concentration Camps, North America: Japanese in the United States and Canada during World War II* (New York: Holt, Rinehart and Winston, 1971; rpt., Malabar, Fla.: Krieger, 1993) and *Prisoners without Trial: Japanese Americans in World War II* (New York: Hill & Wang, 1993); Gary Y. Okihiro, *Storied Lives: Japanese American Students and World War II* (Seattle: Univ. of Washington Press, 1999); Gary Y. Okihiro and Julie Sly, "The Press, Japanese Americans, and the Concentration Camps," *Phylon* 44:1 (March 1983): 66–83; Valerie Matsumoto, "Japanese American Women during World War II," in *Unequal Sisters*, ed. Ellen Carol DuBois and Vicki Ruiz (New York: Routledge, 1990), 373–86; Paul Spickard, *Japanese Americans: The Formation and Transformations of an Ethnic Group* (New York: Twayne, 1996); David Yoo, *Growing Up Nisei* (Urbana: Univ. of Illinois Press, 2000); Bill Hosokawa, *Nisei: The Quiet Americans* (New York: Morrow, 1969).

11. Modell, introduction to Kikuchi, *Diary*, 12.

12. Kikuchi, Hansen interview, 47.

13. Modell, introduction to Kikuchi, *Diary*, 16; Kikuchi, interview by John Modell, New York City, May 9, 1970 (copy in author's possession); the quotation by Modell is from page 15 of the interview.

14. Modell, introduction to Kikuchi, *Diary*, 19.

15. Kikuchi, Modell interview, 5.

16. Quoted in Modell, introduction to Kikuchi, *Diary*, 17.

17. Kikuchi to D. Thomas, June 28, 1945, 1 (Modell file folder, "Kikuchi Biographical Data," copy in author's possession). This is a particularly striking passage, especially in light of "A Young American with a Japanese Face," Kikuchi's contribution to Adamic's collection.

18. Hemesh Patel, "Documentary Highlights Fight by Japanese American in WWII," *Daily Bruin*, November 17, 2000. See Peter Irons, *Justice at War: The Story of the Japanese American Internment Cases* (Berkley and Los Angeles: Univ. of California Press, 1983), 93–9; and Spickard, *Japanese Americans*, 103.

19. *Korematsu v. United States*, 323 U.S. 214, 242 (1944).

20. Sander Gilman, *Making the Body Beautiful: A Cultural History of Aesthetic Surgery* (Princeton, N.J.: Princeton Univ. Press, 1999), 99. See Edward Falces and John Imada, "Aesthetic Surgery in Asians," in *Male Aesthetic Surgery*, ed. Eugene Courtiss (St. Louis: Mosby, 1991), 159.

21. Irons, *Justice at War*, 94.

22. Kikuchi, *Diary*, 136–7.

23. Ibid., 138.

24. Ibid.

25. Kikuchi to D. Thomas, June 28, 1945, 1.

26. Ibid., 4.

27. Ibid., 5.

28. Ibid., 2.

29. Kikuchi, Hansen interview, 104.

30. Kikuchi, Modell interview, 4.

31. Kikuchi, Hansen interview, 118.

32. Mitchell T. Maki, Harry H. L. Kitano, and S. Megan Berthold, *Achieving the Impossible Dream: How Japanese Americans Obtained Redress* (Urbana: Univ. of Illinois Press, 1999), 25.

33. Yuji Ichioka, introduction to Karl G. Yoneda, *Ganbatte: Sixty-Year Struggle of a Kibei Worker* (Los Angeles: Asian American Studies Center, Univ. of California at Los Angeles, 1983), xi–xii.

34. Ibid., 12.

35. Karl G. Yoneda, "The Heritage of Sen Katayama," *Political Affairs: Theoretical Journal of the Communist Party U.S.A.* (March 1975): 23.

36. Yoneda, *Ganbatte,* 97.

37. Ichioka, introduction to *Ganbatte,* xi.

38. James Omura, interview by Arthur A. Hansen, August 22–25, 1984, O.H. 1765, Japanese American Oral History Project, Oral History Program, California State University, Fullerton, published in *Japanese American World War II Evacuation Oral History Project, Part IV: Resisters* (Munich: Saur, 1995), 133–327 (hereafter cited as Omura, Hansen interview); the quotation is from 257. *Current Life* would later change its subtitle to *The Only National Nisei Magazine.*

39. Ibid., 257–62.

40. Ibid., 259.

41. Kikuchi, Hansen interview, 81.

42. Omura, Hansen interview, 258–9.

43. Yoneda, *Ganbatte,* 130–1.

44. Ibid., 80.

45. Denning, *Cultural Front,* 201.

46. Mae Ngai, *Impossible Subjects: Illegal Aliens and the Making of Modern America* (Princeton, N.J.: Princeton Univ. Press, 2004), 41, 49. On quota attempts, see Izumi Hirobe, *Japanese Pride, American Prejudice: Modifying the Exclusion Clause of the 1924 Immigration Act* (Stanford, Calif.: Stanford Univ. Press, 2001).

47. Ronald Takaki, *Strangers from a Different Shore: A History of Asian Americans,* rev. ed. (Boston: Little, Brown, 1998), 212, 214.

48. Ibid., 215. *Kenjinkai* refers to the prefectural-based social associations that "brought its members or people (*jin*) together for social activities such as picnics; more importantly, it provided a network of social relations buttressing economic cooperation and assistance for employment, housing, and credit" (193).

49. Ibid., 214.

50. Hosokawa, *Nisei,* 158.

51. Ibid., 172.

52. Monica Sone, *Nisei Daughter* (Boston: Little, Brown, 1953; rpt., Seattle: Univ. of Washington Press, 1991), 28.

53. Jeanne Wakatsuki Houston, *Farewell to Manzanar* (Boston: Houghton Mifflin, 1973), 94.

54. John Modell, *The Economics and Politics of Racial Accommodation: The Japanese of Los Angeles, 1900–1942* (Urbana: Univ. of Illinois Press, 1977), 132–3, 137–8.

55. Kikuchi to D. Thomas, June 28, 1945, 3.

56. Ibid., 3–4.

57. Ibid., 4.

58. Ibid., 6–7.

59. Ibid., 7–8.

60. Ibid., 8.

61. See Michelle Brattain, *The Politics of Whiteness: Race, Workers, and Culture in the Modern South* (Princeton, N.J.: Princeton Univ. Press, 2001).

62. Kikuchi to D. Thomas, June 28, 1945, 9.

63. Ibid., 10.

64. Kikuchi, "The Japanese American Youth in San Francisco: Their Background, Characteristics, and Problems," National Youth Administration Study, Junior Counseling Service (1941), 4, (JERS Papers, folder W 2.41).

65. Ibid., 68.

66. Ibid., 106.

67. Omura, Hansen interview.

68. Charles Kikuchi, "Joe Nisei Looks for a Job," *Current Life: The Magazine for the American Born Japanese,* (January 1941), 3.

69. Ibid., 4.

70. Kikuchi to D. Thomas, June 28, 1945, 23.

71. Ibid., 24.

72. Kikuchi, Modell interview, 5.

73. Kikuchi to D. Thomas, June 28, 1945, 27.

74. Tsuneishi to the author, June 1, 2004, 9.

75. See Yu, *Thinking Orientals*, 121–3, 140–8.

76. Kikuchi speaks here, as recalled by Kenji Murase in an interview with Arthur Hansen, September 17, 1999, O.H. 2782, Japanese American Oral History Project, Oral History Program, California State University, Fullerton, 47–8 (unpublished version, copy in author's possession; hereafter cited as Murase, Hansen interview).

77. Kikuchi to [D.], May 7, 1942 (CKP, box 11, 1:5; emphasis added).

78. See W. I. Thomas and Dorothy S. Thomas, *The Child in America: Behavior Problems and Programs* (New York: Knopf, 1928); Thomas and Nishimoto, *The Spoilage.* Also see W. I. Thomas and Florian Znaniecki, *The Polish Peasant in Europe and America,* 5 vols. (Chicago: Univ. of Chicago Press, 1918–1920); and Carla Cappetti, "Deviant Girls and Dissatisfied Women: A Sociologist's Tale," in *The Invention of Ethnicity,* ed. Werner Sollors (New York: Oxford Univ. Press, 1989), 124–57.

79. Murase, Hansen interview, 68–9.

80. W.E.B. Du Bois, *The Souls of Black Folk* (1903; rpt., New York: Library of America, 1986), 364–5.

81. Kikuchi to D. Thomas, June 28, 1945, 37.

82. Park, "Migration and Marginal Man," 165.

83. Ibid., 164.

84. Yu, *Thinking Orientals*, 122–3.

85. Sakoda, "Reminisces of a Participant Observer," in Ichioka, *Views from Within,* 221 (emphasis added).

86. Sakoda, interview by Arthur Hansen, August 9–10, 1988, O.H. 2010, Japanese American Oral History Project, Oral History Program, California State University, Fullerton, published in *Japanese American World War II Evacuation Oral History Project, Part III: Analysts* (Munich: Saur, 1994), 370; hereafter cited as Sakoda, Hansen interview.

87. Ibid., 371.

88. Yu, *Thinking Orientals*, 148.

89. Modell, introduction to Kikuchi, *Diary*, 23.

90. Ichioka, *Views from Within*, 12.

91. Modell, preface to Kikuchi, *Diary*, x.

92. Ibid., ix (emphasis added).

93. Married in 1946, Charlie and Yuriko raised two children: Susan, born in 1948, and Lawrence, born in 1955.

94. Park, "Migration and Marginal Man," 166.

95. Tsuneishi to the author, June 1, 2004, 11.

Chapter 2: "A Multitude of Complexes"

1. Kikuchi to D. Thomas, June 28, 1945, 40.

2. Kikuchi, diary entry, December 8, 1941 (CKP, box 11, 1:c). This excerpt also appears in Kikuchi, *Diary*, 43–4.

3. Daniels, *Concentration Camps*, 27.

4. Kikuchi, diary entry, December 8, 1941 (CKP, box 11, 1:b, c).

5. Ibid., c–d.

6. Within a month, the War Department would classify draft-age Nisei as 4-C, or enemy alien, and either discharge or reclassify those already in service, first as 4-F (physically not fit for service) and then eventually as 4-C.

7. Daniels, *Concentration Camps*, 43.

8. Ibid., 47–73.

9. Executive Order 9066, February 19, 1942, in H.R. Rep. No. 77-2124, at 314–15.

10. Kikuchi to D. Thomas, June 28, 1945, 43.

11. Ibid., 42.

12. Kikuchi, diary entry, December 9, 1941 (CKP, box 11, 1:e). Or see Kikuchi, *Diary*, 45.

13. Dorothy Thomas, introduction to Kent and Fitts, "Kikuchi Diary", 19.

14. Kikuchi to D. Thomas, June 28, 1945, 43.

15. See Daniels, *The Politics of Prejudice: The Anti-Japanese Movement in California and the Struggle for Japanese Exclusion* (Berkeley and Los Angeles: Univ. of California Press, 1962); Ngai, *Impossible Subjects*, 47–50 (on the early campaigns of the CJIC); Erika Lee, *At America's Gates: Chinese Immigration During the Exclusion Era, 1882-1943* (Chapel Hill: Univ. of North Carolina Press, 2003), 31–39 (on the racialized rhetoric of nativism); and in general, Grodzins, *Americans Betrayed*, and tenBroek, Barnhart, and Matson, *Prejudice, War, and the Constitution*.

16. Joseph S. Roucek, "American Japanese, Pearl Harbor and World War II," *Journal of Negro Education* 12:4 (1943): 637.

17. Ibid., 641.

18. See tenBroek, Barnhart, and Matson, *Prejudice, War, and the Constitution*, 77–80.

19. Grodzins, *Americans Betrayed*, 20.

20. Ibid., 27.

21. Kikuchi to Louis Adamic, February 21, 1942, 2 (LAP, box 59, folder 7, "Japanese" Subject File).

22. David Levering Lewis, *W.E.B. Du Bois: The Fight for Equality and the American Century, 1919–1963* (New York: Holt, 2000), 470. See W. A. Swanberg, *Norman Thomas: The Last Idealist* (New York: Scribner, 1976), 266–70.

23. Du Bois, "As the Crow Flies," *New York Amsterdam News*, June 10, 1944.

24. Morton Grodzins, "Making Un-Americans," *American Journal of Sociology* 60:6 (1955): 571.

25. Galen Fisher, "Japanese Evacuation from the Pacific Coast," *Far Eastern Survey* 11:13 (1942): 149; "Asks [Atty. Gen.] U. S. Webb, Japanese Lose Citizenship?," *New York Times,* June 27, 1942.

26. Du Bois, "As the Crow Flies," June 10, 1944.

27. 89 Cong. Rec., A358 (1943).

28. "Memorial Bars Japanese," *New York Times,* December 3, 1944; "Hood River's Blunder," *New York Times,* December 9, 1944.

29. Kikuchi to D. Thomas, June 28, 1945, 45.

30. On center statistics, see Thomas, *The Salvage,* 84. On Tanforan, see Sandra C. Taylor, *Jewel of the Desert: Japanese American Internment at Topaz* (Berkeley and Los Angeles: Univ. of California Press, 1993), 67.

31. Miné Okubo, *Citizen 13660* (New York: Columbia Univ. Press, 1946; rpt., Seattle: Univ. of Washington Press, 1983), 35.

32. Ibid., 83.

33. Ibid., 99.

34. Kikuchi to Adamic, December 11, 1941, 1 (LAP, box 59, folder 5, "Japanese" Subject File).

35. Pronounced "AD-uh-mick," although in Yugoslavia, it was properly "Ad-DAHM-mich." Henry Christian reported that Adamic's military experience compelled the name change, since "the military clerk-typists had neither the accent nor the inclination to worry over such details. Thus, without ceremony or any particular regret, he began to be Adamic" (Henry Christian, "Louis Adamic: Immigrant and American Liberal," PhD diss., Brown University, 1967, 6; see also Christian, *Louis Adamic: A Checklist* [Kent, Ohio: Kent State Univ. Press, 1971]).

36. Adamic to Kikuchi, December 15, 1941 (CKP, box 56, folder 3).

37. In Adamic's papers at Princeton, for example, several letters from Kikuchi appear in correspondence files (nine alone between 1939 and 1943), while Kikuchi even sent Adamic his 1940 NYA Report. Keeping in mind that Kikuchi kept nearly every piece of correspondence he ever received, or at the very least transcribed it into his diary, one can conclude that Adamic was far less diligent in replying to Kikuchi's missives. Only three Adamic letters (from the years 1941, 1943, and 1945) appear in the Kikuchi papers at UCLA.

38. Kikuchi, diary entry, September 5, 1951 (CKP, box 21, 33:2–3).

39. Kikuchi, Hansen interview, 2. See Bertha H. Monroe, "A California Playground," *California Teachers Association Journal* 23 (January 1927): 398ff.

40. See Alfred G. Fisk and Howard Thurman, *The First Footprints: The Dawn of the Idea for the Church for the Fellowship of All Peoples: Letters between Alfred Fisk and Howard Thurman, 1943–1944* (San Francisco: Lawton and Alfred Kennedy, 1975); Fisk, "Stereotypes in Intercultural Education," *Common Ground* 7:2 (Winter 1947): 28–33.

41. Louis Adamic, *Laughing in the Jungle: The Autobiography of an Immigrant in America* (New York: Harper, 1932; rpt., Salem, N.H.: Ayer, 1985); and *The Native's Return: An American Immigrant Visits Yugoslavia and Discovers His Old Country* (New York: Harper, 1934).

42. Adamic, *Laughing in the Jungle,* 6.

43. Ibid., 17.

44. Ibid., 189.

45. Louis Adamic, "The Yugoslav Speech in America," *American Mercury*, November 1927, 319.

46. Louis Adamic, "This Crisis Is an Opportunity," *Common Ground* 1:1 (Autumn 1940): 65, 67.

47. Ibid., 66.

48. Dan Shiffman, *Rooting Multiculturalism: The Work of Louis Adamic* (Madison, N.J.: Fairleigh Dickinson Univ. Press, 2003), 14.

49. Fisk to Louis Adamic, October 27, 1939 (LAP, box 59, folder 5, "Japanese" Subject File).

50. Adamic, *From Many Lands*, ii.

51. Kikuchi to Adamic, April 18, 1940, 1 (LAP, box 59, folder 7, "Japanese" Subject File).

52. Adamic to Kikuchi, April 12, 1940, 1–2 (Modell file folder "CK/DST Wartime Correspondence").

53. Kikuchi to Fitts, September 7, 1955, 3 (JERS Papers, folder W 1.15).

54. Adamic to Kikuchi, April 12, 1940, 2–3 (Modell file folder "CK/DST Correspondence").

55. Kikuchi to Adamic, n.d. [February 1940?], 7 (LAP, box 59, folder 7, "Japanese" Subject File).

56. Adamic, *From Many Lands*, 195. This is a citation to Kikuchi's piece "A Young American with a Japanese Face," but given the extent of Adamic's rewriting and outright invention present in the final version—rendering it, in effect, merely a "pseudo-autobiographical" account—crediting the work to Adamic seems justified.

57. Modell, introduction to Kikuchi, *Diary*, 12.

58. Adamic, *From Many Lands*, 232–3 (emphasis added).

59. Kikuchi to Adamic, n.d. [February 1940?], 21.

60. Adamic, *From Many Lands*, 234.

61. Yu, *Thinking Orientals*, 10.

62. I stress "foreign" here, to distinguish Adamic's (or Wirth's) international migration experience from the internal migrant experience (rural to urban) of Chicago sociologists like Park (Red Wing, Minnesota) and W. I. Thomas (Knoxville, Tennessee).

63. Adamic, *My America, 1928–1938* (New York: Harper, 1938), 214.

64. Kikuchi to Hansen, March 1, 1988 (Hansen's personal collection, "Charles Kikuchi/AAH Correspondence" folder; used with permission).

65. Adamic, *From Many Lands*, 187.

66. Kikuchi, Hansen interview, 30.

67. Ibid., 11.

68. Ibid., 30.

69. Kikuchi, diary entry, September 5, 1951 (CKP, box 21, 33:3).

70. Adamic to Kikuchi, April 12, 1940, 4–5 (Modell file folder "CK/DST Correspondence").

71. Mary Oyama, "After Pearl Harbor: Los Angeles," *Common Ground* 2 (Spring 1942): 13.

72. Chester Himes, *If He Hollers Let Him Go* (Garden City, N.Y.: Doubleday, 1945), 3. See Lynn Itagaki, "Transgressing Race and Community in Chester Himes's *If He Hollers Let Him Go*," *African American Review* 37:1 (2003): 65–80.

73. Mike Masaoka, "The Japanese American Creed," *Common Ground* 2 (Spring 1942): 11 (emphasis added).

74. Toshio Mori, "Lil' Yokohama," *Common Ground* 1 (Winter 1941): 54–6.

75. Yuji Ichioka, "'Unity within Diversity': Louis Adamic and Japanese Americans," Working Paper in Asian/Pacific Studies (Durham, N.C.: Asian/Pacific Studies Institute, Duke University, 1987), 25.

76. Ibid., 29.

77. Sollors, "Americans All," 5 (emphasis added).

78. See David Roediger, *The Wages of Whiteness: Race and the Making of the American Working Class* (New York: Verso, 1991).

79. William C. Beyer, "Creating 'Common Ground' on the Home Front: Race, Class, and Ethnicity in a 1940s Quarterly Magazine," in *The Home Front War: World War II and American Society*, ed. Kenneth O'Brien and Lynn Parsons (Westport, Conn.: Greenwood, 1995), 46. The original articles are Mary Oyama, "This Isn't Japan," *Common Ground* 3 (Autumn 1942): 34, and Robert Brown, "Manzanar-Relocation Center," *Common Ground* 3 (Autumn 1942): 27.

80. M. Margaret Anderson, "Democracy Begins at Home—II: Get the Evacuees Out!," *Common Ground* 3 (Summer 1943): 65.

81. Ibid., 66 (emphasis added).

82. Ibid.

83. Ibid.

84. Beyer, "Creating 'Common Ground,'" 53. See David Truman, "A Report on the Common Council for American Unity, August, 1946," Immigration History Research Center, University of Minnesota, St. Paul.

85. Larry Tajiri, "Farewell to Little Tokyo," *Common Ground* 4 (Winter 1944): 94.

86. Ibid., 93.

87. Ibid., 94. See John Howard, *Concentration Camps on the Home Front: Japanese Americans in the House of Jim Crow* (Chicago: Univ. of Chicago Press, 2008).

88. Langston Hughes, "White Folks Do the Funniest Things," *Common Ground* 4 (Winter 1944): 46.

89. M. Margaret Anderson, "Letter to the Reader," *Common Ground* 4 (Spring 1944): 91–2.

90. Ibid., 94–5.

Chapter 3: "Unity within Diversity"

1. John Kikuchi to Louis and Stella Adamic, August 10, 1942, 1–2 (LAP, box 47, folder 4, Correspondence).

2. Stella Adamic, note appended to ibid.

3. Like his older brother, the late Jack Kikuchi began studies at San Francisco State before relocation. He graduated from Drew in 1944.

4. Kikuchi to Adamic, n.d. [February 1940?], 1.

5. Adamic to Charles Kikuchi, March 26, 1940 (Modell file folder "CK/DST Wartime Correspondence"; copy in author's possession).

6. Richard Wright, *Native Son* (New York: Harper, 1940).

7. Kikuchi, diary entry, July 20, 1945 (CKP, box 17, 20:8443–4); see also Wright, *Black Boy* (New York: Harper, 1945).

8. Kikuchi, diary entry, October 25, 1943 (CKP, box 13, 9:3544).

9. Kikuchi, diary entry, May 14, 1945 (CKP, box 16, 18:7729).

10. Kikuchi to Adamic, May 21, 1940, 1 (LAP, box 59, folder 7, "Japanese" Subject File).

11. Ibid., 2.

12. Shiffman, *Rooting Multiculturalism*, 31.

13. Kikuchi to Adamic, mid-February [15?], 1940, 1 (LAP, box 59, folder 7, "Japanese" Subject File).

14. Adamic, *House in Antigua: A Restoration* (New York: Harper, 1937).

15. Adamic, *My America*, 214.

16. Kikuchi to Adamic, April 18, 1940, 1–2 (LAP, box 59, folder 7, "Japanese" Subject File).

17. Adamic, *My America*, 221–2.

18. Werner Sollors, *Beyond Ethnicity: Consent and Descent in American Culture* (New York: Oxford Univ. Press, 1986), 222.

19. Adamic, *My America*, 221.

20. Kikuchi to Adamic, April 18, 1940, 1.

21. Ibid.

22. Kikuchi to Adamic, June 25, 1941, 1 (LAP, box 59, folder 7, "Japanese" Subject File).

23. Ibid., 2.

24. Kikuchi to Adamic, December 11, 1941, verso of 4 (LAP, box 59, folder 5, "Japanese" Subject File).

25. See Sucheng Chan, *Asian Americans: An Interpretive History* (New York: Twayne, 1993), 123; Greg Robinson, *By Order of the President: FDR and the Internment of Japanese Americans* (Cambridge, Mass.: Harvard Univ. Press, 2001), 114; Stephanie Bangarth, *Voices Raised in Protest: Defending North American Citizens of Japanese Ancestry, 1942–1949* (Vancouver: British Columbia Univ. Press, 2008).

26. Kikuchi to Adamic, December 20, 1941 (CKP, box 11, 1:1).

27. Daniels, *Concentration Camps*, 72.

28. Ibid., 72–3.

29. Robinson, *Order of the President*, 115.

30. Thomas, *The Salvage*, 80–1n123.

31. Carlos Bulosan, *American Is in the Heart: A Personal History* (Seattle: Univ. of Washington Press, 1946; rpt., 1991), 275–6.

32. "Filipino Baiting in California Has Started Again," *Nation*, July 28, 1945, 71.

33. Ichioka, "'Unity within Diversity,'" 10.

34. See Carey McWilliams, *Louis Adamic and Shadow America* (Los Angeles: Whipple, 1935); and John Fante, *Ask the Dust* (New York: Stackpole, 1939; rpt., Santa Barbara, Calif.: Black Sparrow, 1980).

35. See the discussion of Mori in chapter 4.

36. Adamic, "The Nisei's Problem Is Difficult but Natural," *Current Life*, January 1941, 5. Kikuchi's article appeared on pages 3–4, 12.

37. Kikuchi to Adamic, February 21, 1942, 2 (LAP, box 59, folder 5, "Japanese" Subject File).

38. Ibid.

39. "New Order on Aliens Awaited," *San Francisco News*, March 2, 1942, available at http://www.sfmuseum.org/hist8/evac16.html.

40. Arthur Caylor, "Behind the News," *San Francisco News*, March 2, 1942, available at http://www.sfmuseum.org/hist8/caylor5.html.

41. Marc Gallicchio, *The African American Encounter with Japan and China: Black Internationalism in Asia, 1895–1945* (Chapel Hill: Univ. of North Carolina Press, 2000), 132.

42. Myrdal, *American Dilemma*, 814–15.

43. See Reginald Kearney, *African American Views of the Japanese: Solidarity or Sedition?* (Albany: SUNY Press, 1998).

44. Kikuchi to Adamic, February 21, 1942, 6.

45. Roger Daniels, "The Japanese Americans, 1942–2004: A Social History," *Law and Contemporary Problems* 68:159 (Spring 2005): 163–4.

46. George Schuyler, "The World Today," *Pittsburgh Courier*, January 17, 1942.

47. Horace Cayton, "White Man's War but Negroes Are Fighting On 2 Fronts for Democratic War," *Pittsburgh Courier*, February 28, 1942.

48. "Is Jap Blood Okay for Fighting Forces?" *Pittsburgh Courier*, March 14, 1942.

49. See Thomas Guglielmo, "'Red Cross, Double Cross': Race and America's World War II–Era Blood Donor Service," *Journal of American History* 97:1 (June 2010): 63–90.

50. Roi Ottley, "The Negro Press Today," *Common Ground* 3:3 (Spring 1943): 18.

51. Philip Gleason, "Americans All: World War II and the Shaping of American Identity," *Review of Politics* 43:4 (October 1981): 500.

52. Ibid., 501–2.

53. Ibid., 502–3.

54. Ibid., 513.

55. Ibid., 513–14.

56. Ibid., 518.

57. Lillian Smith, "Democracy Was Not a Candidate," *Common Ground* 3:2 (Winter 1943): 10.

58. Werner Sollors, *Ethnic Modernism* (Cambridge, Mass.: Harvard Univ. Press, 2008), 194; originally published in *The Cambridge History of American Literature*, vol. 6, *Prose Writing, 1910–1950*, ed. Sacvan Bercovitch (Cambridge: Cambridge Univ. Press, 2002).

59. Ibid., 14–15.

60. Approximately 11,000 German and a few hundred Italian "enemy aliens" were also unlawfully interned. Many of them were immigrants who had been living in the United States or Latin America for many years, like the Issei, while some were American-born citizens (mostly children) who joined their "alien" parents in camp. In comparison to the total population of interned Nikkei, the number of internees of German or Italian descent was indeed smaller, but nevertheless, imprisoning even *one* citizen or enemy alien based solely on racialized suspicion was not merely unconstitutional but morally unconscionable. See Stephen Fox, *America's Invisible Gulag: A Biography of German American Internment and Exclusion in World War II* (New York: Lang, 2000); Lawrence di Stasi, ed., *Una Storia Segreta: The Secret History of Italian American Evacuation during World War II* (Berkeley: Heyday Books, 2001).

61. Roy Wilkins, "Watchtower," *New York Amsterdam Star-News*, April 25, 1942.

62. Alain Locke, "Pluralism and Intellectual Democracy," 206; paper presented at the Conference on Science, Philosophy, and Religion in Relation to the American Way of Life, second symposium, New York, 1942.

63. N. Thomas, "The Fate of the Japanese in North America and Hawaii," *Pacific Affairs* 16:1 (March 1943): 94–5.

64. Roi Ottley, "A White Folks' War?," *Common Ground* 2:3 (Spring 1942): 29.

65. Ibid., 30–1.

66. Roi Ottley, *New World A-Coming: Inside Black America* (New York: World, 1943), 330.

67. Ibid., 331. See Rachel Moran, *Interracial Intimacy: The Regulation of Race and Romance* (Chicago: Univ. of Chicago Press, 2003), 55–56.

68. Langston Hughes, "I, Too" (1925), in *Black Writers of America*, ed. Richard Barksdale and Kenneth Kinnamon (New York: Macmillan, 1972), 519.

69. Kikuchi, diary entry, October 25, 1943 (CKP, box 13, 9:3544). See Bucklin Moon, *The Darker Brother* (New York: Doubleday, 1943).

70. Bucklin Moon, *The High Cost of Prejudice* (New York: Messner, 1947; rpt., Westport, Conn.: Negro Univ. Press, 1970). 164.

71. Lawrence Jackson, "Bucklin Moon and Thomas Sancton in the 1940's: Crusaders for the Racial Left," *Southern Literary Journal* 40:1 (Fall 2007): 83.

72. Ross Wills, "John Fante," *Common Ground* 1:3 (Spring 1941): 84–92; Fante, "Bill Saroyan," *Common Ground* 1:2 (Winter 1941): 64–6.

73. Charles Kikuchi to Yuriko Kikuchi, May 27, 1946, 5 (CKP, box 45, "Letters to Yuriko").

74. Tsuneishi to the author, July 24, 2004.

75. Denning, *Cultural Front*, 238–9. See Henry Roth, *Call It Sleep: A Novel* (New York: Ballou, 1934).

76. Denning, *Cultural Front*, 239.

77. See H. T. Tsiang, *And China Has Hands* (New York: Speller, 1937).

78. Denning, *Cultural Front*, 449.

79. See Carey McWilliams, *Factories in the Field: The Story of Migratory Farm Labor in California* (Boston: Little, Brown, 1939).

80. Carey McWilliams, *Prejudice: Japanese-Americans, Symbol of Racial Intolerance* (Boston: Little, Brown, 1944).

81. Colleen Lye, *America's Asia: Racial Form and American Literature, 1893–1945* (Princeton, N.J.: Princeton Univ. Press, 2005), 156.

82. Carey McWilliams, "Moving the West Coast Japanese," *Harper's*, September 1942, 369; McWilliams, *Japanese Evacuation: Interim Report* (New York: American Council, Institute of Pacific Relations, 1942).

83. Carey McWilliams, *The Education of Carey McWilliams* (New York: Simon & Schuster, 1979), 101.

84. Denning, *Cultural Front*, 450.

85. McWilliams, *Education*, 114–15.

86. Everett C. Hughes, "Queries Concerning Industry and Society Growing out of Study of Ethnic Relations in Industry," *American Sociological Review* 14:2 (April 1949): 220.

87. Carey McWilliams, *Brothers under the Skin* (Boston: Little, Brown, 1943, 1951), 15.

88. Ibid., 15.

89. Adamic, "Plymouth Rock and Ellis Island," in Adamic, *From Many Lands*, 301.

90. See C. K. Doreski, "Kin in Some Way: The *Chicago Defender* Reads the Japanese Internment, 1942–1945," in *The Black Press: New Literary and Historical Essays*, ed. Todd Vogel (Rutgers, N.J.: Rutgers Univ. Press, 2001), 161–87; and Daryl Maeda, *Chains of Babylon: The Rise of Asian America* (Minneapolis: Univ. of Minnesota Press, 2009).

91. Kikuchi to Adamic, August 6, 1945 (CKP, box 17, 20:8572).

92. Adamic to Kikuchi, August 8, 1945 (CKP, box 56, folder 1, "Journal Enclosures").

93. Kikuchi, diary entry, November 23, 1945 (CKP, box 17, 21:460–1).

94. Ibid., 462.

95. Kikuchi, Hansen interview, 42–3.

96. On Caen, see Jason Scott Smith, "New Deal Public Works at War: The WPA and Japanese American Internment," *Pacific Historical Review* 72:1 (February 2003): 63–92.

97. Mike Davis, *City of Quartz: Excavating the Future of Los Angeles* (New York: Verso, 1990), 32.

98. Kikuchi, Hansen interview, 43.

99. Ibid., 43–4.

100. Ibid., 45.

101. "Wife of Adamic Calls It Suicide, Not Plot Killing," *New York Post*, September 6, 1951.

102. Ibid.

103. Carey McWilliams, "Louis Adamic, American," *Nation*, September 21, 1951, 231–2.

104. Kikuchi, diary entry, September 5, 1951 (CKP, box 21, 53:4).

105. Kikuchi, Chicago Diary 1, July 30, 1943, unpaginated (Modell file folder; copy in author's possession).

106. Kikuchi, diary entry, September 5, 1951 (CKP, box 21, 53:1).

107. Ibid., 5.

108. Kikuchi to Adamic, December 11, 1941, 4.

Chapter 4: "Participating and Observing"

1. The Gila Relocation Center was located on land leased by the WRA from the Bureau of Indian Affairs on the Pima Indian reservation (without Indian approval).

2. Dorothy Swaine Thomas to Charles Kikuchi, September 22, 1942, 1 (Modell file folder "CK/DST Correspondence"; copy in author's possession).

3. Kikuchi to D. Thomas, September 17, 1942, 3 (Modell file folder "CK/DST Correspondence").

4. Kikuchi, *Diary*, 25.

5. Kikuchi to D. Thomas, September 17, 1942, 3.

6. D. Thomas to Kikuchi, September 22, 1942, 1–2.

7. Kikuchi to D. Thomas, September 17, 1942, 3.

8. D. Thomas to Kikuchi, September 22, 1942, 1.

9. See Fred H. Matthews, *Quest for an American Sociology: Robert E. Park and the Chicago School* (Montreal: McGill-Queen's Univ. Press, 1977), 160–5.

10. W. I. Thomas, *The Unadjusted Girl: With Cases and Standpoint for Behavior Analysis* (Boston: Little, Brown, 1923), 244.

11. Ibid., 249–50.

12. Cappetti, "Deviant Girls," 153.

13. Matthews, *Quest for American Sociology*, 101.

14. Thomas, *Unadjusted Girl*, 253–4.

15. Thomas and Thomas, *Child in America*, 572.

16. Robert Merton, "The Thomas Theorem and the Matthew Effect," *Social Forces* 74:2 (December 1995): 385.

17. D. Thomas, "Statistics in Social Research," *American Journal of Sociology* 35:1 (July 1929): 2.

18. Ibid., 14.

19. Robert Bannister, "Dorothy Swaine Thomas: Soziologischer Objectivismus: Der harte Weg in die Profession," in *Frauen in der Soziologie*, ed. Claudia Honegger and Theresa Wobbe (Munich: Beck, 1998): 226–57. Also available at http://www.swarthmore.edu/SocSci/rbannis1/DST.html (see sec. 6).

20. D. Thomas to Mark A. May, December 9, 1935 (Dorothy Swaine Thomas Papers [UPT 50 T455], box 1, FF 4 ["Correspondence," 1929–1951], University Archives and Records Center, University of Pennsylvania; hereafter cited as DTP). Charles Cooley (1864–1929) was a University of Michigan scholar who helped establish the American Sociological Association. He explored the interrelationship between the individual and society, emphasizing that one could be understood only in relation to the other; see Cooley, *Human Nature and Social Order* (New York: Scribner's, 1902).

21. See E. S. Lyon, "The Myrdals and the Thomases, 1930–1940: The Trials and Tribulations of a Cross-Atlantic Research Collaboration," in *Mirrors and Windows: Essays in the History of Sociology*, ed. Janusz Mucha, Dirk Käsler, and Włodzimierz Wincławski (Toruń, Poland: Copernicus Univ. Press), 219–34.

22. E. S. Lyon, *Researching Race Relations: Myrdal's American Dilemma from a Human Rights Perspective*, Faculty of Humanities and Social Sciences/Social Science Research Paper 17 (London: South Bank University, 2002), 8.

23. Myrdal, *American Dilemma*, 1:lxxiii.

24. Ibid., 1:117.

25. Other luminaries included Ogburn, Frazier, John Dollard, and Ralph Bunche, to name a few. Dorothy herself recommended Wirth and Everett Hughes. See Lyon, "Myrdals and Thomases," 232.

26. D. Thomas to Gunnar Myrdal, May 14, 1946 (DTP, box 1, FF 4 ["Correspondence," 1929–1951]).

27. Sabagh earned his PhD from the University of California, Berkeley, in 1952. Later the director of the Center for Near Eastern Studies at UCLA, he is credited with cultivating Middle Eastern American studies, a field that has gained prominence since September 11, 2001. He died in 2002. He overlapped with Kikuchi when they both worked on Dorothy Thomas's *The Salvage*.

28. Myrdal did not heavily influence Kikuchi, at least not in the way that Adamic and Thomas had impressed him. On February 12, 1945, he wrote: "I have an idea that [JERS] will be just as significant as the Myrdal study which spent half a million dollars on the Negro problem in America. Two general volumes, 'An American Dilemma' and two monographs have come out of that study and about 60 unpublished monographs. It's supposed to be about the best study done on the Negroes up to now, *but I have only skimmed through parts of it*" (diary entry, February 12, 1945 [CKP, box 16, 16:6962; emphasis added]). By 1947, Kikuchi had apparently read the text, given his bibliographical reference to Myrdal in his master's thesis in social work at Columbia; see Kikuchi, "The Social Adjustment Process of the Japanese American Resettlers to Chicago during the Wartime Years" (MSW thesis, Columbia University, September 1947), 282.

29. Thomas and Nishimoto, *The Spoilage*, v.

30. See Lane Ryo Hirabayashi, *The Politics of Fieldwork: Research in an American Concentration Camp* (Tucson: Univ. of Arizona Press, 1999).

31. The "loyalty question" was more accurately a pair of questions, numbers 27 and 28, on the loyalty registration form distributed by the WRA and the army in February 1943.

32. Sakoda was credited as a research assistant with Kikuchi on the title page of *The Salvage*, although by his own admission, he was never consulted by her on the writing of either volume (while his collected data was used). See two essays by Sakoda in Ichioka, *Views from Within*: "Reminiscences," 219–45, and "The 'Residue': The Unsettled Minidokans, 1943–1945," 247–84.

33. Frank Miyamoto, "Dorothy Swaine Thomas as Director of JERS: Some Personal Observations," in Ichioka, *Views from Within*, 45.

34. Otis Durant Duncan, review of *The Spoilage*, by Dorothy Swaine Thomas and Richard Nishimoto, *Social Forces* 25:4 (May 1947): 458.

35. Rosalie Hankey Wax, *Doing Fieldwork: Warnings and Advice* (Chicago: Univ. of Chicago Press, 1971).

36. Marvin K. Opler, review of *The Spoilage*, by Dorothy Swaine Thomas and Richard Nishimoto, *American Anthropologist* 50:2 (1948): 310.

37. Forrest E. LaViolette, review of *The Salvage*, by Dorothy Swaine Thomas, *Social Forces* 32:1 (October 1953): 98.

38. Oscar Handlin, review of *The Salvage*, by Dorothy Swaine Thomas, *American Quarterly* 5:4 (Winter 1953): 377.

39. John M. Maki, review of *The Salvage*, by Dorothy Swaine Thomas, *Far Eastern Quarterly* 12:4 (August 1953): 437. This is ironic, given Kikuchi's admitted lack of proficiency in Japanese.

40. See Peter Suzuki, "The University of California Japanese Evacuation and Resettlement Study: A Prolegomenon," *Dialectical Anthropology* 10 (1986): 189–213; Francis Feeley, *America's Concentration Camps during World War II: Social Science and the Japanese American Internment* (New Orleans: Univ. Press of the South, 1999); and Hayashi, *Democratizing the Enemy*.

41. Ichioka, *Views from Within*, 22–3.

42. Kikuchi, diary entry, May 24, 1942 (CKP, box 11, 1:100).

43. Kikuchi, "JERS Looking Glass," 188.

44. Kikuchi, diary entry, September 25, 1944 (CKP, box 15, 14:5864).

45. D. Thomas to Kikuchi, January 18, 1943, 1 (Modell file folder "CK/DST Correspondence").

46. Kikuchi, "JERS Looking Glass," 188–9.

47. Kikuchi, *Diary*, April 30, 1942, 51–3.

48. See Ichioka, *Views from Within*, 12–13.

49. Kikuchi, *Diary*, May 7, 1942, 62.

50. Ibid., July 29, 1942, 198.

51. Ibid., May 8, 1942, 67.

52. Okubo, *Citizen 13660*, 53.

53. Ibid., 101.

54. Kikuchi, *Diary*, May 8, 1942, 68.

55. Ibid, May 3, 1942, 54.

56. Ibid., May 8, 1942, 63.

57. Ibid., July 14, 1942, 183.

58. Kikuchi, diary entry, May 24, 1942 (CKP, box 11, 1:98).

59. Ibid., 98–9.

60. Hisaye Yamamoto, "The Legend of Miss Sasagawara," in *Seventeen Syllables and Other Stories* (Latham, N.Y.: Kitchen Table, Women of Color Press, 1988), 20; originally published in *Kenyon Review* 12:1 (1950).

61. Ibid., 32.

62. Ibid., 33.

63. Chan, *Asian Americans*, 117 (emphasis added).

64. See Robinson, "Farewell to L'il Tokyo."

65. Kikuchi, diary entry, May 24, 1942 (CKP, box 11, 1:99).

66. Kikuchi, *Diary*, July 31, 1942, 200.

67. Hansen, interview by the author, November 28, 2010.

68. Kikuchi, *Diary*, June 1, 1942, 98.

69. Kikuchi to Adamic, November 2, 1943 (LAP, box 47, folder 4).

70. Mary Oyama, "My Only Crime is My Face," *Liberty* 20:33 (August 14, 1943): 58.

71. Kikuchi, *Diary*, July 31, 1942, 201.

72. Kikuchi to Thomas, July 17, 1942, 2 (CKP, box 56, folder 5).

73. D. Thomas to Kikuchi, October 31, 1942, 1 (JERS Papers, folder W 1.15).

74. See Kikuchi, diary entries, February 26, 1945, and February 8, 1945 (CKP, box 16, vol. 16).

75. Kikuchi, diary entry, January 30, 1945 (CKP, box 16, 16:6844). Apocryphal as it sounds, W. I. has been credited with inventing "a Manhattan mixer." See Robert Spencer, interview by Arthur Hansen, July 15–17, 1987, O.H. 1958, Japanese American Oral History Project, Oral History Program, California State University, Fullerton, published in *Japanese American World War II Evacuation Oral History Project, Part III: Analysts* (Munich: Saur, 1994), 323; hereafter cited as Spencer, Hansen interview.

76. Kikuchi, diary entry, February 19, 1945 (CKP, box 16, 16:7026–7).

77. Ibid.

78. Kikuchi, diary entry, March 8, 1945 (CKP, box 16, 17:7148).

79. Ibid., 7150.

80. D. Thomas to Kikuchi, January 18, 1944 (JERS Papers, folder W 1.15).

81. D. Thomas to Kikuchi, August 2, 1945 (JERS Papers, folder W 1.15).

82. Kikuchi to D. Thomas, August 29, 1945, 1, 4 (JERS Papers, folder W 1.15).

83. Kikuchi to D. Thomas, September 8, 1945, 2–3 (JERS Papers, folder W 1.15).

84. D. Thomas to Kikuchi, August 31, 1945 (CKP, box 56, folder 1).

85. D. Thomas to Kikuchi, September 26, 1945 (CKP, box 56, folder 1).

86. Charles Kikuchi to Yuriko Kikuchi, August 15, 1948 (CKP, box 45, "Letters to Yuriko" folder).

87. Tule Lake was the "segregation center" to which all "disloyal" internees were sent in 1943. See Frank Miyamoto, "The Career of Intergroup Tensions: A Study of the Collective Adjustments of Evacuees to Crises at the Tule Lake Relocation Center" (PhD diss., University of Chicago, 1950).

88. Miyamoto, "Dorothy Swaine Thomas," 37.

89. Kikuchi, "JERS Looking Glass," 190. *Go* is a traditional Japanese game, akin to chess. *Mochi* are sticky rice cakes, and at New Year's, rice is pounded to make the cakes.

90. Spencer, "Gila in Retrospect," in Ichioka, *Views from Within*, 159.

91. Kikuchi, "JERS Looking Glass," 190.

92. Kikuchi, diary entry, December 7, 1943 (CKP, box 14, folder 2, 10:3850).

93. See Merton, "Thomas Theorem."

94. Matthews, *Quest for American Sociology*, 160.

95. Robert Park, "The Career of the Africans in Brazil," in *Race and Culture* (Glencoe, Illinois: Free Press, 1950), 198–9. This volume of race-related articles by Park was published posthumously, and the date of this particular article was originally 1942.

96. Matthews, *Quest for American Sociology*, 160.

97. Yu, *Thinking Orientals*, 39.

98. Robert Park and Ernest W. Burgess, *Introduction to the Science of Sociology* (Chicago: Univ. of Chicago Press, 1921).

99. Ibid., 508.

100. Ibid., 735.

101. Yu, *Thinking Orientals*, 41; see Park, "Migration and Marginal Man," 164.

102. Matthews, *Quest for American Sociology*, 170.

103. Barbara Ballis Lal, *The Romance of Culture in an Urban Civilization: Robert E. Park on Race and Ethnic Relations in Cities* (London: Routledge, 1990), 59.

104. See, for example, Oliver Cromwell Cox, *Caste, Class, and Race: A Study in Social Dynamics* (New York: Doubleday, 1948; rpt., New York: Monthly Review, 1970).

105. Barbara Ballis Lal, "Black and Blue in Chicago: Robert E. Park's Perspective on Race Relations in Urban America, 1914–1944," *British Journal of Sociology* 38:4 (1987): 558. Also see E. Franklin Frazier, *The Negro Family in Chicago* (Chicago: Univ. of Chicago Press, 1932).

106. Yu, *Thinking Orientals*, 44–5.

107. Ibid., 117ff.

Chapter 5: The Tanforan and Gila Diaries

1. Kikuchi, *Diary*, July 8, 1942, 170.

2. Ibid.

3. Ibid.

4. Ibid., August 31, 1942, 252.

5. Ibid., 253.

6. This quotation and the following ones in this paragraph are taken from Kikuchi, *Diary*, July 11, 1942, 176–7.

7. Kikuchi, Hansen interview, 204 (emphasis added).

8. Ibid., 155.

9. Ibid., 194.

10. Ibid., 194–5.

11. Kikuchi, diary entry, September 2, 1942 (CKP, box 11, 3:647).

12. Ibid., 648.

13. Kikuchi, diary entry, September 4, 1942 (CKP, box 11, 3:654).

14. Evelyn Brooks Higginbotham, *Righteous Discontent: The Women's Movement in the Black Baptist Church, 1880–1920* (Cambridge, Mass.: Harvard Univ. Press, 1993), 196.

15. Kikuchi, diary entry, September 3, 1942 (CKP, box 11, 3:653).

16. Kikuchi, diary entry, September 5, 1942 (CKP, box 11, 3:660).

17. Ibid., 660–1.

18. Kikuchi, Hansen interview, 200.

19. Ibid., 201.

20. Arthur Hansen, personal communications to the author, December 24, 2009, and November 28, 2010.

21. Paul Spickard, "The Nisei Assume Power: The Japanese Citizens League, 1941–1942," *Pacific Historical Review* 52:2 (May 1983): 157.

22. Ibid., 154–5.

23. Hansen, "Cultural Politics in Gila River," 334–5.

24. Kikuchi, *Diary*, June 2, 1942, 100.

25. Spickard, "Nisei Assume Power," 160.

26. Hansen, "Cultural Politics in Gila River," 341–3.

27. Ibid., 343.

28. Kikuchi, diary entry, November 4, 1942 (CKP, box 12, 4:1086).

29. Kikuchi, Hansen interview, 100.

30. Kikuchi, diary entry, November 4, 1942.

31. Kikuchi, Hansen interview, 239–40.

32. Kikuchi, diary entry, December 22, 1942 (CKP, box 12, 4:1581–2).

33. Kikuchi, diary entry, December 23, 1942 (CKP, box 12, 4:1591).

34. Ibid.

35. Kikuchi, diary entry, December 15, 1942 (CKP, box 12, 4:1513–14).

36. Spickard, *Mixed Blood*, 53, 55.

37. See Masako Osako, "Japanese Americans: Melting into the All-American Melting Pot," in *Ethnic Chicago: A Multicultural Portrait*, ed. Melvin G. Holli and Peter d'A. Jones (Grand Rapids, Mich.: Eerdmans, 1995), 423.

38. The foundational historiography includes Quintard Taylor, "Blacks and Asians in a White City: Japanese Americans and African Americans in Seattle, 1890–1940," *Western Historical Quarterly* 22:4 (1991): 401–29; and Gary Y. Okihiro, *Margins and Mainstreams: Asian Americans in History and Culture* (Seattle: Univ. of Washington Press, 1994). Two recent anthologies tackle the subject: Fred Ho and Bill Mullen, eds., *Afro Asia: Revolutionary Political and Cultural Connections between African Americans and Asian Americans* (Durham, N.C.: Duke Univ. Press, 2008); and Heike Raphael-Hernandez and Shannon Steen, eds., *AfroAsian Encounters: Culture, History, Politics* (New York: NYU Press, 2006).

39. Wilder, personal communication to the author, January 2005.

40. Moon-Ho Jung and Greg Robinson, personal communication to the author, American Studies Association Conference, 2003, Hartford, Conn.

41. Kikuchi, diary entry, September 12, 1942 (CKP, box 11, 3:688–9). See John W. Dower, *War without Mercy: Race, Power, and the Pacific War* (New York: Pantheon, 1986), and Akira Iriye, *Power and Culture: The Japanese-American War, 1941–1945* (Cambridge, Mass.: Harvard Univ. Press, 1981).

42. Kikuchi, diary entry, September 12, 1942 (CKP, box 11, 3:687–8).

43. See Richard Wright, *The Color Curtain: A Report on the Bandung Conference* (Cleveland: World, 1956).

44. Kikuchi, diary entry, November 12, 1942 (CKP, box 12, 4:1205–6). This entry is the source for all quotations in this paragraph and the next one.

45. Myrdal, *American Dilemma*, 1:24.

46. See Robinson, *Order of the President*, 163–76.

47. Kikuchi, diary entry, September 12, 1942 (CKP, box 11, 3:687).

48. Kikuchi, diary entry, November 9, 1942 (CKP, box 12, 4:1163–4).

49. Kikuchi, diary entry, September 12, 1942.

50. Ibid.

51. Myrdal, *American Dilemma*, 1:44.

52. Hosokawa, *Nisei*, 159.

53. Takaki, *Strangers*, 214.

54. Kikuchi, *Diary*, June 13, 1942, 125.

55. Ibid., May 31, 1942, 97.

56. See Albert Raboteau, *Slave Religion: The "Invisible Institution" in the Antebellum South* (New York: Oxford Univ. Press, 1978); Tera Hunter, *To 'Joy My Freedom: Southern Black Women's Lives and Labors after the Civil War* (Cambridge, Mass.: Harvard Univ. Press, 1997); Herbert Aptheker, *American Negro Slave Revolts* (New York: Columbia Univ. Press, 1943); and Walter Johnson, *Soul by Soul: Life inside the Antebellum Slave Market* (Cambridge, Mass.: Harvard Univ. Press, 2000).

57. See Cornel West, "Black Strivings in a White Civilization," in Cornel West and Henry Louis Gates, Jr., *The Future of the Race* (New York: Knopf, 1996), 53–112.

58. Kikuchi, diary entry, March 17, 1943 (CKP, box 12, 6:2300–2301).

59. Ibid., 2299.

60. Kikuchi, *Diary*, June 7, 1942, 114.

61. Jeffrey Ferguson, "The Newest Negro: George Schuyler's Intellectual Quest in the Nineteen Twenties and Beyond" (PhD diss., Harvard University, 1998), 85.

62. George Schuyler, "The World Today," *Pittsburgh Courier*, April 25, 1942.

63. Gallicchio, *African American Encounter*, 182.

64. Allison Varzally, *Making a Non-White America: Californians Coloring Outside Ethnic Lines* (Berkeley and Los Angeles: Univ. of California Press, 2008), 125.

65. Lewis, *Du Bois*, 470; David Levering Lewis, interview by the author, June 26, 2001.

66. Kikuchi, *Diary*, June 14, 1942, 127.

67. Ibid., 126. "Jive boys": The camp jazz band was actually named the Tanforan Tooters.

68. Kikuchi, letter to [D.], dated May 2, 1942, (CKP, box 11, 1:7). Club Alabam was one of the jazz clubs in the Fillmore District of San Francisco.

69. Luis Alvarez, *The Power of the Zoot: Youth Culture and Resistance during World War II* (Berkeley and Los Angeles: Univ. of California Press, 2008), 85; Catherine S. Ramírez, *The Woman in the Zoot Suit: Gender, Nationalism, and the Cultural Politics of Memory* (Durham, N.C.: Duke Univ. Press, 2008).

70. Langston Hughes, "From Here to Yonder," *Chicago Defender*, June 19, 1943.

Chapter 6: From "Jap Crow" to "Jim and Jane Crow"

1. "Chicago Japs Gloomy, Hide Behind Doors," *Chicago Daily Tribune*, December 9, 1941.

2. "Chicago Notes on War," *Chicago Daily Tribune*, December 8, 1941.

3. Dominic Pacyga, *Chicago: A Biography* (Chicago: Univ. of Chicago Press, 2009), 276.

4. "Silent Japs," *Chicago Defender*, February 14, 1942.

5. "For Identification," *Chicago Daily Tribune*, December 19, 1941.

6. Beulah Barker, "An Editorial Topic," *Chicago Daily Tribune*, December 13, 1941.

7. Samuel MacClintock, "Moderation!," *Chicago Daily Tribune*, December 15, 1941.

8. See Okihiro, *Storied Lives*, and Allan Austin, *From Concentration Camp to Campus: Japanese American Students and World War II* (Urbana: Univ. of Illinois Press, 2004).

9. See Alice Murata, *Japanese Americans in Chicago* (Charleston, S.C.: Arcadia, 2002); and Brooks, "In the Twilight Zone."

10. War Agency Liquidation Unit, *People in Motion: The Postwar Adjustment of the Evacuated Japanese Americans* (Washington, D.C.: Government Printing Office, 1947), 168.

11. Ibid., 169.

12. Ibid., 168–9.

13. Murata, *Japanese Americans*, 86–87.

14. Ibid., 169. The area actually extended to 47th Street.

15. See Drake and Cayton, *Black Metropolis*.

16. Drake and Cayton, *Black Metropolis*, 379.

17. Green, *Selling the Race*, 58.

18. Ibid., 59.

19. Ibid., 62.

20. Richard Wright (text) and Edwin Rosskam (photo direction), *12 Million Black Voices* (New York: Viking, 1941; rpt., New York: Thunder's Mouth, 1992), 106, 111.

21. Gwendolyn Brooks, "kitchenette building," in *The Norton Anthology of African American Literature*, ed. Henry Louis Gates, Jr., and Nellie McKay (New York: Norton, 1997), 1579. Originally published in *A Street in Bronzeville* (New York: Harper, 1945).

22. See Charlotte Brooks, "Japanese," in *The Electronic Encyclopedia of Chicago* (Chicago: Chicago Historical Society, 2005),

http://encyclopedia.chicagohistory.org/pages/664.html.

23. Thomas et al., *The Salvage*, 295 (case history 31, [CH-31]; emphasis added).

24. Ibid., 295 (CH-31).

25. Ibid., 288 (CH-31).

26. Ibid., 200–201 (CH-45). This is the source for the quotations in this paragraph.

27. Kikuchi, Chicago Diary 1, June 22, 1943, unpaginated (copy in author's possession).

28. D. Thomas to Mrs. Blumenthal, June 26, 1943 (JERS Papers, folder W 1.15, section 1, "Office Correspondence, 1940–1974").

29. Langston Hughes, "From Here to Yonder: America after the War," *Chicago Defender*, May 22, 1943.

30. Kikuchi, Chicago Diary 1, April 17, 1943, unpaginated (copy in author's possession).

31. Kikuchi, diary entry, April 18, 1943 (CKP, box 13, 7:2538).

32. Kikuchi, diary entry, June 21, 1943 (CKP, box 13, 7:2785–6).

33. The translated text of the German announcement is in "'The Shape of Things," *Nation*, July 10, 1943, 31.

34. Kikuchi, diary entry, April 29, 1945 (CKP, box 16, 17:7528–9).

35. Kikuchi, diary entry, April 27, 1943 (CKP, box 16, 7:2569).

36. Kikuchi, diary entry, August 6, 1943 (CKP, box 16, 7:3034–5).

37. Ibid., 3036–7.

38. Ibid., 3041.

39. Ibid., 3038.

40. Kikuchi, diary entry, June 3, 1943 (CKP, box 13, 7:2681).

41. Ibid., 2682.

42. Kikuchi, diary entry, June 5, 1943 (CKP, box 13, 7:2701–3).

43. Gallicchio, *African American Encounter*, 3.

44. Horace Cayton, *Long Old Road* (New York: Trident, 1965), 275.

45. Kikuchi, diary entry, June 5, 1943 (CKP, box 13, 7:2703).

46. Gary Gerstle, *American Crucible: Race and Nation in the Twentieth Century* (Princeton, N.J.: Princeton Univ. Press, 2001), 4–5.

47. Kikuchi, diary entry, April 30, 1944 (CKP, box 14, 12:4899).

48. Kikuchi, diary entry, June 7, 1944 (CKP, box 15, 13:5124–5).

49. On Hayakawa and Hughes, see Doreski, "Kin in Some Way"; on Tajiri and Sugihara, see Robinson, "Farewell to L'il Tokyo."

50. Kikuchi, diary entry, June 2, 1944 (CKP, box 15, 13:5090). See Charles S. Johnson, *Patterns of Negro Segregation* (New York: Harper, 1943).

51. Kikuchi, diary entry, August 11, 1943 (CKP, box 13, 8:3097).

52. Quoted in Kikuchi, diary entry, October 21, 1944 (CKP, box 15, 15:6187–8).

53. Kikuchi, diary entry, May 22, 1945 (CKP, box 16, 18:7801–2).

54. Kikuchi, diary entry, June 6, 1945 (CKP, box 17, 19:7974–5).

55. Kikuchi, diary entry, June 16, 1945 (CKP, box 17, 19:8061–2).

56. Drawing intellectuals from around the world and the United States, International House was part of a movement begun by Harry Edmonds in 1909.

57. Kikuchi, diary entry, February 4, 1945 (CKP, box 16, 16:6898).

58. Ibid., 6903.

59. See Ngai, *Impossible Subjects*, 96–126.

60. Kikuchi, diary entry, February 1, 1945 (CKP, box 16, 16:6864).

61. Ibid., 6859.

62. Kikuchi, diary entry, February 18, 1945 (CKP, box 16, 16:7019–20).

63. See E. Franklin Frazier, *Black Bourgeoisie* (Glencoe, Ill.: Free Press, 1957).

64. Kikuchi, diary entry, February 18, 1945 (CKP, box 16, 16:7018–7019).

65. Ibid., 7018.

66. Ibid., 7020.

67. "Doug Greer," *Sacramento Observer*, February 26, 2003; "Medallion of Honor Recipients," *Sacramento Observer*, September 2, 2003.

68. Robert Matsui, "Tribute to Douglas Robinson Greer," *Congressional Record* 150:105 (September 8, 2004): E1554, http://www.gpo.gov:80/fdsys/pkg/CREC-2004-09-08/html/CREC-2004-09-08-pt1-PgE1554-2.htm.

69. Kikuchi, diary entry, February 6, 1945 (CKP, box 16, 16:6923–4).

70. Kikuchi, diary entry, February 1, 1945 (CKP, box 16, 16:6874).

71. Ibid., 6874–5.

72. Ibid., 6876–7.

73. Ibid., 6875, 6877.

74. Ibid., 6877.

75. Ibid., inserted letter to family, February 2, 1945, 7.

76. Brooks, "In the Twilight Zone," 1687.

77. Alvarez, *Power of the Zoot*, 111.

78. Paul Spickard, "Not Just the Quiet People: The Nisei Underclass," *Pacific Historical Review* 68:1 (February 1999): 89.

79. Ibid., 91.

80. Paul Spickard, personal communication to the author, November 14, 2010.

81. Kikuchi, CH-32 (Tadashi Blackie Najima, pseudonym), February 22, 1944 (CKP, box 47, 32:11).

82. Ibid., April 20, 1945, 112.

83. Ibid., 113.

84. Paul Spickard, personal communication to the author, November 14, 2010.

85. Kikuchi, diary entry, December 22, 1944 (CKP, box 15, 15:6598).

86. Tsuneishi, "In Memoriam: Charles Kikuchi, 1916–1988," in Ichioka, *Views from Within*, vii.

Chapter 7: "It Could Just as Well Be Me"

1. Kikuchi, diary entry, August 16, 1945 (CKP, box 17, 21:31–2).

2. Kikuchi, *Diary*, December 10, 1941, 46.

3. See Warren Tsuneishi and Stanley Falk, eds., *American Patriots: MIS in the War against Japan* (Washington, D.C.: JAVA, 1995).

4. Tsuneishi to Kikuchi, November 8, 1943 (CKP, box 14, folder 1, 10:3719).

5. Ibid., 3720.

6. Tsuneishi to Kikuchi, December 11, 1944 (CKP, box 15, 15:6527–8).

7. Ibid., 6526.

8. Ibid., 6528.

9. Already affiliated with Columbia in 1940, the school was officially renamed the Columbia School of Social Work in 1963.

10. Murase to Kikuchi, February 18, 1945, 2 (CKP, box 16, 16:2).

11. Murase, Hansen interview, 65.

12. Murase, letter to Kikuchi, February 25, 1945, 1 (CKP, box 16, vol. 16).

13. Tsuneishi to Murase, November 17, 1944, 1 (CKP, box 16, vol. 16).

14. Tsuneishi to Murase, December 26, 1944, 1 (CKP, box 16, vol. 16).

15. Tsuneishi to Kikuchi, February 13, 1945, 1 (CKP, box 16, vol. 16).

16. Tsuneishi to Murase, November 17, 1944, 2.

17. Tsuneishi to Kikuchi, February 13, 1945, 1.

18. Murase, Hansen interview, 65–6.

19. Kikuchi, *Diary*, June 23, 1942, 144–5.

20. Tsuneishi to the author, July 24, 2004.

21. Murase, Hansen interview, 65–6.

22. Kikuchi to Tsuneishi, May 8, 1945, 2–3 (CKP, box 16, vol. 18).

23. Tsuneishi to Kikuchi, April 28, 1945, 2 (CKP, box 16, vol. 18).

24. Murase to Kikuchi, September 16, 1945, 2–3 (CKP, box 56, folder 2 ["Journal Enclosures"]).

25. Ibid., 5.

26. Ibid., 6.

27. Tsuneishi to Kikuchi, March 7, 1945, 1–2 (CKP, box 16, vol. 17).

28. Kikuchi to Tsuneishi, May 8, 1945, 5.

29. Ibid., 4.

30. Kikuchi, diary entry, August 16, 1945 (CKP, box 17, 21:31–2).

31. Kikuchi to Tsuneishi, May 8, 1945, 4.

32. Kikuchi, diary entry, August 11, 1945 (CKP, box 17, 21:5–6).

33. Kikuchi, diary entry, August 23, 1945 (CKP, box 17, 21:65).

34. African American enlistment in the army totaled 701,678, with 7,168 officers.

35. Kikuchi, diary entry, August 18, 1945 (CKP, box 17, 21:42–3).

36. Studs Terkel, *"The Good War": An Oral History of World War II* (New York: New Press, 1984), 151.

37. Carina del Rosario, ed., *A Different Battle: Stories of Asian Pacific American Veterans* (Seattle: Univ. of Washington Press, 1999), 91.

38. Kikuchi, diary entry, August 20, 1945 (CKP, box 17, 21:57–8).

39. Kikuchi, diary entry, August 23, 1945, (CKP, box 17, 21:67–8).

40. Ibid., 65–6.

41. Ibid.

42. Kikuchi, diary entry, January 15, 1946 (CKP, box 18, 22:794–5).

43. Kikuchi, diary entry, August 10, 1945 (CKP, box 17, 21:2).

44. Densho, "From Densho's Archives: World War II Volunteers," November 8, 2006, Discover Nikkei, http://www.discovernikkei.org/en/journal/2006/11/8/wwii-volunteered/. Also see updated statistics at Go for Broke, http://www.goforbroke.org/history/history_historical.asp.

45. Kikuchi, diary entry, March 9, 1944 (CKP, box 14, 11:4492, 4494).

46. Tamotsu Shibutani, *The Derelicts of Company K: A Sociological Study of Demoralization* (Berkeley and Los Angeles: Univ. of California Press, 1978), 355.

47. Ibid., 354–5.

48. Kikuchi, diary entry, October 21, 1945 (CKP, box 17, 21:319–20).

49. Kikuchi, diary entry, August 24, 1945 (CKP, box 17, 21:72–3).

50. Thomas Higa, *Memoirs of a Certain Nisei* (Kaneohe, Hawaiʻi: Higa, 1988), 49–50.

51. Kikuchi, diary entry, October 14, 1945 (CKP, box 17, 21:281).

52. See Frank Hines, "Demobilization and the Federal Program of Veteran Aid," *Public Administration Review* 5:1 (1945): 76.

53. Lawrence Kubie, "How Should the Medical Care of Veterans Be Organized?" *Military Affairs* 9:2 (1945): 119.

54. Paul Magnuson, "Medical Care for Veterans," *Annals of the American Academy of Political and Social Science* 273 (1951): 81.

55. Kikuchi, diary entry, October 27, 1945 (CKP, box 17, 21:346).

56. Kikuchi, diary entry, December 26, 1945 (CKP, box 17, 21:611).

57. Kikuchi, diary entry, December 29, 1945 (CKP, box 17, 21:644).

58. Kikuchi, diary entry, December 28, 1945 (CKP, box 17, 21:636).

59. Kikuchi, diary entry, December 31, 1945 (CKP, box 17, 21:649).

60. Kikuchi, diary entry, January 15, 1946 (CKP, box 18, 22:794–5).

61. Kikuchi, diary entry, May 27, 1946 (CKP, box 18, 22:1437–8).

62. Kikuchi, diary entry, May 26, 1946 (CKP, box 18, 22:1432b–c).

63. Kikuchi, diary entry, May 27, 1946 (CKP, box 18, 22:1437–8).

64. Kikuchi, diary entry, April 17, 1946 (CKP, box 18, 22:1185).

65. Du Bois, *Souls of Black Folk*, 526–8.

66. Kikuchi, diary entry, April 7, 1946 (CKP, box 18, 22:1144).

Conclusion: Tatsuro, "Standing Man"

1. Kikuchi, diary entry, March 20, 1943 (CKP, box 12, 6:2323–4).

2. Kikuchi to Yuriko, June 4, 1946, 1 (CKP, box 45, "Original Copies of Letters to Yuriko, 1946–1948").

3. Louis Adamic, *Dinner at the White House* (New York: Harper, 1946).

4. D. Thomas to Kikuchi, September 20, 1946 (CKP, box 45, "Original Copies of Letters to Yuriko, 1946–1948").

5. An accomplished dancer in her own right, Susan Kikuchi married Rick Kivnick in 1980. They have a daughter named Cassey, the oldest of the Kikuchi grandchildren.

After earning a PhD in geography, Lawrence Kikuchi married Victoria Lord in 1982, and the couple has two children, Laura and Walter. Yuriko has regularly taught dance at the Boston Conservatory and all over New York City, well into her youthful nineties.

6. The ties were not completely severed, since he lovingly showed his sister Marji (who was terminally ill with cancer and died a year later in 1974) and mother, Shizuko, around New York. Finally, his brother Jack came to his memorial service in October 1988 to honor his brother's leadership during the war years.

7. Kikuchi, diary entry, June 24, 1948 (CKP, box 20, 28:1).

8. Kikuchi, diary entry, February 7, 1948 (CKP, box 19, 27a: 3382).

9. Kikuchi, diary entry, October 28, 1948 (CKP, box 20, 28:2).

10. Kikuchi, diary entry, July 23, 1951 (CKP, box 21, 33:8–9).

11. Kikuchi, diary entry, August 7, 1950 (CKP, box 21, 31:5).

12. *Brown v. Board of Education of Topeka*, 347 U.S. 483 (1954); *Plessy v. Ferguson*, 163 U.S. 537 (1896).

13. *Mendez v. Westminster School District of Orange County*, 161 F. 2d 774 (9th Cir. 1947).

14. See Toni and Greg Robinson, "*Mendez v. Westminster*: Asian-Latino Coalition Triumphant?" *Asian Law Journal* 10 (2003): 161–83.

15. *Shelley v. Kraemer*, 334 U.S. 1 (1948).

16. *Sweatt v. Painter*, 339 U.S. 629 (1950); *McLaurin v. Oklahoma State Regents*, 339 U.S. 637 (1950).

17. Kikuchi, diary entry, June 6, 1950 (CKP, box 20, 30:2).

18. Kikuchi, diary entry, March 19, 1949 (CKP, box 20, 29:1).

19. Kikuchi, diary entry, July 24, 1950 (CKP, box 21, 31:3–4).

20. Kikuchi, Modell interview.

21. Yuriko Kikuchi, interview by the author, August 28, 2004.

22. Kikuchi, diary entry, October 13, 1950 (CKP, box 21, 31:5–6).

23. Kikuchi, diary entry, December 31, 1951 (CKP, box 21, 33:14).

24. Kikuchi, diary entry, November 13, 1951 (CKP, box 21, 33:2–3).

25. Von Eschen, *Race against Empire*, 186.

26. Ibid., 187.

27. Borstelmann, *Cold War and the Color Line*, 74.

28. Ibid., 74–5.

29. Kikuchi, diary entry, January 15, 1949 (CKP, box 20, 29:1).

30. Kikuchi, diary entry, December 10, 1948 (CKP, box 20, 28:1).

31. Kikuchi, diary entry, June 2, 1948 (CKP, box 19, 27a: 3800).

32. See Von Eschen, *Race against Empire*, 184, 251n116.

33. Austin, *From Concentration Camp to Campus*, 38.

34. Oyama, "A Nisei Report from Home," *Common Ground* 6:2 (Winter 1946): 26–8.

35. See Valerie Matsumoto, "Desperately Seeking 'Deirdre': Gender Roles, Multicultural Relations, and Nisei Women Writers of the 1930s," *Frontiers: A Journal of Women Studies* 12:1 (1991): 19–32.

36. Kikuchi, Hansen interview, 28–35. All the quotations in this paragraph come from this source.

37. Ibid.

38. Kikuchi to Modell, March 25, 1976, 2 (Modell file folder "Kikuchi").

39. Kikuchi to Mr. Kin Yee, Detroit Chinese Welfare Council, April 27, 1983 (CKP, box 59, vol. 105, "Kikuchi—Letters and Notes").

40. While the ACLU's national board adopted an official policy of not questioning the constitutionality of 9066, many of its lawyers were individually involved in defending the plaintiffs in the internment cases: Korematsu, Mitsuye Endo, Minoru Yasui, and Gordon Hirabayashi; see Irons, *Justice at War*. The UNCF was founded in 1944, offering aid to historically Black colleges and universities, while CISPES promoted an alternative to U.S.-backed policies of the El Salvadoran right beginning in 1980.

41. Kikuchi to his family, August 21, 1988, 3 (CKP, box 62, folder 4).

42. Tsuneishi, eulogy, Charles Kikuchi Memorial, Riverside Church, October 17, 1988, videotape courtesy of Yuriko Kikuchi.

Index

Abbott, Edith, 171

Abbott, Robert, 10

Adamic, Louis, 4, 5, 10, 15, 234, 244n35; and
 Americanness, 92–93; analytical framework of, 78–79; and Anderson, 71; army
 service of, 77; and Asian Americans, 64;
 and Caen, 104–5; and Chicago School, 63;
 circle of, 92, 95, 192; and CK, 34; CK and
 circle of, 95, 192; CK and master narrative
 of, 61; and CK and Nisei intellectuals, 84,
 85; and CK and Saroyan, 42; and CK as
 orphan, 64; and CK's "A Young American
 with a Japanese Face," 59–65; and CK's
 desire for active life, 44; CK's experiences
 similar to, 77–78; CK's familial relationship with, 128, 198; CK's first meeting
 with, 59; CK's grateful memories of, 65,
 106–7; as CK's mentor, 56–57, 58–60, 62,
 75–76, 102, 105, 127, 135, 153; CK's opportunities with, 7–8; as CK's parental figure, 9,
 47, 77, 104; CK's practical and emotional
 support from, 74; CK's unequal relationship with, 62, 63; and CK's viewpoint,
 78–81, 102–4; and CK's wedding, 218; and
 Common Council for American Unity,
 66; and *Common Ground*, 63, 65–66, 68,
 84, 92; and Common Ground School, 9;
 and *Current Life*, 41, 84–85; Davis on, 105;
 death/suicide of, 14, 56, 65, 106, 219, 228;
 and diversity, 79, 153; and eastern Europe,
 68; escape from Slovenian home, 77; and
 Fante, 96–97, 104–5; and HUAC, 106; and
 image of Asians, 63; as immigrant, 9, 57,
 63; and immigrants, 64, 77, 79, 92–93; and
 Jack Kikuchi, 74–75, 127; and Japanese

Americans, 66, 67; letter (initial) from
 CK, 75; letter of mid-February [15?], 1940
 from CK, 76–77; letter of n.d. [February,
 1940?] from CK (twenty-six-page letter),
 59, 60–65, 75; letter of March 26, 1940 to
 CK, 75; letter of April 12, 1940 to CK, 59,
 66, 75; letter of April 18, 1940 from CK,
 59, 79; letter of May 1940 from CK, 77;
 letter of June 25, 1941 from CK, 80; letter
 of December 11, 1941 from CK, 56, 81; letter of December 15, 1941 to CK, 56; letter
 of December 20th, 1941 from CK, 81–82;
 letter of February 21, 1942 from CK, 85,
 87; letter of November 2, 1943 from CK,
 102, 125–26; letter of August 6, 1945 from
 CK, 102; letter of August 8, 1945 to CK,
 103; letters from CK, 8, 76–78, 102; master
 narrative of, 61, 62; and McWilliams, 88,
 99–100, 103–4; and minorities, 77; and
 Nisei, 64, 84–85; and Old Americans, 9,
 64, 66, 78–79, 91; and Omura, 84; and
 Orientalism, 63, 64; and Ottley, 94; and
 Oyama, 84; peripatetic existence of, 77;
 and publishing, 77; and Saroyan, 104–5;
 on second-generation Americans, 64, 78–
 79; and Soviet Union, 68, 106; and Stanley
 Rose Bookshop, 97; travels of, 77; and
 unity in diversity, 58, 62, 65–66, 90, 102;
 and War Relocation Authority, 69; work
 experiences of, 77–78; works: *Dinner at
 the White House*, 218; *From Many Lands*,
 9, 19, 59; *Laughing in the Jungle*, 57; *My
 America*, 64; *Nation of Nations*, 100; "The
 Nisei's Problem Is Difficult but Natural,"
 84–85; "Plymouth Rock and Ellis Island,"

263

Made in the USA
Lexington, KY
17 September 2015